EDI DEVELOPMENT STUDIES

# Monitoring and Evaluating Social Programs in Developing Countries

## A Handbook for Policymakers, Managers, and Researchers

Joseph Valadez
Michael Bamberger

The World Bank
Washington, D. C.

Copyright © 1994
The International Bank for Reconstruction
and Development / THE WORLD BANK
1818 H Street, N.W.
Washington, D.C. 20433, U.S.A.

The Economic Development Institute (EDI) was established by the World Bank in 1955 to train officials concerned with development planning, policymaking, investment analysis, and project implementation in member developing countries. At present the substance of the EDI's work emphasizes macroeconomic and sectoral economic policy analysis. Through a variety of courses, seminars, and workshops, most of which are given overseas in cooperation with local institutions, the EDI seeks to sharpen analytical skills used in policy analysis and to broaden understanding of the experience of individual countries with economic development. Although the EDI's publications are designed to support its training activities, many are of interest to a much broader audience. EDI materials, including any findings, interpretations, and conclusions, are entirely those of the authors and should not be attributed in any manner to the World Bank, to its affiliated organizations, or to members of its Board of Executive Directors or the countries they represent.

Because of the informality of the series and to make the publication available with the least possible delay, the manuscript has not been edited fully as would be the case with a more formal document, and the World Bank accepts no responsibility for errors.

The material in this publication is copyrighted. Requests for permission to reproduce portions of it should be sent to the Office of the Publisher at the address shown in the copyright notice above. The World Bank encourages dissemination of its work and will normally give permission promptly and, when the reproduction is for noncommercial purposes, without asking a fee. Permission to photocopy portions for classroom use is granted through the Copyright Clearance Center, Inc., Suite 910, 222 Rosewood Drive, Danvers, Massachusetts 01923, U.S.A.

The backlist of publications by the World Bank is shown in the annual *Index of Publications*, which is available free of charge from the Distribution Unit, Office of the Publisher, The World Bank, 1818 H Street, N.W., Washington, D.C. 20433, U.S.A., or from Publications, Banque mondiale, 66, avenue d'Iéna, 75116 Paris, France.

At the time of writing, Joseph Valadez was on the faculty of the Department of International Health at the Johns Hopkins University School of Hygiene and Public Health, and Michael Bamberger was senior sociologist in the Human Resources Development Division of the World Bank's Economic Development Institute.

**Library of Congress Cataloging-in-Publication Data**

Valadez, Joseph J.
    Monitoring and evaluating social programs in developing countries:
a handbook for policymakers, managers, and researchers /
Joseph Valadez, Michael Bamberger.
        p.   cm.—(EDI development studies, ISSN 1020-105X)
        Includes bibliographical references and index.
        ISBN 0-8213-2989-8
        1. Evaluation research (Social action programs)—Developing
countries.   2. Economic development projects—Developing countries—
Evaluation.   I. Bamberger, Michael.   II. Title.   III. Series.
H62.5.D44V35   1994
361'.0068'4—dc20                                        94-29582
                                                             CIP

# Contents

TABLES

FIGURES

BOXES

# Foreword

The growing concern with social development issues such as poverty reduction, project sustainability, the equal participation of women, and the social costs of economic development has created a need for monitoring and evaluation techniques that are adapted to the special characteristics of social programs. This handbook provides a comprehensive review of the wide range of techniques—many of them worked out within the past few years—available for monitoring and evaluating the main kinds of social development programs.

*Vinod Thomas, Director*
*Economic Development Institute*
*The World Bank*

# Acknowledgments

The preparation of this book spans 10 years, which is more time than we care to remember. A great many factors prevented a speedier completion, including the fact that we had jobs to perform, extensive travel schedules to fulfill, and, probably most important, a great deal to learn. Many of our hard-won experiences have found their way into this volume.

We have a great many people to thank. Joe Valadez would like to thank Amy Leis of the Center for International Studies, Massachusetts Institute of Technology, where he wrote several sections during 1983–84. Also, he would like to thank Hayward Alker, Jr., of the Political Science Department at MIT for his collegiality and advice during his brief period as a visiting faculty member. At Harvard University, he would like to thank Dwight Perkins, the director of the Harvard Institute for International Development, where he was a faculty member during 1986–90. Several of his experiences there are included in this book. At the Johns Hopkins University, he would like to thank Robert Black for supporting his diverse research interests as a member of the international health faculty. And, last but not least, he would like to thank the health and development professionals with whom he has worked in more than 20 countries during the past 15 years.

For his part, Michael Bamberger would like to express his appreciation to Dennis Casley, Pablo Guerrero, Hyung-Ki Kim, Kathryn McPhail, John Middleton, Josette Murphy, John Newman, Dennis Purcell, and Barbara Searle of the World Bank; Krishna Kumar of the U.S. Agency for International Development; and Ram Malhotra, formerly with the International

Fund for Agricultural Development, for their comments on various drafts of this study. He would also like to acknowledge the contributions of many others, including Lawrence Salmen, for stimulating discussions on participatory evaluation methods over more than a decade (during which they worked together on studies in Latin America and Asia); Adil Khan and Viqar Ahmed, with whom he cooperated on studies and seminars on the organization of monitoring and evaluation throughout Asia; Mehdi Al-Bazzaz, with whom he worked on monitoring and evaluation and sustainability assessment in North Africa and the Middle East; Douglas Keare, Stephen Mayo, Stephen Malpezzi, and Emmanuel Jimenez, with whom he worked in developing monitoring and evaluation systems in the Urban and Regional Economics Division; Mila Reforma (Philippines), Johan Silas (Indonesia), Januario Flores (Brazil), Freddy Quiton (Bolivia), Davinder Lamba (Kenya), Mariam Dione (Senegal), Edgardo Gonzalez-Polio, Juan Serrarols, Mauricio Silva, and Alberto Harth Deneke (El Salvador), with whom he worked on evaluations of housing and urban development programs; and Dani Kaufmann, Eduardo Velez, Mari Clark, John Oucho, Mohammed Mukras, and Abdul Aziz, with whom he cooperated on studies of interhousehold transfers and survival strategies of poor households.

Both authors would like to thank Hanna Sarkees, Faythe Calandra, Marie Christine Theodore, and Mike Lewis for their help in preparing and revising the text and graphics, Venka Macintyre for editing the manuscript, and Cynthia Stock for desktopping the book. Special thanks are also due to John Didier for editorial advice and encouragement throughout the long and complex publication process.

# Overview

After several decades of experience in financing, designing, and managing social and economic development projects, international agencies and developing country governments are finding that many such projects still fail to achieve their objectives. The portfolio performance of projects supported by the World Bank, for example, deteriorated steadily from 1981 to 1991, with the share of projects having "major problems" increasing from 11 percent to 20 percent in that period (World Bank 1991). Such figures probably do not even indicate the true size of the problem, as they refer only to the stage of *project implementation* and say little about how well projects are able to *sustain* the delivery of services over time or to produce their intended impacts.

As a result, project impact evaluation has received considerable attention in recent years. This interest has also been fueled by the mounting pressure on governments and donor agencies to broaden the goals of their development strategies to address such issues as the quality of the environment; the level of poverty; and the economic, social, and political participation of women in developing countries. Resource constraints have also heightened interest in the use of cost-effectiveness analysis to help identify more economical and equitable ways of delivering services to priority target groups.

This book is a practical guide for the many groups who are concerned with these broad development issues and who use or produce information on the performance and quality of social development programs. The term "social programs" refers here to the array of programs designed to improve the quality of life by improving the capacity of citizens to participate fully in social, economic, and political activities at the local or national levels. On the one hand, these programs may focus on improving physical well-being and access to services; protecting vulnerable groups from the adverse consequences of economic reform and structural adjustment; or providing education, literacy, and employment and income-generating opportunities. On the other hand, they may focus directly on local empowerment and equity issues by strengthening community organizations, encouraging women to participate in development, or alleviating poverty.

We have written this volume for a broad audience. We hope that policymakers, planners, and project managers from government, nongovernmental, and international development agencies, along with evaluation researchers, project beneficiaries, university teachers and students, will find the discussion useful.

We try to present a comprehensive view of the ways in which information produced by monitoring and evaluation studies is used at the project, sectoral, and national levels, together with the principles of design, data collection, and analysis. The benefits of monitoring and evaluation depend as much on the way the data from these studies are collected, disseminated, and used as on the research methodology. Consequently, we pay particular attention to the organization of monitoring and evaluation at the national, regional, and local levels. We also discuss how to identify potential beneficiaries and their information needs, and how to manage evaluations.

It has been argued, particularly by nongovernmental organizations, that the methods typically used to evaluate economic and infrastructure projects are not appropriate for social programs. Certainly, great strides have been made in developing innovative evaluation techniques, but much remains to be done to ensure that the procedures will respond to the unique characteristics of social development programs and at the same time provide the rigor and reliability needed to accurately compare projects and also integrate these procedures with the conventional quantitative and other methods of economic analysis.

Although there is an abundance of literature on the evaluation of social programs in the United States and other industrial countries, many of the methods described are difficult to apply directly to the conditions under which evaluations must be conducted in developing countries. For the most part, these countries have only modest financial and professional resources for evaluation research and are without access to the extensive data bases and secondary data available in industrial countries. Nevertheless, industrial countries offer a tremendous store of evaluation experience that could be helpful to developing countries. This book draws attention to some of the more useful lessons that can be gleaned not only from the traditional literature on quasi-experimental designs, but also from the debate on the relationships between methods of quantitative and qualitative evaluation. The discussion also covers new developments in qualitative evaluation, stakeholder analysis, the politics of evaluation, and the use of existing research data in meta-analysis and prospective evaluation.

Many international agencies have prepared handbooks for evaluating the projects they finance in accordance with their own administrative requirements. The problem is that few general textbooks are available to show how monitoring and evaluation principles can be applied by national governments and nongovernmental organizations to projects in developing countries. We refer extensively to the few publications that exist and in addition draw on our own experience in helping agencies in developing countries design and use monitoring and evaluation techniques and in organizing seminars and workshops for agencies concerned with project planning, management, monitoring, and evaluation at the national and project levels in Latin America, Africa, Asia, and the Middle East. We also review the monitoring and evaluation literature produced by international development agencies in the United States and by governments and evaluation researchers in a number of developing countries.

Equally important, we discuss a number of topics that have been by and large overlooked in earlier evaluation publications. First, as already mentioned, special attention is given to the *organization of monitoring and evaluation* at the project, sectoral, and national levels. Firsthand experience and research have led us to conclude that the effectiveness and utility of most monitoring and evaluation studies are greatly affected by their organizational arrangements (organization chosen to conduct the studies, location of the monitoring and evaluation unit within the organization, and so on). Second, the book provides information on the *organization and utilization* of the data bases required to select, design, and implement new social projects and programs. Third, a chapter is devoted to the monitoring and evaluation of *project sustainability*. Fourth, we try to draw examples from *all the social sectors* and from all the major developing regions. Fifth, we review *simple and cost-effective methods of estimating project impact*, including the existing rapid appraisal and participatory assessment methods and some of the new methods for working with small samples, such as lot quality acceptance sampling. Sixth, we examine the application of program evaluation methods to the evaluation of poverty alleviation programs and to the assessment of the impact of development policies, programs, and projects on women. Finally, we discuss the role of nongovernmental organizations (NGOs) in the evaluation of development programs and the areas in which they may have a comparative advantage.

## Intended Audience

The book is intended for at least four groups, beginning with *planners* and *policymakers* (particularly at the national and sectoral levels). They are the ones who decide how monitoring and evaluation should be organized (particularly at the national level) and what kinds of studies need to be conducted. They also work closely with international donor agencies, which frequently play a key role in study selection.

The second group consists of the *project managers* who will use the results of the studies to improve the performance of the projects in their charge. Managers are also accountable to their technical ministries and to central planning and financial agencies and are therefore required to prepare monitoring reports on the status of their projects.

The third group comprises the *monitoring and evaluation practitioners* who are directly responsible for the design, implementation, and dissemination of the studies. Practitioners vary greatly in their level of professional training and experience. The book therefore provides an easily understood introduction to the basic principles of evaluation, as well as information on some of the more sophisticated methodologies.

The fourth group the book addresses is composed of the *institutions* that provide training programs in monitoring and evaluation.

The book is organized around the needs of these four groups.

## Scope of the Book

*Part I. Monitoring and Evaluating Social Programs: A Guide for Policymakers, Planners, and Managers*

Part I provides an overview of the utility of monitoring and evaluation to managers, planners, and policymakers concerned with project management, sectoral development, and national economic management. *Chapter 1* assesses the status of monitoring and evaluation (M/E) in developing countries and identifies some of the main weaknesses of current approaches. The M/E approach used in the book is then outlined, together with the main kinds of studies required at each stage of the project cycle. Next, the context in which each kind of evaluation is conducted is described, along with the kinds of questions clients will have, the range of available research methods, the time frame in which each kind of study normally has to be carried out, and the ways in which the studies are typically used. As is emphasized throughout, the needs of the clients and the context are likely to vary from one kind of study to another. Evaluators must fully understand the particular context and the concerns of their clients. Important issues relating to the design and utilization of monitoring and evaluation in developing countries are also discussed, especially as they relate to social programs. *Chapter 2* turns to the practical applications of monitoring and evaluation at the project, sectoral, and national levels and provides examples of the kinds of studies that can be conducted at each stage of the project cycle and their function. The chapter covers evaluation methodologies that have proved useful in industrial countries, such as those that deal with prospective evaluation and meta-evaluation, and notes the benefits of modeling in the design and interpretation of M/E studies. The "PRISM" system employed by the U.S. Agency for International Development illustrates how a set of indicators can be used to develop and monitor medium-term strategic management objectives. Methods for evaluating the different impacts of development policies and programs on women and men are also discussed, together with the principles of gender analysis.

*Chapter 3* explains how modeling can be applied to project evaluation. It points out that development programs are social experiments and that the factors affecting their outcomes are best understood with the aid of models describing the intended project implementation and operational processes. The lessons learned will help improve the selection and design of future projects. The modeling procedures appropriate for social programs include logical framework analysis, quasi-experimental designs, systems analysis, causal networks, process modeling, and path analysis. Structured learning, a comparatively new approach, is also discussed. It employs models to systematically distill the lessons from the experience of ongoing programs as well as from broader policies. This approach has also been used to build experiments into project design that can test and evaluate alternative delivery systems. In the examples discussed, models were used to evaluate the impacts of primary education on girls and of structural adjustment on the poor and to assess housing and urban sector policies.

*Part II. Design and Implementation of Monitoring and Evaluation: A Guide for Practitioners*

The five chapters in Part II focus on the design, implementation, and application of the six most commonly used kinds of monitoring and evaluation studies. *Chapter 4* describes the components of a system for monitoring project implementation. These include monitoring physical and financial inputs and outputs, diagnostic studies of problems that have arisen during project implementation, project completion reports, cost-effectiveness analysis, and the evaluation of project efficiency. Cost-effectiveness analysis is widely used in evaluating social programs to compare the costs of alternative methods of delivering services. By way of example, we show how cost-effectiveness analysis can be used to compare the effectiveness of different methods of expanding primary education in El Salvador. We also discuss the particular problems that can arise in monitoring social programs, particularly in quantifying the outputs and benefits of social programs and in assessing the quality of inputs and outputs. Here, it is vital to consider the perspectives of different stakeholders, as well as the implementation processes and the expected outputs. As the chapter points out, beneficiary assessment is one method that has proved particularly useful in evaluating social programs.

*Chapter 5* presents an in-depth discussion of diagnostic studies, which can play a vital role in providing management with rapid feedback concerning problems or other information required to modify ongoing project components or to design new ones. As is also explained, diagnostic studies can be used to evaluate the efficacy of community organizations and may be of assistance in project identification and design. *Chapter 6* describes the studies conducted during the planning or operational phases of a project in order to assess the project's potential sustainability—in other words, its capacity to continue delivering services and benefits to the intended population groups. Factors affecting sustainability that must be assessed include project design, implementation methods, and organizational decisions, along with external factors such as the economic and political environment in which the project operates and the cultural characteristics of the affected populations. This subject has recently become a major concern of both governments and donors. The chapter describes a scale consisting of 20 indicators that can be used to develop a simple numerical index of sustainability based on four main factors: continued delivery of services and benefits, maintenance of physical infrastructure, long-term institutional capacity of the principal agencies involved in the project, and the support of key stakeholders. These methods of assessing sustainability are then applied to an integrated rural development project in Bangladesh.

*Chapter 7* presents some rapid and cost-effective methods of assessing project impacts, especially the extent to which target groups are receiving the intended benefits. These methods can be used to minimize time, money, or the level of professional expertise required. There are usually tradeoffs between these factors, and the evaluation design must specify which of the three is to be kept to a minimum. Simple and rapid methods include the use of archival sources, automatic recording devices, case studies, community fora, cluster samples and focus groups, key informants, participant observation, physical traces, photographic surveys, and new developments in small-sampling theory.

In recent years there has been a growing concern about what the impact of development assistance has been over the long term, whether investments have achieved their intended results, and whether they have benefited the intended target groups. Among the many particular subjects of concern are long-term environmental impacts, the involuntary resettlement caused by the construction of power projects and irrigation schemes, the impact of development assistance on the poor in general and on poor women in particular, and the sustainability of development programs. *Chapter 8* presents the current state of thinking on the practical utility of the conventional quasi-experimental (QE) impact evaluation designs. Conventional designs are compared with three widely used designs that are simpler and more economical to use but that the QE literature would classify as methodologically "less robust." These simpler designs combine various quantitative and qualitative techniques in an effort to provide the greatest degree of methodological rigor possible in most real-life situations, where the impact must be assessed without access to baseline data collected on project beneficiaries and control groups before the project began.

Despite their usefulness in many operational contexts, these simpler designs at times fail to provide the essential information needed to assess a social program. For one thing, many of them do not include adequate before and after measures of the situation among the groups who did not benefit from the project (such as families who were forced to relocate without compensation, or children who were not vaccinated or did not receive nutritional supplements). Consequently it is difficult to determine how these groups have been affected by the project. Moreover, without an adequate control it is difficult to quantify the level of impacts or benefits, and hence to estimate the economic benefits produced.

The discussion then turns to three evaluation designs that did approximate a quasi-experimental design: the River Blindness Control Program in West Africa, the Rural Education Project (EDURURAL) in northeast Brazil, and three components of the Bolivian Social Investment Fund.

## Part III.  Data Collection for Monitoring and Evaluation: A Guide for Practitioners

As in other areas of the social sciences, many evaluation researchers have a preference for either quantitative or qualitative methods of analysis because they still find it difficult to reconcile the two paradigms behind these methods. The objective of the "positivist-behaviorist" paradigm (often called the "quantitative" approach) is to identify and measure relationships between observable social regularities (participation in projects or community activities, investment in housing, years of education, labor force participation, and the like) that can be interpreted independently of the meanings communities or individuals may attach to them. This approach emphasizes quantitative methods. In contrast, advocates of the "subjectivist-phenomenological" or "constructivist" paradigm (the "qualitative" approach) argue that human behavior and attitudes can be understood only within a particular social context and through the meanings that people attach to particular situations and actions. Researchers in this group prefer qualitative methods of evaluation. Thus, a central issue in evaluation research is to what extent qualitative and quantitative methods can be combined. We strongly recommend that a broad range of quantitative and qualitative methods be integrated into most evaluation designs.

*Chapter 9* describes sample survey methods used in quantitative analysis. It explains how questionnaires and other survey instruments are administered; how questions can be asked; and what kinds of preparatory studies can help analysts understand the issues being studied, identify the key concepts to be measured, and arrive at the most effective and reliable question format. Qualitative methods are then recommended to interpret the results and to explore any inconsistencies in the findings.

*Chapter 10* presents a variety of nonsurvey or qualitative methods of collecting data, including participant observation, unobtrusive methods, direct observation, secondary data sources, photography, the use of key informants, community fora, self-monitoring, and mapping. The complementarities between quantitative and qualitative methods are also discussed. *Chapter 11* examines the principles of sample design and their application to all evaluations, rather than just to conventional quantitative survey designs. The most common methods of sample design are described and assessed and simple guidelines are given for estimating the size of a sample required to achieve a certain level of precision. Recent developments in small sample designs are discussed and are illustrated by lot quality assurance sampling.

## Part IV. Organizational and Management Issues in Program Evaluation: A Guide for Policymakers, Planners, and Managers

*Chapter 12* discusses some of the management issues surrounding monitoring and evaluation, particularly the importance of defining program content and objectives and of identifying the principal "stakeholders" and their information needs. This chapter considers how the monitoring and evaluation program should be organized, where it should be located, and how it should be managed. The management of consultants and the role of nongovernment organizations are other important topics covered here. The chapter also examines national monitoring and evaluation systems, some of the issues arising from the competing demands of the major stakeholders, the role of donor agencies, the effect of national systems on project-level monitoring, and some guidelines for improving national M/E systems.

## Part V. Teaching Monitoring and Evaluation: A Guide for Training Institutions

Many countries have been unable to improve their monitoring and evaluation performance because they lack trained researchers or because their managers, planners, and policymakers do not fully understand how M/E should be organized and used. *Chapter 13* explains how to teach the subject. It reviews current approaches and their weaknesses. The main audiences and their training needs are then identified. The elements of an integrated national M/E training program are presented next, with the different kinds of courses and seminars that should be organized for policymakers, managers, and evaluation practitioners. The chapter concludes with a discussion of some of the main teaching methods.

# Acronyms and Abbreviations

| | |
|---|---|
| ADP | annual development program |
| AVV | Autorité des Aménagements des Vallées des Volta |
| BRAC | Bangladesh Rural Advancement Committee |
| CIDA | Canadian International Development Agency |
| CMEA | central monitoring and evaluation agency |
| EOPS | end of project status |
| EPI | Expanded Programme on Immunization |
| ERR | economic rate or return |
| FSDVM | Fundación Salvadoreña de Desarrollo y Vivienda Mínima (Salvadoran Low-cost Housing Foundation) |
| GAO | General Accounting Office (U.S.) |
| GTZ | German Technical Assistance Agency |
| HP | health provider |
| HW | health workers |
| IDA | International Development Association |
| ILO | International Labour Organization |
| IMED | Implementation, Monitoring, and Evaluation Division (Ministry of Planning, Bangladesh) |
| IRR | internal economic rate of return |
| LQAS | lot quality assurance sampling |
| M/E | monitoring and evaluation |
| MEU | monitoring and evaluation unit |
| NGO | nongovernmental organization |

| | |
|---|---|
| NORAD | Norwegian Agency for International Development |
| NPV | net present value |
| OECD | Organisation for Economic Co-operation and Development |
| OED | Operations Evaluation Department (World Bank) |
| ORS | oral rehydration salt |
| ORT | oral rehydration therapy |
| PAHO | Pan-American Health Organization |
| PCR | project completion report |
| PEO | Programme Evaluation Organization (India) |
| PHC | primary health care |
| PRISM | Program Performance Information System for Strategic Management |
| QE | quasi-experimental |
| QED | quasi-experimental design |
| RAD | Research and Analysis Division (Manila Housing Authority, Philippines) |
| RRA | rapid rural appraisal |
| SDA | social dimensions of adjustment |
| SEWA | Self-Employed Women's Association (India) |
| SIDA | Swedish International Development Agency |
| SIF | Bolivian Social Investment Fund |
| UNCHS | United Nations Centre for Human Settlements |
| UNDP | United Nations Development Programme |
| UNICEF | United Nations Children's Fund |
| USAID | United States Agency for International Development |
| ZOPP | participatory logical framework analysis (German) |

# Part I

## Monitoring and Evaluating Social Programs
### A Guide for Policymakers, Planners, and Managers

# 1

## Evaluating Social Programs
## in Developing Countries

Developing countries and international aid agencies finance, design, and manage large numbers of diverse and complex development projects. In 1987 alone, the central government of India financed more than 3,000 projects and its state governments sponsored another 6,000–7,000, while Pakistan supported some 3,800 projects under its Federal Annual Development Plan (Ahmed and Bamberger 1989). Among the projects financed by international aid groups, approximately 192 were completed under the auspices of the World Bank in 1985, according to its project completion reports (World Bank 1987:xi), and close to 250 are completed every year under the U.S. Agency for International Development (USAID), to judge by its evaluation reports (OECD 1986).

### The Current Status of Monitoring and Evaluation in Developing Countries

The available evidence suggests that a significant proportion of these projects fail to fully achieve their objectives. Of the 192 completed by the World Bank in 1985, approximately 20 percent had unsatisfactory or uncertain outcomes (World Bank 1987:5). Success rates have been even lower for complex projects in low-income countries in need of major social and economic reform, notably in Africa. The success rate for such countries is often less than 50 percent (World Bank 1987:28).

These figures do not fully reflect project performance, however, because they usually refer to the *project implementation* stage (in which infrastructure is constructed, equipment installed, and service delivery systems established). Little is known about how well projects are able to *sustain* the delivery of services over time, and even less about the extent to which projects are able to produce their intended impacts.

The need for such information has grown considerably in recent years, for governments and donor agencies have come under mounting pressure to formulate development strategies that contribute to broad goals, such as protecting the environment, alleviating poverty, and improving the economic, social, and political participation of women—all of which require a thorough understanding of the complex interactions between a project and its environment. Because many governments are also finding that the constraints on their resources are increasing, they are in addition being pressed to use those resources effectively.

In view of these various problems, it has become essential for governments and donor agencies alike to learn as much as possible from past experience that will enable them to identify the kinds of projects and delivery systems most likely to succeed and the factors most likely to contribute to that success. As a result, more emphasis is being placed on monitoring and evaluating (M/E) the extent to which development projects are cost-effective and achieve their intended objectives.

Fortunately, the need for improved monitoring and evaluation systems comes at a time when the industrial nations have made numerous advances in the theory and practice of program evaluation. In the United States and some other industrial nations, program evaluation is emerging as a separate social science and management discipline. Since the early 1970s it has become standard practice in the United States to monitor and evaluate most federal and state-financed projects, and the results of these evaluations are used extensively by both supporters and opponents of these programs (Chelimsky 1988; Rossi and Freeman 1993; Wholey 1979). The U.S. General Accounting Office now publishes more than one program evaluation a day—many of which greatly influence budgetary allocations and the formulation of new programs (Chelimsky 1987). The growing presence of evaluation specialists can be seen in their published works, in professional organizations such as the American Evaluation Association (which now has more than 2,500 members), and in the increasing number of courses on monitoring and evaluation (now offered in at least forty-six universities in the United States).[1]

In the opinion of many leading evaluation practitioners, satisfactory solutions have been found to most of the basic problems of evaluation design and analysis, at least for countries such as the United States. It is possible to produce methodologically sound and operationally useful evaluations for a broad range of development programs. Rossi and Wright (1984:332), in a review of the status of evaluation research, concluded:

> The evaluation research field is beginning to reach a high level of intellectual accomplishment, that is, just as the best evaluation research of the prosperous decades is being published. New developments in techniques and methodology have appeared that promise to raise the overall quality not only of evaluations but of many other areas of social research as well. Evaluation researchers have now learned how to conduct field experiments successfully and how to analyze the resulting complicated data sets, and they have also started to provide solutions to some of the most serious validity problems of non-experimental research.[2]

Perhaps as many as 100 developing countries now perform some kind of regular monitoring and evaluation activities. These range from comprehensive national evaluation systems in countries such as India and Malaysia to basic monitoring of selected projects in many countries in Africa and the Middle East.[3] The national systems in South Asia (see Table 1-1) have one or more central agencies responsible for the coordination and synthesis of monitoring (and less frequently evaluation) data, which are regularly collected from all major development projects (Ahmed and Bamberger 1989; Khan 1989).[4] Many of these countries are also developing national M/E computer networks to increase their capacity for data collection and analysis.

Much of the original impetus behind the move toward monitoring and evaluation in developing countries came from international aid organizations, most of which require M/E in a large percentage of their projects. The Organisation for Economic Co-operation and Development (OECD 1986) has estimated that an average donor agency conducts 10 to 30 evaluations a year, while USAID and the World Bank conduct as many as 250 evaluations a year (Baum and Tolbert 1985). International agencies

## Table 1-1. Organization and Functions of Central Monitoring and Evaluation Agencies in South Asia
(as of December 1987)

| | |
|---|---|
| *Bangladesh* | The *Implementation, Monitoring and Evaluation Division* (IMED) was established in 1984 under the Planning Commission as the successor to an earlier apex monitoring unit. It is responsible for the physical and financial monitoring of all development projects and feedback to line ministries. It focuses on *implementation* monitoring. Public enterprises are monitored by a separate agency. |
| *India* | The *Project Monitoring Division* of the Ministry of Program Implementation (MOPI) was established in 1985 to monitor megaprojects (costing more than 200 million rupees) as well as the prime minister's nineteen-point Poverty Eradication Program. The Management Information Division and the line divisions of the Planning Commission monitor all centrally managed and sponsored projects. The Programme Evaluation Organization of the Planning Commission evaluates social programs. |
| *Nepal* | The *Programme Division* of the National Planning Commission monitors nationally important projects. The *Program Budgeting and Monitoring Cell* of the Ministry of Finance is testing systems that can be used to monitor both physical and financial progress of all major projects. |
| *Pakistan* | The *Projects Wing* of the National Planning Commission oversees the financial and physical progress of national projects funded by the National Development Program and intensively monitors selected projects. Public manufacturing enterprises are monitored through the performance evaluation system of the *Experts' Advisory Cell* of the Ministry of Production. The *Auditor General's Office* is developing a performance evaluation system. |
| *Sri Lanka* | The *Progress Control Division* of the Ministry of Plan Implementation has been responsible since 1986 for the close monitoring of about 140 major projects and programs and for developing indicators of physical progress. Major development programs such as the Mahaweli Irrigation Authority have their own M/E systems. |

*Note*: These systems continue to evolve, and since this report was prepared there have been further changes in how M/E is organized in some of these countries.

*Source*: Ahmed and Bamberger (1989).

have had both a positive and a negative effect on the way M/E systems have evolved and are used in developing countries.

A small but increasing number of developing countries are now beginning to use M/E for their own project control, financial planning, and policy analysis (these countries include Chile, Colombia, Brazil, India and Malaysia). The World Bank, among others, is helping selected countries develop this capacity through its Evaluation Capability Development Program (World Bank 1991a:12).[5] However, the OECD concludes that, with the exception of a small number of countries, "interest in evaluation generally tends to be stronger among those allocating resources than among those using them."

When properly applied, the information produced by M/E studies can be of direct use to policymakers, planners, and managers in at least four ways. First, it can help a country improve its method of identifying and selecting projects and programs by ensuring that these endeavors are consistent with national development objectives, that they will have a good chance of succeeding, and that they are using the most cost-effective strategy for achieving the intended objectives. Second, M/E studies can determine whether the project is being implemented efficiently, is responsive to the concerns of the intended beneficiaries, and will have its potential problems detected and corrected as quickly as possible. Third, they measure whether projects and programs that are under way are achieving their intended economic and social objectives, as well as contributing to sectoral and national development objectives. Fourth, evaluation studies can be used to assess the impact of projects on wider developmental objectives such as protecting the environment and managing natural resources, alleviating poverty, and giving women full economic, social, and political participation in all aspects of development. Examples provided throughout the book illustrate how M/E studies are used in developing countries in different social sectors and geographical regions.

Despite the growing emphasis on national M/E systems, the focus of M/E studies in most developing countries continues to be narrow, the data are underutilized, and the contribution to project management and national development planning is limited. A high proportion of M/E resources are devoted to monitoring the physical and financial implementation of large projects, and little attention is devoted to assessing the sustainability of projects, the quality of social development projects, the distribution of project benefits among various socioeconomic groups or geographical regions, the extent to which projects have achieved their intended impacts, or the effect development strategies have had on the environment. Nor have the recent developments in evaluation methodology in the United States been applied in developing countries. Section F outlines some of the main organizational, managerial, and methodological problems affecting the design, implementation, and use of monitoring and evaluation in developing countries.

## The Current Status of Social Program Evaluation

As mentioned earlier, social programs refer here to the broad range of programs designed to improve the quality of life by improving the capacity of citizens to participate fully in social, economic, and political activities at the local or national levels. Programs may focus on improving physical well-being (health, nutrition); providing access to services (housing, water supply, local transportation); protecting vulnerable groups from some of the adverse consequences of economic reform and structural adjustment; or providing education, literacy, and employment and income-generating opportunities (vocational and technical training, credit, integrated rural development, small business development). Other programs may focus directly on empowerment and equity issues by strengthening community organizations, encouraging women to participate in development, or alleviating poverty.

Development agencies differ in their view of the nature and objectives of social programs and in how they compare with conventional capital investment programs. These differing perspectives determine how social programs are evaluated.

Some donor agencies consider health and education an investment in human capital, for example, and they appraise, design, and monitor these projects in much the same way that they handle a capital investment project. They assume that precisely defined inputs applied by means of a particular implementation methodology will produce predetermined outputs that will generate measurable improvements in indicators of human capital (such as educational attainment, labor market earnings, or morbidity and mortality). An educational project would be appraised on the basis of its economic rate of return and would have a time-bound implementation schedule with precise and easily monitored implementation and financial objectives. The same approach might be used for a health project, although it would probably be appraised using cost-effectiveness analysis rather than economic rates of return. As we discuss in Chapter 4, however, in only a small number of cases are clearly defined output and impact indicators identified and used for education and health projects. Assessment tends to concentrate more on monitoring inputs, or possibly physical outputs.

A second approach adopted by many governments, United Nations (UN) agencies, bilateral organizations, and nongovernmental organizations (NGOs) is based on the concept that things like literacy, primary health, housing, and drinking water are basic human rights that do not require economic justification. Evaluations, if they are conducted, tend to focus on the cost-effectiveness of the delivery systems and accessibility to the intended target groups. Rigorous impact evaluations are rarely conducted because program justification does not depend on a particular economic impact.

Both of the above approaches are "supply-driven." That is to say, the government or the donor decides what services people should receive and what their basic needs are.

A third approach—adopted by many NGOs, a number of bilateral donors, and agencies such as the United Nations Children's Fund (UNICEF) and recently the World Bank—is based on the notion that the principal objective of social development should be to help indigenous communities or underprivileged groups (such as women, landless laborers, and urban slum dwellers) develop the organizational capacity and knowledge needed to identify and satisfy their own needs.

> The goals of many social development projects and programmes involve such things as the development of indigenous sustainable capacity, the promotion of participation, the awakening of consciousness, and the encouragement of self-reliant strategies. How are these to be measured? What are the purposes of evaluations of these sorts of projects? . . . Are the evaluations of these types of projects essentially different from those of more conventional infrastructural projects?
>
> Because we are dealing with development strategies that are rather different from those that emphasize production, new techniques and new methods need to be devised. We are dealing with a changing set of relationships between actors involved in the development process and a changing scientific and social environment where the old orthodoxies associated with Northern liberal

scientific principles of economic development backed by objective analysis no longer hold. We are negotiating new ways in which value can be analyzed, and new methodologies that will provide more appropriate ways of understanding the effectiveness of interventions in the name of social development (Marsden and Oakley 1990:1–2).

Given the great diversity of social development programs and the various objectives and political and social orientations of the organizations involved, there is no standard way of evaluating such programs—nor should one be sought. Some flexibility will always be desirable. A number of new precepts are evolving, and although some have stirred up controversy, they are gaining increasing support and therefore are given close attention in this book.

First, many authorities recognize that the major stakeholders, particularly the intended beneficiaries (as well as groups that may suffer as a result of the project) should be actively involved in project selection, monitoring, and evaluation. *Beneficiary assessment* methodologies, long used by NGOs, are now being adopted by international agencies (Salmen 1987, 1992).

> Beneficiary assessment is a tool for managers who wish to improve the quality of development operations. This is an approach to information gathering which assesses the value of an activity as it is perceived by its principal users. The approach is qualitative in that it attempts to derive understanding from shared experience as well as observation and gives primacy to the centrality of the other person's point of view. As the Bank and others engaged in development activities seek to do their work better, one key indicator will need to be how the ultimate customer, or intended beneficiary, assesses the value of this work, project or policy, as it affects his or her life. The illumination of this customer/user appreciation of developmental activity is the primary objective of beneficiary assessment." (Salmen 1992:1)

Until recently, beneficiary assessment focused mainly on the intended low-income project beneficiaries, but now its methods are also being used to better understand the perspectives of other stakeholder groups such as other government agencies and private service providers. *Environmental impact assessment* is probably the area in which the opinions of all major stakeholders are most systematically canvassed.

Second, *social impact assessment* techniques (also called social analysis or social soundness analysis) are being more widely used before projects begin or during implementation to assess how different social and economic groups are likely to be affected by the project or program (Asian Development Bank 1991; Ingersol 1990). One of the areas in which the use of social impact assessment has expanded is *gender analysis* (Asian Development Bank 1991; Maya Tech Corporation 1991; Overholt and others 1985). Many multilateral and bilateral agencies now require gender analysis, and sometimes even broader social impact analysis, either as part of their country programming exercise or as part of their project approval process.

Third, efforts are being made to strengthen the use of *qualitative* methods in the evaluation of international development programs and to break away from conventional evaluation approaches based on precisely defined *quantitative* indicators of project performance. Although significant progress has been made, the long-standing split between the advocates of quantitative and qualitative approaches to evaluation has not been resolved. Consequently, few evaluation studies have been able to successfully integrate both approaches, and considerable work remains to be done to encourage the practitioners of conventional quantitative evaluations to accept qualitative methods.

Fourth, interest is growing in rapid assessment procedures (also known as Rapid Social Assessment or Rapid Rural Appraisal), which are more cost-effective than most other methods and more responsive to the sociocultural environment of the project (see Kumar 1993).

Fifth, there is pressure for more *holistic* evaluations that will make it possible to understand the complex interaction between a project and the social, cultural, political, and economic environment in which it evolves (Marsden and Oakley 1990).

Although significant progress is being made in all these areas, the evaluation of social programs has not yet been fully integrated into the M/E systems being developed for other public programs in most developing countries. At the same time, NGOs are playing an increasingly important role in the execution and evaluation of social programs. While many believe that NGOs can contribute a new evaluation perspective with greater emphasis on holistic approaches and qualitative methods (ACVAFS 1983; Marsden and Oakley 1990), these new approaches have so far made little impact on how governments and international agencies evaluate social programs. For these various reasons, the methodologies and systems for evaluating social programs have not developed to the same degree, or as systematically, as the so-called conventional evaluation methods.

## A Monitoring and Evaluation Framework for Developing Countries

This section presents a framework for describing various methods of monitoring and evaluation in developing countries. The definitions employed are consistent with most of the main publications in this field, and we have indicated the few areas in which we differ from these sources, or the sources disagree among themselves. In such cases, the diverging opinion is presented in the endnotes. The main sources used in this comparison are Casley and Kumar (1987), the United Nations ACC Task Force on Rural Development (1984), Rossi and Freeman (1993), and OECD (1986).

Monitoring is an *internal activity of program management,* the purpose of which is to determine whether programs have been implemented as planned—in other words, whether resources are being mobilized as planned and services or products are being delivered on schedule. We refer to the former as *input monitoring* and to the latter as *output monitoring.* In more formal terms, monitoring is

> a continuous internal management activity whose purpose is to ensure that the program achieves its defined objectives within a prescribed time-frame and budget. Monitoring involves the provision of regular feedback on the progress of program implementation, and the problems faced during implementation. Monitoring consists of operational and administrative activities that track resource acquisition and allocation, production or the delivery of services, and cost records.[6]

In contrast, *evaluation* may be conducted within the project implementation agency or by an outside organization. It can be used to assess and improve the performance of an ongoing program or to estimate the impacts and evaluate the performance of completed projects or programs (these activities are known as impact evaluation and efficiency evaluation). To assess the appropriateness of design and implementation methods, data are normally collected while the project is going on (by means of *diagnostic studies or process evaluation*). Diagnostic studies often follow an input or output monitoring study that has identified an actual or potential problem. For example, management may request a diagnostic study when a monitoring report has shown an unexpectedly small number of families applying for permission to purchase housing units, a lower proportion of girls than boys attending a new primary school, or low loan repayment rates. The results of a program are measured by the extent to which it achieves its objectives, the other impacts it produces, the costs per program benefit or per program product, and the problems responsible for either the poor quality of program implementation or the failure to achieve program objectives. We therefore define evaluation as

> an internal or external management activity to assess the appropriateness of a program's design and implementation methods in achieving both specified objectives and more general development objectives; and to assess a program's results, both intended and unintended and to assess the factors affecting the level and distribution of benefits produced.[7]

One important question concerns the relationship between monitoring and evaluation. Although it is customary to refer to the two together (as in the term "M/E"), many aid agencies and project implementing agencies treat them as distinct activities conducted by separate agencies and having separate objectives. Casley and Kumar (1987:8) support this separation: "Are monitoring and evaluation such distinctly different functions, serving distinctly different users, that they should be considered independently of each other? The answer to this question, in the light of the definitions given here, is yes. Hence we disapprove of the use of the universal acronym 'M&E' as it can imply that we are dealing with a single function." When the two functions are kept separate, there seems to be substantial support for monitoring project implementation but limited support for evaluation. Evaluation is given much lower priority because it is seen as an activity that would be nice to support if time and resources permitted—which, unfortunately, is seldom the case. As a result, little effort is made either to evaluate the extent to which projects have achieved their objectives, or to use the experience from completed projects to improve the selection and design of future ones.

In contrast, most of the U.S. evaluation literature assumes monitoring and evaluation to be closely related, and frequently the term "program evaluation" is taken to mean both monitoring and evaluation, as in the work of Hatry, Winnie, and Fisk (1981:4): "Program evaluation is the systematic examination of a specific government program to provide information on the full range of the program's short- and long-term effects. While a program evaluation may include consideration of workload measures, operating procedures, or staffing, its chief focus is on measuring the program's impact." This is also the view of Morris and Fitz-Gibbon (1978), Rossi and Freeman (1993), and Wholey (1979). In the United States, organizations such as the General Accounting Office (Chelimsky 1987, 1988) have encouraged the close integration of monitoring and evaluation by creating banks of both monitoring and evaluation data for assessing the potential impacts of proposed new programs (prospective evaluation).

In their studies of developing countries, Freeman, Rossi, and Wright (1979) use the term "project monitoring and evaluation" to stress the close ties between monitoring and evaluation; and Middleton, Terry, and Bloch (1989:38) call for integrated monitoring and evaluation systems with "a central capacity with strong vertical links to intermediate administrative units and schools." The United Nations ACC Task Force (1984) also favors an integrated system, as reflected in its constant use of the acronym "M&E."

Likewise, we believe that monitoring and evaluation should be considered complementary parts of an integrated system. Evaluation is concerned as much with the lessons of project implementation as it is with the degree to which intended impacts have been achieved. Consequently, evaluation should take place either continuously or periodically from the time the project is formulated right through implementation and the operational phase. Also, monitoring information should constantly be fed into the national M/E system to build up a national data bank that can be used to improve the selection and design of future projects. Therefore the acronym M/E is used throughout this book, except when it is necessary to refer specifically to monitoring or evaluation.

We are aware, of course, that resource constraints force many countries to concentrate on project monitoring and prohibit systematic evaluation. But there are also many countries in which the potential contributions of evaluation are poorly understood, and their neglect of this activity is not due simply to a resource constraint. As this volume points out, however, simple and economical methods are now available for estimating project impacts, and many of these methods can be used in countries with limited research expertise and financial resources.

## Monitoring and Evaluation at the Project Level

Monitoring and evaluation studies can be conducted at the project, sectoral, or national levels. This section discusses the uses of M/E at the project level. Applications at the sectoral and national levels are discussed in Chapters 2, 4, 6, 8, and 12.

Baum and Tolbert (1985:333) have defined a project as "a discrete package of investments, policies, and institutional and other actions designed to achieve a specific development objective (or set of objectives) within a designated period." Although this definition is satisfactory for capital investment and economic development projects, it is less adequate for many kinds of social projects and programs. For social programs, the objectives may be partly defined by beneficiaries as the program evolves, and much greater flexibility may be required, depending on the period in which the project or program is to be implemented.

The project concept has evolved from the activities of the international aid agencies and their concern that their financial assistance would be used to achieve specific and monitorable objectives within a given time frame.

Projects generally progress through seven main stages (see Figure 1-1).[8] M/E systems should provide the information that project planners, implementers, and managers need at each of these stages and should help determine whether a project has been implemented as planned, what problems need to be resolved, what expected or unexpected impacts have occurred, and what lessons can be learned for the selection and design of future projects (see Chapter 2).

### Stage 1: Identification and Preparation

Before specific projects are identified, governments—often in consultation with international agencies—define their national and sectoral development strategies. Some countries prepare five-year plans, whereas others plan over a shorter period. In many countries the longer-term strategy is then translated into annual development plans (ADP). These strategies and plans calculate the national and international resources required for new development projects, determine how much is available, and identify sectoral priorities.

**Figure 1-1.  Project Management Cycle**

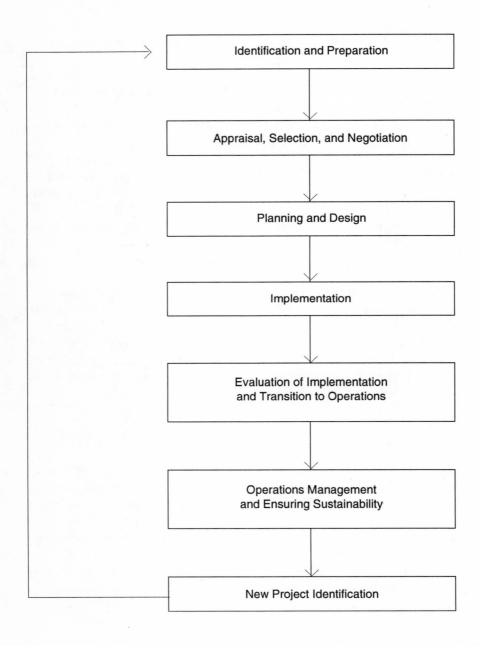

A preliminary assessment should be made of each of the short-listed projects to assess their potential viability on the basis of economic, financial, technical, institutional, social, poverty, environmental, and gender criteria (see project social analysis checklist in Chapter 2, Box 2-3).

## Stage 2: Project Appraisal, Selection, and Negotiation

This stage is devoted to assessing the economic, financial, and technical feasibility of the project. Many aid agencies conduct an economic analysis (see Chapter 2) and calculate the internal economic rate of return (IRR) to determine whether the proposed project can be expected to achieve some minimum acceptable IRR on the resources invested (Gittinger 1982:314).

Conventional appraisal methods often have to be greatly modified when applied to social programs. Gender analysis, social impact assessment, and environmental impact assessment are among the new analytical approaches discussed in this book.

## Stage 3: Project Planning and Design

Once a project has been approved, attention turns to detailed planning and design. Six kinds of activities are performed in this stage.

First, information is collected to define the target population. Second, the condition to be resolved or alleviated by the project is identified. Third, the project's goals and objectives are formulated. *Goals* are the social change to which a project is expected to contribute. For example, a goal of the Pan American Health Organization (PAHO) was to eradicate polio from the Western Hemisphere by 1991. *Objectives* refer to the magnitude of an expected output from a project, expressed in quantitative terms. In the above example, a PAHO objective would be to deliver three doses of polio vaccine to 80 percent of the children in Haiti within the first year of life. Fourth, decisions are made about the duration and sequencing of each stage. Fifth, the most efficient methods of construction and service delivery are selected. And sixth, additional information is collected for formulating the program model that is expected to produce the desired social change in the target population.

Whether explicitly stated or not, every project includes assumptions about the ways in which the target population will respond to it, the relative effectiveness of different implementation methods, and the ways in which the project is likely to affect and be affected by the social, economic, and political environment in which it operates. In order to design and implement the monitoring and evaluation program, the evaluator must work with program planners and managers to develop all the above assumptions and expectations into a model of how the project is expected to evolve; how it will be affected by the social, economic, and political environment in which it will operate; and how the intended beneficiaries will respond to it. Modeling is discussed in Chapter 3.

For the present, we can define a model as a planned intervention based on explicit theories about how to achieve social change or reform, and why that change should be expected. A model of a social program should make explicit how different inputs can be expected to lead to certain impacts. Therefore, a model is a testable hypothesis about a project that can be either refuted or vindicated.

### Stage 4: Project Implementation

According to Baum and Tolbert (1985:834), "The implementation stage covers the actual development or construction of the project, up to the point at which it becomes fully operational. It includes monitoring of all aspects of the work or activity as it proceeds and supervision by 'oversight' agencies within the country or by external donors."

For many projects, this means constructing a physical infrastructure (roads, irrigation systems, schools) and acquiring plant and equipment; but for many social projects this stage may involve training, designing, and testing experimental education programs, and developing delivery systems for health and credit programs. Project implementation involves a number of distinct phases, activities, and decisions:

- Decisions have to be made about how the project will be organized, which will be the lead agency and the project executing agency, what other agencies will be actively involved, and how the project will be coordinated. Another important decision concerns the extent to which project beneficiaries will be involved in the planning, implementation, and management of the project.
- The financial, material, and human resources required for the project must be procured and mobilized. Because the procurement of resources and the contracting of technical assistance are complex tasks and may involve procedures that are unfamiliar to borrowers, the

procurement phase tends to be the source of many of the cost overruns and delays that arise in projects and also affects the quality and maintenance of equipment.

- Facilities and equipment must be constructed and installed.
- The most effective methods of service delivery must be selected and implemented.
- Physical implementation and service delivery need to be supervised and financial control established for all aspects of project implementation.

Figure 1-2, which shows a simplified form of the project implementation model, indicates the principal components of concern for monitoring and evaluation, namely, project inputs, implementation methods, outputs, and impacts. For the purposes of monitoring and evaluation, it is often convenient to use a simpler definition of project implementation:

- *Implementation* refers to the transformation of project inputs, through a set of technical and organizational systems and procedures that produce a specified volume and quality of project outputs.

**Figure 1-2.  Simplified Model of the Project Implementation Process**

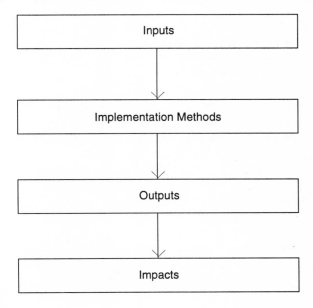

**Table 1-2. The Context in Which Input-Output Monitoring
Takes Place**

*Questions on the minds of clients*

- Are financial resources being released on time? What causes delays?
- Is the procurement of equipment and materials keeping to the planned timetable and budget? What is causing the delays and cost overruns?
- What problems, if any, are there in the contracting, training, and retention of staff?
- Are there any major delays or cost overruns in the production of the main outputs?
- How do implementation delays affect the disbursement of foreign assistance?

*Kinds of studies*
- Gantt charts.
- Logical framework analysis.
- Network-based systems for physical and financial monitoring.

*Timing of the studies*
- Monthly or quarterly progress reports are prepared from the time the project starts up to the completion of project implementation.

*How the studies are used*
- Progress reports are discussed in management review meetings. Delays, cost overruns, and related problems are identified and discussed.
- Follow-up diagnostic studies may be requested if the reasons for the delays are not clear.
- Information is forwarded to central monitoring and financial agencies where it is aggregated with other project reports to provide a global picture of the status of all (or major) development projects.

- *Inputs* are defined as financial, human, and material resources available to implement the project as planned.
- *Outputs* are the services or products that a project delivers to a target population to produce the expected impacts.

Table 1-2 indicates the context in which input-output monitoring studies are normally conducted. The following are some of the questions clients may ask: Are the financial resources being released on time? Is the procurement of equipment and materials proceeding according to schedule? and Are there any major cost or time overruns? Where projects have foreign financing, the Ministry of Finance will also wish to know whether implementation delays are likely to affect loan disbursements.

The monitoring reports are discussed in management meetings, which give special attention to delays, cost overruns, and other kinds of problems. Follow-up diagnostic studies are often requested to obtain feedback on the causes and possible solutions of the identified problems.

Table 1-3 indicates the context in which diagnostic (process evaluation) studies are normally conducted and the kinds of questions on the minds of clients.

**Table 1-3.  The Context in Which Diagnostic Studies Are Conducted**

*Questions on the minds of clients*
- How might prospective beneficiaries react to the proposed project and to its different components?
- Why are certain components of the project falling behind schedule or suffering cost overruns?
- Why are there large differences in loan and service charge payment rates in different communities?
- What impacts is the project having on different groups? Who benefits and who does not? Are any groups worse off as a result of the project?

*Kinds of studies*
- Participant observation.
- Rapid surveys.
- Direct observation.
- Interviews with key informants.

*Timing of the studies*
- During project identification and design.
- During implementation, when problems have been identified by the input-output monitoring reports.
- Continuous panel studies conducted to provide continuous feedback on the attitude of beneficiaries.
- Ad hoc studies conducted whenever management needs a better understanding of certain aspects of the project.

*How the studies are used*
- During project identification, studies help identify components and services of interest to beneficiaries, as well as communities that are likely to respond favorably to the project.
- During implementation, problems are examined and possible solutions recommended; continuous feedback is obtained from beneficiaries and adjustments are made in project implementation and service delivery systems; and feedback is obtained on any groups that are being left out or negatively affected, and the appropriate adjustments are made.

*Stage 5: Evaluation of Project Implementation and Transition to Operations*

Once project implementation has been completed, most donor agencies and central government financing agencies ask for a project completion report that will describe and evaluate each component of project identification, appraisal, and implementation. At this point decisions may be made about how the operational phase of the project will be managed. The involvement of many donor agencies ends with the formal closing of their loan, once implementation is completed. The evaluation helps authorities decide how the operational phase of the project is to be managed. Ideally, the transition to operations should have been planned at an early stage in the project cycle, but as explained in the discussion of project sustainability in Chapter 6, in many cases little attention is given to this phase until implementation is nearing completion.

Table 1-4 shows the context in which studies are conducted to evaluate the efficiency with which outputs and impacts are produced and the kinds of questions on the minds of clients.

The results of the studies are used to select new projects and to determine how benefits are distributed among various socioeconomic groups.

*Stage 6: Management of Project Operations and Ensuring Sustainability*

After implementation, the project may continue as a separate activity or it may be absorbed into the general operations of the responsible ministry or agency. If the project is to be successfully sustained (see Chapter 6), organizational and financial arrangements must be made for managing service delivery; for ensuring that the infrastructure, plant, and equipment will be maintained on a regular basis; and for assisting the formal and informal agencies and organizations involved with the project. As discussed in Chapter 6, many projects are unable to keep operating because they paid far less attention to sustainability than to implementation.

Through its continued operation, the project is intended to produce one or more *impacts* (or *outcomes*). An impact is defined as the expected effect (or effects) of a project on a target population. Impacts can be further classified as short-term and long-term (depending on when they occur and how long they last); intermediate and final (depending on the objectives of the project); and intended and unintended (depending on whether or not they were planned or expected).

**Table 1-4.  The Context in Which Studies Are Conducted to Evaluate Project Efficiency in the Production of Outputs and Impacts**

*Questions on the minds of clients*
- How much does it cost to produce each project output?
- Are there other ways to produce the same outputs more economically?
- How would the cost-effectiveness of the project be affected by a large-scale replication?
- Does the project produce a good return on the resources invested?
- Could the resources have produced a higher yield if they had been invested in a different project?
- How are project benefits distributed between different geographical and income groups?

*Kinds of studies*
- Cost-effectiveness studies.
- Cost-benefit studies (economic analysis).

*Timing of the studies*
- During project identification and appraisal to assess the likely costs and benefits of alternative projects.
- During the preparation of the project completion report.
- When the project has been operating for several years, to reassess the economic rate of return as an indicator of project sustainability.

*How are the studies used*
- To help in the selection of projects and delivery systems offering the highest potential outputs and benefits at the lowest costs.
- To assess (before the project begins) and to evaluate (after the project is completed) the distribution of benefits.
- To assess the sustainability of ongoing projects.
- To improve the data base for the selection of new projects.

Table 1-5 indicates the contexts in which impact evaluation studies are conducted and the kinds of questions on the minds of clients.

The results of the preliminary impact studies (conducted during the implementation phase) are used to assess whether impacts are likely to be achieved and whether the intended target groups will benefit. If the prospects in this regard look poor, corrective measures can be taken. Since most impact studies are conducted after projects are operating, however, their main purpose is to help improve the selection and design of future projects.

## Table 1-5.  The Context in Which Project Impact Evaluations Are Conducted

---

*Questions on the minds of clients*
- Is the project producing the intended benefits?
- How large are the benefits?
- Who actually receives the benefits? Who does not?
- What factors account for the variations in impacts?
- How can impacts be increased or stabilized?
- How likely is it that similar impacts would be produced in another similar project?

*Kinds of studies*
- Rigorous quasi-experimental designs with before and after measurements and a carefully selected control group.
- Continuous panel studies.
- Rapid and economical impact assessments.
- Qualitative impact assessments using participant observation and related techniques.
- Broader studies to assess environmental impacts.

*Timing of the studies*
- Preliminary impact estimates can be made while the project is still being implemented.
- For quasi-experimental designs baseline data should be collected before implementation begins and at least one, and ideally several, repeat measurements should be made once the project is operating.
- Rapid ex-post evaluations can be conducted at any time after the project becomes operational.
- A panel of respondents can be re-interviewed periodically throughout implementation and the early years of project operation.

*How the studies are used*
- Preliminary impact studies are used to assess whether impacts are likely to be achieved. Corrective measures can be taken.
- Panel studies and qualitative evaluations can identify at an early stage groups who are not benefiting or who are negatively affected by the project.
- Since most impact studies are conducted after projects are operating, their main purpose is to help improve the selection and design of future projects.
- Macro studies are used to monitor environmental impacts and to take corrective measures at the national, regional, or local levels.

---

*Stage 7: New Project Identification*

Decisions concerning the selection and design of future projects seldom take full advantage of the M/E information from earlier projects. Chapter 12 discusses these issues and explains how central data banks can be created to make use of the lessons learned in earlier projects.

## Problems with Current Approaches to Monitoring and Evaluation

In view of the rapid proliferation of monitoring and evaluation systems, it is not surprising that many of them have had difficulty living up to the ambitious demands placed on them. Many project M/E systems have been criticized for their inefficiency and limited utility. In some cases the information arrives too late, does not answer the right questions, or is too costly to collect. In other cases the attention is narrowly focused on certain quantitative and financial aspects of the projects, and most of the information refers only to the period of physical implementation. These problems can be classified into four main groups, each of which is referred to frequently throughout the book.

### Organizational and Political Problems

Although the "politics of program evaluation" has been widely discussed in the United States (Palumbo 1987), the political dimensions of evaluation have been by and large neglected in developing countries. Needless to say, one cannot expect to understand the dynamics of program evaluation without recognizing that many central monitoring and evaluation agencies (CMEAs) exercise considerable influence over resource allocation and over decisions concerning the future fate of the programs they are evaluating. However, the CMEAs are frequently perceived as a threat or as a powerful resource that needs to be controlled (Bamberger 1988a). As a result, CMEAs are often switched from one ministry or department to another or have their powers or resources greatly reduced. Ahmed and Bamberger (1989) found none of the CMEAs in South Asia operating in their present location for more than three years.

Other organizational problems arise when the M/E functions are located in an inappropriate agency, when functions are assigned to different agencies and thus are difficult to coordinate, or when coordination problems restrict the flow of information between the central agency and the intended users. Chapter 12 discusses in some detail the links between where M/E is located and how it is organized, on the one hand, and the kinds of studies produced and how they are disseminated, on the other. It is also common to find nongovernmental organizations—many of which have extensive evaluation experience—excluded from collaborating in the evaluation of public sector programs.

Donor agencies have considerable influence on the content and organization of M/E systems. The fact that donors and borrowers often need different kinds of information can create a further set of problems.

### Managerial Problems

Many M/E agencies at the project, sectoral, and national levels have failed to establish clear procedures for identifying the main users of the information they produce, for comparing the importance of studies requested by different national and international organizations, and for defining the kinds of information required by each potential user. Consequently, the potential users complain that the studies do not provide the information they require or that information is produced too late or in a form that is not easily understood. The highly centralized nature of many CMEAs means that M/E information is used mainly by central government agencies to *control* line ministries and project units and is not considered a management tool to be used by project managers. Many managers thus see M/E as a threat, or at least an inconvenience, and they are unwilling to cooperate in data collection or analysis. This has also created concern about the quality and reliability of the M/E information provided by line agencies. Most of these problems are also found in the United States. Even though a broad range of federally and state-funded programs have mandated that such evaluations be conducted, and even though the potential utility of evaluation is widely recognized, many program managers still seem reluctant to initiate evaluations, for the following reasons (Carlson and Crane 1989):

- *Minimization of accountability.* The pressure to reduce the size of government has brought a new sense of risk. Managers are aware that legislators and budget departments are seeking programs that can be cut or scaled down. Consequently, there is a fear that any kind of evaluation result could be used to justify closing the program. At the same time, no benefits are expected from a positive evaluation.

- *Lack of confidence that evaluation products will yield practical benefits exceeding their cost.*
- *Lack of rewards associated with sponsoring evaluations.*
- *Length of time required to begin an evaluation.* In U.S. government agencies, the process of obtaining approval to conduct an evaluation, and then to complete the procurement process for contracting consultants, is often very slow and cumbersome. Many managers do not feel that the evaluation results are likely to justify the effort involved.
- *Length of time to produce results.*

Another set of managerial problems relates to the difficulties of recruiting and retaining qualified staff for the M/E units. Often the kinds of researchers required for these units are not appropriately defined in the civil service structure. As a result, it can be difficult to offer competitive employment conditions. Also the lack of a clearly defined career path for evaluators can discourage qualified staff from entering this field.

### Problems of Focus

CMEAs usually focus on the monitoring of project implementation, and few studies are conducted to determine how programs operate, how they are sustained, or whether they are able to produce their intended impacts. Thus, although a great deal of information is collected on whether programs are implemented on time and within their budgets, little is known about whether the massive social and economic development programs actually achieve their intended objectives and produce the benefits or changes for which they were designed (Bamberger 1989).

One reason for this implementation bias is that in most developing countries the capital investment budget (for the construction of new roads, schools, factories, and hospitals) is usually far greater than the operations or revenue budgets from which funds are obtained for operations and maintenance. Because most government resources go into project implementation, this is the area in which there is most demand for careful monitoring. And because international aid agencies are mainly involved with project implementation, they, too, are more interested in monitoring implementation. Many M/E units are thus located in agencies created to oversee project implementation. Since many of these agencies are disbanded once implementation is completed, they cannot manage long-term impact evaluations.

Another constraint on the use of evaluation is the fact that most governments and implementing agencies focus more on the assessment of *inputs* than on the evaluation of *outputs* and products. This limits the demand for evaluations of the quality or cost-effectiveness of outputs or the estimation of impacts.

A broader problem arises from the fact that most governments and policymakers operate within a one-year or at most two-year time horizon. Most countries continue to operate on annual budget cycles, and consequently planners and operational agencies tend to focus on short-term implementation objectives. This means that one of the most powerful applications of evaluation—namely long-term prospective studies—is rarely used. Osborne and Gaebler (1992) point out that an important recent development in the U.S government is that some of the more innovative local and state authorities have moved toward ten-year planning and budget cycles. This approach, when combined with *strategic planning*, can generate demand for a whole new range of prospective and retrospective evaluation studies that will help planners and managers project the future on the basis of a systematic analysis of past and present experience.

## Methodological Problems

During the 1970s a number of large-scale impact evaluations using quasi-experimental designs were financed by international aid agencies in sectors such as health, housing, and agriculture. The results of most of these evaluations were disappointing, and now many government authorities and donors argue it is impossible for *rigorous impact evaluations* to be cost-effective and operationally useful. Thus, the proponents of impact evaluations are required to defend the technical feasibility of rigorous impact evaluations, while at the same time responding to criticisms that the results of such evaluations are too academic or arrive too late to be of any operational use.

Some of the other methodological problems discussed in subsequent chapters include the *mono-method bias* that arises from relying on a single (or small number of) data collection method(s); the preference for *quantitative methods* and the tendency to ignore the many valuable qualitative methods; the preference for *static comparisons between points in time* rather than analyses of processes of change; and *excessive reliance on computers* and the lack of concern for the constraints that computerization imposes on the kinds of data collected, or on the quality and validity of the data.

## Evaluating Social Development Programs: Further Problems and Recommended Approaches

The monitoring and evaluation of social development programs can run into still other kinds of problems of a less general nature.

### Further Problems

First, owing to the large number of donor or nationally funded programs that must be monitored, social development programs are often monitored using the same procedures and reporting formats employed in capital investment and economic development projects. These monitoring systems are based on a set of easily quantified physical and financial indicators, many of which are not entirely appropriate for social development projects, since their outputs are not easy to identify or measure. For example, the performance of health or education projects should in part be assessed on the basis of qualitative indicators such as the *quality* of teachers or health extension workers, the quality and utility of the textbooks or curricula, the effectiveness and representational character of community organizations, or the quality and utility of the technical assistance provided for entrepreneurs. It is inappropriate and misleading to monitor these programs *exclusively* through quantitative indicators (as is frequently done in national monitoring systems), such as the number of patients or clients assisted or the number of people attending community meetings.

Second, many social development programs use a flexible, participatory approach in which project objectives are defined in consultation with intended beneficiaries, and often over a period of time as the project evolves. This makes it difficult to establish objectives at the start of the project and to define a set of criteria for evaluating the objectives. To complicate matters further, different stakeholder groups may have different objectives (see the discussion of stakeholder analysis in Chapters 4 and 10).

Third, it is often difficult to assess the links between project outputs and the production of desired impacts. For example, infant mortality, school performance, or household income are affected by so many factors that it is extremely difficult to isolate the contribution of a particular project. The contribution becomes even more difficult to evaluate when programs have broad objectives, such as alleviating poverty or improving the social and economic participation of women.

*Recommended Approaches*

Before discussing specific recommendations for social program evaluation, we note some general recommendations concerning the organization, design, and management of evaluations. These are taken from a number of recent studies on evaluation experience in the United States and Europe. The interested reader is referred to Wholey, Newcomer and Associates (1989); Osborne and Gaebler (1992); Rist (1990); Stokke (1991a); and Barkdoll and Bell (1989). The following are some of the key lessons and recommendations derived from these and other similar recent publications:

- It is essential to involve all major stakeholders in the evaluation process from the initial stages of identifying the need for studies and defining objectives.
- Without, of course, eliminating input and process evaluation, much greater attention should be given to the evaluation of outputs and products. It must not be forgotten that programs are funded and organized to achieve certain objectives—and that an effective evaluation program must provide policymakers and managers with consistent feedback on the extent to which these objectives are being achieved and on the factors that are interfering with that endeavor.
- Greater attention must be devoted to assessing the *quality* of programs rather than simply examining the quantitative indicators of inputs and outputs.
- Evaluators must help managers understand how evaluation can become a management tool for improving performance. Evaluators must also maintain a much closer relationship with managers than they normally do.
- More emphasis should be put on *policy evaluation*. One of the greatest potential uses of evaluation data is in the systematic analysis of what is known about a particular problem or type of program so as to help policymakers select the policy or program most likely to achieve the desired objectives.

Although it is important to incorporate social programs into established national M/E systems, these systems must be enhanced in a number of ways to reflect the special characteristics of social development programs.

- The intended beneficiaries should be involved in the planning, execution, and interpretation of the M/E studies. This means that the perspectives of different stakeholders should be identified and incorporated into the planning and interpretation of the studies. The beneficiary assessment methods being developed by the World Bank are among the many examples of how this approach can be applied.

- Social analysis should be incorporated as a standard component of project appraisal. Thus an assessment of the social and institutional soundness of a project should be evaluated in exactly the same way as its economic and financial soundness.
- Social development projects are frequently more concerned with institution building at the community and local level than with achieving precisely defined outcomes. Consequently, much greater attention is placed on the evaluation of the *processes* of project selection, implementation, operation, and replication. Closely related to this is the emphasis on institutional assessment. However, these projects should also be concerned with the outcomes they hope to sustain.
- Rapid appraisal methods should be developed and standardized so that they can be used as a regular part of data collection and analysis during the appraisal, monitoring, and diagnostic phases.
- More flexibility must be introduced in the M/E process in recognition of the fact that the objectives of the program will evolve as the program develops. This means that the evaluation must describe and assess the implementation *process* as well as the outputs.
- It will often be helpful to develop a *model of the project implementation process*. Such a model (described in Chapter 3) identifies the assumptions on which the project is based, describes the intended methods of project implementation, and identifies the assumed links between inputs, implementation, outputs, and impacts. The intended model is then compared with actual implementation experience and the reasons for deviations, and unexpected outcomes are examined and explained.
- Nongovernmental organizations should be asked to participate in all stages of the evaluation.
- It is important to establish a number of independent indicators of key outputs and impacts so as to obtain more reliable ways of assessing and explaining project performance and outcomes. This will normally involve both quantitative and qualitative indicators. The methodology for reconciling the different indicators is often referred to as *triangulation*.

These various strategies for improving M/E are the subject of this book.

## Recommended Reading

Ahmed, Viqar, and Michael Bamberger. 1989. *Monitoring and Evaluating Development Projects: The South Asian Experience.* Seminar Report Series. Washington, D.C.: World Bank, Economic Development Institute.

A description and assessment of how monitoring and evaluation is conducted in the countries of South Asia.

Casley, Dennis, and Krishna Kumar. 1987. *Project Monitoring and Evaluation in Agriculture.* Baltimore, Md.: Johns Hopkins University Press.

One of the standard texts on the evaluation of international development projects.

Osborne, David, and Ted Gaebler. 1992. *Reinventing Government: How the Entrepreneurial Spirit Is Transforming the Public Sector.* New York: Addison-Wesley.

Reviews innovative approaches to local and state government in the United States and shows the new roles that evaluation is coming to play.

Rossi, P. H., and H. E. Freeman. 1993. *Evaluation: A Systematic Approach.* 5th ed. Beverly Hills, Calif.: Sage.

One of the standard U.S textbooks on program evaluation.

Rossi, Peter, and James Wright. 1984. "Evaluation Research: An Assessment." *Annual Review of Sociology* 10:331–52.

A useful overview of the development and current status of program evaluation in the United States.

Wholey, J., K. Newcomer, and Associates. 1989. *Improving Government Performance: Evaluation Strategies for Strengthening Public Agencies and Programs.* San Francisco: Jossey-Bass.

Describes innovative methods that are being used to improve the design and utilization of evaluation in U.S. public sector agencies.

## Notes

1. See Davis (1986). Of the 46 evaluation programs identified in U.S. universities in 1984, 25 were located in education departments, 14 in psychology, 3 in sociology, 2 in social work, 1 in medicine, and 1 in a multidisciplinary setting.

2. Ironically, Rossi and Wright concluded that this high level of evaluation expertise was being achieved at a time when the evaluation field was suffering a decline, owing to budgetary cutbacks in human service and entitlement programs and to corresponding cutbacks in related evaluation activities.

3. Cited by the International Development Research Centre in the Evaluation Research Society Annual Meeting in Toronto (October 1985).

4. The M/E systems have continued to evolve and there have been further changes in how M/E is organized in several of these countries.

5. In 1991 the Operations Evaluation Department of the World Bank helped six countries (including Brazil, Morocco, and the Philippines) and one regional development bank to strengthen their evaluation capability, and requests are being considered from three more countries (World Bank 1991a:12–13). In most countries the emphasis is initially on taking over responsibility for the preparation of project completion reports, but some countries (such as Brazil) have broader interests and the National Planning Secretariat is seeking to integrate evaluation within the national planning framework.

6. The United Nations ACC Task Force (1984:13) defines monitoring as "the continuous or periodic review and surveillance (overseeing) by management at every level of the hierarchy of the implementation of an activity to ensure that input deliveries, work schedules, targeted outputs and other required actions are proceeding according to plan." Casley and Kumar (1987:2) define monitoring as "a continuous assessment both of the functioning of the project activities in the context of implementation schedules and of the use of project inputs by targeted populations in the context of design expectations. It is an internal project activity, an essential part of day-to-day management."

7. The OECD (1986:65) defines evaluation as "an examination as systematic and objective as possible of an on-going or completed project or programme, its design, implementation and results, with the aim of determining its efficiency, effectiveness, impact, sustainability and the relevance of its objectives. The purpose of an evaluation is to guide decision makers." Casley and Kumar (1987:2) also point out that "evaluation is a periodic assessment of the relevance, performance, efficiency, and impact of the project in the context of its stated objectives. It usually involves comparisons requiring information from outside the project—in time, area or population."

8. The discussion of the project cycle is based on Baum and Tolbert (1985). They conclude their work with the evaluation of project implementation, since this is the point at which donor involvement normally ends. For the purposes of the present discussion, two extra stages have been added: management of project operations, and selection and design of new projects.

# 2

# Practical Applications of Monitoring and Evaluation at the Project, Sectoral, and National Levels

As pointed out in Chapter 1, monitoring and evaluation can be conducted at the project, sectoral, and national levels. At the *project level*, the emphasis is on monitoring project implementation (to ensure that resources are used efficiently), assessing the quality and timeliness of the production of outputs, identifying and correcting problems, and ensuring that benefits and services are accessible to the intended target groups. At the *sectoral level*, the goals are to monitor performance across different projects and geographical regions, identify areas requiring greater attention, assess the complementarities between different services and use the results to identify the most effective "package" of components to include in projects, and determine whether broader sectoral objectives have been achieved, such as environmental conservation, poverty alleviation, better health conditions, and the full participation of women as economic producers and as project beneficiaries.

## Levels at Which Monitoring and Evaluation Are Used

A number of distinct M/E activities are conducted at the *national level*. The Ministry of Finance normally monitors the implementation of all foreign-funded projects to estimate the flow of foreign loan disbursements. The Central Planning Agency or the Ministry of Program Implementation monitors project implementation to identify possible delays or cost overruns and prepares recommendations for the prime minister's or president's office indicating what corrective actions must be taken. The Central Planning Agency may also be required to assess the overall progress and impacts of the national development program (the Five-Year Plan, for example) and to cooperate with line agencies in conducting sector reviews. In recent years many heavily indebted countries have been seeking to evaluate the social and economic impacts of the structural adjustment programs they have been forced to implement.[1]

Many federal systems have an evaluation office operating in each state or province, thus creating a fourth level of evaluation.

International agencies such as the World Bank and the Asian Development ment Bank and bilateral agencies such as the U.S. Agency for International Development (USAID), Canadian International Development Agency (CIDA), Norwegian Agency for Development (NORAD), and Swedish International Development Agency (SIDA), among others, have been helping countries establish national evaluation offices having a range of functions, including the preparation and analysis of project completion reports, and the development of standardized monitoring and evaluation procedures. As yet, few countries look to their central evaluation offices to conduct the kinds of policy analysis that are becoming increasingly important in the United States, and to a lesser extent in Europe. However, *policy analysis* and *strategic planning* are areas in which evaluation can make an important contribution. One step toward this end would be to develop a systematic response to the economic and social problems resulting from structural adjustment programs. This suggestion is discussed on pages 56–66 and in Chapter 3.

Note that nongovernmental organizations (NGOs) and academic research institutions also conduct M/E activities. Many NGOs are particularly concerned with the social and environmental issues surrounding development, which usually receive little attention in government studies. NGOs and academic institutions have performed some important evaluations of the environmental impact of development strategies (World Resources Institute 1990; Centre for Science and Environment 1985). They have also studied the effect of development on women (Heyzer 1985, 1987; Azad 1986) and on the poorest sectors of society (Bangladesh Rural Ad-

vancement Society 1983; Getubig and Ledesma 1988). These nongovernmental groups play a vital role in evaluating and monitoring national
development strategies.

The purpose of this chapter is to describe the practical applications of
monitoring and evaluation at each of these levels and to illustrate how they
can help project managers, planners, and policymakers improve the selection, design, implementation, and sustainability of development projects,
programs, and policies.

## Practical Applications of Monitoring and Evaluation at the Project Level

Because international agencies provide most of their loans and grants
through projects, they have helped promote the project concept (that is, the
package of investments, policies, and institutional and other actions designed to achieve particular development objectives within a particular
time frame) in order to ensure that their financial assistance is used to
achieve specific and monitorable objectives within a given time frame.

M/E can provide the information project planners and managers need
to determine whether a project has been implemented as planned. It can
also help them identify the problems that need to be resolved, the expected
or unexpected impacts that have occurred, and the lessons that should
guide them in selecting and designing future projects.

Chapter 1 identified the seven stages through which projects evolve (see
Figure 1-1). The following paragraphs describe how M/E studies can
provide the kinds of information required by project managers, planners,
and policymakers at each of these stages (summarized in Table 2-1).

### Stage 1: Project Identification and Preparation

During project preparation, alternative projects are compared and alternative implementation strategies are evaluated. Attention is given to identifying and assessing risks and to determining the viability of the proposed
methods for reducing the risks. Stakeholders are identified and the process
of consensus building begins.

An important step in project identification is to *review the experience of
earlier projects.* When the intended objectives of earlier projects are compared with the actual outcomes, valuable insight is gained into the kinds

**Table 2-1.  Practical Applications of Monitoring and Evaluation at Each Stage of the Project Cycle**

| Stage | Practical Applications of M/E Studies |
|---|---|
| 1. Project identification and preparation | A "prospective evaluation" draws lessons from earlier projects to identify the kinds of projects most and least likely to succeed. "Evaluability assessment" assesses whether the project is likely to produce measurable results that can be evaluated. |
| 2. Project appraisal, selection, and negotiation | Appraisal identifies projects most likely to achieve national and sectoral objectives; and ensures that projects are environmentally and socially sound, and that they are likely to be sustainable. |
| 3. Project planning and design | Rapid "diagnostic studies" and "beneficiary assessment" assess the "social soundness" of projects and anticipate how different target groups are likely to respond. |
| 4. Project implementation | "Input-output" studies provide regular feedback indicating whether resources are being used correctly and whether the intended outputs are being achieved. Delays, cost-overruns, or other problems can be rapidly identified. "Diagnostic studies" provide rapid feedback on the causes and possible solutions of problems that have been identified. |
| 5. Evaluation of project implementation and transition to operations | "Project completion reports" assess the overall design and implementation of the project, providing guidance on how to improve the design of future projects. The assessment of institutional arrangements helps improve the operational phase of the project. "Cost-effectiveness" studies assess the most economical ways to deliver the intended services. |
| 6. Management of project operations | "Sustainability assessment" studies monitor the factors affecting the ability of the project to continue delivering the planned services and benefits to the intended beneficiary groups and identify and correct factors inhibiting the project's sustainability. |
| 7. New project identification | "Impact" or "summative" evaluations assess how well the project has achieved its intended benefits and impacts and identify factors affecting their achievement. Conclusions contribute to the selection and design of new projects. |

of services or components that have proved most effective in achieving the specified objectives. Such comparisons also indicate which groups have or have not benefited from previous projects, which factors have most affected the successful implementation and operation of previous projects, and the degree to which intended beneficiaries have responded as anticipated in the project design.

Poverty alleviation is an area in which great efforts are being made to learn from past experience. During the past few years many African countries have found it necessary to introduce drastic economic adjustment programs to correct worsening economic and social conditions. Most of these structural adjustment programs have called for substantial reductions in government expenditures on the social sectors as well as in public sector employment. Inevitably, these measures, however beneficial in the medium and long term, have imposed severe burdens on the poorest sectors of society. The World Bank, the African Development Bank, and the United Nations Development Programme (UNDP) jointly sponsored the Social Dimensions of Adjustment in Africa (SDA) Program to help countries that were implementing structural adjustment programs develop data bases with which to monitor the impacts of adjustment programs on the poor (see pages 56–66) and to assess the impacts of different kinds of programs for protecting the poor (such as those devoted to nutrition, the basic social infrastructure, public works, and credit to promote microenterprises; see World Bank 1990c). The results of these evaluations are now being used to assist in the selection of "social action programs," which are designed to produce a rapid impact on the conditions of vulnerable groups affected by these social costs of adjustment.

Box 2-1 illustrates the kinds of lessons that can be learned from a review of earlier integrated rural development projects in Bangladesh. For example, projects appear more likely to succeed if they have only a small number of components, but it is also essential to complement credit with irrigation and other inputs that will enable farmers to use the credit to improve their incomes.

Such reviews can indicate which projects will be most likely to achieve top-priority sectoral objectives and can help project planners avoid making unrealistic assumptions about potential project impacts. If a national project data base has been established (see Chapter 12), this information should be readily accessible. If the data base covers a large number of projects, it may be possible to conduct a *prospective evaluation* to assess whether pro-

---

### Box 2-1.  Using Lessons from Earlier Integrated Rural Development Projects

The following lessons from earlier rural development projects in Bangladesh could be useful in the selection and design of new projects:

- The number of components should be limited to simplify organization and coordination.
- Agricultural credit must be coordinated with the provision of irrigation and other inputs. Otherwise farmers will be unable to repay loans.
- Integrated rural development projects require a longer implementation period and closer supervision than infrastructure projects. Managers should not be under pressure to generate certain volumes of loans or to create certain numbers of cooperatives within a given time period.
- High priority must be given to institutional development.
- The financial support for infrastructure such as roads, markets, and buildings should include funds for maintenance.
- Tight discipline is required in the administration of loan programs.
- Project appraisal procedures must place greater emphasis on social analysis and the assessment of institutional capacity.
- Considerable attention must be given to mechanisms that will ensure the equitable distribution of project services and benefits because there is a strong tendency for most of the resources to be monopolized by high-income and politically powerful farmers.

*Source:* Bamberger and Cheema (1990).

---

jects are likely to achieve certain kinds of objectives. If no such data base exists, the review can still be conducted by reading reports on completed projects and talking to those involved in designing and implementing them.

Another important and somewhat related approach is *evaluability assessment* (Wholey and Newcomer, 1989:7). This activity helps planners, policymakers, and other stakeholders clarify program goals and estimate the likelihood that program performance will affect these goals. In this way evaluation priorities are identified in terms of the program's likely impacts.

*Diagnostic, beneficiary assessment, or rapid rural appraisal* studies can be also be used to obtain feedback from intended beneficiaries regarding their likely responses to different kinds of projects.

Economic analysis (cost-benefit analysis) has been defined as the study of the macroeconomic significance of microeconomic projects (Sang 1988:30). The need for economic analysis of projects arose from the recognition that macroeconomic instruments of monetary and fiscal policy might not achieve the desired level of investment in an economy (Squire and Van der Tak 1975:6) and that market prices do not necessarily reflect national development priorities. Consequently, financial soundness is no guarantee that a proposed project is using scarce resources in the way most likely to make the maximum contribution to national development objectives. For example, a forestry project that has a high financial rate of return may still have a negative effect on the environment, may dislocate large numbers of people, or benefit only higher-income families.

An important step in this kind of analysis is to estimate *shadow prices* that reflect the true economic costs to society of the resources invested in a project and the true economic benefits of the outputs produced. For traded goods, this is achieved by calculating "border prices," which reflect the world prices at which products could be bought and sold. For "nontraded" goods, this is achieved by computing "conversion factors," which remove distortions in the relative prices and convert them to border prices.

The great advantage of this approach is that different projects can be compared on the basis of their economic contribution to the economy. Authorities can thus identify the project that will produce the highest "rate of return" on the resources invested.

Furthermore, "social weights" can be computed to indicate the distribution of project costs and benefits among different socioeconomic groups or to assess the project's impact on consumption and investment. In practice, however, little use has been made of social weights, and a World Bank task force recently recommended that efforts to further refine social weights should be dropped (World Bank 1992a:18).

Donors and governments conduct economic and sectoral studies to identify areas that might qualify for support. Rapid economic analysis can then be used to screen potential projects and to assess their potential contribution to development objectives. This kind of analysis normally involves "back-of-the-envelope" calculations. When a short list of potential projects has been identified, a minimum internal economic rate of return (IRR, often 10 or 12 percent) can be used to eliminate economically unsound projects. Issues requiring further study are then identified.

Currently, project analysis at this and later stages tends to emphasize economic and financial criteria and pays limited attention to environmental and institutional issues, or to poverty, gender, or sustainability. Ideally, policymakers and planners should use a chart such as the one presented in Box 2-2 to assess each of the possible projects on the basis of their economic, financial, institutional, social, poverty, environmental, gender and risk considerations. At this point, most variables would be simply rated as "high," "acceptable," and "low," although numerical ranges might be estimated for economic and financial viability. The final indicator, "risk," summarizes the overall assessment of how likely the project is to achieve its objectives. This and other assessments would be discussed in the text accompanying the chart.

As this chart makes clear, economic and financial rates of return, while extremely important, are only two of at least eight criteria that a project must satisfy. It is quite possible for a project to receive a satisfactory economic and financial rate of return and yet be given a low rating where other criteria are concerned. Similarly, another project might be rated high in terms of its contribution to alleviating poverty, avoiding environmental damage, and promoting institutional development, but have a low economic rate of return.

Each of the components included in Box 2-2 must be considered and steps taken to ensure that potential problems are eliminated and that all criteria are taken into account in the ranking.

Criteria will be established for assessing success in the case of each variable (criteria, dimension/component). Stakeholders must be actively involved in this process.

### Stage 2: Project Appraisal

*Economic analysis* (Gittinger 1982; Squire and Van der Tak, 1975) or *cost-benefit analysis* (Thompson 1980) may be used to assess the economic viability of projects.[2] These techniques ensure the most economically efficient use of scarce resources by identifying those projects that offer the highest economic rate of return on the investment. Economic analysis is also routinely repeated when project implementation is completed in order to compare the original and reestimated rates of return. The results are used as one indicator of the potential sustainability of a project.

Box 2-2. Components to Be Evaluated during Preliminary
Assessment of Potential Investment Projects

| Component | Indicator | Potential Projects | | | | | | |
|---|---|---|---|---|---|---|---|---|
| Financial viability | Acceptable range for IRR or NPV | | | | | | | |
| Economic viability | Acceptable range for IRR or NPV | | | | | | | |
| Institu-tional | Qualitative rating on scale | | | | | | | |
| Tech-nical | Qualitative rating on scale | | | | | | | |
| Poverty impact | Quantitative estimate of percentage of beneficiaries below poverty line or qualitative assessment of impacts | | | | | | | |
| Environ-mental impact | Quantitative or qualitative assessment | | | | | | | |
| Gender impacts | Quantitative estimate of percentage of benefits going to women or qualitative assessment | | | | | | | |
| Sustain-ability | Sustainability checklist: reestimate IRR or qualitative assessment | | | | | | | |

Although seldom employed, "social weights" may be used to assess
what the project contributes to development objectives in the way of
promoting investment or making project benefits accessible to low-income
households (Squire and Van der Tak 1975:chap. 10).

Despite the fact that economic analysis is a valuable tool for selecting and
evaluating projects, its results must be interpreted with care, particularly
in projects whose social benefits are difficult to quantify. Economic analysis
has also been criticized for having an anti-environmental bias (Tisdell

1988), in that the method of discounting future costs and benefits tends to greatly undervalue any long-term environmental impacts.

Although economic analysis is widely used by international development agencies, and by a few developing-country governments, a number of criticisms have been expressed concerning how the economic analysis is implemented and interpreted.[3]

*Cost-effectiveness analysis* (Levin 1984), or the somewhat similar procedures of least-cost analysis, may also be used to select implementation methods that can deliver the desired services or produce the intended outputs at the lowest cost (Chapter 4).

In addition, *social analysis* can be used to evaluate (a) the social soundness of a project with respect to the attitudes and likely response of intended beneficiaries; (b) the feasibility of implementing the project through existing social organizations; and (c) the cultural, administrative, and political factors likely to support or hinder project implementation and operation. USAID (Ingersoll 1990), the World Bank (Baum and Tolbert 1985:chap. 22; Cernea 1991), the Asian Development Bank (1991), and many other agencies have developed guidelines for social analysis. Even so, it still plays a smaller role in the project selection process than does conventional economic analysis. Box 2-3 summarizes USAID and World Bank guidelines for social analysis and illustrates how this information can be applied in the planning and implementation of a project. For example, many projects fail because the proposed benefits are of lower priority to the target population than had been assumed or because the proposed implementation methods are not compatible with the values and social organization of the communities.

With the growing concern about the impacts of development lending on the poor, these issues are now receiving greater attention during the project appraisal stage. Although poverty impacts can be assessed through various kinds of social analysis, particularly beneficiary assessment, a number of specific approaches are also being developed. To some extent, poverty concerns can be incorporated into conventional project analysis through the use of social weights to assess the distribution of benefits and costs between different income groups. The problem here, however, is that there are few reliable data on how benefits are likely to be distributed. Efforts are now under way, particularly in Africa, to develop data bases and monitoring systems that will provide feedback to indicate how completed and ongoing projects are affecting the poor. Public expenditure reviews are

---

Box 2-3.  USAID and World Bank Guidelines for the Social Analysis of Projects

USAID guidelines

- The project must be compatible with the way of life of the people, and ways should be found to improve the mutual fit.
- Project results should be capable of extending beyond the initial intended beneficiaries.
- The project should have the potential to alleviate poverty and to increase social equity.

World Bank guidelines

- The sociocultural and demographic characteristics of the affected populations must be taken into account.
- Greater emphasis should be placed on the social organization of productive activities.
- The project must be culturally acceptable.
- The social strategy of the project (commitment and participation, diffusion and sustainability, long-term effects) must also be considered.
- Attention must be given to special or sensitive project populations (tribal minorities, involuntary resettlement).

*Source:* Ingersoll (1990).

---

another valuable source of information on the impacts of different investment and expenditure strategies on different target groups (World Bank 1991b).

In recent years there has also been more interest in the potential impacts of development strategies on women. Many international organizations such as USAID, the Asian Development Bank, and the World Bank are now using *gender analysis* in formulating their country strategies. Because of the growing need to assess the potential environmental impacts of projects, many international agencies and national governments have also begun introducing methods of *environmental impact assessment* in the project appraisal stage. In addition, more emphasis is being placed on *assessing project sustainability* (Bamberger and Cheema 1990; Honadle and VanSant 1985; Winpenny 1991; World Bank 1989b).

The concerns of social analysis are closely linked to the belief that the target population of a project should be fully involved in all stages of its planning and implementation (Cernea 1991; Honadle and VanSant 1985; Salmen 1987). Consequently, increasing attention is being given to *beneficiary assessment, stakeholder analysis,* and *community participation,* all of which are referred to throughout this book.

### Stage 3: Project Planning and Design

Information from previous projects can be used to select socially acceptable and operationally practical implementation methods, to avoid inappropriate assumptions about the needs or forms of cooperation of the target population, to choose appropriate implementing agencies, and to involve the intended beneficiaries. Planners can save considerable time and resources and can improve the effectiveness of project implementation and operation by taking advantage of the experience gained in earlier projects.

*Rapid diagnostic studies and rapid appraisals* and other forms of social analysis (see Chapter 5) can be used to assess the social soundness of the project by the likely reaction of intended beneficiaries, the capacity of community organizations to participate in the project, and any social conflicts or problems that may have an effect on implementation or operation.

### Stage 4: Project Implementation

Once a project is approved, the required financial, material, and human resources (inputs) are authorized and the outputs to be produced with these resources and the time frame are specified. At the completion of the project, the executing agency may be legally required to show that all resources have been used in the proper way. Most governments and donor agencies also have an agency (auditor general, a central Audit Bureau, or General Accounting Office) conduct an independent assessment of how the resources were used.

Governments and donors usually require periodic (monthly or quarterly) *input-output monitoring* reports on the status of resource utilization and the production of outputs (Chapter 4). Many countries also ask a central monitoring and evaluation agency to prepare periodic reports for the cabinet or the prime minister indicating the status of all major projects (Chapter 12).

It is important to monitor output since the disbursement of foreign loans or the release of funds from the Treasury is normally contingent on the completion of certain components of the project. Consequently, the concerned line ministry and the Ministry of Finance both wish to ensure that implementation proceeds according to the preestablished schedule.

In some cases, input-output monitoring is used in the budgetary process to determine which projects should be cut (where implementation has fallen so far behind schedule that the project may never be completed) or to identify sectors in which new investments would not be justified until the backlog of ongoing projects is reduced.

*Process evaluations* or *diagnostic studies* (see Chapter 5) help uncover implementation and operational problems and identify other factors exogenous to the program that could have a bearing on project implementation or its impacts. Process evaluation can also provide an early indication of whether the intended impacts are being produced and can track the trends of these impacts while the project is still under way. This enables managers to determine whether an impact is occurring as expected and whether it is benefiting all sectors of the intended beneficiary population.

Consider the example of urban planners who expect the purity of local groundwater to increase to a certain standard over a twelve-month period following the installation of a new sanitation system and water treatment facility. Planners could chart the trend in improvement by measuring water purity at various intervals during that period and could thereby detect whether changes in water purification are occurring at the prescribed intervals.

Diagnostic studies are often conducted when managers detect programmatic problems—for example, when milestones are not reached, when negative feedback is obtained from beneficiaries, or when loan repayment rates are poor. The main purpose of diagnostic studies is to identify the underlying causes of the problem and to propose solutions. Diagnostic studies can also be conducted on a regular basis to help managers control quality or better understand the social, cultural, political, and economic factors affecting the way a project is being implemented and how different groups are responding to it. Box 2-4 shows how a diagnostic study was used in El Salvador to help the managers of a low-cost housing program understand why so few families participated in a new project in one of the interior cities when the level of demand had been much higher for earlier projects in other cities.

---

**Box 2-4.  Diagnosing the Reasons for the Low Level of Demand for a Low-Cost Housing Project in El Salvador**

A monitoring study conducted by the El Salvador Foundation for Low-Cost Housing (FSDVM) estimated that less than 5 percent of households currently living in low-quality housing in the city of Usulutan were participating in the project. A rapid diagnostic study by the monitoring unit found that the following factors were responsible for the low demand:

- Only 60 percent of the target population had heard about the project. The people who were aware of the project were at a somewhat higher economic level and therefore were more likely to own a radio or visit the cinema, two of the media used to advertise the project.
- Only 18 percent of the families living in squatter areas and 40 percent of those living in rented tenements were interested in the project once the price, size of unit, and service level had been explained. Cheap, centrally located land was readily available, water could be obtained from shallow wells, and pit latrines provided adequate sanitation. For the price of purchasing an FSDVM house with piped water and sanitation on a 75-square-meter plot, a family could purchase a 200-square-meter plot, construct a house of equal size and quality, dig a well, and construct a pit latrine.
- About 43 percent of the households that initially expressed interest in the project did not apply because of their low income.
- About 25 percent of the families selected for the project dropped out because they found it difficult to participate in the mutual-help construction required by FSDVM. Most of these families worked on weekends and either could not obtain leave from their employer or were self-employed and obtained a substantial part of their income during the weekends.

*Note:* All these factors were taken into consideration in the redesign of the second phase of the project.
*Source:* Bamberger, Gonzalez-Polio, and Sae-Hau (1982).

---

*Stage 5: Evaluation of Project Implementation and Transition to Operations*

Most agencies call for a *project completion report* (PCR) at the end of the implementation phase (see Chapter 4). The PCR describes and assesses each stage of project identification, appraisal, and implementation; identifies the main problems and issues that arose; and provides guidelines and recommendations for future projects.

*Cost-effectiveness analysis* (Chapter 4) compares projects according to the costs of producing a unit of output or service. Such analyses are particularly useful for evaluating the results of a pilot project and deciding which, if any, of the delivery systems could be replicated in a cost-effective way on a larger scale (see Box 2-5).

As mentioned earlier, *cost-benefit analysis* is used during project appraisal to ensure that a satisfactory internal economic rate of return will be obtained on the resources invested. The IRR is often reestimated at the time of project completion to determine whether the project is still economically viable. If the IRR has fallen, managers, planners, and policymakers will want to find out why (was it due to changes in the costs of production, reduced prices at which outputs can be sold, changes in the terms of trade, and so on) so that they can decide whether the project should be canceled, modified, or put into operation as originally planned.

It is also useful to compare the IRR at the time of project appraisal with the IRR at the completion of the implementation phase for all projects in a particular sector or country. This can help planners and policymakers identify any general trends or problems affecting all projects and thus make more realistic estimates of the likely rates of return from future projects.

A vital step during the transition to a project's operational phase, is to assess its capacity to sustain its operations and to continue delivering

---

**Box 2-5. Using Cost-Effectiveness Analysis to Assess Whether Pilot Projects Could Be Replicated on a Larger Scale**

- A cost-effectiveness analysis was used in El Salvador (Carnoy 1975) to compare educational reform and teacher retraining with educational television as a means of providing education for a significant proportion of the population of primary school age.
- A number of traditional public housing schemes were compared with self-help housing projects to identify the most cost-effective way of providing housing for low-income families in El Salvador (Bamberger, Gonzalez-Polio, and Sae-Hau 1982).
- Beginning on an experimental basis, the Bangladesh Rural Advancement Committee (BRAC) set up informal rural education programs designed to increase enrolment and reduce dropout rates, with a view to developing models that the Ministry of Education would be able to replicate on a large scale. Given the huge rural population of school age and the limited educational budget, it was essential to compare the cost-effectiveness of these models with that of conventional educational programs.

services and benefits over its intended economic life. Consequently, researchers are giving more attention to *sustainability assessment* methodologies (see Chapter 6 for a general discussion of sustainability assessment techniques and Chapter 5 for some of the diagnostic techniques for assessing institutional capacity). Such methodologies take into account a broad range of factors—including institutional development, beneficiary participation, provision for recurrent cost financing, adequacy of maintenance procedures, and accessibility of services to the intended target groups—which together affect the sustainability of a project.

*Impact evaluation* studies can also be used at the completion of project implementation to assess the initial evidence on the capacity of a project to produce its intended impacts, but they are more commonly used when the project has been operating for several years and are therefore discussed in the next section.

### *Stage 6: Management of Project Operations and Ensuring Sustainability*

In recent years it has been found that the effective operating life of many projects is much shorter than expected, and consequently many projects are able to deliver only a small fraction of their intended benefits and services. International agencies, and perhaps to a lesser extent governments, are therefore beginning to assess the *long-term sustainability of projects* once they have been operating for several years (Bamberger and Cheema 1990; Honadle and VanSant 1985; World Bank 1985). Sustainability is affected by many financial, economic, technical, organizational, social, and political factors, and rapid detection of those factors enables managers and policymakers to correct problems early on and hence to increase the effective life of a project (Box 2-6).

*Impact evaluation*, which is sometimes referred to as summative evaluation, is usually conducted after a project has been operating for some time, although it is possible to evaluate probable impacts as they begin to occur. Here the evaluator determines whether a project's objectives have been reached, and if not, the reasons for the failure. This activity consists not only of establishing whether expected changes occurred in the target population, but also whether the changes can be attributed to the presence of the project rather than to extraneous factors.

Such factors may be other projects or external events that are having an influence on the variables being studied. For example, the evaluation of

---

**Box 2-6.  The Utility of Sustainability Assessment Studies**

Sustainability assessment can improve project performance in the following ways:

- Maintenance problems can be detected and corrected before they become more serious and more expensive to resolve.
- Factors causing beneficiaries to withdraw their support for a project can be detected and corrected so that participants will be more willing to cooperate in project maintenance and to pay service charges.
- Factors affecting the capacity of organizations to manage the project or problems of interagency coordination can be identified and resolved.
- Groups that are not benefiting from the project can be identified and measures taken to ensure their participation.

---

impacts in a housing project could be affected by maternal and child health programs organized by the Ministry of Health and voluntary organizations, by an increase in housing starts in the private sector (which would be generating employment but also raising rents), and by an upcoming political campaign that resulted in the provision of a number of new community services and facilities.

A carefully planned and executed impact study will indicate what effects can realistically be expected from different kinds of projects and the conditions under which they are most likely and least likely to be observed (see Box 2-7). This information can improve the cost-effectiveness of future investments and prevent communities from wasting resources on kinds of projects that are likely to produce less impact than would have been assumed without the impact study.

*Stage 7: Selection and Design of New Projects*

As already mentioned, new projects can benefit greatly from the lessons learned during the design and implementation of earlier projects. It is therefore important to coordinate the work of the project monitoring unit, which is responsible for collecting information on a particular project, and that of the sectoral and national monitoring agencies, which can incorporate this information into a national data base that will be easily accessible when new projects are being selected and planned (see Chapter 12). Unfor-

---

**Box 2-7. The Practical Benefits of Impact Evaluation**

A carefully planned and executed impact evaluation can produce the following benefits:

- Will provide a precise assessment of the nature and extent of the impacts that can be expected and hence can help planners identify the projects likely to produce the best return on the resources invested.
- Can show whether the observed changes were not due to the project (but to external factors) and can thus avoid investment in projects not likely to produce desired benefits.
- Can assess the factors contributing to project impact and can thus help planners improve project design.
- Will identify those groups that tend to benefit least from certain kinds of projects and thus propose the special measures needed to encourage these groups to participate.
- Can estimate the time period over which the impacts are likely to occur and thus increase the precision of project analysis procedures.

---

tunately, a number of factors may prevent planners from using such information in designing new projects. First, new projects are often approved before the earlier projects have been fully evaluated. Second, staff changes (at the government and donor levels) disrupt continuity with the result that earlier information is less accessible to the new staff. Third, monitoring is often considered the donor's task, and the value of the information for planning future projects is overlooked.

## Using Monitoring and Evaluation at the Sectoral Level

A sectoral analysis brings together information on the experience of all projects in a particular sector. Because projects are frequently funded by different agencies, or are carried out by different state or provincial authorities, no one is likely to have a clear view of all the project experiences and programs in a particular sector. A sectoral review and synthesis can help policymakers and planners understand the successes and failures in a sector and the factors affecting project outcomes and potential areas for new investments.

Except in the case of government or private agencies working in a limited geographical area (such as a small voluntary organization in only one community or a local government with only one rural water supply project), policymakers expect a project to contribute to broad sectoral objectives as well as to improve the conditions of the people or households immediately affected. Thus a low-cost housing project is usually part of a general strategy to provide affordable housing for the low-income urban families in a city, region, or nation. Similarly, an innovative primary education project, primary health care project, or small business credit program will also be expected to develop and test service delivery systems that, if found to be successful and cost-effective, may be replicated on a larger scale.

Consequently, an important function of project evaluation is to assess the *potential replicability* of projects on a larger scale. Box 2-8 illustrates some of the replicability questions a sectoral evaluation might address.

International agencies have made a substantial contribution in this field by preparing surveys of sectoral issues at the international and national level. The U.S. Agency for International Development regularly produces impact evaluation studies, program evaluation reports, and sector discussion papers. Examples in the agricultural sector include *Central America: Small Farmer Cropping Systems* (USAID 1980a); *Agricultural Credit in the Dominican Republic* (USAID 1985a); *A Synthesis of USAID Experience: Small Farmer Credit 1973–85* (USAID 1985b); and *Philippines Small-Scale Irrigation* (USAID 1980b).

The Operations Evaluation Department (OED) of the World Bank, in its Annual Review of Project Performance, summarizes the overall experience

---

Box 2-8.  Questions Relating to Project Replicability in Sector
Evaluation

- Which of the alternative methods of service delivery are the most cost-effective?
- How would cost-effectiveness be affected by the implementation of the project on a larger scale?
- Which conditions cause the different methods of service delivery to be most effective and least effective? What are the implications for replicating the project on a large scale?
- Which groups are most and least likely to benefit from the project if it is replicated on a larger scale?

of project implementation by region and sector and identifies the main lessons learned in each sector. For example, the Twelfth Annual Review (World Bank 1987:46–50) found that project performance in the agricultural sector was affected by the following factors (among others): political problems, adverse pricing policies, too complex a design, weak interagency coordination, insufficient preparation time and lack of knowledge of local conditions, and increases in the scale of the project.

In addition, the OED has begun producing international sectoral reviews, the first of which were *Rural Development: World Bank Experience 1965–86* (World Bank 1988); *The Sustainability of Investments Projects in Education* (World Bank 1991c); *Forestry: The World Bank Experience* (World Bank 1991d); and *Population and the World Bank: Implications from 8 Case Studies* (World Bank 1992b).

Governments can compile national sectoral reviews at little cost, although the ease of preparation will depend on the accessibility of monitoring and evaluation information from completed and ongoing projects. The Programme Evaluation Organization (PEO) of India's Planning Commission has produced a number of such reviews, some which have covered integrated rural development projects (IRD; see Box 2-9). The PEO drew its information from the concurrent evaluation studies conducted periodically on the major IRD projects. National sectoral reviews normally include the following tasks: a review and synthesis of existing studies and reports; interviews with central planning agencies, line ministries, and executing agencies; interviews with and possibly sample surveys of project beneficiaries; the preparation of a synthesis paper; and often a national workshop organized to review the final report.

Line ministries and sectoral agencies also need to monitor programs that are under way to assess their overall performance and to obtain rapid feedback on any significant differences among projects so as to learn from those that are performing well how to identify and correct problems arising in others. Such monitoring studies can also be used to identify any sectors of the target population that have more limited access to project services or whose members are not receiving the intended benefits. The concurrent evaluations of integrated rural development programs in India, for example, collect information regularly on the progress being made in introducing basic social services and on the accessibility of these services to populations in various areas.

Box 2-9. Using Sectoral Analysis to Monitor the Poverty
Impact of a National Integrated Rural Development Program:
Concurrent Evaluation in India

In order to assess the impact of credit and supporting services for the rural
poor, the Department of Rural Development of the Indian Ministry of Agriculture commissions approximately 1,440 household interviews per month
in 36 districts in different parts of the country. Among the findings of the
studies are the following:

- Sixty-five percent of the households receiving credit increased their incomes by at least 50 percent, but 22 percent of households felt no effect on
  income.
- Sixty percent of beneficiaries were able to raise their incomes above the
  poverty line.
- Eighty-one percent found the loan sufficient to accumulate assets, and 72
  percent of the households still had the assets intact at the time of the study.
- Loan repayment was good in comparison with other programs, with 73
  percent of the borrowers having no, or very low, arrears.

The surveys identified these areas of concern:

- Eight percent of loans were given to ineligible borrowers.
- Only 25 percent received working capital although 65 percent required it.
- Only 25 percent obtained insurance although 70 percent required it.
- Program benefits were significantly lower than expected because few areas
  had supporting infrastructure.

*Source:* India, Department of Rural Development (1985).

A sectoral review may compare all the projects implemented in a particular sector to determine what kinds of benefits and impacts have been
achieved, which areas have made less progress, and what factors are
responsible. Such reviews frequently focus on integrated rural development at the national level (India, Department of Rural Development 1990)
and the international level (Honadle and VanSant 1985; Jha 1987; World
Bank 1988), or on irrigation programs, primary health care (Satia 1993),
primary education, and low-cost housing (Cheema 1986), among others.

Sectoral analysis may also be used to determine what different kinds of
programs have contributed to broad development objectives such as alleviating poverty, strengthening the economic participation of women, and

protecting the environment. Many studies of integrated rural development programs have shown, for example, that most of their services do not reach the poorest families but benefit mainly farmers with medium or large farms (Jha 1987). Other studies have shown that irrigation schemes and other forms of agricultural modernization may have negative effects on women by taking away many of their traditional forms of land use rights or access to the income from the sale of certain kinds of agricultural outputs (Heyzer 1987). Similarly, it has been argued that projects in a particular sector can have negative long-term environmental impacts (Centre for Science and Environment 1985).

## Using Monitoring and Evaluation at the National Level

### The Main Agencies Involved

At the national level, at least six kinds of agencies (central banks, planning, program implementation, finance, audit bureau, and line ministries) normally generate and use monitoring and evaluation data. They are linked to a multitude of regional, local, and project-level organizations. A national monitoring and evaluation *system* usually has most of the components listed below.

a.  A central agency is usually responsible for defining and coordinating the national monitoring and evaluation strategy. This entity is normally the Ministry of Planning. Central planning agencies have the task of preparing long-term national development plans and consequently are interested in studies that assess the overall performance of the economy and the achievement of national development objectives. In some countries the Ministry of Planning may also have to design and supervise the national monitoring and evaluation system, whereas in others it may be more concerned with evaluating project impacts.

b.  A central agency is also responsible for implementing and coordinating the *monitoring* of development projects. This organization may be the Ministry of Planning, the Ministry of Plan or Program Implementation, or, less commonly, the Ministry of Finance. Many countries have established a special *project implementation* ministry or agency devoted to increasing the efficiency of project implementation. This agency is responsible for monitoring all major national investment projects and may also monitor programs initiated by the president or prime minister (in India, for example, the Ministry of Program Implementation was responsible for monitoring the prime minister's 20-Point Program, which included high-priority programs such as Rural Poverty Alleviation, Rainfed Agriculture, Better Use of Irrigation, and the Two-Child Norm).

c. A central agency should be responsible for implementing and coordinating the *evaluation* of development projects and programs. This is normally the Ministry of Planning.

d. A central agency should be responsible for monitoring the use of resources and aid disbursements, assessing capacity of agencies to implement projects, and defining future resource allocation. This is usually the *Ministry of Finance.* A primary concern of the Ministry of Finance is to monitor the flows of foreign aid and to ensure that the maximum amount of approved funds is actually disbursed. The disbursement of approved foreign aid is greatly affected by the speed of project implementation, and consequently the Ministry of Finance normally develops a system to monitor project implementation performance and the effects of implementation delays on the schedule of foreign aid disbursements. In countries where project monitoring systems are well established, the Ministry of Finance will only monitor financial flows. If a centralized monitoring system does not exist, the Ministry of Finance will often develop a project monitoring system with a much broader base. Monitoring systems developed by the Ministry of Finance tend to focus on the physical implementation of projects since these are the components financed by foreign aid.

e. One or more agencies should be responsible for ensuring *accountability* to donors and to the national legislature and executive for the use of project funds. This is normally the Ministry of Planning working in tandem with the auditor general. Most governments require that project expenditures be subjected to an independent audit by the *auditor general* or the *Audit Bureau of the Ministry of Finance* to ensure that funds have been used correctly. Traditionally, the audit function is limited to conventional financial auditing so as to ensure that all expenditures are subject to the appropriate administrative controls and correspond to the line items indicated in the loan agreement or parliamentary authorization.

In recent years the auditing function has been expanded to assessing whether funds have been used efficiently. Some audit authorities are beginning to develop indicators of the extent to which the nation has received "value for money" from different programs and expenditures. One way is to assess the cost-effectiveness of different programs or delivery systems, as the Bureau of the Budget does in Thailand, or to monitor the performance of ongoing public enterprise projects to highlight potential financial or marketing problems, as is done in Pakistan. A recent innovation is to have the Auditor General's Office develop a data base on the implementation performance of completed projects to determine whether the proposed implementation schedules and expenditures for new projects are realistic.[4]

f. Most public investment projects are implemented through *line ministries or state enterprises* at the national or state (provincial) levels. Consequently, the line agency normally has the primary responsibility for implementing the project and for providing the monitoring information required by central government agencies and by international lending agencies. The range of monitoring responsibilities varies, depending on the resources available, but can cover the physical and financial implementation of all projects for which the ministry is responsible, the operation and sustainability of projects, project impacts, and the sectoral impacts of large programs consisting of numerous separate projects. It may also be necessary to interact with consultants or central government agencies conducting more specialized or large-scale evaluation studies.

A principal responsibility is to coordinate the monitoring of the donor-funded projects for which the agency is responsible. If the ministry does not have a strong central evaluation unit, donor agencies may request that special monitoring and evaluation units be created within each project. In sectors where donor agencies are active, the ministry may have to coordinate the activities of large numbers of separate donor-sponsored monitoring and evaluation units.

Although the majority of line ministries in developing countries with a strong research tradition (such as Brazil, Mexico, India, and the Philippines) are primarily concerned with the implementation of projects, certain line ministries also conduct sectoral evaluations and review studies and design more sophisticated studies to assess the impacts of projects or broader programs.

Participants at a performance evaluation seminar in Kuala Lumpur in 1991 indicated that many Asian countries are interested in strengthening their capacity for performance and ex-post evaluation. Although most countries reported that they had experimented with performance evaluation, usually on an ad hoc basis, China was one of the few that had applied it in any systematic way. Even there, it was used only on a pilot basis in twenty-three foreign-financed and large state-financed projects, and no decision was made as to how performance evaluation would be used in the future.[5]

g. Although a greater effort is being made to have *nongovernmental organizations* participate in the design and execution of development projects, governments and donor agencies have made little use of the considerable experience of NGOs in the areas of monitoring and evaluation.

## *The Need to Strengthen Policy Analysis*

At present most countries are using monitoring and evaluation to monitor the performance of operational projects and programs, but the United States and some countries of Europe have been applying M/E in *policy analysis* and strategic planning. Fishman (1989:30-31) identifies six "windows of opportunity" where evaluation can influence congressional policymaking in the United States:

- *Development of new legislation.* The process of developing new legislative solutions to identified problems provides an opportunity to present the findings of evaluations to congressional committees.
- *Reauthorization of existing legislation.* Deadlines are often set for the review of evidence to decide whether a program or law should be renewed.
- *Annual appropriations and budget cycle.* Programs are attacked and defended on the basis of their perceived impacts and cost-effectiveness. Both sides often rely on evaluation findings to support their positions.
- *Oversight hearings.* These hearings are particularly important for programs that do not have a fixed statutory life, such as Social Security.
- *Congressionally mandated evaluations.* Congress frequently initiates large and complex evaluation studies, the findings of which can have an important influence on the long-term survival and development of a program.
- *Expansion of the body of knowledge.* Congressional committees routinely seek to broaden their knowledge and understanding of the problems and program areas for which they are responsible. Existing or specially commissioned evaluation studies are often one of their main sources of information.

An EDI-Korean Development Institute seminar held in Seoul in November 1987 (Lamb and Weaving 1992) examined the process of policy reform in six Asian countries. The seminar attributed the successful formulation of trade liberalization policies in Korea and the smooth implementation of tax reform in Indonesia to the systematic collection and analysis of relevant economic and social data. In contrast, authorities in Thailand were unaware of the inherent contradictions of their rice policies and thus found it more difficult to anticipate conflicts and to achieve the necessary compromises (Boeninger 1992:11).

Seminar participants concluded that policymakers require *sound anticipatory analysis* and also *quick access* to the relevant information. In all the Asian countries studied, policymakers (particularly in central banks and ministries of finance) tended to rely on market-oriented economists for advice and policy analysis. These economists were committed to economic growth and macroeconomic equilibria and paid little attention to the political dimensions of policy reform—such as the distribution of costs and benefits and the reactions of major stakeholders—which are of greater concern to politicians.

The seminar proposed the following guidelines for policy analysis (Boeninger 1992:13):

- Be economical in the use of economics.
- Discount for political demand.
- Dare to be "quick and dirty."
- Think like a manager.
- Analyze equity as well as efficiency.
- Know your market (who you are trying to influence).
- Pay your organizational dues (have your minister's or organization's interests at heart).
- Profit from action-forcing events.
- Do not oversell economic analysis.
- Learn policy economics by practicing it.

Two main lessons emerged (Boeninger 1992:15). First, the synoptic, rationalist, view of policymaking is rather unrealistic, and the neat distinctions embodied in that view—means versus ends, political decision versus bureaucratic execution, and a neat sequence of information-decision-implementation-evaluation—do not correspond to how policies are actually made and implemented. Second, there are many kinds of economic policy decisions; they vary in complexity, and decisionmaking styles are heavily influenced by the traditions, political context, and governmental systems in which they are situated.

If evaluation data are to be used effectively in policy analysis, it is essential that the system of data collection and analysis "be firmly set within an administrative routine that explicitly assigns responsibilities to departments and individuals for collecting, processing and transmitting the information needed" (Boeninger 1992:10).

It is often assumed that policy analysis entails long and complex study. In fact, many of the most useful studies can be conducted cheaply and rapidly and still provide up-to-date information and options to policymakers faced with impending decisions. As one new administrator discovered when he took over the Delaware Department of Economic Services (Bell 1989), all it took was three weeks of progressive "brain-storming" to learn the views of staff and management concerning the agency's perceived mission and to identify the barriers to the achievement of this mission. By starting at the lower levels and then providing the opinions of staff at these levels as an input to the meetings at the next highest level, he was able to turn the attention of senior management to key issues and problems and to the alternative lines of action that could be taken.

## USAID's Program Performance Information System for Strategic Management (PRISM)

PRISM, which was created by USAID in 1991, illustrates how a major international assistance agency developed a set of indicators for formulating, monitoring, and evaluating strategic objectives (USAID 1993). Whereas systems such as logical framework analysis (see Chapter 3) operate at the level of individual projects and hence have a short-term focus, PRISM operates at the level of the *strategic objectives* to be achieved over a time frame of five to eight years.

PRISM is a system for monitoring program performance and for reporting and managing information. It was designed by USAID for senior managers both in Washington and in the field. Its purpose is to improve USAID's ability to clarify objectives, measure performance, and apply performance information in decisionmaking at all organizational levels. Under the PRISM system, Missions routinely collect data that can be used to measure their actual progress in achieving strategic objectives and program outcomes. In the PRISM strategic planning process, Missions, often assisted by USAID Washington, define their own strategic objectives and program outcomes, select their own indicators, and set targets. By periodically gathering data to measure and compare actual progress with the targets or expected results established at the outset of the strategic planning process, Missions can obtain "early warnings" indicating that programs are not going as planned. Gaps between actual and target per-formance will alert Mission managers to the need for more in-depth eval-uations explaining why programs are succeeding or failing. These assessments would then lead the authorities to either adjust or terminate the program (and shift funds to more promising projects within the Mission's portfolio).

Fifteen clusters of strategic objectives have been developed under the PRISM system. Policies are defined and assessed in terms of appropriate sets of these objectives. Objectives themselves are assessed on the basis of their effectiveness, impact, efficiency, sustainability, relevance, and replicability. The steps of the procedure are similar to those followed in logical framework analysis: An *objective tree* is developed linking different levels of results or outcomes according to a causal theory that specifies that a certain set of activities will result in certain program outcomes that will achieve a strategic objective. A *strategic objective* that is developmentally significant and that can be achieved and measured over a period of five to eight years is defined. A *program* consisting of an entire set of development activities designed to achieve this objective is then developed. A set of *program outcomes* that are directly attributable to the program and can be measured over a period of two to five years are defined. Next, the *indicators* needed to measure these outcomes are defined. And finally, the *results expected* within a specific time frame are defined.

The initial results obtained when the system was introduced are consid-ered to have been successful and thus have helped planners develop a uniform framework for formulating and evaluating strategic objectives and broad policy goals that can be compared across sectors and countries (USAID 1993).

### The Potential Value of National Data Bases

Most national M/E systems fail to use the data they have collected, often at considerable expense. When project implementation is completed, in many cases the extensive monitoring information that has been compiled, sometimes over a period of three to five years, is filed away and never used again. Consequently, the persons responsible for the planning and selection of new projects are unable to benefit from past experience, and many wrong assumptions and mistakes may be repeated. Data are not fully used because most agencies do not have good data bases and also because the activities of the line ministries that conduct the monitoring studies are not coordinated with those of the central planning agencies responsible for selecting future projects.

With the rapid spread of microcomputers and the development of national computer networks, it is now technically feasible to collect and synthesize data from a large number of geographical regions and projects. Indeed, a number of countries have started building national data banks. Most of these data banks have limited objectives, however, and their full potential has not yet been recognized.

An example of the potential utility of a national data base can be seen in the recent efforts to monitor the impacts of structural adjustment programs on the poor and vulnerable groups in Africa. These cases are described later in this volume.

## Structured Learning

Structured Learning is a systematic way to learn from the experience of ongoing projects or sector programs and policies, and to use this knowledge to improve the way in which future projects, programs, and policies are formulated, implemented, and evaluated. This approach is described in Chapter 3, pages 103–8.

## Prospective Evaluations and Evaluability Assessment

A prospective evaluation synthesizes M/E information from earlier studies to assess the likely outcomes of proposed new projects. Prospective evaluation is said to be one of the most rapidly growing and productive uses of evaluation information in the United States (Chelimsky 1988). Congressional committees and individual congressmen frequently ask the U.S. General Accounting Office (GAO) for advice in forecasting the likely outcomes of proposed legislation designed, for example, to encourage mothers to reenter the labor force, to promote housing investment, or to reduce teenage pregnancies. After reviewing evidence from previous studies, the GAO will state whether these findings indicate the new legislation seems likely to succeed or fail, or whether there is not enough evidence to form an opinion one way or the other. In many cases the evidence has been strong enough to persuade Congress to withdraw or modify its legislation and thus has possibly saved large sums of money.

The GAO has access to time-series data on socioeconomic variables such as labor force participation, income and expenditure, family size, and education, all of which can be linked to economic and fiscal variables such as tax rates and the introduction of government programs at the federal and state levels. In addition, it has access to the findings of large numbers of evaluations of programs similar to one being proposed.

Prospective evaluation has a number of features in common with *evaluability assessment,* a method used to advise program planners whether a program can be evaluated. The purpose of an evaluability assessment is to ensure, by means of a preliminary evaluation of a program's design, that the design meets three criteria: (a) it clearly defines program objectives; (b) the underlying assumptions and objectives are plausible; and (c) the intended uses of evaluation information are well defined (Wholey 1979:2:17). The experience of previous projects will have to be examined in order to determine whether the assumptions and objectives of the new project seem plausible.

Prospective evaluations and evaluability assessment are seldom used in developing countries, even though the required information is usually available—at least in part. Although few countries have time-series data, many have access to large numbers of monitoring and evaluation reports on earlier projects that could be used to conduct evaluability assessments and simple prospective evaluations.

### Meta-Analysis and the Use of Secondary Data

Many evaluation professionals have begun to synthesize the findings of evaluation studies to determine what is known about the impacts of different kinds of program interventions. One approach, called *meta-analysis,* is based on the notion that the individuals included in all available evaluation studies of a particular kind of program or intervention form a population and that the findings of single studies can be treated as observation points (Cordray 1985; Yeaton and Wortman 1984). All observations are combined to estimate the magnitude and range of effects produced by a particular intervention. It is argued that the average effect levels observed in a large number of studies will be more reliable than the findings of any individual study. Light (1984) identifies six program evaluation issues that synthesized studies can resolve better than single studies:

- *Analyze the interactions between treatment variables and the different attributes of the target population.* Program impacts are affected by the interactions between the combinations of treatments and how they are applied, on the one hand, and the characteristics of the recipients, on the other. Synthesis studies can examine a wider range of interactions and hence shed more light on when and how these interactions operate.
- *Help match treatment types with recipient types.* Different recipients respond differently to different treatments, and a larger sample of observations can help identify what treatments work best for each type of recipient.
- *Determine which features of a treatment matter.* Although some aspects of a program are crucial, others may be insignificant. Synthesis can help identify crucial factors and can help eliminate other (sometimes costly) program components.
- *Help explain conflicting results.* Apparently conflicting results are often a consequence of different designs or differences in the context in which the two programs operate. The analysis of a wide sample of programs can elucidate these contextual factors and how they operate.
- *Compare the short-term and long-term impacts of programs.* Programs can be assessed either in terms of whether they have achieved their immediate goals (improved reading skills) or in terms of their long-term impact on beneficiaries (did improved reading skills help participants obtain better paying jobs?). The comparison of a large number of studies is helpful in this respect.
- *Ensure that treatment effects remain stable.* A synthesis study can assess the variability of treatment effects. Do certain treatments always produce certain effects, or is there great variability?

Besides meta-analysis, which is normally concerned with the statistical comparison of studies, more descriptive and qualitative analysis can be used to identify the factors affecting program success. Some of the analytical procedures described in Chapters 5 and 6 (also see Miles and Huberman 1984) are useful for this kind of qualitative assessment.

## Gender Analysis: Ensuring the Full Participation of Women in Development Policies and Programs

Many development policies and programs have different effects on men and women because social roles in various economic activities are frequently associated with gender. Men and women may also have different food consumption patterns, different kinds of education, and different kinds of housing. Moreover, in most societies women are socially, economically, and politically weaker than men and have less control over resources and less influence on decisionmaking.

There is increasing evidence that women do not automatically benefit from development policies and programs and that some policies may even make life worse for significant numbers of poor women (Heyzer 1987; Rao, Anderson, and Overholt 1991). In almost every developing country, women make up a disproportionately large share of the poor and very poor. Women are particularly vulnerable to many factors that create and perpetuate poverty.

The principal economic reason for focusing on gender in development programs is that poorer families tend to rely on the earning capacity of women. Even with effective economic development policies, most poor families would not be able to survive without the help of their female members.

Women typically earn lower wages, however, and have more limited access than men to productive resources such as land, credit, fertilizers, and higher technology, with the result that their productive capacity and their ability to contribute to the survival or improvement of their families are severely constrained. Despite the evidence indicating the crucial economic role of women in low-income families, governments still tend to associate women with "income-generating activities" that they can perform in their spare time as extensions of domestic activities. In contrast, men are said to require "employment" that can provide for the needs of their families. Strategies for alleviating poverty must therefore make an all-out effort to understand and remove the constraints on productive female employment.

According to a number of studies, not only do women have less access than men to the benefits of economic modernization, but many poor women are even worse off as a result of economic modernization programs introduced to benefit the poor. In a number of large irrigation projects, including the Mahaweli Accelerated Irrigation Program in Sri Lanka, plots are indivisible and property rights are normally vested in the man—even in societies where women traditionally have quite extensive property rights (Heyzer 1987:chaps. 4 and 5). In such cases, women have not only lost their rights to the ownership and use of land, but they now have difficulty obtaining the credit they need to purchase productive inputs because they have no land to use as collateral.[6]

While the "Green Revolution" has clearly had a significant impact on agricultural output and productivity (World Bank 1990d:chap. 4), agricultural modernization, with its new technology, has also displaced female labor or relegated these workers to the less skilled and heavier kinds of manual labor.[7] The following quotation from the 1990 *World Development Report* summarizes both the positive and negative effects of agricultural modernization:

Modern seed varieties, irrigation and the increased commercialization of crops have commonly been accompanied by the greater use of hired labor, mostly from landless households. The new technologies have also had important implications for the division of household labor. Wage labor has replaced unpaid labor, and in some cases male labor has replaced female labor. This has raised concerns that technological change has harmed women.

The substitution of hired labor for family labor usually improves the household's standard of living. In the Philippines, for example, the new technologies raised farming incomes, allowing households to hire labor and purchase labor-saving farm implements. This reduced the number of hours worked by family members in low-productivity jobs on the farm and allowed them to engage in other, more productive, activities such as trade or raising livestock. In addition, greater demand for hired labor provided jobs to landless workers.

Modern varieties have, in general, raised the demand for hired female labor. They usually require more labor per acre—particularly in tasks typically done by women, such as weeding, harvesting, and postharvest work. A study of three Indian states concluded that the use of hired female labor was greater on farms that had adopted modern varieties than on those that had not. Other studies for India and Nepal have found that the overall use of hired female labor rose substantially with the introduction of modern varieties.

**Table 2-2.  Contents of Bangladesh Strategy Paper on Women in Development**

1. *Greater Participation of Women in Development: An Economic Imperative*
   Defining women's dilemma
   Government position on development and the role of women
   Strategic considerations and directions

2. *The Situation of Women in Bangladesh*
   Social, cultural, and economic context
   Poverty context
   Health, nutrition, and fertility status
   Legal status

3. *Women in the Labor Force*
   Enumeration of women in official labor statistics
   Observed magnitude of women in labor force participation
   Causes of underenumeration in official statistics
   Employment patterns of women: wage and self employment
   Concerns about the conventional wisdom of employment generation programs
      for women

4. *Government Strategies to Incorporate Women into National Policy and Program Planning*
   Focus of government policies and programs
   Institutions
   Future approaches

5. *Education and Technical Training*
   Structure and characteristics of the education system
   Government programs
   Issues and recommendations

6. *Water Supply and Sanitation*
   Characteristics of the sector
   Government institutions, policy, and programs
   Issues and recommendations

7. *Agriculture*
   Characteristics of the agricultural sector
   Nature and extent of women's involvement in agriculture
   Government policy, institutions, and programs
   Issues and recommendations

8. *Industry*
   Characteristics of the industrial sector
   Female employment in manufacturing industries
   Government policies and programs
   Issues and recommendations

9. *Credit*
   Special credit programs and issues concerning women
   Recommendations

*Source*: World Bank (1990a), abridged table of contents.

In some cases, however, mechanization has led to lower female employment. The outcome has often depended on the tasks mechanized. When predominantly female tasks were given over to machinery, women were displaced. This happened in Bangladesh, Indonesia and the Philippines with the replacement of the finger knife as a harvesting tool and the introduction of direct seeding and portable mechanical threshers. In Bangladesh most of the postharvest work had been done by women using the *dheki* (a foot-operated mortar and pestle). When the dehusking and polishing of grain were mechanized, these operations were turned over to men, who now operate the modern mills. A study in the Indian states of Kerala, Tamil Nadu, and West Bengal found that where chemical fertilizers have replaced cow dung, men rather than women now apply the fertilizer because women lack access to the information provided by extension services.

When women were displaced, the effect on their incomes and on household welfare depended on whether they found more productive jobs elsewhere. Overall non farm employment did increase, but data classified by gender are scanty. (World Bank 1990d:61)

In many rural areas women control the household budget and are responsible for providing food and other basic necessities for their families. Agricultural modernization, which normally involves an increasing commercialization of crops, shifts the control of the revenue to the husband. Thus, even though total household income may increase, women will control a smaller proportion of the total income, and household expenditures on food and other basic necessities may actually decrease.

For all of the above reasons, any development strategy that overlooks the many and complex links between gender and poverty is likely to fail. Far-reaching policies and large-scale programs are needed to provide women with the outlook on life, skills, and resources they need to overcome the scourge of poverty. Furthermore, project identification, planning, monitoring, and evaluation must all take into account the differential impacts on men and women (as well as on different socioeconomic and cultural groups). *Gender analysis* methodologies have been developed to address these issues.

Table 2-2 illustrates how gender analysis was used by the World Bank in Bangladesh in the design of a gender-responsive national development strategy. It shows the status and factors affecting the participation of women in the labor force, education, sanitation, agriculture, and industry and their access to water supply and sanitation, as well as credit. Similar analyses have been conducted by governments and multilateral and bilateral agencies in many developing countries.

Gender analysis is also being used to assess the impacts of structural adjustment policies on women. A recent review of structural adjustment programs found that women frequently bear an excessive burden during the first stabilization and demand management phase owing to the following factors (USAID 1991:xiv):

- Women and members of female headed-households tend to suffer relatively more during the economic contraction associated with the stabilization phase of adjustment. Because women are frequently poorer to start with, reductions in living standards are more critical for them.
- Women act as "shock-absorbers" during adjustment, curtailing their own consumption and increasing their work effort to compensate for losses in household income.
- Women are often more dependent on public services because of their child-bearing and child-rearing roles. The reductions in social spending that accompany adjustment efforts therefore affect them more directly than men. The shrinkage of government services "off-loads" responsibilities to the private sector, usually to women.
- Education represents one of the most important factors in women's economic and social advancement, and it is often a victim of economic restraint.
- Where there is relatively higher representation of women in the public sector, public expenditure restraints may have a greater impact on women than on men.

Gender analysis is also used in the selection and design of projects, and in their monitoring and evaluation. Overholt and her colleagues (Rao and others 1991) propose an analytical framework that can be used for this purpose as well as for national and sector planning. This framework (described in Chapter 4, Section D) provides information on four important components of gender analysis:

- *Activity profile.* Describes the extent and nature of women's participation in the production of goods and services, and their role in the reproduction and maintenance of human resources (child rearing and household management).
- *Access and control profile.* Describes the access that women and men have to the resources required for carrying out these activities and the control they exercise over the benefits produced from these activities.

- *Analysis of factors influencing activities, access, and control.* Describes the factors determining who does what and who will have access and control over resources.
- *Project cycle analysis.* Examines the role of women in project identification, design, implementation, and evaluation.

This book makes frequent reference to the ways in which gender analysis can be incorporated into monitoring and evaluation studies at the national, sectoral, and project levels, and at all stages of the project cycle.

## Recommended Reading

African Development Bank, UNDP, and World Bank. 1990. *The Social Dimensions of Adjustment: A Policy Agenda.* Washington, D.C.: World Bank.

Explains how policymakers and planners can use evaluation to assess the impacts of structural adjustment programs on vulnerable groups in Africa. Good example of how to create and use national data banks.

Ahmed, Viqar, and Michael Bamberger. 1989. *Monitoring and Evaluating Development Projects: The South Asian Experience.* Washington, D.C.: World Bank, Economic Development Institute.

Describes how monitoring and evaluation information is used in the countries of South Asia.

American Council of Voluntary Agencies for Foreign Service. 1984. *Evaluation Sourcebook for Private and Voluntary Organizations.* New York.

Describes how evaluation data can be used by NGOs.

Bamberger, Michael, and Eleanor Hewitt. 1986. *Monitoring and Evaluating Urban Development Programs: A Handbook.* Washington, D.C.: World Bank.

Identifies the principal stakeholders and describes the kinds of information they require and how it is used.

Chelimsky, Eleanor. 1989. *Evaluation and Public Policy: The Uses of Evaluation Products in the Executive and Legislative Branches of the United States.* Washington, D.C.: World Bank, Economic Development Institute.

Explains how evaluation is used by legislators and policymakers in the United States. Good discussion of prospective evaluation.

Lamb, Geoffrey, and Rachel Weaving. 1992. *Managing Policy Reform in the Real World: Asian Experiences.* Economic Development Institute Seminar Series. Washington D.C.: World Bank.

Discusses the role of evaluation in policy reform with concrete examples from Asian countries.

Rossi, Peter, and Howard Freeman. 1982. *Evaluation: A Systematic Approach*. Beverly Hills, Calif.: Sage.

Reviews the main ways in which monitoring and evaluation can be used.

Salmen, Lawrence. 1987. *Listen to the People: Participant Observer Evaluation of World Bank Projects*. New York: Oxford University Press.

_____. 1992. "Beneficiary Assessment: An Approach Described." Washington, D.C.: World Bank .

Discusses the design and use of beneficiary assessment evaluations.

World Bank. 1989. *Annual Review of Evaluation Results*. Washington, D.C.: Operations Evaluation Department.

_____. 1991. *The Sustainability of Investment Projects in Education*. Washington, D.C.: Operations Evaluation Department.

_____. 1991. *Forestry: The World Bank's Experience*. Washington, D.C.: Operations Evaluation Department.

_____. 1992. *Population and the World Bank: Implications from Eight Case Studies*. Washington, D.C.: Operations Evaluation Department.

Shows how lessons from completed projects can be used in the selection and design of new projects.

## Notes

1. The Social Dimensions of Adjustment Program initiated by the World Bank, UNDP, and African Development Bank to evaluate the impacts of structural adjustment programs in Sub-Saharan Africa on the poor and vulnerable groups is the largest program of this kind. For a description, see World Bank (1990c).

2. This section draws heavily on the report of the World Bank Task Force on Economic Analysis (World Bank: 1992b).

3. The following are some of the main criticisms about how economic analysis is applied. (1) Even when fully operational in the late 1970s and early 1980s, project analysis never fully adopted all of the methodological rigor proposed by Little and Mirlees and by Squire and Van der Tak (Little and Mirlees 1991). (2) Project analysis, at least in the World Bank, provides an overoptimistic assessment of a project's likely internal rate of return. For projects completed in the late 1980s and early 1990s, the reestimated IRR at the time of project completion was on average eight to nine percentage points higher than the original IRR estimated at the time of project

appraisal (World Bank, 1992:2). This was due to overoptimistic assessment of a stable macroeconomic environment and fulfillment of required policy measures. (3) It makes narrow and limited use of risk analysis, particularly with regard to the ways in which projects will be affected by slippage, weak macroeconomic policy, or inadequate financial and institutional capacity. (4) The methodology for applying project analysis to social projects (for example, in the area of health, education, or rural development) has not been adequately developed. (5) Until recently, the environmental impacts of projects were not adequately addressed. However, significant progress has been made during the past few years (World Bank 1992e).

4. The Auditor General's Office in Pakistan is creating such a data base to compile information on the average time and cost overruns of the main categories of projects. This information is used to review the proposed budgets and implementation schedules of new projects.

5. See the papers presented at the Operations Evaluation Seminar for descriptions of experiences in Indonesia (Sjamsu and Rantetana 1991), Pakistan (Khan, 1991), Sri Lanka (Ramanajuam, 1991), Nepal (Nepal and Nepal 1991), and China (Li Ruogu 1991). As far as the present authors are aware, these papers have not been published.

6. There are also broader questions about the benefits of large-scale irrigation projects, which suggest that women are not the only group that may be negatively affected by some of these projects.

7. See Heyzer (1987:chap. 1) for a summary of ways in which women can be negatively affected by agricultural modernization.

# 3

## *Using Models to Learn from Experience*

To reiterate the point made at the outset of this volume, governments and donor agencies are responsible for the financing, design, and management of hundreds, and in some cases thousands, of development projects, a significant proportion of which fail to achieve their main objectives.[1] Furthermore, many governments are under growing pressure to use their resources as efficiently as possible. These and other constraints make it essential for governments and donor agencies to learn as much as possible from the experience of completed projects. They need to be able to identify the kinds of projects and delivery systems that are most likely to achieve their objectives, and to understand the factors contributing to the success and failure of projects.

### The Need to Learn from Completed Projects

Governments and donor agencies are also under pressure to ensure that their investment strategies contribute to broader developmental goals such as protecting the environment, alleviating poverty, and increasing the economic, social, and political participation of women—all of which require a clear understanding of the complex interactions between a project and its environment.

As discussed in Chapter 2, anticipatory analysis (prospective evaluation) can also play an important role in ensuring that policy reform is anchored in effective planning and undergoes smooth implementation. Such analysis draws on the lessons of earlier policies or programs to anticipate the likely impacts and potential problems of proposed reforms.

Although few would deny that completed projects offer a wealth of information on the possible impacts of and obstacles to development projects, some might ask why the lessons cannot be learned from techniques that are currently available and whether new evaluation research procedures are really needed? Indeed, a great deal of useful information is already available from monitoring activities, project completion reports, and the overview studies conducted by governments and donors, but, for a number of reasons, this information has limited application with respect to improving the capacity of projects to achieve their development objectives.

First, as mentioned earlier, most of the available information refers only to the project *implementation* phase and little is known about the factors affecting the sustainability of project operations or their success. In other words, there are adequate guidelines on how to make project implementation more efficient, but little advice on how to design sustainable projects that will achieve their objectives. There is no guarantee that improving the efficiency of implementation will improve sustainability and project results. In some cases (discussed in Chapter 6), the emphasis on implementation has even had an adverse effect on sustainability.

Second, projects operate in highly complex economic, social, administrative, and political environments that make it difficult to assess the extent to which successful (or unsuccessful) outcomes were the result of project design and management. It is often hard to tell whether the higher incomes of small farmers were a consequence of the rural development project being assessed or whether they were caused by national agricultural pricing policies, varying credit rates, or rapid urban growth (and its effects on the demand for rural labor and the demand for basic food products), or some other factor.

Third, complementary or competing projects may enhance or reduce the effects of a particular project. Other international organizations and government agencies may also be organizing health, credit, employment, nutrition, industry, and infrastructure projects that will affect families living in the geographical areas covered by the project being assessed.

Fourth, projects are never implemented exactly as planned and are subject to significant variations in different geographic areas, so that it is often difficult to determine exactly how the project was implemented. It is possible that in region A the credit program was implemented efficiently, but that there were serious problems with the construction and management of the minor irrigation component; whereas in region B the irrigation component worked much better, but the number of loans authorized was much smaller. Another complicating factor is that the efficiency of implementation varies over time. For all of these reasons, it is extremely difficult to pinpoint the components operating in each area at different points in time and know how well they were operating. This in turn makes it difficult to draw lessons from the past for the design of future projects.

A number of factors hamper the systematic evaluation of the processes and impacts connected with development projects. One of the more serious concerns is how to identify and maintain a control group that is reasonably comparable to the intervention group. Many projects either try to cover the entire target population (all urban squatters or all small farmers), or they operate in areas that cannot easily be matched to a control area. Furthermore, many projects do not have a clearly defined beginning or end, so it is difficult to devise a "before" and "after" evaluation design. In large urban development projects, it is not uncommon for the first beneficiaries to receive some services such as water or sanitation three or four years ahead of other beneficiaries. Still another problem is that many of the services, outcomes, and impacts are not easy to capture and measure, so there may be some disagreement as to the level of benefits or impact of the intervention actually produced. This happens particularly when the *quality* of services or outcomes is important, as in the case of education, extension services and technical assistance, and medical services.

Thus, the lessons and conclusions that should be drawn from the apparent successes or failures of a project may not be at all clear. There may even be little consensus of opinion about what project activities have actually been implemented and what factors affected the outcomes. Would the project have been more successful if there had not been a municipal election campaign? What effect did the increase in the official market price of rice have? Was the project implemented better in area A than in area B? New methods of analysis are obviously needed to help planners and managers better understand how the project was implemented, how different stages of implementation or operations were affected by different outside events, what impacts can be attributed to the project (rather than outside events), and what factors affected the level and distribution of impacts. The best way to understand these complex processes and issues is to construct a model of the process of project design, implementation, and operation.

## Potential Applications for Modeling in the Evaluation of Development Projects

### Models Provide Insight into Development Projects

A social development program can be defined as a planned intervention based on explicit theories that will foster social change or reform and explain why that change should be expected. A model of a social program should make explicit how different inputs are likely to lead to certain impacts. Therefore, a model can be described as a set of testable hypotheses about a project that can be either refuted or vindicated.

Programs for improving social, physical, and health conditions are based on models of social change. Although the theoretical assumptions under-lying the project's design may not be stated explicitly, decisions concerning the amount and type of inputs, implementation procedures, and even the size and characteristics of target or client groups are based on assumptions about how a project is affected by, and interacts with, the environment in which it operates. That is to say, these design decisions are based on an *implicit model* of how the program will work, why it will achieve its impacts, and how different groups will respond.

A *project model* is an explicit *theory of how* a set of resources and activities will produce a specific impact on a society or environment. The model makes explicit the population or environmental conditions that a project is intended to affect (that is, infants under three years of age, residents of a slum, water resources), the direction of the effect (for example, infant mortality is declining, the size of the housing stock is increasing, or the provision of clean water is increasing), and the input or intervention variables that lead to this effect (for example, infant immunization, a sites and service program, and a water purification facility, respectively).

Once the intended project implementation model has been defined (which is a major step in itself), the actual implementation and operation of the project should be carefully documented to determine how closely the activities correspond to the intended model, to evaluate the quality of implementation, and to assess the production and quality of intermediary outputs and services. If required, an evaluation design with appropriate statistical controls can then be developed to assess the extent to which observed outcomes can reasonably be assumed to have been produced (or at least affected) by the project intervention rather than by factors unrelated to the project. Finally, an analytical framework can be developed to assess what each project stage and component contributes to the final outcomes, and to estimate how these outcomes were affected by the interactions between the project and the economic, social, and political environment in which it evolves. Thus, a well-designed social model can provide a rigorous framework for interpreting the experience of completed and ongoing projects and for gleaning lessons and guidelines from them to help with the formulation, design, and implementation of future projects.

Suppose that a nation has a high rate of infant mortality, attributable to vaccine-preventable diseases. Immunization programs are known to be an effective means of reducing such infant mortality, and a program is designed to obtain the vaccinations in sufficient quantity, administer funds, train and manage personnel, publicize the vaccination program to attract mothers, and plan the logistics for vaccinating the target population. The model in this instance should describe the entire immunization program and make explicit the assumptions about how different population groups will respond to it. The program's expected impact is based on medical knowledge about the etiology of infectious diseases and their control; on logistics that maximize the potential for effective coverage of the population with vaccines; and on the provision of adequate monetary, human, and material resources for implementing the plan. In this example the logistics could consist of activities such as estimating the amount of vaccine required for a target population, preparing a cold chain, a host of organizational actions dealing with the delivery of the vaccine to the target population, and the vaccinating of the population itself.

*Types of Models and Their Applications in Program Evaluation*

Within this broad framework, a number of approaches to social modeling can be distinguished by their objectives, structure, and kinds of analysis (Table 3-1). Models can be of assistance in project planning and design, in studying and assessing the implementation process, in making quantitative estimates of a project's impact, or in identifying the factors affecting the success of implementation and the production of impacts. They can also be helpful in presenting evaluation findings to policymakers, planners, and managers. A model can take the form of a matrix, graph, network diagram, or a series of mathematical or statistical equations, among other formats. The analysis can be descriptive, use simple numerical indicators, or employ mathematical or statistical analysis.

The following examples (see Table 3-1) illustrate the wide range of possible approaches.

*Logical framework analysis* (described below in more detail). This approach, originally developed by USAID but now used by many international agencies (including CIDA, the Asian Development Bank, and the German Development Agency) requires project planners to complete a

**Table 3-1. Some of the Common Approaches to Social Modeling**

| Model | Use | Form | Analysis |
|---|---|---|---|
| Logical framework analysis | Project planning and performance evaluation | Matrix | Descriptive and numerical |
| Quasi-experimental design | Quantitative estimates of project impact | Statistical | Univariate or multivariate analysis |
| Systems analysis | Project planning and performance evaluation | Graphic and mathematical | Descriptive and mathematical |
| Causal networks | Ongoing planning and revision of evaluation design and synthesis of hypothesis and findings | Graphic or matrix | Descriptive or simple numerical |
| Process modeling | Evaluation planning and defining format for presenting findings | Graphic | Descriptive and numerical |
| Path analysis | Estimating the contribution of project components and nonproject variables to project outcomes | Graphic and statistical | Multivariate analysis |

matrix defining the sector goals, the project purpose, inputs, and expected outputs. Important assumptions are stated and a list of objectively verifiable indicators are specified. The progress of the project is periodically monitored.

"Log frame" analysis was originally used by international agencies in planning and monitoring their own internal projects. In recent years, however, the approach has been modified to ensure that project beneficiaries actively participate in selecting, planning, and monitoring projects.[2]

*Quasi-experimental designs.* This is a statistical procedure designed to estimate the size and distribution of project impacts by statistically controlling for the effect of other factors that could affect project outcomes. This is generally considered to be the ideal way to estimate project impacts, even though it is not practical to use in many circumstances (see Cook and Campbell 1979). Examples are given in Chapters 8, 9, and 11.

*Systems analysis* (see below). This approach uses graphic and mathematical techniques to describe the process of project implementation and to assess factors affecting project outcomes. It is extensively used for planning and monitoring health and infrastructure programs, among others.

*Causal networks.* This is a simple graphic system applied mainly in evaluations using qualitative data to help clarify hypotheses about the links between implementation variables and their impacts on project outcomes. Examples are given in Chapter 5. (For applications in education, see Miles and Huberman 1984).

*Process modeling* (see below). This is a simple graphic method used to define the factors affecting the outcome of particular project components and to assess the contribution of various factors to these outcomes. Examples are given in Chapters 5 and 6.

*Path analysis.* The purpose of this widely used statistical technique is to estimate the quantitative impact of project components and nonproject variables on project outcomes. The relative contributions of each component and interaction term are expressed as multiple regression coefficients. (For an example of how this can be used to assess the impacts of vocational training and small business credit programs, see Instituto SER 1981.)

*Structured learning.* Structured learning is a systematic way to learn from the experience of ongoing projects or sector programs and policies, and to use this knowledge to improve the way in which future projects, programs, and policies are formulated, implemented, and evaluated. This technique consists of creating a model of the causal process that will describe how

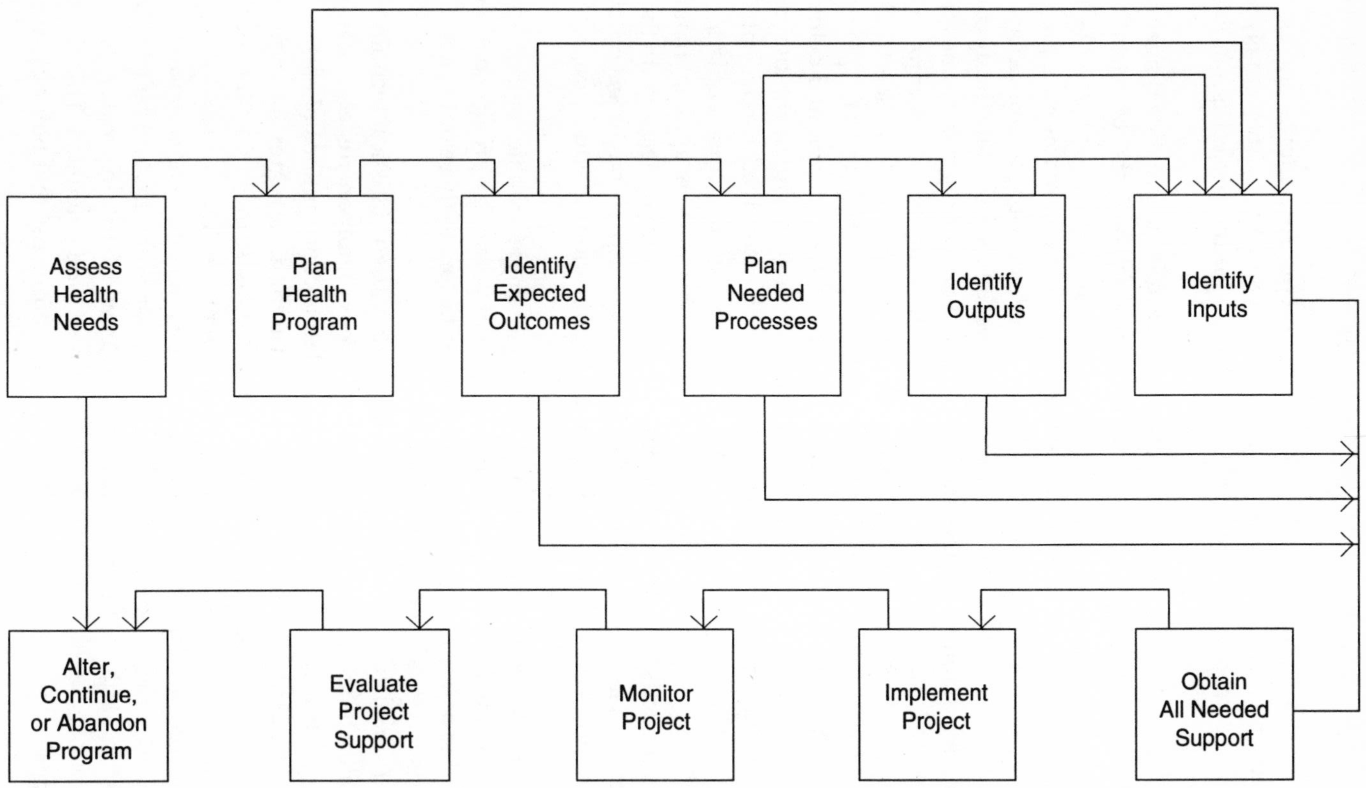

Figure 3-1. Systems Analysis Model of the Cycle of a Health Project

projects and programs are expected to be implemented and to operate. On the basis of this model a set of hypotheses are developed and tested on a large number of projects and programs so as to gradually improve the data base on which future activities are planned and evaluated. This approach is discussed in more detail in Section E of the present chapter.

## Constructing a Model

*A Systems Analysis Approach*

The systems analysis approach to constructing a program model consists of five basic tasks:

- *Define program goals.* Goals are the ultimate achievements or reforms that a program is expected to produce. For example, the goal of an immunization program may be to eradicate polio from the nation.
- *List program objectives.* Objectives are the quantifiable benchmarks that determine whether a program has been successful.
- *List program inputs for each expected reform.* Inputs are all the necessary program resources (such as money, material, personnel, infrastructure); hence, they are the independent variables of the program. Inputs are generally derived from interdisciplinary sources (medical, administrative, logistical, and so on).
- *Outline the temporal phasing of each input.* A time chart or a flow chart should be constructed indicating the quantity of input required, the point in time it is required, the length of time it takes to receive the input, and whether any input is dependent on preceding inputs. In short, this step specifies the quantity of inputs required and the order in which they should be introduced. Inputs can vary greatly in this respect. Some (for example, program management and operating capital) will persist throughout the project at a constant quantity, whereas others (for example, computer programmer) will be present at one time or intermittently at different phases and in variable quantities (as in the case of program evaluators).

  Figure 3-1 illustrates one typical way of displaying the temporal ordering of the ten main categories of activity for a health project. The flow moves clockwise, the first activity being to "assess health needs." The connecting lines indicate dependent relationships; that is to say, they show which activities must precede another activity. Activities that are not connected can be performed independently. Although Figure 3-1 is a simple diagram, international development projects can be so complex that it takes computer and microcomputer programs to construct the flow charts and thereby identify dependencies.

An alternative approach is to use a Gantt chart to display the chronological order of activities, their duration, and dependencies and to indicate whether they overlap (see Chapter 4, Table 4-2).

* *Identify impacts.* The impacts expected from the intervention program constitute the dependent variables. Impacts, as defined in Chapter 1, consist of both expected and unexpected results. The program model should identify all expected impacts. Subsequent analyses of results may refine the model by making explicit any impacts that were produced by the model but were not anticipated or stated previously. Conversely, when objectives are not achieved, the model needs to be edited either to eliminate this unrealistic objective and the program components that were supposed to produce it or to augment the model by adding additional support components that could increase the possibility of achieving the objective.

In sum, a systems analysis model explicitly identifies inputs, outputs, processes, and impacts; explains how they are related; and defines the role of each component in the program plan. From a social science perspective, development programs are considered action theories about how to effect change within society. Probably the most distinctive feature of a model is its explicit description of how its variables interact to produce impacts. One notable characteristic of a development program is that it is expected to produce societal changes, either through new institutions (such as clinics) or delivery systems, or by removing already existing ones (for example, a squatter settlement). Whether the social program is in the field of housing, public health, water and sanitation, or small business development, a model identifies what should be introduced or eliminated from the environment, and why.

Development projects formulated as models are sometimes easier to streamline than projects that are not so precisely delineated. This advantage is the result of having to spell out separate activities and their relative priorities and dependencies. With this level of precision, it is easier to identify potential bottlenecks and compare different delivery systems according to their cost-effectiveness and required duration. Systems analysis can also help planners identify and eliminate components that will make little contribution to the final outcomes. Other advantages of using a model become clearer when a program is expanded from one location to another. A model makes it easier to determine whether components have to be added or eliminated to coincide with environmental constraints or population needs.

Because development programs are implicitly or explicitly social models describing how to effect change in society, both the independent variables that instigate change and the dependent variables that are the hypothesized effects should be clearly stated, or at the very least they should be explicitly deducible from a program's statement of purpose or plan of action. The independent variables consist of all inputs, outputs, and processes—namely, the components that lead to an expected outcome. During the implementation stage of a project, the evaluator's role is to determine whether there are enough inputs, whether outputs are being delivered, and whether the quantity of outputs is sufficient. By establishing a monitoring system, the evaluator is able to judge whether the model has been implemented. During the operational stage, he assesses whether the expected outcomes occurred and identifies additional unexpected outcomes. If the hypothesized effects do not occur, the evaluator attempts to determine why the social model failed to obtain the expected impact. In so doing, he may then offer recommendations for reformulating the model.

### Constructing a Model for Logical Framework Analysis

Logical framework (log frame) analysis is a technique originally developed for the U.S. Agency for International Development (Practical Concepts Incorporated 1979). Its distinctive feature is that it requires an explicit statement of the changes that a project is supposed to produce, along with each step that leads toward achieving them. This method divides a project into four components:

- The GENERAL GOALS to be achieved.
- The PURPOSE of the project (that is, how it will achieve these goals).
- The OUTPUTS to be produced to achieve this purpose.
- The INPUTS to be used to achieve these outputs.

The logical sequence of these activities is stated in the following way:

- If INPUTS are provided at the right time and in the right quantities, then OUTPUTS will be produced.

- If OUTPUTS are produced, then PURPOSE (impacts/benefits) will be obtained.
- If PURPOSE is obtained, then GENERAL GOALS will be achieved.

Log frame analysis typically divides its information into four columns: a narrative summary of project goals, purposes, outputs, and inputs; objectively verifiable indicators of whether each of the above has been achieved, produced, or obtained; the means of objectively verifying the indicator; and assumptions on which the verification is based.

The log frame is specifically designed to facilitate monitoring and evaluation in that all the intended outcomes (called "end of project status"), as well as the sequence of events through which they should be achieved, are clearly defined. Thus if an outcome is not achieved, it is possible to determine whether this was because the required inputs were not provided or whether important assumptions were not satisfied.

Table 3-2 illustrates how log frame analysis might be applied to a project intended to reduce infant mortality. In this example, the *general goal* of the project is to reduce infant mortality in the Dominican Republic from 90 to 75 per thousand and child mortality from 24 to 10 per thousand. The *purpose* of the project, through which the goals will be achieved, is to organize child survival activities in two rural areas and one urban area by establishing sustainable primary health care (PHC) systems for education in the use of oral rehydration therapy, for monitoring the growth of infants, and for controlling acute respiratory diseases. The *outputs* through which this purpose would be achieved include improved private voluntary organizations (PVOs) engaged in PHC, a strengthened primary health care directorate in the Dominican Ministry of Health (SESPAS), and a quality control system for monitoring community health. The *inputs* that would achieve these outputs include curriculum materials for classrooms and field practice, family record sheets, household visit record sheets, computer software, questionnaires, and sampling frames. Vehicles, equipment, and operating costs are also considered inputs. Log frame analysis is structured to help planners formulate programs logically and to think through each step of a program model, beginning with the desired impact and then working backward through each step needed to achieve it.

Column 2 consists of empirical measures of the goals, purposes, outputs, and inputs. The last three components are subsumed in Figure 3-2 as end-of-project status (EOPS). The EOPS defines the program's objectives on a set of numerical targets that the program is expected to achieve or produce. The final INPUT in column 2 is the budget, which is a necessary condition for successful project implementation.

Column 3 indicates the source of the data used in verifying whether objectives have been attained and whether resources have been committed by donors. For example, health records collected at the community level and kept in the community center will be one of the main sources of information on changes in the infant mortality rates and disease-specific mortality rates. Column 4 lists the assumptions on which the various components of the program model are based, including the mitigating circumstances that could delay implementation or evaluation of the project.

## *Participatory Project Planning and Design*

Log frame analysis was originally developed for the internal use of international donor agencies, and consequently the objectives and implementation methods were largely defined by the donor agency. The approach has now been adapted to permit the intended beneficiaries to participate in the identification and planning of the project. The German Development Agency (GTZ) has developed a goal-oriented planning version known as ZOPP (Zielorientierte Projekt Planung). ZOPP uses a four-phase method for ensuring beneficiary involvement:

*Problem analysis* confirms or amends the project concept by identifying the core problem of the target group and depicting the causes and effects of this problem visually in the form of a problem tree. This will build on the findings of the rapid social assessment or other exploratory studies and involves in-depth and systematic consultations with representative samples of each subpopulation the project is intended to benefit, as well as with other stakeholders.

*Objectives analysis* develops specific objectives that relate directly to the problems identified above. This and the following stages normally involve consultation workshops with the intended beneficiary groups.

*Alternatives analysis* assesses alternative or competing strategies so as to achieve the previously agreed objectives in the most efficient and equitable manner.

*Planning matrix* spells out detailed action plans to achieve the above objectives and identifying indicators to measure the progress in achieving these objectives.

Table 3-2. Application of Logical Framework Analysis to a Health Project to Reduce Infant Mortality

| Narrative Summary | Objectively Verifiable Indicators | Means of Verification | Important Assumptions |
|---|---|---|---|
| *Program Goal* | *Means of Achieving Goal* | | |
| • Reduce infant mortality from 90/1,000 to 75/1,000<br>• Reduce child deaths from 26/1,000 to 10/1,000 | • Infant mortality rates<br>• Disease-specific mortality rates | • Project's community record system for verifying: birth, age-specific deaths, target population age distribution, distribution of malnutrition, and diarrhea episodes | • Access to government and PVO records<br>• Access to community archives<br>• Access to families in target areas<br>• Availability of training space |
| *Project Purpose* | *End of Project Status* | | |
| • Child survival activities in 2 rural and 1 urban area<br>• To develop sustainable systems for ORT and growth chart monitoring<br>• Improve government and NGO primary health care for infants, women, and children at the community level | • Grade II and III malnutrition reduced by 40% and 25%<br>• Prevalence of diarrhea reduced by 20%<br>• 80% coverage in target population by all program activities<br>• 100% coverage of all catchment areas with child survival quality control<br>• 80% of all diarrheal episodes treated with ORT | • Project's community record system for the following variables: birth, age-specific deaths, target population age distribution, frequency distribution of malnutrition, and diarrhea episodes<br>• Credibility of PVOs | • Availability of technical assistance in community-based public health and epidemiology<br>• Excellent coordination between public and PVO programs |

*Inputs*

- Curriculum and materials for classroom and field practice
- Family record sheets, household visit record sheets, growth charts and computer software
- Quality control instruments: questionnaires, sampling frame
- Vehicles and equipment
- Operating costs

- 80% of communities with community health programs
- 80% communities receiving regular health assessments for women and children
- 80% of staff participating in annual further education
- 80% communities covered by social marketing materials
- 80% of promoters and supervisors with regular transportation
- Budget disbursement

- Ministry of Health and PVO data
- Resource accounting system should provide all data regarding training and continuing education
- Cooperative agreements with participating agencies

- Allocation of promoter's time by all organizations expected to participate in training and coaching activities

*Outputs*

- Train government and PVO promoters in health concepts and practice and in management of community-based information systems
- Establish quality control system for monitoring community-based PHC delivery
- 80% of all communities covered by primary health care organization

- 80% referral of all pregnant women and neonates to a physician at least once

- Surveys for measuring the following variables: use of ORT, mother's knowledge of ORT use, measurement of all variables in the above health records

- Legitimization of the management—teacher roles of the technical advisers, PVOs and project managers
- Population motivated to participate and receptive to social marketing
- Funds available

Figure 3-2. Using a Process Model to Examine Factors Affecting the Sustainability of a Social Development Project

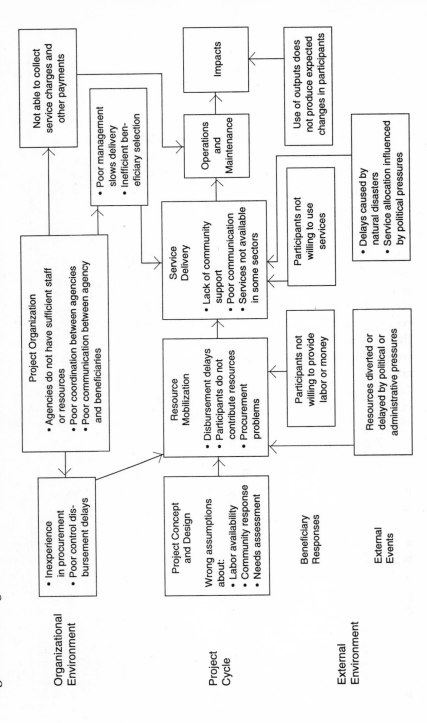

The overall ZOPP methodology has been described by the GTZ (1987), while O'Sullivan (1993) has explained how the participatory approach is implemented. The beneficiary assessment approach (Salmen 1992) can also be used to collect the information required for the objectives analysis.

## Constructing a Process Model

Figure 3-2 shows how a process model can be used to assess factors affecting project sustainability (see Chapter 6). Such a model has been used to analyze the sustainability of rural development, irrigation, housing, and education projects in Bangladesh (Bamberger and Cheema 1990), Viet Nam, Kuwait, Jordan, and Tunisia. With appropriate modifications, the general model in Figure 3-2 can be used to evaluate the implementation and sustainability of most kinds of social development projects. The model is divided into central, upper, and lower sections. The central section describes the stages of the project cycle: project concept and design, resource mobilization, service delivery, operations and maintenance, and the achievement of project impacts. This is a simplified version of the seven-stage project cycle model presented earlier. The first three stages are combined into "project concept and design"; stage 4 is divided into "resource mobilization" and "service delivery"; stages 5, 6, and 7 are combined into "operations management"; and "project impacts" is presented as a separate component. For each of the first three stages, factors are identified that might affect sustainability. For example, wrong assumptions during project design about the community's potential response to the project might lead project beneficiaries to reject some of the project maintenance responsibilities that the planners had assumed they would accept.

The upper section of the model identifies ways in which the project is affected by the organizational environment in which it operates. This refers both to the internal organization of the project (discussed in Chapter 12) and to the influences of the broader institutional environment. For example, poor administration might make it more difficult to collect water user charges that were to be used to finance routine maintenance. Other problems might arise because it is difficult to coordinate the project with other government, private, or community projects.

The lower section of the model describes ways in which sustainability may be affected by the economic, political, social, and cultural environment in which the project develops. Consider an urban development project that

Figure 3-3. Using Path Analysis to Evaluate the Impacts of a Small Business Credit Program in Colombia

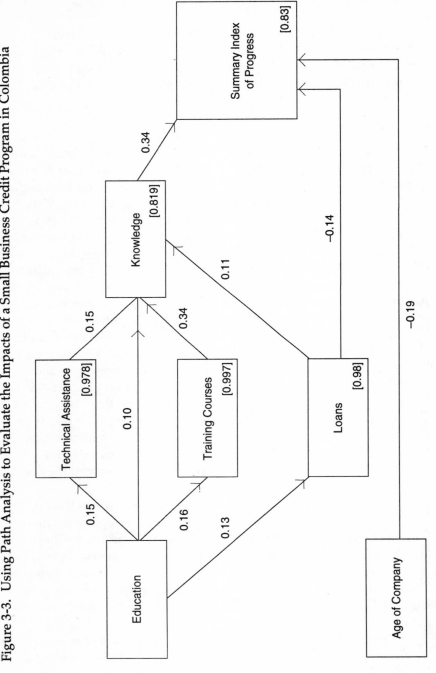

*Source:* Instituto Ser (1984).

provides cost-effective sanitation through communal toilets and washing facilities and through communal standpipes supervised by community leaders. Because of religious and cultural differences, these facilities may be acceptable to only certain cultural groups. Other groups may refuse to accept such facilities because of their hygienic practices and concepts of privacy. Responses may also vary in culturally mixed as opposed to homogenous communities. Similarly, sustainability may be affected by external political events, by changes in the economic environment, or by natural disasters.

The model is used in its present form as a checklist to assist analysts in designing the process of evaluation and is later modified to adapt to the specific characteristics of the project being studied. Once the evaluation has been conducted, the main findings are entered into the model, which is then used as a visual aid in the written assessment and during the verbal presentations of the findings.

### Path Analysis

Figure 3-3 shows how path analysis was used to evaluate the effectiveness of different components of a small business development program in Colombia (Instituto SER 1984). The program sought to promote and strengthen small businesses through technical assistance, loans, and training courses. The effectiveness of these project inputs was expected to be affected by the education of the entrepreneur, the age of the company (assuming it already existed), and the previous knowledge the entrepreneur possessed.

A diagram like the one in Figure 3-3 is prepared to identify the links to be examined. In the present example it was assumed that the progress of the small businesses (defined in a summary index) would be affected by the three program inputs (technical assistance, training courses, and loans); and also by the education of the entrepreneur, his knowledge of the field before the start of the project, and the age of his company. It was assumed that education would influence the effectiveness of the courses, technical assistance, and loan programs.

Multiple regression analysis is then used to assess the strength of the statistical association between the different elements in the model. The numbers on the lines linking two variables are the *standardized regression coefficients*, which indicate the strength of the association between the two variables (the proportion of the total variance). The closer to 1.0, the stronger the association. Thus previous knowledge has more influence on the index of progress than does the amount of the loan. The age of the company is negatively associated with progress (that is, the longer a company has been established, the less likely it is to be affected by the project). The numbers in each box are the *residual coefficients*, which refer to the proportion of the total variance *not* explained by the variables in the model. In this case, 83 percent of the variance in the summary index is not explained by the variables in the model.

Path analysis is a useful way to visualize relationships between the different variables in the model, test the statistical strength of the relationships, and present the findings in a way that is easily understood. When expected links are weak or go in the opposite direction to what was expected, the design of the project needs to be modified, and perhaps the way in which certain services are organized needs to be improved or additional services provided.

## Using Models to Evaluate Social Development Programs

The models described in the previous sections should play a central role in all stages of the evaluation of a social development program. Although models are useful for evaluating any kind of development project, they are particularly important for social programs. To begin with, in social programs the *process* of implementation can be almost as important as the final outcomes, particularly with respect to institution-building objectives. Social programs are concerned with process. During the preparatory stage, when the focus and design of the evaluation are being discussed, a *process model* or *causal network* can be useful in identifying the processes through which the project will be implemented; the organizational structure through which it will be implemented; and the political, social, and economic environment in which it will operate. This kind of model can also identify the key assumptions about how it will operate and the factors likely to affect its success. Such information provides the essential foundation on which discussions of objectives and methodology should be built.

Garaycochea (1990:66–67) argues that models can contribute a great deal to our understanding of the dynamics of social development programs, but that many technical difficulties have to be overcome in developing models that are expected to capture the complexities of the implementation process:

> To evaluate social development means to evaluate a process, that is to say to understand the process which unfolds when [an] intervention has taken place. If evaluatory exercises are integrated into a social development process, they become part of it. . . . It is not concerned as an isolated or external element in an organic body, it is more like a "process within a process" situation. Compared to traditional forms of evaluation (cost-benefit analysis), social evaluation does not conclude in a specific "canned" product, because it has the nature of being simultaneously an output and an input contained in a continuous process.

Some of the major difficulties that social development projects face are the process and the qualitative objectives they pursue. In fact, the "difficulty with objectives such as participation is not only that they are difficult to characterize, but also that it is not possible at the beginning of a project to predict what the outcome or effect might be" (Oakley 1988:5). In addition to this, the results of the project would not be visible during its life span or by the time it has finished. Effects can appear later in the future and in a context where we will not be able to determine to what extent changes or actions taking place are due to the project's past intervention.

Another problem related to this topic arises in asking to what extent project members have control of the processes taking place in it. We might know when and how to switch on the mechanisms to start a social development process, but we do not know when and where it is going to finish. Social development projects are dynamic and do not necessarily follow a predetermined direction. We should take into account that social development projects can develop unexpected results. Even though a project might not accomplish its initial goals (the predetermined parameters against which evaluation is supposed to rest), the project can still be a success (in that it contributes to developing or strengthening community institutions).

Efforts to construct this kind of model often reveal that some of the essential information (for example, about how beneficiaries are likely to respond to the services offered) is missing, in which case a rapid diagnostic study may be conducted.

Once the objectives of the program and the evaluation have been defined, it is possible to undertake a *logical framework analysis or systems analysis* to

Figure 3-4. Framework for the Analysis of the Impacts of Education on Women

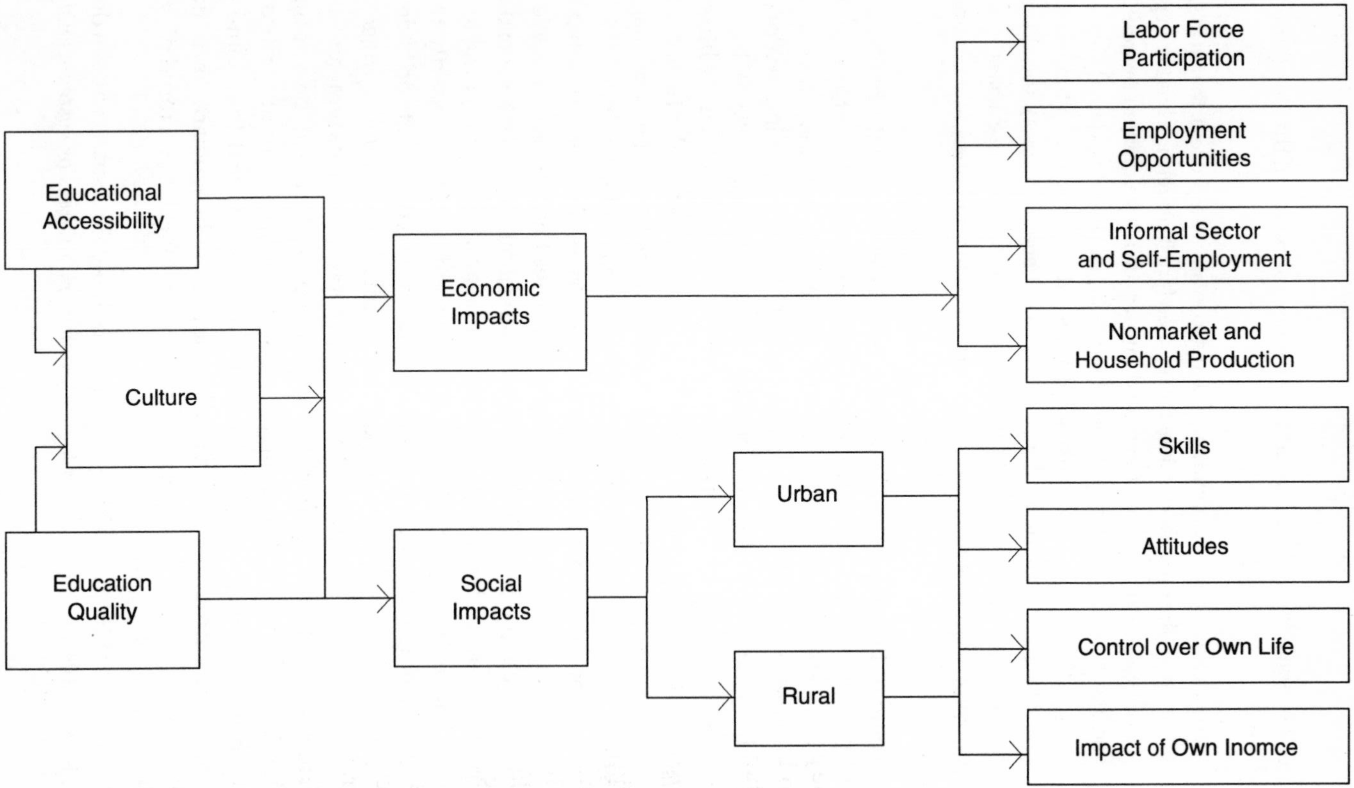

Labor Force Participation

Employment Opportunities

Informal Sector and Self-Employment

Nonmarket and Household Production

Skills

Attitudes

Control over Own Life

Impact of Own Inomce

Urban

Rural

Economic Impacts

Social Impacts

Educational Accessibility

Culture

Education Quality

*Source:* Based on USAID (1990).

specify in more detail how the evaluation will be conducted and which indicators will be used to assess project performance. If more precise statistical estimates of project impact are required, *path analysis* or *quasi-experimental designs* can also be used.

As the evaluation progresses, continuous reference should be made to the models to determine the extent to which the key assumptions on which the program is based are proving correct. For example: Are beneficiaries responding as expected? Are delivery systems performing as planned? When inputs are delivered, do they produce the intended outputs? Whenever deviations are identified, this suggests the need for additional studies. Thus the model should be used as a reference point throughout the implementation of the evaluation.

When the project is completed, the models can provide a framework for the systematic analysis of the lessons learned. In particular, an analysis can be presented of all the initial assumptions that proved incorrect or that had to be modified to determine why they were wrong, and to suggest how they should be modified in future projects.

*Using a Model to Assess the Impacts of Primary Education on Girls*

Figure 3-4 illustrates how a model can be used to help in the design and interpretation of an evaluation of the impact of primary education on girls. The example is based on the findings of a study conducted under the USAID Advancing Basic Education and Literacy (ABEL) Project (USAID 1990).

A primary education project provides two main kinds of inputs. The first is to increase the accessibility of education through the provision of more schools, the reduction of economic barriers to attendance, outreach programs, and the like. The second is to improve the quality of education through the increased supply and better training of teachers, more school books, a curriculum that is more relevant to the culture and economic opportunities of each region, and so on.

The present study did not evaluate these inputs, but the proposed model can easily be expanded to assess the effects of accessibility and quality on the production of the intended impacts. Chapters 4 and 5 describe the use of monitoring and diagnostic studies to assess input variables.

The effectiveness of educational or other kinds of human development projects will be affected by cultural variation and the extent to which local culture supports or is in conflict with the programs being developed. As an illustration, the USAID report cites considerable variations between regions in Nepal with respect to the cultural expectations regarding the extent to which women should become involved in trading and other economic activities outside the home (see Acharya and Bennett 1981). These variations are likely to affect the willingness of families to send their daughters to school (rather than keeping them at home to help with housework), and also the extent to which women can capitalize on their improved education. In another example, "superior health achievers" in ten societies appear to come from cultures with an ideology that encourages greater status and autonomy for women and that places a high value on female education (Caldwell 1986).

In the analysis of girls' primary education, two kinds of impacts were assessed: economic and social. Economic impacts were assessed in terms of increased female labor force participation, greater employment opportunities, performance in the informal sector and in self-employment, and nonmarket activities and household production. A literature review was conducted in each of these areas to develop hypotheses concerning the ways in which improved education could affect the economic status of women. In the area of self-employment and informal economic activities, for example, there is considerable evidence that low literacy levels are one of the major barriers to women's access to credit (Lycette and White 1989). Educational level has a less clear impact on women's participation or performance in the informal sector.

Education is also expected to produce social impacts on girls. The model suggests that the impacts may be different in rural and in urban areas. In both cases four main types of impacts are examined: skill acquisition, attitudes, control over one's own life, and the effects of controlling one's own income. For example, a number of hypotheses are proposed as to the potential impacts of women having direct control over income. Earlier studies are cited suggesting that a greater proportion of a woman's earnings are used for the nutrition and education of her children, and that the autonomy resulting from control over income tends to reduce fertility.

This model makes explicit testable hypotheses to explain both the kinds of impacts that are expected, and the social and economic factors that influence the extent to which the changes occur. If expected impacts are not produced or if unanticipated changes do occur, it is then possible to reexamine each stage of the model to determine where and how reality departed from expectations. In this way the model can be continually revised and adapted to the cultural and economic variations of particular countries or regions.

*Using a Model to Monitor the Impacts of Structural Adjustment Programs on the Poor*

During the past few years more than thirty African countries have found it necessary to introduce far-reaching structural adjustment programs to correct chronic deteriorations in their economic and social conditions. Most of these adjustment programs have involved substantial reductions in government expenditures on the social sectors, cutbacks in public sector employment, and large increases in the price of basic commodities such as food, clothing, and public transportation. These measures, however beneficial in the medium and long term, may have imposed severe burdens on the poorest and most vulnerable sectors of society in the short run. In order to help countries that are undertaking structural adjustment programs reduce the "social costs of adjustment," the World Bank, African Development Bank, and the United Nations Development Programme (UNDP) jointly sponsored the Social Dimensions of Adjustment in Africa (SDA) Program. The SDA program is helping the more than thirty participating African countries develop data bases to monitor the impacts of adjustment programs on the poor, to identify and implement social action programs (such as nutrition, the maintenance of basic social infrastructure, public works programs, and credit to promote microenterprises) designed to have a rapid impact on the identified vulnerable groups, and to assess the impacts of these social action programs.

One of the primary objectives of the SDA program is to help countries establish national data bases that can

- Monitor the changes in the social and economic conditions of different population groups that appear to be associated with structural adjustment and related economic policies.
- Identify the groups most seriously affected by different measures and describe the main kinds of pressures or problems to which they appear to be subjected (for example, increased prices of basic commodities, falling prices or markets for their products, loss of primary and secondary employment).
- Monitor the performance of social action programs, evaluate their impacts, and seek to assess the factors contributing to their outcomes.

**Figure 3-5.  Framework Showing Links between Policy Interventions, Market Factors, Poverty Programs, and Impacts at the Community and Household Levels**

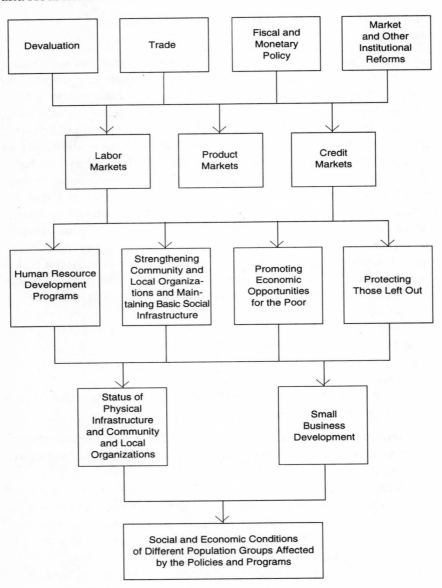

*Source:* Adapted from World Bank (1990).

- Identify the programs needed to protect or benefit vulnerable groups and suggest ways in which the effectiveness of current programs could be increased.

Figure 3-5 presents a framework adapted from SDA (World Bank 1990c:86) that can be used to define the data required to meet these four objectives. The framework identifies the ways in which structural adjustment policies are likely to affect poor and vulnerable groups by identifying the potential links between

- Four sets of *macroeconomic policy interventions* (devaluation, trade policy, fiscal/monetary policy, market and other institutional reforms).
- The operation of labor, product, and credit markets—showing how they are affected by project interventions.
- Poverty alleviation interventions at the sector, program, and project levels. Four main kinds of interventions are identified: (1) enhancing and maintaining human capital (such as education, population, health, and nutrition); (2) strengthening local and community organizations and maintaining basic social infrastructure; (3) promoting economic opportunities; and (4) providing programs to protect those who are left out (such as the old, handicapped, and sick).
- Potential outcomes at the *community* level (strengthening community organizations, maintenance of physical infrastructure) and *small business* level (for example, increased employment, provision of a wider range of services to local communities).
- Potential outcomes at the household level for different affected population groups (impacts on income, employment, consumption, health, education, access to basic services, and the like).

The SDA program has developed a *priority survey system* that can provide the basic information required at each of the above levels (for a detailed description of the objectives, content, and methods of analysis of this survey program, see Grootaert and Marchant 1991; and for an illustration of how this method was applied in Ghana, see Boateng and others 1990). Information is collected through three main survey instruments:

- The SDA *priority survey system* (PSS) is used to rapidly collect the information needed to identify target groups during the process of adjustment. It is designed to identify *what* is occurring without necessarily explaining *why*. The survey is normally administered in less than one hour and is intended to provide rapid feedback on the effects of the adjustment process. Box 3-1 summarizes the main information categories covered by the PSS.

- The social dimensions *integrated survey* aims at providing a complete and integrated data set needed to better understand the mechanisms of the adjustment process at the household level. The focus is on *diagnosis* and the reasons that certain impacts or effects are produced. Data collection is time-consuming in that information is collected at different times of the year. The integrated survey covers the size and composition of the household; health; education; employment status of each household member; housing; valuation of durable, productive, and financial assets; productive activities, both agricultural and non-agricultural; income, transfers, and savings; and food and nonfood consumption and other expenditures.
- The social dimensions *community survey* is intended to provide community-level data on prices and infrastructure that can easily and readily be integrated with the data collected through the household surveys.

The surveys produce several kinds of outputs:

- They rapidly identify vulnerable groups and provide rapid feedback on how each group is affected by structural adjustment policy interventions.

---

**Box 3-1.  Information Covered by the SDA Priority Survey**

1. Household roster: demographic characteristics, education, health, and employment
2. Employment
3. Housing and facilities: occupancy status; access to water and fuel; access to food market, school, health facilities, and transportation
4. Migration
5. Agricultural enterprises
6. Nonfarm enterprises
7. Household expenditures: expenditure and changes for five key food items and essential nonfood items.
8. Income by source
9. Assets
10. Anthropometrics: weight and height of children 3–59 months

*Source:* Grootaert and Marchant (1991:21).

---

- They can be used to monitor the implementation of policies and programs and rapidly identify problems and possible solutions.
- They help the authorities evaluate different policies and programs, with recommendations on how they might be improved.

## Structured Learning

In recent years international development agencies and national governments have become increasingly aware of their lack of success in learning from the experience of the projects and programs they finance and implement. Even when individual projects and programs are well monitored and evaluated (which in any case is the exception rather than the rule), they tend to be treated in isolation. Few agencies have mechanisms in place that will allow them to systematically learn from the experience of these activities and to use these lessons to improve the design, implementation, and evaluation of future projects, programs, and policies. The PRISM system introduced by USAID, and described in Chapter 2, is one such attempt to develop a learning system.

Another approach, which the World Bank has begun exploring, is known as Structured Learning (SL). Although the approach is still quite new and has not yet been formalized, a number of its elements can be identified. Basically, it is a *comparative method* of systematically drawing information from a large number of similar projects, programs, or policies. This information is then used to provide a framework for improving the formulation, implementation, and evaluation of future activities. SL also involves the development of a model of the process of project/program/policy implementation, operation, and sustainability. The model should specify the causal links between different stages of the implementation process and the identification of factors affecting outcomes. A series of indicators are also defined for measuring performance and outcomes.

Information on the performance of the model can be obtained in various ways. In some cases experiments have been introduced into the project to test the efficiency and outcomes of different delivery systems or designs. This has been done, for example, in road construction projects where different design standards (such as road surfaces) have been used and outcomes such as maintenance costs have been systematically compared. In other cases, systems have been compared on the basis of differences in the environment in which different projects, programs, and policies are carried out; or differences in implementation and operation that happen to

Box 3-2.  Using Structured Learning in the Indonesian Water
Supply and Sanitation Project for Low-Income Communities
(WSSPLIC)

The aim of this $120 million World Bank–financed water and sanitation
project in Indonesia was to provide sustainable water and sanitation services
to poor people in six Indonesian provinces.

The Structured Learning approach started with a modest and as yet imperfect conceptual framework for considering factors that affect both the
demand for services (how social, economic, hydrological and policy decisions
affect the services people want and are willing to pay for) and the supply of
services (incentives, risk, accountability, transactions costs, and principal-
agent factors). In the project preparation phase, this framework is used to help
digest the lessons of relevant experience both in Indonesia and in other
countries. This is a rich and relatively untapped source of information, with
many large and costly failures, and some modest successes. As a result of this
review, some potential options are eliminated as proven losers and a range
of promising options are identified. Rather than "pick a winner," the process
indicates the uncertainties involved. It does so in part by encouraging diversity. That is, each of the six provinces involved were allowed to design their
own set of institutional arrangements (starting from the previously identified
menu of promising options). At the same time, it acknowledges that within
each province the chosen option is not a rigid arrangement, but a sensible
starting point for incorporating a "learning process" that will lead to modifications, and one in which adjustments can be made as experience accumulates. An important component of the project in each province would then be
learning both internally (from its own experiences) and externally (from the
experiences of subprojects in other provinces).

For the moment, only a temporary set of indicators is being used to assess
performance; the medium-term objective is to develop a more rigorous set of
performance indicators that can be used not only to measure progress, but
also to uncover the reasons for less satisfactory performance. Since the testing
of the different institutional alternatives is undertaken on the basis of an
explicit conceptual framework, SL in this project can be more easily transferred to and compared with others. In fact, a proposal has been put forth for
an Asian Rural Water Learning Process, which would initially include six to
seven Bank-financed projects.

*Source:* World Bank data.

occur. In the Housing Indicators Program, described below, indicators were collected on housing programs and the urban and macroeconomic environment in fifty-three countries. This programs is probably the largest and most systematic example of this approach (United Nations Centre for Human Settlements 1992).

Proponents of SL distinguish it from the Classic Research Mode, which favors an extensive and expensive analysis of a particular situation in a project. While detailed and useful information may be obtained on this particular activity, the fact that outcomes are always, in some degree, situation-specific usually makes it difficult to produce operational guidelines that are applicable to other contexts. The Highways Design Model developed by the World Bank, which by the mid-1980s had cost an estimated $25 million, is often cited as an example of the limitations on the Classic Research Mode. Although the computer model has proved extremely popular, a number of its parameters, such as the maintenance component, were calibrated with maintenance data only from Brazil. Proponents of the SL approach argue that it would have obtained data on maintenance performance and requirements for a wide range of countries and operating conditions, and at considerably less cost.

To use SL, a distinction must be made between "hard" and "soft" activities and between situations in which the scope is "narrow/simple" and "broad/complex." A "hard" activity would be one such as the Highways Design Model, which features a clearly defined conceptual framework, precise hypotheses, and specified outcomes. In contrast, examples of "soft" activities would include rural development, poverty alleviation, and resettlement programs. In each of these cases it is difficult to specify the conceptual framework or to define precise hypotheses and outcomes. Scope refers to the size and diversity of the areas covered by the activity and the number of variables included. An education project that seeks to improve reading skills through a small number of innovations would be a simple project, whereas an integrated urban development program involving housing, water supply and sanitation, road construction, and housing construction loans would be a complex project. Box 3-2 illustrates the application of SL to a complex and "soft" water and sanitation project in Indonesia.

*Applying Structured Learning to the Development of Housing and Urban
Sector Policies: The Housing Indicators Program*

Although international development agencies such as the World Bank have
invested billions of dollars in support of urban housing programs, their
investment represents only a very small fraction (probably less than 1
percent) of total investments in this sector by governments and the formal
and informal private sector in these countries. Consequently, if donors are
to make any significant contribution, they need to understand how to use
their resources to support or promote a favorable policy environment in
the urban sector of developing countries. The Housing Indicators Program
(United Nations Centre for Human Settlements 1993), which is a joint
program of the United Nations Centre for Human Settlements (UNCHS)
and the World Bank, demonstrates how structured learning can be applied
to the collection and analysis of Housing Indicators on some fifty-three
countries. Box 3-3 lists the indicators on which information is collected
(where available) on all fifty-three countries covered by the study.

The comparative analysis of these indicators has the following objectives
(UNCHS 1992):

- To provide governments with a conceptual and analytical tool for
  measuring the performance of the housing sector in a comparative,
  consistent and policy-oriented perspective.
- To establish baseline data in participating countries for new national
  shelter strategies and new housing sector loans.
- To create a framework for comparing housing sector performance
  between countries and cities, as well as between different time periods.
- To create a typology of countries with similar housing sector profiles.
- To contribute toward establishing a new institutional framework
  within countries for formulating and implementing sector-wide housing policies.
- To work toward the creation of an international network of experts
  and institutions capable of overseeing the development of the housing
  sector.

The indicators and the comparative analysis offer policymakers and
planners at the national and international level a number of tools for
structured learning. First, the comparative analysis shows how the housing
sector in a particular country performs in comparison with the same sector
in other countries (or cities) with similar economic and demographic

Box 3-3. Indicators Used for Comparative Analysis in Housing Indicators Program

| | |
|---|---|
| 1. New household formation | 24. The skill ratio |
| 2. Homelessness | 25. Households per dwelling unit |
| 3. Housing production | 26. Persons per room |
| 4. Housing investment | 27. Squatter housing |
| 5. Ratio of house price to income | 28. New housing credit |
| 6. Ratio of rent to income | 29. Mortage to prime differences |
| 7. House price appreciation | 30. Mortgage to deposit differences |
| 8. Floor area per person | 31. Mortgage default rate |
| 9. Permanent structures | 32. Land concentration |
| 10. Water connection | 33. Import share of construction |
| 11. Journey to work | 34. Construction time |
| 12. Unauthorized housing | 35. Restrictiveness index |
| 13. Residential mobility | 36. Institutional development index |
| 14. The vacancy rate | 37. Rent control index |
| 15. Owner-occupancy | 38. Public housing stock |
| 16. The housing credit portfolio | 39. Public land ownership |
| 17. The credit to value ratio | 40. Urban area growth rate |
| 18. Housing subsidies | 41. Household size |
| 19. Targeted subsidies | 42. Median unit size |
| 20. The land development multiplier | 43. Median annual rent |
| 21. Infrastructure expenditures per capita | 44. Median house price |
| | 45. Developed land price |
| 22. Construction cost | 46. Raw land price |
| 23. Industrial concentration | 47. Median unit reproduction cost |

*Source:* UNCHS (1992a).

characteristics. This helps policymakers define objectives (for example, to achieve at least an average performance compared with similar countries) and also indicates how much improvement can reasonably be expected. Second, if indicators continue to lag behind other countries, this indicates the policy issues that need to be addressed. Third, where countries are performing above average, this suggests that there are some important lessons to be learned.

Finally, the indicators can be of use to international agencies in demonstrating the links between housing indicators and macroeconomic variables. These links indicate why it is important to consider the housing sector within a broader set of macroeconomic policies, and also provide clear benchmarks for assessing the comparative impacts of different kinds of interventions.

## Summary

The principal message of this chapter is that social programs ought to define their activities, resources, outputs, and inputs explicitly, since their ultimate objectives are to have a measurable effect on society. Therefore, social programs should be designed to include testable hypotheses, the accuracy of which may be improved upon over time. Since social programs include testable hypotheses, they can and should be portrayed as models to clarify how specific resources and activities are related to the production of program outputs, and how these outputs lead to measurable beneficial effects.

Several approaches were discussed. We did not attempt to rank them by our own preferences since our main concern has been to underscore the value of modeling, rather than to promote a single approach to doing so.

## Recommended Reading

Asher, Herbert. 1983. *Causal Modeling.* Quantitative Applications in the Social Sciences 3. Beverly Hills, Calif.: Sage.

A relatively technical explanation of how path analysis is used.

Bamberger, Michael, and Abdul Aziz. 1993. *The Design and Management of Sustainable Poverty Alleviation Programs; The South Asian Experience.* EDI Seminar Series. Washington, D.C.: World Bank, Economic Development Institute.

Detailed discussion of participatory approaches to project planning and evaluation and of social development applications of logical framework analysis.

Cook, Thomas, and Donald Campbell. 1979. *Quasi-Experimentation: Design and Analysis Issues for Field Settings.* Chicago: Rand McNally.

Explains the logic and application of quasi-experimental designs. Although many examples are included, they are all drawn from the United States, and many of the techniques would be difficult to replicate in developing countries owing to the lack of data.

German Development Agency (GTZ). 1987. *ZOPP: An Introduction to the Method.* Frankfurt am Main.

An explanation of how logical framework analysis can be combined with participatory planning.

Miles, Matthew, and Michael Huberman. 1984. *Qualitative Data Analysis: A Sourcebook of New Methods.* Beverly Hills, Calif.: Sage.

Describes how modeling techniques can be used with qualitative data. All the examples are drawn from the education sector, but the principles can be applied more generally.

O'Sullivan, Neil. 1993. "Identification and Design of Poverty Alleviation Projects," in Bamberger, Michael and Abdul Aziz. 1993. *The Design and Management of Sustainable Poverty Alleviation Programs; The South Asian Experience.* EDI Seminar Series. Washington, D.C.: World Bank, Economic Development Institute.

Explains how participatory approaches can be incorporated into the planning and design of development projects.

Practical Concepts Incorporated. 1979. *The Logical Framework: A Manager's Guide to a Scientific Approach to Design and Evaluation.* Washington, D.C.

Simple explanation of how Log Frame Analysis is used. The discussion is oriented toward the international donor agencies and does not address issues relating to participatory planning.

## Notes

1. The Operations Evaluation Department (1987) reported that only 80 percent of World Bank projects completed in 1985 could be classified as "worthwhile" and that the proportion was significantly lower for complex projects in low-income countries where major social and economic transformations were required.

2. See GTZ (1987) for a discussion of the participatory planning approach to log-frame analysis. See also the chapters by Neil O'Sullivan in Bamberger and Aziz (1993).

# Part II

## Design and Implementation
## of Monitoring and Evaluation
### A Guide for Practitioners

# 4

## Monitoring Project Implementation to Ensure Efficient and Timely Production of Outputs

In Chapter 1 monitoring was defined as a continuous management activity that helps a project achieve its defined objectives within a prescribed time frame and budget. Monitoring provides regular feedback on the progress of project implementation and on the problems faced during implementation. It consists of operational and administrative activities that track resource acquisition and allocation, the production or the delivery of services, and cost records.

### Defining Management Information Needs

The purpose of a monitoring system is to provide, in a timely manner, the information needed (a) to ensure that a project is implemented efficiently and economically and is achieving its objectives and (b) to help in the selection and planning of future projects. Before a monitoring system can satisfy these criteria, it is necessary to identify the intended users ("stake-holders") and to fully understand the information they need and how they will use it. A number of recent reviews of evaluation experience in the United States and Europe have emphasized that the successful outcome and usefulness of evaluations depend on close cooperation between the evaluators and their clients at all stages of the evaluation (Osborne and Gaebler 1992; Rist 1990; Wholey, Newcomer, and Associates 1989).

### Defining Project Stakeholders and Their Information Needs

Most development projects involve at least four categories of agencies: international agencies (donors, NGOs, and research foundations); national and sectoral agencies (central government ministries, financial agencies, line ministries, local NGOs, and national consulting and research groups); project implementing agencies; and intended beneficiaries. These groups are often referred to as *stakeholders* to emphasize that they have an interest in the outcome of the project and, consequently, in the orientation and interpretation of the monitoring and evaluation studies.

Now that evaluators have come to understand the political nature of their profession, they are focusing more attention on identifying the myriad of stakeholders whose interests and concerns affect the fate of evaluations. They realize that stakeholder groups often have conflicting political interests in whether the evaluation should be done at all, what should be studied, and how the results should be interpreted and disseminated (or not disseminated). There is also a growing consensus that the evaluator must identify the principal stakeholders and understand their information needs to ensure that evaluation is *focused on utilization*. This sensitivity increases the likelihood that the results of an evaluation will be used to influence the project. Different users have different perspectives—which may be contradictory—and the evaluator must often negotiate with various stakeholders to reach a consensus on what is to be studied. The evaluator must also try to reflect fairly some of these different points of view.

A number of fundamental issues continue to be hotly debated. One concerns what might be called "objective truth versus fairness." Many continue to believe the evaluator should be an objective and impartial outsider, who applies rigorous (and unbiased) research methods in an effort to provide objective answers to questions about how well a program has performed. Others (for example, Guba and Lincoln 1987; Palumbo 1987; and Patton 1987) argue that the search for objective truth is meaningless and that the role of the evaluator is to represent fairly the perspectives of each of the principal stakeholders.

Those who advocate stakeholder analysis have raised other questions about the role of the evaluator. Is it appropriate to work for a single client and to adopt his or her conceptual framework? Should evaluators pass judgment on programs and their underlying assumptions, or should they try to be ethically neutral? To what extent should evaluators try to control the way in which information is used? Patton (1978, 1982, 1987) believes that the evaluator should try to ensure that the results of the evaluation are properly used, and he discusses in considerable detail how this can be done. Chelimsky (1987), while fully aware of the political nature of evaluation, emphasizes that different kinds of evaluation can be used at different stages of the policy cycle. The intelligent evaluator who understands these applications, Chelimsky argues, can increase the likelihood that the evaluation findings will be used rationally. Weiss (1987) believes the evaluator has much less control over how the information will be used.

Although most of the stakeholder literature refers to the United States, there has been some discussion of the influence that donors—often among the largest and most influential stakeholders—have had on the scope and objectives of international evaluations (Bamberger 1988a).[1] Gran (1983:303–4) states that World Bank evaluations

> focus on the degree to which productive targets and implementation schedules have been met. Time permits only the enumeration of a few simple variables such as the number of loans to "small farmers" or number of wells dug. Little or no investigation takes place that would lay bare the quality of the activity. If a road is built the entire community is assumed to benefit. No thought goes to building up the capacity and legitimacy of local organizations so that regular repairs on the road would take place. If production does rise, the project gets the credit as though simple direct links can be proven. If there are minimal gains, local conditions or limited extension systems are to blame. Blaming the victims avoids system contradictions and dangerous political issues.

Gran's point is that the World Bank adopts a "developmentalist, neoclassical economic approach" that implicitly accepts the political and economic system in which projects are planned and implemented. Consequently the evaluations focus mainly on economic, technical, and financial issues and deliberately (or inadvertently) avoid broader political and economic considerations that are much more important in explaining project failures. He also claims that because of the Bank's international nature it is isolated from the kinds of criticism to which bilateral agencies are subjected and hence can determine its own agenda of topics to cover in the evaluations.

Turning to USAID, Gran (1983:309–10) states that

> AID's environment . . . impels evaluators to try to please the U.S. Congress
> and AID administrators. Professionals also see some need for information that
> will appease AID auditors and a more skeptical US public. . . . Most projects
> get little external scrutiny. Routine post-project summaries follow a standard
> form and mix descriptive, quantitative and subjective judgments. Rarely has
> baseline data been there that would permit really rigorous measurement. The
> system does not reward brilliance or thoroughness, so few of these reports are
> noteworthy or much used thereafter. . . . AID performs regular evaluations
> with an assortment of agency personnel versed in the region or the project
> types. On average they cannot afford to be too critical; the players have to
> continue working together. The system is, however, far more open, so that
> provocative critical work appears irregularly throughout the project cycle.

Gran cites examples such as the effort begun in 1979 by the Office of
Evaluation in the Bureau for Program and Policy Coordination to assess
the results of development evaluations and to provide guidelines for
building new standards. However, Gran (1983:310–11) concludes that

> these reports are also quite limited in certain crucial ways. It is not just that
> they focus largely on donor agency needs, slightly on host country needs, and
> very little on needs of project participants. There is a consistent pattern of
> bureaucratic timidity about concluding policy recommendations, an unwill-
> ingness to go where much of the evidence pointed. As an occasional consultant
> I understand reasonably well the pressures to bureaucratize language and
> substance in order to be found acceptable. . . . It is a neat circular pattern by
> which new ideas and the interests of the poor remain excluded or poorly
> represented.

In a recent review of the approach of OECD countries to the evaluation
of the development programs they finance, Rist (1990:42) argued that
donors mainly use evaluations to satisfy their own domestic information
needs and make little effort to involve the beneficiary countries in the
design, implementation, or interpretation of the results:

> The record of DAC countries on this account is not impressive. As noted by
> the Expert Group (OECD 1986), recipient country involvement in defining the
> purpose and scope of evaluations has been very limited in all but the most
> operations-focussed evaluations and even there their involvement has often
> been confined to a *pro forma* review and approval of the terms of reference

which have been drafted by donors. Recipients have not been encouraged to participate in formulating issues and questions on some of the most influential determinants of project and program success. They are explicitly excluded from the planning of certain types of evaluation, particularly those which address the donor's program, policy, management or procedures.

Other critics show how the design, management, and evaluation of projects are affected by the culture and operating procedures of these agencies and of the governments with which they interact. Chambers (1983:13–22) says the following six biases limit the capacity of donors to effectively design or evaluate agricultural and rural development projects:

- *Spatial bias.* Project staff and researchers do not stray too far from urban centers, tarmac roads, and roadside projects.
- *Project bias.* Agencies plan in terms of, and evaluate, projects and show little interest in what happens to the rural poor who are usually not affected (at least directly) by projects.
- *Person bias.* "Rural development tourists," as Chambers calls them, tend to get most of their information from elite groups, males, and users and adopters of new technology; and from people who are active, well, and present.
- *Dry-season bias.* Experts make few visits during the rainy season so they rarely get to appreciate the impacts of flooding.
- *Diplomatic bias.* A combination of politeness, fear, embarrassment, and language problems frequently deter visitors from speaking to the poor, the underprivileged, or those who are not directly involved in the projects. Often it is considered discourteous to insist on meeting with people not on the itinerary prepared by your hosts.
- *Professional bias.* Professional visitors are frequently drawn to the wealthier, better-educated, and more progressive farmers, since they are the ones best able to discuss the topics of interest to the outside agronomist, extension worker, or economist.

As a result, many outside experts fail to perceive the true dimensions of rural poverty and are often overoptimistic about the potential impacts of their projects or skeptical about estimates of the severity of rural poverty. Similar biases surround urban development. Salmen's (1987) participant observation studies of housing upgrading projects in La Paz and Guayaquil found that government executing agencies and donor project staff both tend to rely heavily on contacts with "community leaders" (sometimes self-designated) and house-owners who are better off, rather than on low-income squatters and renters who are difficult to locate.

### The Information Needs of Major Stakeholders

At the *international level*, stakeholders include multilateral and bilateral agencies, foundations and research institutions, and international NGOs.[2] *Donor agencies* are made up of different departments, each with their own information requirements. The project divisions, which are responsible for supervising project implementation, require periodic information on the physical and financial progress of projects in relation to the targets specified in the loan agreement. In contrast, programs or policy divisions may require broader economic or social data to assess the degree of intended impacts achieved or to help in the selection of future projects.

Donor and lending agencies also vary considerably in their orientations. In Bangladesh, for example, a number of donor agencies, concerned with what they considered too narrow an economic focus of the donor community, created the "Like-minded Group" to sponsor broader program evaluations that focus on social, political, and cultural needs, as well as the economic dimensions of development.

*NGOs* at both the international and national levels have become increasingly concerned about their access to information needed to identify and plan projects; they feel that their ability to participate in policy formulation is seriously constrained by their limited access to information on projects being prepared and appraised by international agencies. The kinds of questions asked in NGO evaluations are often quite different from those covered in government and donor M/E systems (Marsden and Oakley 1990).

At the *national level*, the *planning ministries* or the policymaking units in the line ministries are usually interested in receiving a summary of progress in the physical implementation of a project and how this is affecting loan disbursements. The more sophisticated agencies are also interested in comparisons of cost-effectiveness or the economic rates of return of alternative projects. Although there is still very little demand for the kinds of *prospective evaluations* used in policy research and strategy planning in the United States and some other industrial nations, an increasing number of countries are becoming results-oriented rather than input-oriented and in recent years have expressed considerable interest in strengthening ex-post evaluation capacity, particularly in Asia.

All countries have a government agency (usually the *Ministry of Finance*) in charge of monitoring the financial performance of their projects. Monitoring is often limited to standard auditing, but in some cases it employs cost-effectiveness techniques. A number of developing countries have created separate watchdog agencies to take care of monitoring, such as the Programme Evaluation Organization in India (see World Bank 1983). Pressed to obtain maximum utility from their scarce resources, governments are beginning to pay more attention to cost-effectiveness in their project monitoring. Countries such as Colombia and Brazil (among others) are beginning to tie future budget allocations to the assessment of project performance.

As evaluations begin to focus on *anticipatory analysis* and *prospective evaluations,* policymakers, including central banks, may become an important consumer of evaluation outputs—assuming that the information can be produced in the format, and within the time frame, they require.

*Line ministries* such as Housing, Irrigation, and Health are usually responsible for coordinating and supervising projects, and for preparing information required by central planning and financial agencies. The kind of monitoring and evaluation information that ministries require varies greatly, from basic monitoring tables to sophisticated research projects.

In many countries, the research community is the main source of data on projects and on their links to overall development strategies. The academic community may also press their evaluation colleagues to make their studies more sophisticated and academically "interesting." In addition, there may be pressure to ensure that the evaluation follows a particular ideological line.

Women's organizations, too, are becoming important stakeholders at both the national and project levels. In India, for example, the Self-Employed Women's Association (SEWA) and the Working Women's Forum have both been able to persuade the government and donors to address gender issues. Largely as a result of pressure from SEWA, the government of India prepared a study on the economic and legal status of the self-employed.

At the *local level,* implementing agencies require short- and medium-term information to monitor progress and to detect and help resolve problems

**Table 4-1.** The Timing and Purpose of the Main Kinds of Monitoring Studies

| Study | Purpose | Timing |
|---|---|---|
| Performance monitoring | To track the use of project inputs and production of outputs and to identify delays and problems. | Reports produced monthly or quarterly throughout the period of project implementation. |
| Financial monitoring | To monitor the correct use of funds, disbursements, and internal cash flow and assess cost-effectiveness. | Weekly or monthly, quarterly and annually. |
| Diagnostic studies | To understand why implementation and sustainability problems have occurred and propose solutions. | Follow-up to examine problems identified in performance monitoring; or conducted periodically to assess implementation performance. |
| Midterm assessment of project performance | To assess the overall progress of the project in order to identify key issues and required changes. | Midpoint of the implementation phase. |
| Project completion report (PCR) and project audit | To assess project implementation performance of the executing agency; followed by an independent audit to evaluate the extent to which loan agreement terms are being met. | PCR prepared within six months of final loan disbursement; audit follows submission of PCR. |
| Monitoring operations, maintenance, and sustainability | To assess the capacity of the project to continue delivering intended services and benefits throughout its planned economic life. | Once project is operational, studies can be conducted on a periodic basis or at one point in time (for example, after five years). |

when they arise. These agencies are also required to produce monitoring data for agencies at the national level. All these agencies are made up of various divisions, each of which has different information needs and different expectations from a monitoring unit.

Authorities often make little effort to consult with *project beneficiaries* in the design or discussion of the monitoring studies. However, they are beginning to recognize that beneficiaries have an important role to play in all stages of the design, implementation, and interpretation of the evaluation. Many community development organizations are already helping beneficiaries develop their own systems for monitoring projects, particularly for ensuring that benefits reach the intended population groups.

## Components of a Project Monitoring System

Table 4-1 summarizes the timing and utilization of the main kinds of monitoring studies.

### Monitoring Project Implementation

Most projects have a clearly defined set of inputs (money, materials, equipment, staff, technical assistance) that are expected to produce a given set of outputs (houses, roads, children vaccinated, small business loans authorized) within a given period of time. Project management requires periodic reports comparing actual and planned progress toward each of these implementation targets. The production of these reports is usually referred to as *input-output monitoring,* or sometimes *performance monitoring.*

Table 4-2 illustrates a simple way to monitor progress using a two-bar chart (often called a Gantt chart). It compares actual and intended progress for each project component. The chart lists twelve components and shows the planned start and completion dates, and the actual or expected start and completion dates. Expected delays (in weeks) are also given, along with the present status of each component. Casley and Kumar (1987:45–49) show how Gantt charts can be used in monitoring agricultural projects. Several software packages now exist for the personal computer market to help managers develop and update Gantt charts (for example, Timeline, Harvard Total Project Manager).

An alternative approach uses three bars instead of two. This extra bar shows the percentage of work completed for each component. The disad-

Table 4-2. Using a Two-Bar Gantt Chart to Plan and Monitor the Main Phases of a Housing Project

| Phase | 1986 1 2 3 4 | 1987 1 2 3 4 | 1988 1 2 3 4 | 1989 1 2 3 4 | 1990 1 2 3 4 | Revised Estimate (weeks) | Status |
|---|---|---|---|---|---|---|---|
| Approval of contract | | | | | | +8 | Completed |
| Earth moving | | | | | | +16 | Completed |
| Installation of water | | | | | | +18 | 82% of domestic water connections completed |
| Installation of sewage system | | | | | | +15 | 72% of sewage pipes laid |
| Installation of drainage | | | | | | +13 | 44% of drains laid |
| Road construction | | | | | | +6 | Roads 65% complete but steep terrain will slow completion |
| Selection of participants | | | | | | +6 | 6,000 to 12,000 participants already selected |
| Construction of core housing units | | | | | | +12 | 20% of core units constructed |
| Group house construction | | | | | | +18 | Lag due to delays in earlier stages |
| Construction loan approval | | | | | | +12 | |
| Plot occupation | | | | | | +17 | |
| Community facilities | | | | | | +18 | |

Note: Column headings indicate year and quarter.

Planned start and completion dates     Actual or projected start and completion dates

122

vantage of this method is that the bar representing the percentage of work completed can often be misleading. For example, if 82 percent of domestic water connections have been completed, this does not necessarily mean that the component is 82 percent completed. Work in the remaining sectors may be much slower because of legal problems relating to the removal of houses obstructing the work, or the terrain may be much steeper, and so the remaining work will be slower and more expensive.

Another widely used approach is *logical framework analysis* (described in Chapter 3). In this case, all project goals for a given time period are spelled out together with the criteria for measuring the degree to which each objective has been achieved. At the end of the period, the actual and intended progress are compared and the reasons for any differences are examined. The logical framework approach is particularly well suited to social development programs because it emphasizes processes and forces the program manager and the evaluator to define and assess the assumptions concerning how the project will be implemented and how different groups will respond. This is a simple and useful example of the application of models in the evaluation of social programs.

In more complex projects a logical network (PERT chart) may be constructed in which all the components of a project are laid out in logical sequence. The network shows which stages must be completed before others can begin and also estimates the time required to complete each component and the total time it should take to complete the project. Figure 4-1 illustrates a relatively simple logical network for a sites and services project involving thirty-four activities of which only the first fourteen are included in the figure.[3] The complete project consists of ten main components (land acquisition, design, offsite services, tendering, construction of core units, selection of participants, material loans, completion of habitable unit, occupation of units and start of cost recovery) of which only the first four are included in Figure 4-1. Each component comprises a series of activities that must be carried out in a certain logical sequence. The number of weeks it will take to complete each activity is also estimated. A "node" indicates the estimated minimum and maximum number of weeks up to the completion of each activity. For example, activity 1 consists of defining the types and numbers of housing units to be constructed. The number between nodes 0 and 1 indicates that this activity is expected to last four weeks. However, the numbers in node 1 indicate that it could last up to six weeks. Similarly, activity 2, general housing unit design and estimate of costs, is expected to last four weeks, but it could last up to seven weeks, so

Figure 4-1. Using a Logical Network Chart to Plan the Implementation of a Sites and Services Housing Project

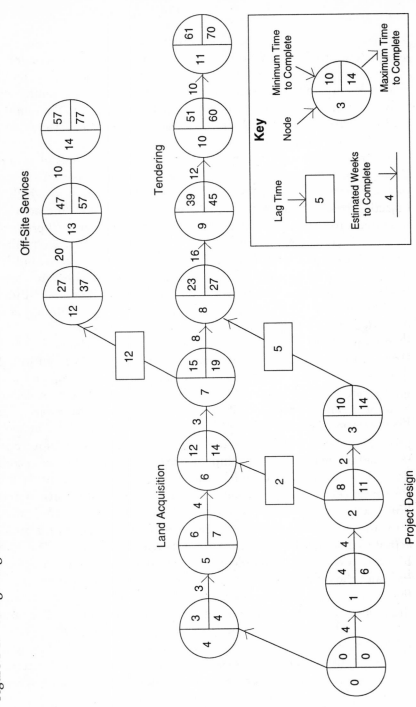

*Note:* The example only covers the first 14 nodes. The complete chart has 31 nodes and also covers the phases of construction of the core unit, selec-

124

that the total elapsed time up to the completion of this activity will be between eight and eleven weeks.

The logical network is a useful tool for project planning and monitoring. It indicates the links between project components and hence the potential bottlenecks. A variety of computer software is available for constructing networks and for monitoring programs, and thus eliminates the tedious and error-prone manual work involved in designing and updating these charts.

### Excessive Emphasis on Monitoring Inputs and Physical Outputs

Recently a number of writers (for example, Osborne and Gaebler 1992: chap. 5) have criticized conventional approaches for placing too much emphasis on monitoring inputs and physical outputs and not enough on evaluating the *quality* of outputs or achieving the intended products or objectives. They argue that as long as performance is evaluated in terms of numbers there will be a tendency to ignore quality and to lose sight of the ultimate goal of the program—namely to produce a particular product. They cite innovative methods used in a number of U.S. cities and states to develop objective indicators suitable for monitoring the quality of services such as street cleaning, road maintenance, and community security.

### Financial Monitoring

Project managers, central government agencies, and donors all periodically require information on the financial performance of projects. The *project cost summary chart* given in Table 4-3 illustrates one of the simpler systems for financial reporting and control. For a more detailed discussion, see Bamberger and Hewitt (1986:Annexes G and I). The example of a hypothetical housing project is used to illustrate how this chart is used. The chart was prepared at the end of year 2 of a five-year project. The chart compares expected and actual costs for each project component in different financial periods. The reasons for changes in actual or expected costs should be given in an accompanying written report. The chart permits the following kinds of analysis:

- Changes in the expected total cost of each line item and of the total project. By the end of year 2 it can be seen that the actual projected total cost has increased by 11 percent in comparison with the original estimate. The biggest increase is in the price of land and in the cost of management and administration (both increased by 19.9 percent).

Table 4-3.  Example of a Project Cost Summary Chart: Year 2 of a Five-Year Housing Project

| Line Item | Expected Total Project Cost (thousands of dollars) | | | Budget for Financial Year (Year 2 of Project) | | | Cumulative Expenditures | | | Year 3 Budget (thousands of dollars) |
|---|---|---|---|---|---|---|---|---|---|---|
| | Plan | Actual | % change | Plan | Actual | % change | Plan | Actual | % change | |
| Land | 1,983 | 2,181 | +19.1 | 500 | 950 | +90 | 1,983 | 3,500 | +76 | |
| Civil works | 5,788 | 6,400 | +10.5 | 4,100 | 3,500 | -15 | 5,200 | 4,500 | +86 | |
| Materials loan program | 788 | 906 | +14.9 | 550 | 350 | -37 | 650 | 400 | -39 | |
| Community facilities | 679 | 747 | +10 | 450 | 250 | -45 | 500 | 300 | -40 | |
| Design and engineering | 710 | 781 | +10 | 500 | 650 | +13 | 650 | 900 | +38 | |
| Management | 1,042 | 1,250 | +19.1 | 250 | 350 | +14 | 450 | 780 | +73 | |
| Technical assistance | 490 | 539 | +10 | 200 | 50 | -75 | 350 | 100 | -72 | |
| Total | 11,480 | 12,804 | +11.1 | 6,550 | 6,100 | -7 | 9,783 | 10,480 | +7 | |

- Comparison of planned and actual budget for current financial year. It can be seen that while expenditure on land is almost twice the planned expenditure for the current year (year 2), expenditure on many line items are lower than expected. The accompanying written report would explain that this was due to delays in project implementation and not to cost savings.
- Comparison of actual and planned cumulative expenditures to the end of the second year. There has been an overall increase of only 7 percent, which is again due to delays in implementation.

*Cost variance analysis* can be used to investigate any observed departure from planned costs (Bamberger and Hewitt 1986:Annex G). Cost variances are decomposed into price variation, contractor variations in quantity or quality, and changes in project design. Similar formats can be used to monitor contractor payments, loan repayments, and the like.

Many projects provide loans to families, cooperatives, or enterprises. In order to facilitate loan repayment, it is essential to have a reliable, up-to-date record of loan authorization and repayment. By classifying borrowers into income groups, it is possible to monitor whether loans are going to the target income groups (rather than to higher-income groups, as often happens). Casley and Kumar (1987:42–43) give an example of a more complex monthly credit record form for an agricultural project. It distinguishes between short- and medium-term credit and the purpose of the loan (purchase of seeds, fertilizer, tractors, irrigation pumps), and also between loans given under each of three different projects.

Whereas the traditional emphasis of financial monitoring was on auditing, emanating from the desire to ensure that funds were not being misappropriated, there is now greater interest in assessing whether taxpayers or the nation as a whole are receiving "value for money." This approach—which probably originated in England with the 1983 Financial Management Initiative and since then has been adopted by Norway and a number of other European countries—seeks to introduce private sector managerial principles into the management and evaluation of government.[4]

*Project Monitoring Systems Used by the Implementation, Monitoring, and Evaluation Division of the Ministry of Planning in Bangladesh*

Bangladesh, like many other developing countries, has developed a system to monitor all projects financed under the Annual Development Plan (ADP).[5] Responsible executing agencies must submit a quarterly statement

(IMED Pro Forma 01) to the Implementation, Monitoring, and Evaluation Division (IMED) of the Ministry of Planning containing the following information for the Quarterly Progress Monitoring Report:

- General information on project approval (when approved and initial project cost)
- Funds allocated, released, and expended
- Physical targets and progress
- Contracting of technical staff
- Problems and factors affecting the achievement of project objectives.

Similar information must be submitted for the Annual Progress Reports (IMED Proforma No. 02), but in somewhat more detail. Bar charts are used to compare actual progress with planned progress, and bottlenecks and delays are highlighted in the regular reports submitted to the National Economic Council. IMED staff also make periodic field visits to meet with project staff and to check on the validity of the data included in the pro forma report. In practice the frequency of the field visits is affected by staff shortages.

Similar project-monitoring systems are operating in most of the countries of South and Southeast Asia. These systems are described in more detail in Khan (1989, 1990) and Ahmed and Bamberger (1989).

*Diagnostic Studies ("Process Monitoring") to Identify and Correct Problems Arising during Project Implementation*

The procedures for monitoring project implementation can identify discrepancies between the planned and actual progress of implementation, but they cannot explain why the problems have occurred. For example, Table 4-2 shows a three-month delay in the selection of project beneficiaries and an eight-month delay in the occupation of the houses in this project, but in neither case is there an explanation of what has caused the delays. The delays could have been the result of a simple administrative problem (a delay in the delivery of the microcomputer used for processing applicants) that has now been resolved, or a more serious problem, such as a lack of interest in the houses being offered. These administrative monitoring studies should be complemented by *diagnostic studies* of the causes of problems and suggestions for corrective actions. (See Chapter 5 for a more detailed discussion of diagnostic studies.) These studies must usually be conducted quickly because project delays are costly. As a result, they are sometimes called *rapid feedback* or *rapid reconnaissance studies.*

More complex problems may require a more careful and more detailed analysis. Rapid diagnostic studies may be used to find out why participants dropped out from a project; why farmer demand for agricultural credit is unexpectedly low; or how community work groups have been organized to construct drainage ditches and whether they are effective. More comprehensive diagnostic studies might be concerned with assessing the effectiveness of a production cooperative program; analyzing the organization and effectiveness of a small business credit program; or determining the factors affecting the willingness of farmers to participate in the management of different irrigation projects.

Diagnostic studies can also be used as a form of quality control and can be conducted periodically, even when no problems have been detected. (See Chapter 11 for a discussion of LQAS, a quality control method used in industry to control the quality of development projects.)

### Midterm Assessment of Project Performance

Government finance and planning agencies and international donors often require a midterm assessment of the overall progress of a project. Its purpose is to identify actual or potential problems and to provide a sound basis for changing the design or resource allocations. Since many projects last at least four to five years, the assessment report is often needed two to three years after the project has started up. The assessment covers all aspects of implementation and financial performance, the effectiveness of project organization, and its accessibility to intended beneficiaries. This assessment is largely based on a compilation of existing implementation, financial, and diagnostic reports, but in some cases additional studies may be commissioned.

### Project Completion Report

Most government funding and planning agencies require some kind of report from the agency that executed the project once implementation is completed. The purpose of the report is to certify that the project has been satisfactorily completed and to identify any deviations from the planned implementation schedule, outputs, and budget. In Bangladesh, for exam-

**Table 4-4. Components of a Typical World Bank Project Completion Report on a Hypothetical Integrated Rural Development Project**

1. The context and the Integrated Rural Development Project

2. Project identification, preparation, and appraisal

3. Project implementation
   Project start-up
   Changes in project design
   Project implementation
   Monitoring and evaluation
   Procurement
   Performance of consultants
   Performance of contractors (roads, drainage, rural markets,
       fish ponds, local government buildings)

4. Operating performance

5. Financial performance and disbursements

6. Institutional performance and development
   Management and organization effectiveness
   Institutional development

7. Impact of the project
   Agricultural impact
   Development of new varieties of rice
   Expansion of irrigated areas
   Crop yield and production
   Employment generation
   Institution building
   Impacts on the landless and women

8. Economic reevaluation

9. Conclusions
   Achievement of project objectives
   Project design
   Implementation capacity
   Performance of the World Bank
   Lessons learned

ple, the Implementation, Monitoring, and Evaluation Division of the Ministry of Planning is responsible for providing a series of progress and completion reports for all projects included in the Annual Development Program. The reports have a standard format for all sectors and include a project description; financial analysis (comparison of actual and planned expenditure by year and category of expenditure); manpower analysis (estimated and actual manpower utilization); and physical analysis for each work component and benefit analysis. Benefit analysis includes a benefit-cost analysis and an estimate of foreign exchange savings due to the project. The format is largely quantitative and intended to ensure that resources have been properly used, rather than to yield lessons useful for the design of future projects (Ahmed and Bamberger 1989; Khan 1989).

Donor agencies also require a project completion report (PCR) on the projects they have helped finance (for a description of World Bank procedures for preparing PCRs, see Van der Lugt 1990; and for a description of procedures used by the Asian Development Bank, see Asian Development Bank 1991). Depending on the experience and the available professional resources in each developing country, most of the PCR may be prepared either by the borrower or by the donor agency. In all cases, the draft PCR will be discussed with government officials, and agreement will be reached on its final form. Table 4-4 gives the table of contents for the PCR on a typical World Bank–financed project. The PCR seeks to assess the implementation experience of the project and to draw lessons for the selection and design of future projects. In the case of World Bank–financed projects, the preparation of the PCR is the responsibility of the operational department that supervised the project. After the PCR has been approved by the competent authorities of the borrowing country, it is reviewed by the Operations Evaluation Department of the World Bank, which then prepares a project performance audit report for submission to the World Bank Board of Directors.

The following are typical remarks from the concluding section of a PCR on a hypothetical integrated rural development project. A hypothetical example is used because the PCRs are internal documents that are normally not published.

*Achievement of Project Objectives.* Despite the countrywide entrenchment of privileged village groups into the key management of the cooperatives over which the project had no control, the project has been able to strengthen the capacity of local government agencies to service the small farmer, particularly with respect to irrigation and rural credit. Rice production targets were met by introducing high-yielding varieties and by expanding the rice-growing areas through minor irrigation works.

*Project Design.* The original project failed to build into the design the degree of flexibility that is essential for a pilot project. It was assumed uncritically that the proposed structure was appropriate for replication and ignored the budgetary implications on government recurrent annual costs—a situation that is now creating serious problems for the local government agencies responsible for project operation.

*World Bank Project Supervision.* World Bank supervision was variable. During the start-up period, insufficient attention was devoted to the need to assist a largely inexperienced project staff, and problems over implementation quickly emerged. The Bank was forced to adopt more flexible attitudes to the enforcement of the loan covenants.

*Government Performance.* Most of the ministries and departments involved in the project had no previous experience of the conditions associated with a World Bank loan. The frequency of changes in the incumbent holding the post of executive director of the project can be interpreted as a measurement of the government's waning commitment to the project.

A great deal of time was spent attempting to meet the loan covenants, particularly with respect to the eligibility of existing cooperatives to participate in the project, and, as a result of these factors, implementation of the project fell behind schedule.

The implementing agency was unable to maintain financial records to standards acceptable to the Bank, and a number of problems remain with respect to the auditing of project accounts.

*Lessons Learned.* If the principal objective of a project is to create an institution to provide farmers, particularly small farmers, with the means to adopt new technology and undertake efficient irrigation development to augment production, it is counterproductive to combine investments directed toward many different activities under the same project. For example, the investments should probably have focused only on crop production and should not have included other activities such a livestock and fisheries.

A future project should not concentrate all of the investments in a few areas of an administrative district. Because of administrative problems, the concentration on a few areas was confusing to local officials in terms of providing services and inputs, and coordinating overall development of the district.

It is evident from the project that rural development cannot take place without an assured supply of inputs and services to farmers.

Although the Bank does not publish individual project completion reports, its Operations Evaluation Department issues an annual review of project performance results (see, for example, World Bank 1987). This report uses project completion reports to review overall project performance (the proportion of projects achieving satisfactory results, cost and time overruns, and so on); overall economic, policy, social, technological, environmental, and institutional impacts of development; and project sustainability. The review also includes a detailed analysis of progress for each of the major sectors (agriculture; industry; development finance companies; transportation; power, water supply, and waste disposal; education; and population, health, and nutrition).

Some governments produce similar annual reviews (see, for example, India, Ministry of Programme Implementation 1987).

## Monitoring Project Operations and Sustainability

For most projects, systematic monitoring ends with the preparation of the project completion report (which covers only the implementation stage), and little information is collected on project operation, cost recovery, and maintenance. Because project implementation is frequently financed by an international donor or from the national budget, these external sources insist that the use of their funds be monitored. In contrast, operations and maintenance are normally financed from the operating budget of the implementing agency, and there is little external pressure to see that the project actually achieves its intended objectives once it begins to operate.

Both donors and borrowers are coming to recognize that even when implementation has been completed according to plan, many projects do not produce their intended volume of benefits, or the benefits do not continue over the intended lifetime of the project. For example, a recent report by the Operations Evaluation Department of the World Bank found that only 52 percent of the 557 projects audited for all economic sectors and regions during 1986–88 were considered likely to be sustained, 15 percent were classified as unlikely, and 33 percent were uncertain or difficult to assess (World Bank 1990a). Some of the problems here were inappropriate organizational arrangements for project operation (including reductions in staff and authority once implementation was complete), inadequate budgets and resources, inappropriate technology, lack of community participation and support, a negative reaction among intended beneficiaries for social or cultural reasons, the lack of financial provisions for operating and maintenance costs, and incompatibility between the project and the policy environment in which it operated. An example of this last problem would be a small farmer credit program that assumed farm prices would be allowed to rise so that it would be profitable for farmers to increase production, when in fact government policy kept food prices from rising to ensure a lower cost of living in the rapidly growing and politically volatile cities.

It is strongly recommended that most projects be systematically monitored during at least the first five years of operation. Several aspects of the project should be studied during this period:

- The quantity and quality of outputs and benefits produced in comparison with the project targets.
- The social and economic characteristics of actual beneficiaries and of the target population. Depending on the type of project, some of the key indicators may be household income, sex of the beneficiary, size and type of agricultural holding, family size, and economic sector.
- The capacity and resources (human, financial, equipment) of the organizations responsible for operations and maintenance.
- The participation of intended beneficiaries in project management and maintenance.
- Cost recovery performance.
- Adequacy of recurrent cost financing.
- Adequacy of the maintenance of physical infrastructure and capital.

Chapter 6 describes how projects can be compared in terms of a numerical index of sustainability.

# Assessing the Efficiency of Project Implementation

*Increasing Interest in Efficiency and Institutional Development*

Over the past ten years, development planners have become increasingly concerned with issues related to organizational efficiency and institutional development. One factor behind this trend is that public sector institutions have been steadily growing in size and importance ever since governments became more involved in complex economic and social activities. At the same time, some experts have expressed concern about a decline in the efficiency (productivity) of many of these institutions (World Bank 1983:4). Second, many of the first generation of social development projects (particularly urban and health projects) failed to achieve their objectives because the organizational arrangements had not worked or could not be replicated on a larger scale.

Third, donors and lenders have come to realize that the resources they could provide or that developing countries could afford to borrow are in most cases insufficient to make a large direct impact on the supply of basic services such as shelter and health. Consequently, development agencies have begun to focus their efforts on strengthening the institutional frameworks for development management to help countries maximize the effectiveness of their available resources.

Fourth, as mentioned earlier, it is now believed that project beneficiaries need to be more actively involved in decisionmaking and project implementation. Increased community participation, many argue, can improve the efficiency of cost recovery and the quality of community infrastructure maintenance. Participation can also help ensure a more equitable distribution of project benefits.

In this and the following section we explain how to assess the efficiency of individual project components and how to handle indicators of the performance of multicomponent projects.

*Assessing the Efficiency of Implementation of Individual Project Components*

Five measures of project performance can be used to compare the performance of different components.

*Speed of implementation.* Delays in almost any component tend to increase costs as well as affect the completion of other components. Speed can usually be measured quite easily through Gantt charts or networking procedures described on pages 121–25 of this chapter.

*Cost of implementation.* Cost-effectiveness can be measured by comparing actual costs with the original budget estimates or with the costs of similar projects. Some of the methods for monitoring and analysis of costs were also described on pages 125–27. The techniques of cost-effectiveness analysis (described in the following section) are especially useful as they measure the unit cost of each output.

*Quality of the final product or service.* Quality is usually more difficult to measure than speed or the costs of implementation. One possibility is to ask consumers to rank the quality of the services (for example, using a 5- or 6-point scale ranging from "very good" to "very bad"). Or one or more experts could be asked to rank the services. Jimenez (1980) asked a group of five experts (including architects, contractors, and engineers) to estimate the monetary value (a good proxy for quality) of a sample of houses in an upgrading project in Manilla. In economic analysis, changes in quality are often estimated through changes in rental values. The amount of rental increase following the installation of water or other urban services is assumed to indicate the additional benefits households obtain from these services.

*Accessibility of services to intended beneficiaries.* An objective of many projects is to ensure that project services or benefits reach a certain target population—defined in terms of its geographic, economic, or demographic characteristics. When income or demographic characteristics are used in selecting beneficiaries or in approving loans, it may be relatively easy to monitor accessibility. In other cases, however, special sample surveys or other data collection procedures may be required to determine who is actually benefiting from the project. A drawback of such assessment, however, is that people may distort information on income or other similar variables used as selection criteria so as to be eligible for the project.

*Replicability of the project.* Many development projects are designed as pilot projects, which, if successful, are expected to be replicated on a larger scale. However, many pilot projects are implemented through special units or under specially privileged arrangements that could not be replicated on a larger scale. Consider, for example, what might happen when participants are selected for a housing project: speed can be measured either as the average number of staff and hours required to select a family or the total elapsed time of the selection phase; and cost can be defined as the cost per family selected. The quality of selection is more difficult to assess and could be defined in terms of the fairness of the procedures and their reliability. Accessibility is defined by comparing the target objectives, with respect to income, family size, and time of residence in the city with the actual characteristics of the families selected. Replicability is determined by assessing whether the selection procedures could be used on a larger scale.

## Assessing the Overall Efficiency of a Multicomponent Project

Most projects have three broad sets of development goals: to achieve the efficient implementation of the project (construction of houses, vaccination of children, authorization of loans); to ensure efficient operation and maintenance of the project; and, in many cases, to promote the replication of successful projects on a larger scale. In order to assess a project's efficiency in achieving each of these three objectives it is necessary to estimate not only the degree to which outputs and impacts have been achieved, but also the progress toward the creation of sustainable and replicable organizational arrangements. Factors affecting institutional performance and outcomes can be measured with both qualitative and descriptive quantitative methods.

The evaluation will normally examine the following factors:

- Achievement of program goals: usually evaluated by using management by objectives or one of the related methods described earlier in this chapter.
- Satisfaction of other participating agencies regarding their relations with the agency being studied.
- Community satisfaction with the performance of the agency.
- Effectiveness of coordination with other agencies.
- Effectiveness and efficiency of monitoring and evaluation arrangements (at each of the three levels discussed earlier).
- Financial administration and control.
- Overall efficiency and effectiveness of the agency's organization and management procedures.
- Flexibility of the organization and its ability to modify the project in the light of changing circumstances.
- The effectiveness of beneficiary participation in project planning and implementation.
- Achievement of project goals. This would be assessed using the approaches described earlier in this chapter.

- General efficiency of organizational procedures. This would assess the financial administration and control, internal organization, effectiveness of monitoring and evaluation, coordination with other agencies, and responsiveness to intended beneficiaries (Table 4-5).

Each of these indicators can be measured separately and can then be combined to produce an overall index of project efficiency. Often there will be tradeoffs between different indicators. For example, it may be possible to implement the project more quickly and cheaply if less attention is paid to ensuring that selected families fall within the targeted income ranges. Similar tradeoffs may exist between replicability and the speed or cost of implementation. And it may be possible to complete the project more rapidly by setting up a special implementation unit not subject to normal administrative controls (and delays), but once the first project is completed, the special unit will often be disbanded and no base will have been created for replicating the project.

### Table 4-5.  Indicators of the Efficiency of Project Organization and Administrative Procedures

*Internal Organization*
  Clarity of the organizational chart, definition of functions, and forms of coordination
  Extent to which the actual system conforms to the organizational chart
  Numbers and qualifications of staff at different levels
  Numbers of unfilled vacancies at different levels and the time they have been unfilled
  Staff turnover at different levels

*Financial Administration and Control*
  Quality and comprehensiveness of information collected on financial performance
  Speed with which financial information is obtained and reports prepared
  Time taken to prepare and process disbursements and the main obstacles to disbursement
  Achievement of financial goals

*Effectiveness and Efficiency of Monitoring and Evaluation Systems*
  Comparison of planned and actual production of reports
  Quality of reports
  Regularity and effectiveness of meetings to review and take action on the evaluation reports
  Opinions of managers and other intended users on the usefulness of the reports

## Cost-Effectiveness Analysis

Cost-effectiveness analysis enables policymakers to compare alternative projects on the basis of the cost of producing a given output, or set of outputs. The method can be used in any situation where the outputs can be clearly defined and are easily measurable, as in constructing housing, improving reading skills, or providing credit for fishermen or small artisans. The procedure is usually relatively simple and economical because information on both costs and outputs can be obtained from project records. Cost-effectiveness analysis is widely used for health, education, and other human resource development programs where it is not feasible to assign a monetary value to all of the benefits and costs involved, and consequently where cost-benefit analysis is not practical.

### *Identifying and Measuring Costs*

The worksheet used for estimating costs in an urban housing project in Table 4-6 is equally valid for other kinds of projects. The main steps are as follows:

- Identify all costs, whether or not they will be charged to the project. For example, even if the municipality provides the land at no cost to the project, it should be included as a cost to the nation.
- Estimate the accounting cost. This is the actual amount paid for the good or service (salaries plus benefits for staff, annual rent or purchase price for land, and the like).
- Where costs are paid over a period of years, prepare a separate cost stream for each year. The costs in future years should be discounted in order to compute the net present value of the costs.
- Indicate who actually pays each cost. A project may appear to have a high cost-effectiveness ratio if many of the costs are being paid by other agencies.

### *Identifying and Measuring Outputs*

It is important to keep in mind the distinction between *outputs*, which are the tangible products of a project (school buildings, number of students receiving literacy classes), and *benefits*, which are the increases in welfare (living standards) the project is intended to achieve. Outputs can be measured in several ways.

Table 4-6.  Cost-Worksheet for Cost-Effectiveness Analysis:
The Example of a Housing Project

| Item | Account-ing cost | Cost to client | Cost to other agencies | Shadow cost | Net present value of costs |
|---|---|---|---|---|---|
| Personnel | | | | | |
| Land | | | | | |
| Rent, purchase, or construction of buildings | | | | | |
| Infrastructure | | | | | |
| Materials and equipment | | | | | |
| Professional services | | | | | |
| Other (specify) | | | | | |
| Total cost (NPV) | | | | | |

*Source:* Adapted from Levin (1975).

a. Cost-effectiveness analysis may be used to compare the costs of producing a particular output through various projects. The question is, which output should be used? In other words, what priority or weight should be assigned to each output? Suppose that an artisan project is more cost- effective than other programs when it comes to delivering loans, but is less cost-effective in providing technical assistance and helping develop new marketing outlets. What weight should we give to each of these results? In practice, most cost-effectiveness analysis uses only one outcome indicator. How should this be chosen? If the wrong indicator is chosen, the results could obviously be misleading. Thompson (1980:232) suggests that where the number of indicators is small, it may be better to present them without any weights. For example, "$64,000 spent per death averted and 400 nonfatal flu cases averted."

b. When weights are assigned to different indicators, the exercise is called *cost-utility analysis.* For an artisan cooperative, the main outcome indicators might be the number of credits authorized, the volume of credits authorized, the provision of technical assistance, and access to new markets. Suppose that a panel of experts is asked to rate the importance of each of these four outcomes on a scale of 1 to 10 (where 10 is the most important and 1 the least important) and the mean scores of their ratings are as follows:

| Outcome | Mean Rating |
|---|---|
| Number of credits | 8.2 |
| Volume of credits | 5.4 |
| Technical assistance | 4.9 |
| New markets | 7.1 |

These ratings indicate the relative importance (utility) of each outcome and show that on average the evaluators considered the number of credits authorized to be the most important indicator of the project's success. The ratings can then be used to calculate the cost-effectiveness ratio for the delivery of the number of credits (the most important outcome according to the judges). Or the weighted scores can be combined to form a more complex index. For example, the composite cost-effectiveness index (I) could be defined as

$$I = W_1 * R_1 + W_2 * R_2 + W_n * R_n$$

where $W_n$ = the weight of the nth project component and $R_n$ = the reciprocal of the cost-effectiveness ratio of the $n$th component. The reciprocal of the cost-effectiveness ratio is used because lower ratios (that is, lower costs of producing a given output) indicate greater effectiveness.

c. Problems may arise in comparing the outcomes of different programs. Take the example of technical assistance. One program might give artisans bookkeeping assistance by having them participate in a course, whereas another might provide assistance during the visits of promoters to their business. Although both of these approaches might be classified as technical assistance, they are likely to differ in quality and in specific content.

Similar differences may exist with respect to the delivery of credit. The credits might be given through community offices set up by a government agency or through a commercial bank with which the artisan must open an account. In the latter case the program may help the artisan enter the commercial credit market and thus may make it easier for him to obtain future loans.

d. Another problem relates to *scalability*. The output of many literacy programs is measured by the scores on a scale of reading ability. But some have questioned whether the intervals on this type of scale can be compared. For example, an increase from 10 to 15 points for children with reading difficulties may be much more significant than an increase from 40 to 45 points for children with average reading ability. Yet both of these increases would be given the same value in the analysis.

### Computing the Cost-Effectiveness Ratio

The cost-effectiveness ratio $(R)$ is defined as

$$R = C/U$$

where $C$ = the average cost per case (student, house constructed, and so on) and $U$ = the average number of units of output produced per case. In the evaluation of the El Salvador educational television (ETV) program discussed in Section E, the average cost per student of using television to teach math was $22, and the average math test gain score was 3.7 points (Table 4-7). The cost-effectiveness ratio was therefore

$$R = 22/3.7$$
$$= \$5.9.$$

### Using Cost-Effectiveness Analysis as a Decisionmaking Tool

Cost-effectiveness analysis is used to judge whether a certain kind of project is worthwhile (summative evaluation) and to select the best version of a project (formative evaluation).

To determine whether a project is worthwhile, one must estimate the costs of producing a given output. This can be done in two ways: by measuring the *constant effects*, that is, the costs of producing a given output or service in different projects; or by measuring the *constant cost*, which is the cost per unit of output. A common methodological problem here is the choice of unvalued output. Thompson (1980) suggests four possible outputs that could be used for assessing the cost-effectiveness of a hypothetical cancer screening program: cost per case discovered and treated ($18,000), cost per cure ($30,000), cost per life saved ($22,500), and cost per year of life gained ($6,000). The choice of program might well depend on the output indicators used. A variant used to assess programs that may cause a certain

Table 4-7. The Cost-Effectiveness of Educational Television
and Educational Reform for Improving Educational Performance
in El Salvador

| Area of Improvement | Gain | Gain over Traditional Methods |
|---|---|---|
| *Mathematics* | | |
| Traditional classes | 1.95 | — |
| Experimental ETV classes | 5.70 | 3.7 |
| Educational reform | 5.20 | 3.2 |
| *Science* | | |
| Traditional classes | 1.34 | — |
| Experimental ETV classes | 4.20 | 2.9 |
| Educational reform | 5.10 | 3.8 |
| *Social studies* | | |
| Traditional classes | 2.61 | — |
| Experimental ETV classes | 6.40 | 3.8 |
| Educational reform | 3.10 | 1.5 |
| *Cost-effectiveness analysis* | ETV | *Reform only* |
| Math | $ 22/3.7 = $ 5.9 | $ 16/3.2 = $ 5.0 |
| Science | $ 22/2.9 = $ 4.2 | |
| Social studies | $ 22/3.8 = $ 10.7 | |

*Note*: The cost-effectiveness ratios indicate the cost to produce a one-unit gain. The *lower* the ratio the more cost-effective the program.

*Source*: Adapted from Carnoy (1975).

number of lives to be lost (for example, a high-risk treatment) is *risk-benefit analysis* (Thompson 1980:233–34). If a program produces benefits estimated at $10 million but causes ten deaths through accidents or premature death, there would be a risk-benefit ratio of one life per $1 million of benefits produced.

Cost-effectiveness analysis can also be used to select the best version of a program. First, it can help determine the *optimal intensiveness* of the program, such as the minimum level of loan below which farmers, small businessmen, or participants in a self-help housing program cannot make worthwhile investments, or the maximum level above which borrowers may make less productive investments, or the optimum number of hours of literacy education, or the volume of water for irrigation. Second, cost-effectiveness analysis may be used to select the alternative that produces the required output at the lowest cost. Third, it can be used to compare the costs of producing different levels of benefit or output. For example, various methods of selecting participants for a low-cost housing program could be compared to establish which ones ensure that all families admitted into the program are poor and have incomes below a specified level. Visits to the houses of applicants would almost certainly be more effective than office interviews as a way of checking on family income but would greatly increase program costs.

### Applying Cost-Effectiveness Analysis to Social Programs

Cost-effectiveness analysis is, in principle, well suited to the evaluation of social development programs, particularly since benefits need not be monetized. However, a number of methodological issues must be addressed in this case as well.

First, it is important to ensure that the appropriate indicator is selected. In a job placement program, for example, one must decide whether the output indicator should be the number of people who receive counseling, the number who obtain jobs, the amount of time people stay in the job, or the level of job (income) they obtain. The results may vary according to the output indicator used.

Second, care must be taken to ensure that all costs have been identified and quantified. Among the costs that can be overlooked are goods and services provided free or below cost; time and money spent by clients getting to, and waiting at, the project facility; the opportunity cost of the time spent by participants (for example, in a self-help construction project); and social costs such as environmental deterioration, health hazards, family dislocation, and community conflict.

Third, the output indicators from different projects must be comparable. There may be significant qualitative (professional qualifications of the counselors) or quantitative (amount of time spent with each client) differences between the kinds of job counseling various programs offer, and their apparently similar outcomes (numbers of clients receiving counseling) may actually be significantly different.

A fourth question is how to evaluate a project that has a number of outcomes. Should only the most important outcome be assessed? Should a separate analysis be conducted for each major outcome? Or should weights be assigned to each outcome so that a composite score can be obtained?

Fifth, a number of issues must be addressed relating to the scalability of outputs. A problem already mentioned was that of comparing a relatively small increase in reading skills for a person with a low initial reading level with a numerically greater increase for someone starting from a higher initial reading level. The scalability problem has to do with many social output indicators, including improvements in the organizational capacity of community groups, improvements in the quality of housing, changes in the health status of a community, the quality of services provided by a health center, and the volume of loans provided by a cooperative.

Sixth, a basic question to consider is how to interpret a cost-effectiveness ratio. What do we mean when we say it costs $5.9 to produce a 1-unit gain on a math aptitude test? The experimental TV program described in the next section produced an average math gain score of 3.7 points. Is this a large number or a small number? Perhaps this increase is too small to be of any practical significance, or perhaps it indicates a major improvement. How does the policymaker decide whether it is worth investing $5.9 to produce each unit gain? This takes us back to the difference between outputs and impacts. Normally, the reason for trying to produce a certain output is that this output is expected to have some benefit. However, it will often be necessary to test whether such a benefit will follow from the outcome before the full meaning of the cost-effectiveness ratio can be understood.

## Using Cost-Effectiveness Analysis to Compare Methods of Expanding Primary Education in El Salvador

Table 4-7 illustrates how cost-effectiveness analysis was used to compare two alternative methods for expanding primary education in El Salvador (Carnoy 1975): *educational reforms* involving the retraining of teachers and revision of the curricula, and the use of *educational television*.

The quality of the education under each method was measured by applying a set of standard achievement tests at the beginning and end of the school year and by calculating a *gain score*. Gain scores were calculated for math, science, and social studies. The costs of the two methods were estimated to be $22 per year per student per subject for ETV and $16 for educational reform.

Three groups were examined: traditional classes (which were used as a control group), the educational reform group, and the ETV group (see Table 4-7). For social studies, the gain from ETV (3.8) was more than twice that obtained in the educational reform group (1.5), but the difference between the two groups was quite small for mathematics and science. These findings show that the effects vary considerably by subject; therefore care must be exercised when generalizing from the results. Scores for all three subjects showed a gain over traditional teaching methods.

The lower section of the Table 4-7 compares the cost-effectiveness of the two methods. The cost was divided by the gain score to compute the cost of producing a one-unit gain by each method. The lower the cost-effectiveness ratio, the more economical the method. Educational reform is the most cost-effective method for teaching math (5 pesos per unit gain compared to 5.9) and science (4.2 compared to 7.6), whereas ETV is more cost-effective for social studies (5.7 pesos compared to 10.6).

This is a useful tool for the policymaker because it shows that, even though ETV produces a larger gain for mathematics, the unit cost of producing the gain is higher. Thus it would be more cost-effective to invest in educational reform.

## Issues and Approaches in Monitoring Social Sector Programs

Although many social programs are monitored using the same quantitative procedures employed in economic and physical infrastructure projects, the characteristics of most social programs are such that the standard monitoring techniques are usually unable to capture their objectives and implementation processes. Some countries clearly recognize this problem. India, for example, tends to appraise social programs by different criteria (they need not be assessed in terms of their economic rates of return), finances them differently (until recently foreign loans were rarely used for social programs), and evaluates them according to different criteria (such as the accessibility of their benefits to the intended target population).

In this section we consider the limitations of conventional monitoring systems for social programs, identify some of the monitoring approaches being used or developed for social analysis, and describe some of the monitoring issues and approaches in different social sectors.

Although it is often important to compare social programs with other kinds of development programs to determine their overall contributions to national development objectives, standard monitoring procedures may not be appropriate.

For one thing, the outputs and benefits of social programs are often difficult to quantify. For programs such as primary education, rural and health extension, and self-help housing, the *quality* of the product is at least as important as the *quantity*. However, most monitoring systems do not look at quality. In programs that use a participatory planning and implementation approach, some of the outputs may not even have been defined at the start of the project. Many social projects (such as rural nutrition programs, the provision of primary education or primary health) are part of broader social development programs, and the outputs of a particular project may be difficult to isolate and assess.

In addition, social programs need to be assessed from the perspective of their different stakeholders, each of whom may use quite different criteria for this purpose. Although conventional monitoring systems assume that a standard set of indicators can satisfy the information needs of all interested parties—an adequate monitoring system for a social program normally requires a stakeholder analysis to identify stakeholder perspectives and information needs.

Recall, too, that conventional systems do not adequately monitor implementation *processes*, only inputs and outputs. Furthermore, conventional monitoring systems fail to consider whether projects have the capacity to continue delivering the intended services and benefits to target populations. This is a particularly serious issue for social programs.

A number of techniques have been or are being developed for monitoring and evaluating social programs. These techniques, many of which are known as "social analysis," are described briefly here but are discussed more fully in later chapters.

*Institutional analysis* is used to assess the institutional capacity and performance of participating agencies and community organizations in the formulation, implementation, and operation of the project. Some of the techniques were described earlier in this chapter (see also chapters 5 and 6). Institutional analysis can also be used to compare the merits of integrated social development programs that offer a wide range of services but require complex coordination arrangements between different agencies, on the one hand, and the merits of specialized programs that may be more efficient but address only one component of a complex social problem having many causes and requiring many kinds of services, on the other.

Efforts are also being made to develop indicators of the *quality* of inputs and outputs. These combine assessments and rankings of project performance by staff, supervisors, and beneficiaries with assessments of staff performance. An example of the latter was a study in Bangladesh comparing the actual use of time by staff in a primary health program with the allocation of time specified in their official job descriptions (BRAC 1990). Similar ranking and assessment procedures can be used to monitor the quality of outputs. It is also possible to develop detailed observational guidelines for monitoring the physical outputs, and the frequency and quality of utilization. A promising approach in urban development is to monitor changes in assessed rental and sale values as an indicator of quality (Jimenez 1982).

*Beneficiary assessment* techniques are also used to provide regular feedback on the opinions and experiences of beneficiaries and victims as a project evolves (Finsterbusch, Ingersoll, and Llewellyn 1990; Salmen 1987). The range of techniques is being expanded to incorporate simple quantitative indicators into the earlier qualitative approaches. (These techniques are discussed in Chapters 5, 7, and 10.)

Various techniques are also being developed for monitoring the *sustainability* of projects, both the capacity of the project to continue delivering services and the capacity of the institutions involved to operate and further develop the project. These approaches are now being widely used in assessing project impacts on the environment (Wallis 1989). Although to date the techniques have mainly been used in project appraisal and to some extent for impact evaluation, many of them could be used to monitor environmental impacts on a regular basis (Centre for Science and Environment 1985; World Resources Institute 1990; the approaches are discussed in Chapter 6).

It is also important to determine whether projects are alleviating poverty and reaching the intended low-income groups. Some of these concerns can be built into regular monitoring reports (for example, to report on the income levels of families receiving loans or services). It is usually difficult to assess the reliability of this information, however, because families may deliberately distort information on their income to make sure they are eligible for the project. This is particularly problematic when powerful economic or political groups are involved (BRAC 1983). In such cases it may be necessary to conduct in-depth studies to better understand and assess who is benefiting and to identify the factors affecting access to the project. (These approaches are discussed in Chapters 5 and 10.)

Many countries are also assessing project impacts on women, and a wide range of *gender analysis* techniques are now available for this purpose (Asian Development Bank 1991; Heyzer 1992; Maya Tech Corporation 1991). Rao, Anderson, and Overholt (1991) propose an analytical framework for analyzing the gender issues during the project identification and design phases (Table 4-8). This indicates the kinds of information required to assess how well project identification and design respond to women's needs and promote women's active participation in implementation and how women are likely to be positively and negatively affected by the projects. The purpose of collecting this information during the preparatory phase of a project is to allow time for the selection or design to be modified to correct any potential problems or to further increase the participation of women. Table 4-9 presents similar recommendations on the kinds of information to be collected during project implementation and evaluation.

Of particular interest are the questions relating to whether gender issues are adequately addressed in the project monitoring and evaluation. Emphasis is placed on ensuring that women stakeholders are involved in the definition of the evaluation questions and also in the interpretation of the findings. This means the evaluation reports must be presented in a clear and simple format. The results must also be made available in a timely manner so that problems can be identified and corrected.

*Sector Approaches*

Although most of the above techniques are widely applicable, each social sector has tended to focus on a specific set of issues and to rely on sector-specific assessment strategies.

In the *urban* sector, project affordability and accessibility of shelter and water to low-income households have always been of concern, and efforts have been made to develop more reliable methods for estimating income and for monitoring the economic level of project beneficiaries.

Beneficiary assessment techniques, including participant observation, are used to obtain feedback from beneficiaries on project design and implementation. These techniques are also sometimes used to monitor the efficiency of community organizations and to determine whether they fairly represent the target population. The kinds of diagnostic studies described in Chapter 5 are also used to provide rapid feedback on the causes and possible solutions of implementation and operational problems identified by input-output monitoring.

A question frequently raised, but rarely studied, concerns the long-term impact of projects on the poor. When land and property values rise as a result of project investments in infrastructure and housing, little is known

Table 4-8.  Gender Issues in Project Identification and Design

Women's Dimension in Project Identification

*Assessing women's needs*

What needs and opportunities exist for increasing women's productivity and/or
   production?
What needs and opportunities exist for increasing women's access to and control
   of resources?
What needs and opportunities exist for increasing women's access to and control
   of benefits?
How do these needs and opportunities relate to the country's other general and
   sectoral development needs and opportunities?
Have women been directly consulted in identifying such needs and
   opportunities?

*Defining general project objectives*

Are project objectives explicitly related to women's needs?
Do these objectives adequately reflect women's needs?
Have women participated in setting those objectives?
Have there been any earlier efforts?
How has the present proposal built on earlier efforts?

*Identifying possible negative effects*

Might the project reduce women's access to, or control of, resources and benefits?
Might it adversely affect women's situation in some other way?
What will be the effects on women in the short and longer run?

---

about the impact on the original low-income beneficiaries—whether they
will sell to achieve a capital gain or be forced to leave because of pressure
from speculators or because they cannot afford to pay higher rents and
service charges.

In *rural development* and in many of the *agricultural subsectors*, a primary
concern is to find efficient and economical ways to obtain rapid feedback
on the implementation, accessibility, and impacts of projects affecting large
numbers of rural families in small and widely scattered communities. (For
general discussions of cost-effective sampling methods for monitoring and
evaluation in agriculture, see Casley and Kumar 1988; for applications in
social forestry, see Slade and Noronha 1984; and for agricultural extension,
see Murphy and Marchant 1988.)

In addition to the basic logistical problems of monitoring widely scattered populations, a number of political and cultural factors further complicate monitoring. In many rural areas the allocation of project resources

**Table 4-8** (*continued*)

| |
|---|
| **Women's Dimension in Project Design** |

*Project impact on women's activities*

Which of these activities (production, reproduction and maintenance,
sociopolitical) does the project affect?

Is the planned component consistent with the current gender denomination for
the activity?

If it plans to change the women's performance of that activity (locus of the
activity, remunerative mode, technology, mode of activity), is this feasible, and
what positive or negative effects would it have on women?

If there is no change, is this a missed opportunity for women's roles in the
development process?

How can the project design be adjusted to increase the above-mentioned positive
effects, and reduce or eliminate the negative ones?

*Project impact on women's access and control*

How will each of the project's components affect women's access to and control
of the resources and benefits engaged in and stemming from the production of
goods and services?

How will each of the project's components affect women's access to and control
of the resources and benefits engaged in and stemming from the reproduction
and maintenance of the human resources?

How will each of the project's components affect women's access to and control
of the resources and benefits engaged in and stemming from the sociopolitical
functions?

What forces have been set into motion to induce further exploration of
constraints and possible improvements?

How can the project design be adjusted to increase women's access to and
control of resources and benefits?

*Source*: Rao, Anderson, and Overholt (1991:18–19).

---

may be controlled by local power groups whose influence is difficult to
monitor because villagers and small farmers are reluctant to denounce their
employers and patrons, even when significant amounts of project resources
are being misappropriated (Getubig and Ledesma 1988).

Rural development practitioners have pioneered the use of rapid rural
appraisal methods for providing rapid and economical feedback during the
appraisal, monitoring, and evaluation of rural projects (Chambers 1985;
Gow 1990). Many of these techniques are now being applied in health,
nutrition (Scrimshaw and Hurtado 1987), and urban programs. The early
advocates of these techniques tended to stress speed and economy and to
adopt a somewhat iconoclastic attitude to conventional research methods

### Table 4-9.  Gender Issues in Project Implementation and Evaluation

**Women's Dimension in Project Implementation**

*Personnel*

Are project personnel sufficiently aware of and sympathetic to women's needs?
Are women used to deliver the goods or services to women beneficiaries?
Do personnel have the necessary skills to provide any special inputs required by women?
What training techniques will be used to develop delivery systems?
Are there appropriate opportunities for women to participate in project management positions?

*Organizational structures*

Does the organizational form enhance women's access to resources?
Does the organization have adequate power to obtain resources needed by women from other organizations?
Does the organization have the institutional capability to support and protect women during the change process?

*Operations and logistics*

Are the organization's delivery channels accessible to women in terms of personnel, location and timing?
Do control procedures exist to ensure dependable delivery of the goods and services?
Are there mechanisms to ensure that the project resources or benefits are not usurped by males?

*Finances*

Do funding mechanisms exist to ensure program continuity?
Are funding levels adequate for proposed tasks?

---

such as sample design, but recently a number of questions have been raised about the methodological validity of rapid assessment methods. Researchers are now trying to develop cost-effective ways to incorporate a greater degree of methodological rigor to respond to some of these concerns (Valadez 1991).

The influence of sociocultural factors on the selection, design, and implementation of projects has been another subject of interest in these sectors (Cernea 1991). In addition, more attention is being given to beneficiary assessment and to beneficiary participation in operations and maintenance. Irrigation maintenance, in particular, has emphasized participatory approaches, and a large number of evaluation studies have been conducted in this area (Uphoff 1989).

**Table 4-9** (*continued*)

Is preferential access to resources by males avoided?
Is it possible to trace funds for women from allocation to delivery with a fair
degree of accuracy?

*Flexibility*

Does the project have a management information system that will allow it to
detect the effects of the operation on women?
Does the organization have enough flexibility to adapt its structures and
operations to meet the changing or newfound situations of women?

**Women's Dimensions in Project Evaluation**

*Data requirements*

Does the project's monitoring and evaluation system explicitly measure the
project's effects on women?
Does it collect data to update the activity analysis and the women's access- and-
control analysis?
Are women involved in designating the data requirements?

*Data collection and analysis*

Are the data collected with sufficient frequency so that necessary project
adjustments could be made during the project?
Are the data fed back to project personnel and beneficiaries in an understandable
form and on a timely basis to allow project adjustments?
Are women involved in the collection and interpretation of data?
Are data analyzed so as to provide guidance in designing other projects?
Are key areas for research on women in development identified?

*Source*: Rao, Anderson, and Overholt (1991:19–20).

These sectors have also demonstrated the importance of monitoring
environmental impacts and assessing the sustainability of projects.

The sizable investments in rural development, in particular, have created
an opportunity to develop some comprehensive monitoring techniques
(for example, the concurrent evaluation of all integrated rural development
programs in India) and to assess and compare different programs. A
number of reviews have been published in this regard (Asian Development
Bank 1988; India, Programme Evaluation Organization 1985; Jha 1987;
World Bank 1985).

In the *population, health, and nutrition* sectors, precise techniques have
been developed for monitoring the distribution and accessibility of clearly

defined inputs and services such as vaccination, primary health care, and contraceptives (Valadez 1991). In addition, cost-effective techniques and impact assessment techniques have been devised in this field (Briscoe and others 1986). Advances have also been made in developing and testing project implementation models that specify the behavioral links between inputs and outputs. Among the earliest examples were the "KAP studies" (of knowledge, attitude, and practice) that were used to monitor population programs and that are now fundamental components of many HIV/AIDS control projects.

Methods have also been devised to assess the targeting techniques of poverty alleviation programs. For example, the Tamil Nadu Integrated Nutrition Program in South India uses anthropometric techniques to target nutrition programs toward children diagnosed as suffering from malnutrition and to monitor the impacts of the administration of nutritional supplements on the physical development of poor children (Heaver 1988).

In addition, these sectors have focused on assessing the organizational and institutional systems used for implementing the programs, and on the difficulty of developing integrated multiservice programs that may have lost some of their effectiveness because of problems with interagency coordination.

Two recent studies in Latin America (Grosh 1992; Pfefferman and Griffin 1989) have shown that it is possible to develop rigorous methods for comparing the cost-effectiveness and equity of different methods for targeting health, nutrition, and education programs. One technique somewhat analogous to statistical significance testing compares targeting methods in terms of their *exclusion error* (the percentage of eligible families or individuals who are excluded) and their *inclusion error* (the percentage of noneligible families or individuals who receive benefits).

In *education and vocational training,* the emphasis has been on the accessibility of education, particularly on monitoring regional and urban-rural differences, the impact of the household economic level, and factors affecting the participation of girls. The efficiency of the operation and the organization and the quality of education (Hunting, Zymelman, and Martin 1986) and its effect on employment and income are also being studied. Tracer and cohort studies, in which employment and earnings histories of students are studied over years or even decades, have been widely used.

# Recommended Reading

## General

Ahmed, Viqar, and Michael Bamberger. 1989. *Monitoring and Evaluating Development Projects: The South Asian Experience.* Washington, D.C.: World Bank, Economic Development Institute.

Grosh, Margaret. 1992. "From Platitudes to Practice: Targeting Social Programs In Latin America." World Bank, Washington, D.C.

Khan, Adil. 1990. *Monitoring and Evaluation of Development Projects in Southeast Asia.* Washington, D.C.: World Bank, Economic Development Institute.

Levin, Henry. 1984. *Cost-Effectiveness Analysis.* Beverly Hills, Calif.: Sage.

## Agriculture and Rural Development

Casley, Dennis, and Krishna Kumar. 1987. *Project Monitoring and Evaluation in Agriculture.* Baltimore: Johns Hopkins University.

————. 1988. *The Collection, Analysis and Use of Monitoring and Evaluation Data.* Baltimore: Johns Hopkins University.

Cernea, Michael, ed. 1991. *Putting People First: Sociological Variables in Rural Development.* 2d ed. New York: Oxford University Press.

Cernea, Michael, and Benjamin Tepping. 1977. *A System for Monitoring and Evaluating Agricultural Extension Projects.* World Bank Staff Working Paper 272. Washington, D.C.

Chambers, Robert. 1985. *Shortcut Methods of Gathering Information for Rural Development Projects.*

Murphy, Josette, and Tim Marchant. 1988. *Monitoring and Evaluation in Extension Agencies.* Technical Paper 79. Washington, D.C.: World Bank.

Ng, Ronald, and Francis Lethem. 1983. *Monitoring Systems and Irrigation Management: An Experience from the Philippines.* Washington D.C.: World Bank.

Slade, Roger, and R. Noronha. 1984. "An Operational Guide to the Monitoring and Evaluation of Social Forestry in India." World Bank, Washington, D.C.

## Population, Health, and Nutrition

Briscoe J., R. G. Feachem, and M. M. Rahaman. 1986. *Evaluating Health Impact: Water Supply, Sanitation and Hygiene Education.*

Pfefferman, Guy, and Charles Griffin. 1989. *Nutrition and Health Programs in Latin America: Targeting Social Expenditures.* Washington, D.C.: World Bank.

Scrimshaw, Susan, and Elena Hurtado. 1987. *Rapid Assessment Procedures for Nutrition and Primary Health Care: Anthropological Approaches to Improving Programme Effectiveness.* Tokyo: United Nations University.

Valadez, Joesph. 1991. *Assessing Child Survival Progress in Developing Countries: Testing Lot Quality Assurance Sampling.* Cambridge, Mass.: Harvard University Press.

### Education and Vocational Training

Hunting, Gordon, Manuel Zymelman, and Martin Godfrey. 1986. *Evaluating Vocational Training Programs.* Washington, D.C.: World Bank.

Miles, Matthew, and Michael Huberman. 1984. *Qualitative Data Analysis: A Sourcebook of New Methods.* Beverly Hills, Calif.: Sage.

### Housing and Urban Development

Bamberger, Michael, and Eleanor Hewitt. 1986. *Monitoring and Evaluating Urban Development Programs: A Handbook.* (Available in French: a Management Summary is available in French, Spanish, and Chinese.) World Bank Technical Paper 54. Washington, D.C.

Perrett, Heli. 1984. "Monitoring and Evaluation of Communication Support Activities in Low-Cost Sanitation Projects." Technical Assistance Group Technical Note 11. UNDP Interregional Project for the International Drinking Water Supply and Sanitation Decade. World Bank, Washington, D.C.

World Health Organization. 1983. *Minimum Evaluation Procedure for Water Supply and Sanitation Projects.*

## Notes

1. See Gran (1983:chap. 11) for a review of some of the critiques of donor-sponsored evaluations.

2. See Rossi and Freeman (1982:chap. 9, "The Context of Evaluation Research") for a similar classification of stakeholders.

3. This example is described in more detail in Bamberger and Hewitt (1986: Annex H).

4. See Hans-Ulrich Derlien, "Genesis and Structure of Evaluation Efforts in Comparative Perspective" (in Rist 1990:150–51).

5. The national monitoring and evaluation systems in Bangladesh and in all other South Asian countries are described in detail in Khan (1989). See also Khan (1990) for a description of systems used in the countries of Southeast Asia. In addition, see

World Bank (1983:5, "The Role of the State"). Between 1900 and 1980 public expenditure in industrialized countries increased from about 10 to 40 percent of GDP. Between 1960 and 1980 the proportion increased from about 15 to 25 percent for middle-income countries, and from about 12 to 17 percent for low-income countries.

# 5

# Diagnostic Studies of Problems Affecting Project Implementation, Operation, and Sustainability

The successful implementation, operation, and sustained delivery of a program's activities depend as much on what happens during implementation as on how carefully the program was planned and designed. Implementation problems are often due to unexpected responses on the part of intended beneficiaries; difficulties in obtaining or using human, financial, or material resources; inappropriate service delivery systems; and external events largely beyond the control of project management. Box 5-1 illustrates some unanticipated events that necessitated changes in designs or method of execution while project implementation was in progress.

## The Purpose of Diagnostic Studies

Given the complexities and unpredictability of the program environment, managers require constant feedback on the factors affecting project implementation and on the corrective actions taken when problems arise. This feedback can be provided through *diagnostic studies*, which are conducted either when problems have already been detected or on a regular basis as an early warning system to detect potential problems. Diagnostic studies are also called *process studies* or *evaluations* (Rossi and Freeman 1993) and *formative evaluations* (Morris and Fitz-Gibbon 1978).

---

**Box 5-1.  Unanticipated Events That Have Caused Project Design or Implementation Methods to Be Modified**

- A housing project in El Salvador was designed for families currently living in tenement houses in which they shared washing and toilet facilities. In order to make the project housing affordable, units were designed with communal washing facilities on the assumption that these would be acceptable, as they were similar to those in the tenements currently lived in. To the surprise of the planners, families objected strongly. They were well aware of the number of arguments and other problems arising from shared facilities. The new houses had to be redesigned in the face of this opposition.
- Baum and Tolbert (1985) cite examples in which project designers had seriously overestimated the availability of labor. In India, for example, farmers could not plant the new crops promoted by an agricultural development project because the peak labor demand coincided with the rice harvest. Similarly, road construction projects have been delayed in rural areas when construction can only take place during the dry period, which is often the time of peak agricultural activity.
- A footbridge in Nepal was not completed because the government assumed that the villages would welcome the bridge and would be willing to provide timber and complete the construction. As it turned out, villages were annoyed that they had not been consulted about the location of the bridge and refused to cooperate.
- It was recently discovered that an immunization program proposed in Bolivia could not be implemented as planned. Vaccines were to be administered by nurse auxiliaries. However, because there was not enough fuel to run the generators, the cold chain could not be maintained. Replanning was therefore necessary to either improve the local supply of fuel or to organize the program through a higher level of the health system.
- In Venezuela, the design, scope, and method of selection of beneficiaries for many low-income housing projects had to be drastically modified when the project sites and nearby land were invaded by squatters. The invaders were numerous and well organized, and so they could not be evicted. Thus their presence had to be taken into account in the implementation of the project and the allocation of houses.
- A USAID-funded agroforestry project in Haiti was designed to help 6,000 peasants plant three million trees in four years to combat deforestation. However, by using an innovative approach in which promoters (animateurs) worked with local peasant organizations, it was possible to help 75,000 peasants plant some 20 million trees.

Diagnostic studies can be subdivided into *diagnostic monitoring studies,* whose purpose is to improve the performance of an ongoing project, and *diagnostic evaluation studies,* whose purpose is to help interpret the reasons for the success or failure of a completed project and to help in the design of future projects.

Diagnostic evaluation studies are usually part of an ex-post evaluation. Most of the quantitative evaluation procedures described in Chapters 8, 9, and 11 are designed to measure the extent to which intended outputs or impacts were achieved (and some of the intervening variables affecting the level or direction of impact), but they cannot explain why the intended effects were not achieved. For example, a multiple regression analysis can estimate the proportion of the variance in housing investment explained by household income or education, but it cannot assess why the average family only invested, say, 1,000 pesos in housing instead of the 5,000 pesos estimated when the project was being planned.

Diagnostic studies can complement quantitative evaluation methods by pinpointing the reasons for a project's poor performance—whether it be poor project design, implementation problems, lack of receptivity of the target population, problems of coordination with other agencies, or unexpected external events.

## The Design and Implementation of Diagnostic Studies

### Identifying an Implementation Problem

Since managers need some means of rapidly detecting implementation problems before they become too serious, one of the functions of monitoring studies (see Chapter 4) is to identify actual or potential problems, such as delays, cost overruns, or beneficiary dissatisfaction. Often management will decide that special studies are required to provide a more detailed analysis of the causes or to propose possible solutions. To make such an assessment, management may need to examine the preliminary results of the diagnostic studies within a few weeks. Box 5-2 shows a typical sequence of events in a diagnostic study of a development program for a hypothetical small business.

Salmen (1992:21) notes that beneficiary assessment was used in Ethiopia to help explain why pregnant women almost never visited health centers during their pregnancy:

---

**Box 5-2.  Defining the Scope, Objectives, and Timing of a Diagnostic Study for a Hypothetical Small Business Development Project**

- The quarterly monitoring report highlighted the unexpectedly low rate of applications for small business loan applications as one of the key issues to be addressed by management.
- The management meeting considered various explanations as to why the application rate was so low but failed to reach agreement on the principal cause. One manager claimed that the main problem was poor publicity while others put the blame on cumbersome administrative procedures, the minimum loan (which they said was too large), the maximum loan (which was too small), or the unwillingness of businesses to pay for the technical assistance and training required as part of the loan package.
- The general manager explained that there would be visits from the donor agency in three months, at which time the possibility of the following changes in project design would be considered: changes in the minimum and maximum loan sizes, increased expenditures on publicity, and changes in the kinds of training offered. The donor would probably not agree to having technical assistance eliminated, and it would be difficult to make rapid changes in the administrative procedures because these had to comply with banking regulations. Consequently, the diagnostic study should focus on those issues where changes could be made.
- All agreed that a diagnostic study was required to obtain more information. The evaluation unit was asked to submit the results of a preliminary study at the next management meeting in four weeks. A further four weeks would be available if a follow-up study was necessary.
- A budget was approved for the study, and it was agreed that staff could be loaned from the social services of credit divisions to conduct interviews or to help with data analysis.

---

On the basis of in-depth discussions held with men and women in the community in which they lived, it was discovered that the major reason for the low visitation rate lay in the cultural belief that it was considered weak and improper for women to admit to any pain or discomfort. This information, which was new to the public health officials in Addis Ababa, was considered useful to help orient health education among rural communities.

The need for diagnostic studies can be identified in other ways as well. Managers may call for such studies when they have identified a problem or when they need additional information to help them make a decision, or the evaluation unit may suggest what topics need to be studied.

Exploratory studies may also be conducted from time to time to assess the progress of a program's activities and to identify possible problems. This approach is strongly recommended for innovative projects for which there is little previous experience to guide project design and implementation. Such diagnostic studies employ two basic methods: participant observation and panel studies in which a sample of subjects are interviewed periodically to obtain feedback on those aspects of the project that are going well or badly. Box 5-3 describes some typical panel studies.

*Defining the Conceptual Model of a Program and Identifying Possible Causes of the Problems*

The model of the implementation process in Chapter 3 (Figure 3-2) can help management identify the factors contributing to problems. The figure identifies six sets of such factors: conceptualization and design, resource mobilization, service delivery, program organization, unanticipated responses by the target population, and the influence of external events.

---

**Box 5-3. Examples of Panel Studies to Monitor Project Implementation**

- In the Tondo upgrading project in Manila, approximately 100 families were asked to keep a daily record of their income and expenditures over a period of two years. The data were used to study the sources of housing investment and to identify any negative effects that these expenditures might have on the ability of families to purchase basic necessities such as food and clothing (Reforma and Obusan 1981).
- To monitor the process of house construction and to identify any problems arising during the self-help construction period, panels of households have been selected in a number of countries. In some cases (for example, Nairobi), information on the progress and quality of construction was obtained by direct observation, whereas in other cases (for example, El Salvador), observation was combined with interviews (FSDVM 1979).

---

*Alternative Designs for a Diagnostic Study*

SINGLE-SITE ANALYSIS. Many diagnostic studies are conducted at a single site, either because the program is located in a single site, or because there is not enough money or time for a cross-site analysis. An exploratory single-site study may also be conducted in preparation for a more comprehensive cross-site study. If management requires a rapid initial response (in time for the next monthly management meeting), the single-site analysis may be the only feasible option. Box 5-4 gives examples of single-site studies.

The drawback of such studies is that they do not reveal whether problems are general or are site-specific. Without comparative data, it is difficult to choose between alternative explanations or to assess the plausibility of a particular causal hypothesis.

---

### Box 5-4. Examples of Single-Site Diagnostic Studies

- *A study of the causes of absenteeism and dropout among participants in a self-help housing project in El Salvador* (FSDVM 1976). Interviews were conducted with families actively participating in the project, those who were frequently absent from communal work days, and those who had dropped out of the project. Application forms were analyzed to compare the age, education, and family size of the participants and dropouts. Project staff were also interviewed.
- *Analysis of the causes of the slow-rate of house construction and occupation in Dakar, Senegal* (Bureau d'Evaluation 1977). Families were interviewed at the project site and in their homes. Application forms were analyzed to compare the characteristics of families that were building quickly and slowly. The process of house construction was observed and project staff were interviewed. The problems in contracting and supervising building contractors were also analyzed.
- A participant observation study was conducted in La Paz Bolivia (Salmen 1983) to shed light on the *attitude and experiences of different sectors of the community with a squatter upgrading project.* By living in the project site for several months, Salmen was able to learn who was and who was not benefiting from the project. Such details could not have been learned from a survey.

---

CROSS-SITE ANALYSIS. If a program is operating in a number of sites, a cross-site analysis can be conducted to assess the extent of the problem (Does it occur in all sites? Are there differences in the intensity of the problem between sites?). The following contributing factors also need to be examined to assess their influence on the problem being studied:

- *Resources and their utilization.* Were there differences in the volume or kinds of financial, human, and material resources available in each site? Were the resources used in different ways?
- *Project implementation methods.* Were different methods used to organize the community, select participants, and provide technical assistance?
- *Services delivered.* Did the level or quality of services (outputs) delivered vary?
- *Characteristics of the beneficiary population.* Did the social, cultural, economic, and political characteristics of the population differ from site to site?
- *Political and administrative characteristics.* Were different kinds of community and political organizations operating at each site? Were sites managed in different ways (Did they have different administrative areas? Were different central or local government agencies involved)?
- *External events.* Were there any significant natural, economic, social, or political events that might have affected project implementation at particular sites?

For multicomponent projects that are implemented in different cities or regions, it is also possible to compare *relationships between city characteristics and program performance.* Box 5-5 gives some examples of multisite studies.

LONGITUDINAL AND CROSS-SECTIONAL DESIGNS. Since most diagnostic studies must be completed within a relatively short period of time, they are not normally used to analyze the evolution of a program over time. In longitudinal studies, however, the evaluation can describe how the program evolved and assess the extent to which the current problems are due to the way the program was implemented or to external events that occurred during implementation.

Even when a longitudinal study is not possible, an effort should be made to locate and use historical data. Sometimes such data can be found in

---

**Box 5-5.  Examples of Multisite Diagnostic Studies**

- A comparison was made of the factors affecting the performance of seven urban cooperatives in El Salvador (Urban and Regional Economics Division 1978). The records of the cooperatives were examined, members were asked to complete a short questionnaire, in-depth interviews were conducted with a sample of members, meetings were attended, and interviews were conducted with the cooperative promoters.
- In a study of a number of fishing cooperatives in Recife, Brazil, the factors affecting performance were examined to determine why the cooperative program had developed more slowly than expected. A participant observer lived in one of the fishing villages for several months, and additional interviews were conducted with fishermen who were and were not members of the cooperative, and with the various organizations involved in the promotion of the program. The records of the cooperatives were examined and a study made of the role of the middlemen and moneylenders who were competing with the cooperative (Nucleo de Acompanhamento 1983).

---

program records (records on credit operations, minutes of meetings, supervision reports) or through interviews with affiliated organizations. Newspapers and other secondary sources of data can also be useful for certain kinds of projects.

### Defining the Kinds of Information to Be Collected

Data collection procedures cannot be defined until one know what kinds of information are required. In diagnostic studies, the data usually cover at least several of the following topics:

*Indicators of project performance.* In order to determine whether problems are general or site-specific, it is necessary to establish criteria for measuring how well different sites are performing with respect to the problem being studied.

*Resource allocation.* Information is needed on the kinds and levels of resources actually allocated to and used at each project site.

*Indicators of implementation.* In some cases, it is sufficient to determine which of several implementation methods was used (for example, were loans administered through banks or through community based offices), but usually it is also necessary to develop indicators of the quality or intensity of implementation methods.[1] Valadez (1991) developed lot quality assurance sampling for this very purpose (see Chapter 11).

*Service delivery.* Evaluators also need indicators of the quantity and quality of services delivered and of the distribution of services among different sectors of the population.

*Characteristics of the target population.* Social, economic, and cultural characteristics of the population need to be considered.

*Community organizations.* Attention must also be given to the types of organizations operating in the community, their activities, their interrelationships, and their attitudes to the program's activities. For quantitative cross-site analysis it may be necessary to develop a more rigorous system for classifying and comparing organizations. This might include indicators such as the number of members, frequency of meetings, kinds and scale of activities, and value of resources mobilized.

*External events.* For some kinds of analysis it will be sufficient to identify the important events and describe how they might have affected the project. In the case of statistical analysis, however, it may be necessary to develop quantitative indicators such as numbers of families affected by natural disasters, number of new jobs created in the area, and amount of government investment in related projects.

*City or sectoral characteristics.* Per capita income, per capita investment, the proportion of the population with access to particular services, and the sectoral distribution of employment all need to be examined.

*Perceived causes of the problems affecting the program.* It is particularly important to seek the opinions of all the main groups involved in the program's activities about the causes of the problems being studied. The data may be obtained from sample surveys or from a small number of key informants.

## Methods of Collecting Data

Diagnostic studies can use any of the methods of collecting quantitative or qualitative data described in Chapters 7 and 10. The following list outlines the main methods.

*Use of secondary data.* Before embarking on the collection of data, the researcher should check to determine what kinds of information are already available from existing records and reports, records of community organizations, government documents, previous studies, newspapers, and the like.

*Sample surveys.* These surveys consist of interviews with a sample of mothers, businessmen, farmers, and the like, about how they have been affected by the program activities and how they think the program is performing. Care must be taken to ensure that the correct respondents are being interviewed, namely, those whose responses are most pertinent to implementing the project or to benefiting from it. However, there are many issues to consider. For example, should it be the household head or the household member most actively involved in the activity? Is it necessary to interview more than one person in the family? Should the survey include people who are not involved as well as those who are?

*Panel studies.* A sample of respondents is interviewed periodically to document how they are affected by program activities and what they think about the program at different stages in its evolution.

*Direct observation.* Physical changes in the community or the maintenance of infrastructure can often be monitored through an observation guide. It is sometimes possible to conduct a statistical analysis of the resulting information. Other data can be collected by observing the conduct of community meetings, the organization of community work groups, the use of community facilities, or the way program staff are utilized.

*Participant observation.* Living in a project site or becoming directly involved in community- or project-related activities is one of the most effective ways to learn what the beneficiaries and the community think about programming activities and the various agencies involved in their implementation. This is also an excellent way to assess the validity of the more structured methods of data collection. Evaluators should maintain regular contact with representatives of all the major "stakeholders" to obtain rapid feedback on how the program is progressing and to gain insight into the causes and consequences of its various problems. Informants should represent all groups, such as the main population groups in the community, and should not just be the community "leaders."

*Group meetings.* People respond differently in groups than in individual interviews. In a one-on-one interview, the researcher is more likely to impose his or her agenda on the respondent. However, the respondent is more likely to behave in a more unbiased manner than in a group. In a group interview, the group will take a more active role in directing the discussion, and the interactions between group members will bring forth many issues that would not otherwise have arisen.

As always, a multimethod approach should be used so that information from a number of independent sources can be compared.

## Data Analysis

Data analysis encompasses several activities, which take place from the time the data are still being collected. This section draws heavily on Miles and Huberman (1984), who offer a more detailed discussion of many of the procedures.

ANALYSIS DURING DATA COLLECTION. The data used in diagnostic studies are by and large qualitative. Usually they are collected by a single person or a small number of interviewers using a checklist. Rapid feedback methods should be devised so that the initial findings and impressions can be reviewed and discussed by the data collection team and by program leaders. The following are some examples.

*Contact summary sheets* can prepared by data collectors for each contact so that a brief and systematically organized report (usually no more than one page long) will be available for reviewers. Information should be recorded on topics such as the background of the project, problems in collecting the data, and new issues that should be covered.

A simple system should be used for *coding reports* (for example, different categories of information can be highlighted in different colors or tagged with numbers or letters) so that the reader can easily identify the information each report contains on a particular topic. Where secretarial support is available, the information can be retyped by topic, or a microcomputer coding system can be used to print out all the data on a particular topic. Patterns and themes in the data can be identified and coded. One theme might be the methods a committee uses to encourage families to participate in a project; another theme could be disagreements within households about whether to invest in a particular project (for example, take out a loan, buy fertilizer).

*Memos and aid memoirs* can be used to record ideas or hypotheses that occur to the researchers at the time they occur. They should be written down so that they can be discussed with other members of the team. They also help the lone researcher systematize his or her thoughts about patterns emerging from the data.

*Site analysis* is required when the study is being conducted at a number of different sites. A site includes any unit of analysis, whether the household, group, or community. The purpose is to produce an interim summary of what is known about each site, what the problems are, and what contextual factors appear to be affecting outcomes. This is also a useful way to review what information still needs to be collected. This assessment brings together a number of different strands of research and helps evaluators formulate hypotheses and decide how to use the remaining time and resources. It can also identify biases due to data collection methods. For example, a selection bias may arise when interviews are conducted with members of the cooperative and nonmembers are overlooked.

WITHIN AND BETWEEN SITE ANALYSIS. Data collection at a particular site normally produces large amounts of information in the form of written reports on individual interviews, observations of meetings, and the like. Often reports go to great lengths to include as many detailed cases as possible to give a "feel" for the data, but cumbersome reports are usually not what a busy policymaker has time to read, and they turn out to be a wasted effort. Nor do cases provide an overview of the situation. Whenever possible, analyses should synthesize data in simple charts, tables, or matrices that are easily digestible. Some further examples follow.

*Context charts* can show the overall structure of the organization being studied or the external factors affecting project development.

*Checklist matrices* are a convenient way of scanning all the field data as a first step in defining how they should be analyzed and presented. For example, a matrix might consist of rows representing the different groups involved in a village water supply project (for example, small farmers, large farmers, extension workers, local political leaders) and columns representing attitudes toward the project (for example, general receptivity, belief in its viability, expected benefits). The analyst would then fill in each cell with a phrase or two to indicate the attitude of each group. This would provide an overview of the differences between groups and might also point up missing information or remaining questions.

*Time-ordered matrices* trace the evolution of the project. Rows represent different groups and columns different stages of the project. The comments in each cell summarize the actions or opinions of groups at different points in time.

*Conceptually ordered matrices* are used for more complex analyses, for example, to uncover the reasons for different responses to a fishing cooperative. Rows might refer to the groups surveyed, such as boat owners, crew members, small independent fishermen, and leaders of the cooperative. The columns can represent the factors affecting motivation, such as perceived economic effects, and relationships to groups promoting and opposing the project.

*Effects matrices* summarize the different types of effects. A simple form would use the rows for different groups and columns for different economic, demographic, and organizational effects.

*Site-dynamic matrices* describe the underlying processes necessary for interpreting the results. The matrix might examine problems and their solutions, or the way that the phases of the project were organized.

*Causal networks* describe the causal links between the phases and activities of the project. Figure 5-1 illustrates how a causal network was used to describe the links between antecedent variables, intervening variables, and outcome variables for a credit and technical assistance program for small business development. The (+) and (–) signs indicate whether a particular factor had a positive or negative influence. For example, the education of the entrepreneur had a positive impact on the progress of the company, whereas the level of political activity in the community or sector had a negative effect on the progress of the company.

An advantage of the network chart is that all the links between the different factors are clearly identified and easy to understand. The reader should compare this causal network with the discussion in Chapter 3 of how path analysis could be applied to this same project. Network diagrams or similar types of causal explanations should be examined by the various groups involved with the project. Their opinions can serve to check any discrepancies in the interpretations and the supposed causal links and thus enable researchers to spot the weaknesses in their causal model and revise it accordingly.

UNDERSTANDING THE CONTEXT AND THE EFFECT OF EXTERNAL FACTORS ON PROJECT OUTCOMES. A weakness of many quantitative survey methods is that they are unable to control for, or perhaps even identify, the external

**Figure 5-1.  Using a Causal Network to Examine Factors Affecting the Success of a Small Business Development Program**

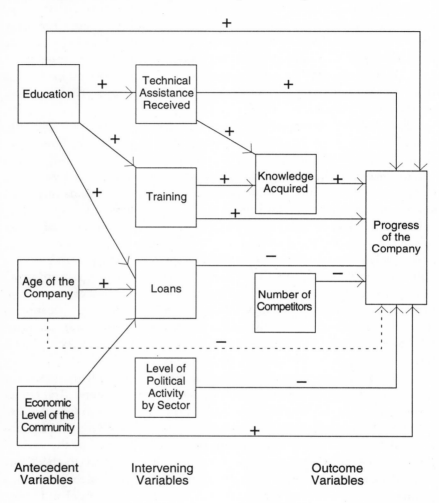

events that can drastically alter a program's outcomes. During the period of implementation there may be an election campaign, a flood, the opening of a number of new factories, or a land invasion in one of the areas close to the project. All of these events may have serious impacts on implementation. Qualitative methods can describe and monitor such events and help assess their impact on the project.

DIAGNOSING THE INFLUENCE OF COMMUNITY OR CITY CHARACTERISTICS ON THE IMPLEMENTATION OF ACTIVITIES. Other important external factors that affect implementation are the characteristics of the target population, the kinds of community and political organizations that are active in the area, and the characteristics of the cities or sectors in which the projects are located.

When the number of project sites is sufficiently large, a statistical analysis can help determine which of these characteristics are associated with performance indicators. Such an analysis was used to assess factors affecting the performance of an integrated urban development program in twenty-three secondary cities in Colombia (Instituto SER 1981). The summary indicators of project performance in this case were water pipes installed, small business loans, numbers of groups organized, and houses constructed. These were compared with some of the principal economic characteristics of the cities (per capita income, investment in infrastructure, percentage of houses with water connections) through a correlation matrix. The analysis found a number of these relationships were constant in most cities. For example, the performance of the house construction component of projects was related to the rate of employment generation in each city.

This kind of comparative analysis pays due attention to the unique characteristics of each city, which are usually overlooked. However, it sometimes overemphasizes the uniqueness of each community, assuming, for example, that good or poor performance can be explained by unique factors such as a conflict between the mayor and the Ministry of Housing. This approach has also been used to analyze the impact of community characteristics on the vaccination status of children under the age of three throughout Costa Rica (Valadez, DiPrete, and Weld 1990; Valadez and Weld 1992), the impact of regional factors on the management of irrigation projects (Bottrall 1981), and the influence of city characteristics such as size and income level on housing demand and the performance of housing projects (Mayo 1983).

In this kind of study, it is important to combine the statistical analysis with a qualitative analysis because a great deal of significant information can be overlooked when some of the variables are reduced to a simple quantitative form. For example, the way in which a local political party committee operates can be more important than whether one exists. And how financial or material support is provided and administered by a government or project donors can be more important than the amount of support.

## Assessing the Performance of Community Organizations

A primary objective of many social programs is to create or strengthen local community organizations that can help in the planning, implementation, and sustainability of their own programs. A monitoring system should therefore be able to assess the *performance* of these community organizations in their design, implementation, and operation of the project. Two reliable indicators of the *performance* of a community organization are the amount of community participation in project design, implementation, and operation and the effectiveness of community communication networks.

### Evaluating Community Participation in the Planning and Management of Projects

Because many of the causes of participation or nonparticipation are complex, it is often difficult to know whether the low participation of certain groups is due to deliberate exclusion policies or to the lack of interest among these groups. In many cultures participation occurs through traditional informal channels rather than through the easily observable formal structures set up by the program. In Indonesia, where it is the custom for people to regularly visit the RT (block leader) in his house to discuss problems, they would be reluctant to air such things in public, even in community meetings.

*Sample surveys* are often used to estimate the level of participation of different groups, the attitudes of the community toward community organizations and their activities, and the degree and form of community participation in decisionmaking in communal projects.

The above indicators can be used to compare participation between socioeconomic groups, between communities, and between types of projects or organizations over time.

Many community organizations keep membership and attendance records that contain useful information on certain kinds of participation (for example, how many people pay their dues, attend meetings, vote, participate in committees and construction groups). Community promoters or implementing agencies also keep records. These records must be interpreted with care for sometimes they are used as a supervision tool, in which case there may be an incentive to distort the information so as to present the project in a more favorable light. Also, many are not up to date or maintained regularly.

*Participant observation* is a useful method for assessing the dynamics of community participation in decisionmaking and project implementation and management (see Box 5-6).

The more formal aspects of community organizations (such as meetings and work groups) can be studied through *passive observation*. The observer may attend meetings and record what takes place either in the form of a general description or an outline based on predetermined categories, such as the number of people attending, the number of active participants who speak and vote, the number of items on the agenda that are discussed, and on which a decision is reached, the methods by which decisions were reached (for example, through a formal vote, through an informal indication of agreement, imposed by group leaders), and the degree of formality of the meetings (for example, whether minutes are taken and read and approved at subsequent meetings; whether a quorum is established).

The advantage of the above categories is that they can be used by different researchers and hence make it easier to compare the results. It is important, however, to have an adequate conceptual framework to explain why these indicators were selected and how they will be interpreted.

Other observational indicators include the types of election publicity used, the number of people attending elections and political meetings, and the degree of openness or coercion used in election campaigns. Similar

---

Box 5-6. Examples of the Use of Participant Observation to Study Community Participation in Decisionmaking

The researcher may observe a group from outside to analyze how it is perceived by other groups inside and outside the community. Parris (1984) lived in the community affected by an upgrading project and sought to understand and describe the attitudes of the community to the implementing agency and to the way in which the project was organized. He had direct contact with the implementing agency itself.

Lisa Peattie (1969) became an active member of the junta opposing the construction of a sewage outlet in the community in which she lived in Venezuela. She was able to observe the response of different government agencies and individuals to the group. However, it was clear that her participation altered significantly the way in which the group operated, thus illustrating the difficulties of using this active role to understand "normal" group functioning in her community.

types of observational procedures can be used to evaluate work groups and other types of community activities. A study of a mutual-help ditch-digging project in Lusaka (Lusaka Housing Project Evaluation Team 1977) included variables such as the proportion of participants working at any point in time, the degree of coercion in persuading people to participate, and the efficiency with which work was planned. Another study of mutual-help house construction in El Salvador (FSDVM 1979) included variables such as efficiency of work compared with that of the professional contractor, frequency of supervision, leadership style, and number of participants actually working.

Important information can also be obtained by studying the processes by which particular decisions were made (often referred to as *case histories*). Nelson Polsby (1963) emphasized the importance of studying issues on which no action was taken as well as those in which a decision was made, for certain people or groups may have a negative or veto power but stay in the background and therefore are difficult to identify.

### Studying Communication Networks and the Dissemination of Information about Community Programs

Effective communication within the community is essential to ensure that all groups are aware of the project and have the opportunity to participate. Groups vary significantly in their access to information, and some groups may be excluded from an intervention because they were not aware of its existence. For example, Valadez found that 28 percent of the children in Costa Rica under the age of three years were unknown to local health workers. Therefore their households were never provided basic health services such as vaccinations.

Communication between the community and the implementing agencies is essential to ensure that the community is aware of the content and objectives of the project and that community views are taken into account in project design and implementation. A striking example of the problems that can occur when the community is not well informed about the nature of the project comes from a squatter settlement in Guayaquil. Since the project had been delayed for more than three years, program managers thought the community had no interest in individual water connections. In fact, the problem "lay with the leaders who misrepresented the project to their followers due to their wish to obstruct any Governmental undertaking which they saw both as jeopardizing their own hold on the population and as inimical to the interests of the radical political party most of them followed" (Salmen 1983:8).

Many social program managers have found it difficult to accept the idea of community involvement in project design and implementation. In their view, experts know best and should design interventions that are then "sold" to the community. Even when executing agencies are committed to involving the community, they may make the common mistake of working through community organizations that represent only a small number of people, or that are strongly identified with one political, religious, or ethnic group, although they have titles such as Junta or Community Association. The very active junta of a community being upgraded in La Paz, for example, represented only house owners. It failed to consult renters, who did not wish to pay the higher service charges proposed by the junta (Salmen 1983). And in Zambia (Bamberger, Sanyal, and Valverde 1982) it was found that the community consultation process for deciding the route of roads to be constructed in squatter areas was sometimes used to expel unpopular religious minorities.

A good indicator of the effectiveness of communication networks is the level and distribution of knowledge on topics relating to community activities. Box 5-7 illustrates questions that measure general awareness about the existence and kinds of activities of a community organization.

The effectiveness of community networks can be detected through changes in knowledge about community affairs among the residents. The simplest way to quantify such knowledge is to use a set of binary Yes/No questions. For example, Was the respondent aware of a proposal to start a consumer cooperative? Could he or she name the president of the cooperative? Did he or she know who was eligible to participate in the project? A value of 1 is given to each Yes and a score of 0 is given for each No.

It is often useful to examine the networks through which information flows and the sources of information used by various people. The analysis must be related to a specific issue because different networks are used for different purposes. For example, people often use quite different sources to obtain information on job opportunities and to gossip about what is happening in the neighborhood. Box 5-8 illustrates questions that might be used to identify communication networks that disseminate information on a family planning program.

A number of studies have examined the socioeconomic characteristics of opinion leaders and compared them with the characteristics of the rest of the group (Rogers 1962). Other studies have tested the extent to which a

---

**Box 5-7.  Examples of Questions to Measure General Awareness about Community Organizations and Their Activities**

1. Is there an organization in this community that is working to improve the conditions of life of community residents? _____
2. Could you tell me the name of the organization and where meetings are held? _____
3. Do you know the name of the director (president)? _____
4. What are the main activities? _____
5. Have you received any information (within the last month) on the possibility of organizing a consumers cooperative? _____

(If "YES")
6. Could you tell me what you have heard? _____
7. What services would be offered by the cooperative? _____
8. Who would be eligible to join? _____
9. Who is organizing it? _____

---

certain type of network is used. For example, respondents may be asked which types of communication they have with members of their kinship group, church, political party, or immediate neighbors. A chart can be constructed in which all members of the group are listed and the respondent would be asked to indicate the kind of communication he/she has had with each person. Although it is more time-consuming, this approach provides more complete information.

Various quantitative indicators can be used to compare networks in different communities:

- The proportion of the community involved in the network.
- The average number of network contacts of each individual.
- The kinds of information flowing through the network.
- The proportion of opinion leaders residing in the community.

Most of the previous types of analysis examine access to information at a particular point in time, but it is also useful to examine the dissemination of information over time. Rogers (1962) plotted the time taken by different groups of farmers to adopt a new weed spray. Whereas the groups defined as "early adopters" and the "early majority" were using the sprays after three to four months, the "laggards" and the "late majority" were delaying

Box 5-8. Questions Used to Study Communication Networks for Disseminating Information on Family Planning Programs

1. How did you first hear about (the family planning clinic)?
   a. Told by another person.
   b. Heard about it on the radio (or through other mass media).
   c. Read about it (where?).
   d. Saw the clinic.

(If told by another person)
2. What is the name of the person who told you?

3. Is this person a
   a. Relative (state relationship).
   b. Friend.
   c. Other (explain).

4. How did this person hear about (the family planning clinic)?
   a. Told by another person.
   b. Heard about it from the mass media.

5. Have you told anyone else about the program? (details of people told—kinship, where they live, etc.).

by up to five years. Early adopters and laggards often have quite different socioeconomic characteristics, and their behavior can be predicted with respect to a wide range of innovations.

*Sociometric studies of friendship and influence* can be used to determine how alliances are formed and community organizations structured. This is particularly important in areas with strong regional, ethnic, or religious ties. One of the objectives of community organizations is to transcend some of these ties. Typical sociometric questions include, Who do respondents go to when they need advice (for example, on family or personal affairs, community activities, and employment)? and Who would respondents recommend to run a community association if one was organized?

For each of the people named, information is then obtained on kinship relations, socioeconomic characteristics (for example, age, sex, education, religion), where they live, and what formal positions they hold in community or other types of organizations. Various kinds of data on organizational behavior can be used in describing (a) the size of different types of networks—for example, the number of contracts reported by different sociocultural groups; (b) the socioeconomic characteristics of the supporters of different community leaders; and the degree of "openness" or "closedness" of different groups (with respect to the number of people included whose social or economic characteristics differ from those of the majority of group members) and whether groups become more "open" after participation in an intervention.

In a study of the structure of social networks in a squatter area in Cartagena, Colombia (Bamberger and Kaufmann 1984), "support networks" were constructed by obtaining information on all households with whom money, goods, or services were exchanged. The social and economic characteristics of receivers and givers were compared and an analysis made of factors determining the size and usage of the networks (Bamberger and Parris 1984).

Respondents often have difficulty in recalling or explaining the details of their communication networks because these follow customary patterns that have never been questioned. For example, a woman may always gossip with her neighbors while washing clothes, but if asked about her sources of information she may overlook the neighbors. For this reason, *participant observation,* in which such communication is observed directly, can be an effective analytical technique. The main difficulty in applying it is that many communications take place in situations to which the outside observer has no access.

An alternative to participant observation is to ask selected members of the community to report on their activities and conversations during a particular period of time or on a particular topic. In some cases the respondent can be asked to write or to tape-record the report, but usually the information is verbally reported to the researcher. In an analysis of how a decision was reached on whether or not to form a consumer cooperative, the respondent could be asked to list all the people he or she talked to about this issue, whether specific people were sought out or themselves initiated a discussion of the matter, and whose opinions were considered most reliable, and the like. The problem here is that the results may be distorted owing to selective recall or the fact that the person may wish to create a certain impression (for example, that he was or was not very involved in the issue). However, these biases can be controlled to some extent by cross-checking information from a number of different informants. The method becomes much more effective if the information can also be cross-checked with the results of sample surveys or with direct participant observation.

In addition to interviewing people about their own communication behavior, it is sometimes possible to locate informants who can provide a general view of the communication networks in the community with respect to a particular issue. For example, the local storekeepers or community leaders may know what sources of information are used for seeking rental accommodation or for hiring certain types of labor; and religious leaders or health workers may know who people go to for advice on health-related problems. When using such informants, the researcher must be aware of the possible biases. The information will be much more reliable if data from different sources can be cross-checked.

## Recommended Reading

Miles, Matt, and A. M. Huberman. 1984. *Qualitative Data Analysis: A Sourcebook of New Methods*. Beverly Hills, Calif.: Sage.

Describes how evaluation questions are formulated, how they are revised as the studies progress, and simple methods of analyzing and presenting the findings. Although the book focuses on education, most of the methods can be applied in other social sectors.

Naroll, Roaul, and Ronald Cohen. 1970. *A Handbook on Cultural Anthropology*. New York: Natural History Press.

Salmen, Lawrence. 1987. *Listen to the People: Participant Observer Evaluation of Development Projects*. New York: Oxford University Press.

Shows how many of the diagnostic techniques can be applied to the study of urban projects. Extensive discussion of the role of the evaluator, his/her relationships with the different stakeholder groups, and the participant observer methodology.

## Note

1. In a study of factors affecting the performance of a sample of 150 rural organizations Esman and Uphoff (1984) point out the difficulties of using simple statistical comparisons: "Even a factor like political support, thought to be a sine qua non for participation, showed no correlation because *how* any support is given turns out to be more important than *whether* support is given, or *how much* is given." Cited in Uphoff (1988:33).

# 6

## Monitoring and Evaluating Project Sustainability

Although many countries have developed quite elaborate systems for monitoring project implementation, few produce regular information on project operation and maintenance or on the extent to which projects are actually producing the intended benefits (see Bamberger 1989; Khan 1989, 1990).[1] This lack of attention to monitoring sustainability is surprising in view of the large numbers of projects that have clearly been unable to continue delivering their intended services over the intended lifetime of the project (see Table 6-1). The first review of project sustainability conducted by the World Bank's Operations Evaluation Department (OED) found that only nine out of twenty-seven of the agriculture projects studied were classified as "sustained," eight more were "doubtful," and the remaining ten were "not sustained" (World Bank 1985).[2] And of a total of seventeen education projects covered by this and a later study (World Bank 1989b), nine were classified as likely to be sustained, five were doubtful, and three were unlikely to be sustained.

## The Concept and Importance of Project Sustainability

*The Importance of Project and Program Sustainability*

The largest OED sustainability study to date covered 557 World Bank projects completed and assessed between 1986 and 1988 (World Bank

Table 6-1.  Findings of World Bank Operations Evaluation Department
Studies on Project Sustainability

| Project | Number of Projects | | | Total |
| | Sustained | Not Sustained | Doubtful | |
| --- | --- | --- | --- | --- |
| Agricultural projects[a] | 9 | 10 | 8 | 27 |
| Educational projects[b] | 9 | 3 | 5 | 17 |
| Fertilizer production[c] | 7 | 2 | 2 | 11 |
| All sectors[d] | 291 | 83 | 183 | 557 |

Note: 1985, 1986, and 1990 studies are based on assessments of sustainability of projects which had been operating for several years. The 1989 study assessed projects at the point when implementation was completed.
  a. Data from OED, 1985.
  b. Data from OED, 1985 and 1990.
  c. Data from OED, 1986.
  d. Data from OED, 1989.

1990a). In contrast to earlier assessments, which did not look at a project until it had already been operational for several years, the 1990 study chose a point just after implementation from which to evaluate whether a project was likely to be sustained. Of the 557 projects studied, 291 were considered likely to be sustained, 83 not likely to be sustained, and 183 doubtful. Although the OED fully recognized the drawbacks of a *prospective* assessment, its study represented the first systematic attempt to assess the sustainability of World Bank–financed projects in all sectors.

Earlier, Honadle and VanSant (1985) had reported that sustainability was a serious problem in twenty-one integrated rural development projects financed by USAID. Most of these projects were designed at a time when careful planning and well-designed implementation strategies were considered the keys to success. The complexities of project operation and institutional development had not yet been fully appreciated.

When sustainability is ignored, the life of roads, schools, irrigation, and similar infrastructure projects is significantly reduced, the quality of services declines, and fewer project staff are assigned to extension and other support services (see Bamberger and Cheema 1990:chap. 5; World Bank 1990a:chap. 4). The political process of deciding how to allocate project benefits when their volume (water, school places, small business credits, and so on) is reduced often has a negative effect on the economically, socially, or politically weaker groups.[3] In some cases, allocations will be made on political grounds, whereas in others it will be necessary to eliminate some of the outreach services, which means denying access to the disadvantaged groups whose participation depends on such services.[4] The results of such neglect are particularly severe where the natural environment is concerned, as the next section explains.

## Defining Sustainability

PROJECT SUSTAINABILITY. Project sustainability is often defined as the capacity of a project to continue to deliver its intended benefits over an extended period of time. According to the Operations Evaluation Department of the World Bank (1986:1),

> The term "Sustainability" describes the ability of a project to maintain an acceptable level of benefit flows through its economic life. While this may often be expressed in quantitative terms involving the internal economic or financial rates of return, benefits may also be qualitatively assessed. For projects in the productive sectors such as industry, the principal measure of performance is output, generally expressed in terms of capacity utilization, but Bank-supported projects normally have other objectives such as sub-sectoral policies, technology transfer and institution building, which must be assessed qualitatively.

As a more recent study (World Bank 1990a) points out, sustainability also depends on whether a balance can be achieved in the use of the principal forms of capital—namely, human, natural, cultural, institutional, physical, and financial. Sustainability is more difficult to define and measure in projects designed to develop human resources because qualitative indicators must be taken into account alongside quantitative ones.[5] The degree of sustainability of a project has been defined as "the percentage of project-initiated goods and services that is still delivered and maintained five years past the termination of donor resources, the continuation of local action stimulated by the project, and the generation of successor services and initiatives as a result of project built local capacity" (Honadle and VanSant 1985:2).

The principal idea behind all these definitions is that any project—whether it is in the agricultural, urban, industrial, transport, or power sectors—is designed to produce a continuous *flow* of outputs, benefits, or services throughout its intended lifetime. For some projects, the intended economic lifetime may be as long as thirty years, whereas for others it may be considerably shorter. The sustainability of a project must be judged by its ability to sustain this flow of benefits over time.

For many kinds of industrial and commercial projects, sustainability must be defined by an enterprise's ability to remain profitable. Depending on the nature of the enterprise, this translates into maintaining or expanding markets, competing in terms of price and quality, securing sources of materials and labor, and so on. Sustainability is a dynamic concept in that enterprises must continually develop new products or services.

Of the various benefits a project is expected to produce, some are easily quantified (industrial output, volume of water, number of houses constructed), but others are more difficult to measure because they are of a qualitative nature. If a project delivers only some of these benefits, it must be assessed by attaching *relative weights* to the different services.

Another factor to consider in evaluating sustainability is the institutional capacity to sustain the delivery of services. That capacity depends on the quality and stability of staff, the adequacy and stability of financial resources for recurrent expenditures, coordination with other government agencies, and links to local community organizations and beneficiaries.

The success of a project may also be affected by its ability to mobilize the *support of* the central and local government, trade unions and business organizations, religious organizations, local community groups, and international organizations. But note that "political support" can be a mixed blessing because political alignments can shift and key officials can be reassigned, and thus a project strongly supported by one administration may quickly lose its support following a change of government or a reassignment of key figures. Projects that are able to maintain a low political profile may be more stable over time.

SUSTAINABLE DEVELOPMENT. Economists and international development agencies are frequently criticized for focusing on the sustainability of individual projects and ignoring the impacts of these projects on broader developmental objectives. As Anil Agarwal (Centre for Science and Development 1985:362) has pointed out in the case of India:

> Development can take place at the cost of the environment only up to a point. Beyond that point it will be like the foolish man who was trying to cut the very branch on which he was sitting. Development without concern for the environment can only be short-term development. In the long term, it can only be

anti-development and can go on only at the cost of enormous suffering, increased poverty and oppression. India may be rapidly approaching that point.

Ecologists are critical of the approach of most economists: "In a world where the economy's environment support systems are deteriorating, supply-side economics—with its overriding emphasis on production and near blind-faith in market forces—will lead to serious problems" (Brown and Shaw 1982:12, cited in Tisdell 1988:374). *The World Conservation Strategy* (1980; quoted in Tisdell 1988:373) defined conservation (sustainability) as "the management of the human use of the biosphere so that it may yield the greatest sustainable development to present generations while maintaining its potential to meet the needs and aspiration of future generations."

Ecologists say it is important to assess whether development strategies can sustain and reproduce the resource base on which they depend, as does society in general. Much of modern agriculture, they argue, obtains its increases in crop yields at the cost of environmental damage. The intensive cultivation of a single, high-yielding variety forces communities to depend on a narrower genetic base, which is likely to be more vulnerable to disease or to the effects of climatic change (Harlan 1977). According to Conway (1983:12, quoted in Tisdell 1988:375), the key to sustainability is to reduce the vulnerability of agricultural and other systems:

> Sustainability can be defined as the ability of a system to maintain productivity in spite of a major disturbance such as that caused by intensive (maintained) stresses or a large perturbation. . . . Satisfactory methods of measuring sustainability have still to be found, however. Lack of sustainability may be indicated by declining productivity but, equally, collapse may come suddenly and without warning.

Greater attention to ecological issues—such as the need to conserve the resource base, protect the broader ecosystem, maintain genetic variety, and develop systems that can survive intensive stress—would significantly affect how projects are evaluated and designed. Tisdell (1988) points out that a rigorous methodology for applying ecological criteria to project evaluation has not yet been developed—although a number of qualitative guidelines are available.

Even within a narrower sectoral framework, sustainability cannot be fully assessed at the level of an individual project. Any meaningful analysis must focus on the broader issues of *sustainable* development. First, if an experimental project is not achieving its objectives, perhaps it should be terminated and a different approach adopted in later projects. Such action may contribute to long-term sectoral development even though the pilot project is not successful.

Second, many social development projects encourage beneficiaries to participate in planning and implementation; and sometimes community organizations may decide to change the priorities defined in the original project plan. In the World Bank–assisted Lusaka Upgrading and Sites and Services Project in Zambia (Bamberger, Sanyal, and Valverde 1982), many community groups worked only half-heartedly on the planned drainage system, but several decided to organize other projects such as health clinics on their own initiative. Although the self-help component failed to contribute to the construction and maintenance of the drainage infrastructure, the creation of effective community organizations was important to the long-term development of the community.

Third, a project might achieve its specific objectives without contributing to sectoral development. For example, donor agencies often encourage countries to establish special project implementation units (PIUs) to ensure that their projects are effectively and speedily implemented. If such PIUs are able to offer more attractive salaries, are given licenses to import supplies and equipment, and are freed from many bureaucratic procedures, they often do complete high-quality pilot projects at considerable speed. In the process of achieving this short-term objective, however, the PIUs may disrupt normal planning and operational procedures and alienate the central and local government agencies whose support is essential for the long-term success and replication of the project. Thus they may make it almost impossible to replicate the project or keep it going after the support of the donor agency ends.

For the above reasons, it is important not only to assess the sustainability of particular projects but also to analyze the contribution to broader sectoral or national development goals.

## Factors Affecting Project Sustainability

The sustainability of any project is affected by four broad groups of factors: how the project is designed and implemented; how the project is organized; external factors operating at the local, national, and international levels; and the responses of intended and actual project beneficiaries.

## Project Design and Implementation

If the primary function of a project is to achieve precisely defined physical and economic objectives, the emphasis will be on speedy and cost-effective implementation, and not on institutional development or the creation of structures that can ensure the project will continue operating. In other cases, however, project objectives explicitly call for institutional development at the community and local government levels, and systems are proposed for generating the resources needed to cover recurrent costs.

One objective of the First Bangladesh Integrated Rural Development Project (see pages 202–6) was to increase food production as rapidly as possible. Therefore, short-term quantitative objectives were established that encouraged the implementing agencies to create the maximum number of cooperatives and to authorize as many loans as possible for the purchase of irrigation equipment. This action created a large number of weak and financially unsound cooperatives and jeopardized the long-term sustainability of the project.

Sustainability can also be adversely affected by wrong assumptions about labor availability, community responses to the project, assessments of community needs, the efficacy of different service delivery systems, and the short- and long-term effects of the provision of certain services. Many sustainability problems can be traced to *procurement*. Delays in obtaining equipment, approving contractors, or acquiring materials frequently lead to implementation delays, cost overruns, poor-quality services, or reduced accessibility for certain target groups.

In addition, sustainability can be affected by the *choice of implementation methods*. Decisions about the degree of beneficiary involvement in construction and other implementation activities can have an important effect on their later support (or lack of support) for the project. Choices must also be made concerning the procedures for participant selection and the distribution of benefits. Sometimes a more cost-effective method of participant selection (such as office interviews rather than house visits) can produce a bias against low-income or weaker groups and can again affect long-term support for the project.

## Project Organization

It is often difficult to decide which ministry or agency should oversee a project, what kinds of coordinating mechanisms should be established between agencies, and whether the project should be implemented through an existing department or through a specially created project-implementing agency. Because high priority is given to project implementation, many countries establish special management units to speed up project implementation. Frequently, these units are disbanded as soon as the physical implementation is completed, and no adequate organizational arrangements are made for the period of project operation. Instead, the newly implemented project is handed over to a line ministry or administrative agency without any of the necessary financial or staff support.

In addition, little attention is paid to the institutional arrangements needed to give beneficiaries a role in the planning and implementation of the project. The literature amply demonstrates the close tie between beneficiary involvement and successful implementation and sustainability (Bamberger and Shams 1990; Martin 1989; Moser 1989; Uphoff 1989). Norman Uphoff (1986:3–4) describes irrigation management as a sociotechnical process: "The benefits from irrigation are few unless the ultimate water users employ their own labor and capital in ways that make good use of available and anticipated land and water resources. It is the users who decide in the final analysis if the prices are 'right' and who judge the suitability of soils and physical structures for growing irrigated crops."

### External Factors

Sustainability is affected by a wide variety of *national and international factors* over which project planners and managers have very little control. The most notable of these are economic changes. A change in the international price of goods produced by the project or in the price of imported materials can seriously affect the profitability of projects. The oil crises beginning in the early 1970s illustrate just how severe the impacts can be. National economic policy changes—which are usually beyond the control of project managers—can suddenly lower the price at which outputs can be sold or the price that must be paid for materials or labor. Political events such as national or local elections or civil unrest can also affect projects. Government changes can rapidly erode or strengthen the base of support for a project—with significant effects on budgetary provisions, access to foreign exchange, or access to materials and equipment in short supply.

Natural phenomena such as droughts and flooding regularly affect output and the condition of roads, irrigation systems, and equipment, as illustrated by the Bangladesh Integrated Rural Development case study, among others. Bangladesh's good harvests encouraged loan repayment, but flooding destroyed those harvests, and the sinking water table made ineffectual large numbers of shallow tubewells and handpumps.

## The Response of Actual and Intended Beneficiaries

The social and political organization of rural communities can either facilitate or impede the creation of cooperatives and the organization of rural development programs. Take the case of Bangladesh, where political and economic power is concentrated in rural areas. Cooperatives and irrigation programs are difficult to promote since the wealthier farmers tend to band together or to undermine such programs—with the result that the associated projects are less accessible to low-income farmers (BRAC 1983). In contrast, the long tradition of community organization and self-help in Indonesia (*gotong royong*) has greatly facilitated the development of community-managed minor irrigation projects (Dilts and others 1989, summarized in Bamberger and Shams 1989:chap. 6) and self-help urban development programs (Bamberger and Shams 1990).

There is also considerable evidence that the traditional roles of the sexes create barriers to the full participation of women in many income-generating projects. Heyzer (1987) reports that Asian women tend to lose their traditional land-use rights during agricultural modernization. As the Grameen Bank and the Bangladesh Rural Advancement Committee (BRAC) programs have revealed, there are cultural barriers to the participation of Bangladeshi women in credit programs designed to promote small businesses. In India, organizations such as the Self-Employed Women's Association (SEWA) and the Working Women's Forum have demonstrated the cultural, legal, political, and economic problems facing Indian women seeking to participate in labor unions or to start their own small businesses.

## Designing a Study of Project Sustainability

Sustainability studies can be divided into two main types. The first is an in-depth study of the current sustainability of a single project. Its purpose is to identify factors likely to affect future sustainability and to ensure corrective actions will be taken to keep services flowing to the intended populations. The second is a comparative analysis. It draws some general lessons from different projects that can be used to improve the sustainability of future projects.

### *Developing a Conceptual Framework to Describe the Project and Its Environment*

The simple model in Chapter 3 (Figure 3-1) includes the main phases of project design, implementation, and operation, along with the main internal and external factors likely to affect sustainability. The central part of the figure shows the principal stages of project design and implementation (project concept and design, procurement of goods and services, implementation, and so on) and identifies some of the key assumptions and procedures at each stage that may affect sustainability. During project design, for example, a number of assumptions are made about the availability of labor, beneficiary responses to the services to be provided, and their response to the financial and organizational responsibilities they will be asked to bear. The upper part of the figure indicates how the project is organized and how this may affect sustainability. The lower section of the figure identifies some of the external events (political, social, and economic) affecting sustainability. The figure also shows how sustainability may be affected by the responses of intended and actual beneficiaries. A model of this kind can easily be developed for any kind of project and can serve as a checklist so that no important factors have been overlooked. It can also help focus discussions with project officials and other key informants on the factors likely to affect sustainability and on the possible causal relationships between internal and external factors.

Once the model has been developed, the following kinds of questions may be asked:

- To what extent were issues relating to sustainability specifically taken into consideration at each stage of project implementation?
- How did the implementation of each stage affect sustainability? What changes could have been made at each stage to have improved sustainability?
- What external factors are likely to have affected sustainability? How?

An OED assessment of the sustainability of education projects (World Bank 1989b) illustrates how a descriptive model of this kind can be expressed as a regression equation of the form

$$Y = f[\ I_1...I_{10},\ E_1...E_4\ ]$$

where $Y$ is an index of project sustainability (discussed below) and where the explanatory variables include internal ($I$) factors within the control of project management (adequacy of appraisal procedures, project design, initial funding, existing monitoring and evaluation, adequacy of planning and management, timeliness of procurement, flexibility of implementation procedures, effectiveness of technical assistance, adequacy of recurrent funding, and institutional support) and external ($E$) factors largely outside the control of project managers (level of government support, macroeconomic conditions, educational conditions, and level of policy commitment).[6]

## Defining Indicators of Project Sustainability

As the preceding discussion makes clear, sustainability is a multidimensional concept that cannot be defined in terms of a single variable. Table 6-2 proposes a sustainability checklist for most kinds of social development projects. Four groups of indicators are proposed. Group A consists of five indicators relating to the ability of the project to continue delivering the intended benefits or services: a *comparison of the actual and intended volume* (level) of each service (A-1); the *stability of service levels* over time (A-2); the *quality* of the services (A-3); beneficiary satisfaction (A-4); and the *distribution of benefits* among different economic or social groups (A-5). Table 6-3 illustrates the application of the Group A indicators to the First Integrated Rural Development Project in Bangladesh.

The second group of indicators (Group B) pertains to the maintenance of physical infrastructure and includes the condition of physical infrastructure (B-1) and of plant and equipment (B-2). To assess long-term sustainability, it is also necessary to determine whether adequate procedures and resources have been provided to ensure continued maintenance (B-3). For some kinds of projects (for example, irrigation and housing), it is also important to assess coordination with community organizations (B-4) and the extent to which beneficiaries are involved in project maintenance (B-5).

Group C indicators reflect the long-term institutional capacity of the executing agencies to sustain the project. These indicators include technical capacity and appropriate mandate of the operational agencies (C-1); stability of staff and budget of the operational agencies (C-2); adequacy of interagency coordination (C-3); adequacy of coordination with commu-

## Table 6-2.  An Index for Assessing Project Sustainability

| | Rating | | | | |
|---|---|---|---|---|---|
| | 1 | 2 | 3 | 4 | 5 |
| A. *Continued delivery of services and benefits* | | | | | |
| A-1  Volume/stability of actual and intended benefits | | | | | |
| A-2  Efficiency of service delivery | | | | | |
| A-3  Quality of services/benefits | | | | | |
| A-4  Satisfaction of beneficiaries | | | | | |
| A-5  Distribution of benefits among economic and social groups | | | | | |
| *Subtotal* | | | | | |
| | | | | | |
| B. *Maintenance of physical infrastructure* | | | | | |
| B-1  Condition of physical infrastructure | | | | | |
| B-2  Condition of plant and equipment | | | | | |
| B-3  Adequacy of maintenance procedures | | | | | |
| B-4  Efficiency of cost-recovery and adequacy of operating budget | | | | | |
| B-5  Beneficiary involvement in maintenance procedures | | | | | |
| *Subtotal* | | | | | |
| | | | | | |
| C. *Long-term institutional capacity* | | | | | |
| C-1  Capacity and mandate of the principal operating agencies | | | | | |
| C-2  Stability of staff and budget of operating agency | | | | | |
| C-3  Adequacy of interagency coordination | | | | | |
| C-4  Adequacy of coordination with community organizations and beneficiaries | | | | | |
| C-5  Flexibility and capacity to adapt project to changing circumstances | | | | | |
| *Subtotal* | | | | | |
| | | | | | |
| D. *Support from key stakeholders* | | | | | |
| D-1  Stability and strength of support from international agencies | | | | | |
| D-2  Stability and strength of support from national government | | | | | |
| D-3  Stability and strength of support from provincial and local government | | | | | |
| D-4  Stability and strength of support at the community level | | | | | |
| D-5  Ability of project to avoid becoming politically controversial | | | | | |
| *Subtotal* | | | | | |

*Note:* Rating code: 1=very poor; 2=poor; 3=average; 4=good; 5=very good.

**Table 6-3.** Application of Component A of the Sustainability Index (Continued Delivery of Services and Benefits) to the Rural Works Component of the First Bangladesh Rural Development Project

| Indicator | Sustainability Status of Rural Works Component | Ranking on 5-point scale |
|---|---|---|
| A-1, provision of services and stability over time | Most roads and drainage were provided. Only 70 percent of fish ponds. | 2.5 |
| A-2, efficiency of service delivery | Deterioration and underutilization of roads owing to poor location. Inefficient dredging of fish ponds. | 1.5 |
| A-3, quality of services | Many roads poorly built and maintained. Fish ponds badly excavated. | 2.0 |
| A-4, beneficiary satisfaction | Users of roads and fish ponds satisfied but complaints from other potential beneficiaries about poor location and monopoly by certain groups. | 3.0 |
| A-5, accessibility to intended low-income beneficiaries | Mainly private landowners who benefited from fish ponds. Access to roads limited by poor location. | 2.5 |

*Source:* Khan, Chowdhury, and others (1988:Table 5-3); Bamberger and Cheema (1990:chap 3).

nity organizations and beneficiaries (C-4); and flexibility and capacity to adapt (C-5).

For many projects, particularly large and highly visible ones, long-term sustainability often depends on the strength and stability of support at the international (D-1), national (D-2), provincial (D-3), and community levels (D-4). Changes of government or of policy can rapidly deplete the budget, cause conflicts with other agencies, reduce access to resources, and possibly cause key staff to leave. By its very nature, political support is highly volatile and must be constantly reassessed if the long-term prospects of a project are to be ascertained. Consequently, the final indicator (D-5) refers to the capacity of the project to develop a broad base of support and to avoid becoming politically controversial.

Box 6-1 summarizes a similar approach the OED uses to assess the sustainability of education projects. In this case, five sets of indicators are used: production of inputs, production of outputs, operational efficiency, qualitative aspects, and demonstration effects and spin-off activities. When applied to different kinds of projects in different countries, the indicators

Box 6-1.  Sustainability Indicators Used in the Assessment
of Educational Projects

| | Level of Measurement | | |
| --- | --- | --- | --- |
| *Indicator* | *Interval* | *Ordinal* | *Dichotomous (1–4 scale)* |
| 1. *Production of inputs* | | | |
|    Physical facilities | X | | |
|    Teachers | X | | |
|    Materials and equipment | X | | |
| 2. *Production of outputs* | | | |
|    Enrollment | X | | |
|    Graduates | X | | |
|    Placement of graduates | X | | |
|    Administrative services | | X | |
| 3. *Operational efficiency* | | | |
|    Teacher/student ratio | X | | |
|    Textbook/student ratio | X | | |
|    Retention rates | X | | |
|    Cost/efficiency | X | | |
|    Utilization rates | X | | |
| 4. *Qualitative aspects* | | | |
|    Relevance of curricula | | X | X |
|    Relevance of project | | X | X |
|    Project flexibility | | X | X |
|    Project adaptability | | X | X |
| 5. Demonstration effects and spin-off | | X | X |

*Source:* World Bank (1989b).

may need to be tailored to the specific characteristics of the project(s) being studied. The number of indicators for a particular component can also be adjusted to the objectives and priorities of each project. In a large transportation project where maintenance is a central concern, the number of indicators for Group B may be increased. If the project is to be implemented through a well-established agency, however, and no major institutional changes are envisaged, the number of Group C indicators might be reduced. If the indicators are applied to the assessment of industrial and commercial projects, other modifications may be required.[7]

Two points should be made about interpreting these indicators. First, the indicators are used to assess the extent to which the project is able to continue delivering its intended benefits. They do not suggest whether the original project design was, or is, economically or environmentally sound. A steel mill that continues to produce the intended output may be assessed as sustainable even though it may be producing some long-term environmental hazards. Second, different stakeholders will attach different priorities to different indicators. Thus, whereas one group may assess the project mainly in terms of its ability to maintain a certain level of benefits, another may be more concerned about the distribution of benefits between different economic groups, and a third may attach more weight to institutional development and the participation of beneficiaries in project management. The interpretation of the sustainability analysis depends on the weights to be given to each indicator, as discussed in the following section.

## Developing an Index of Project Sustainability

THE REESTIMATED ECONOMIC RATE OF RETURN AS AN INDICATOR OF SUS-TAINABILITY. The World Bank's Operations Evaluation Department has assessed sustainability of large numbers of projects by comparing their internal economic rate of return (IRR) at the time project implementation was completed with the reestimated IRR when the project had been operational for several years (World Bank 1986). If the reestimated IRR was greater than the IRR at the time of project completion, the project was classified as "sustained"; if the reestimated IRR was lower, the project was classified as "not sustained"; and if the two IRRs were similar or difficult to estimate, the project was classified as "sustainability uncertain."

Although IRR is a convenient indicator because of the overview it provides, it does not fully reflect project sustainability. One problem is that at the time of project completion many of the future costs and benefits have to be estimated with limited data. Thus, if it is found five years later that the reestimated IRR is lower than at the time of project completion, this might not indicate that the project performance has deteriorated but simply that the quality of the data has improved. Many of the economic parameters used to calculate conversion factors will also have changed, thus affecting the estimation of costs and benefits.

A more fundamental criticism is that the use of the IRR encourages evaluators to focus on short-term benefits, since those received early in the life of a project are more highly valued than those produced later. Tisdell (1988) points out that IRR calculations pay almost no attention to long-term environmental impacts since normal discount rates mean that long-term costs or benefits have almost no effect on the IRR. Dunu Roy (1985) cites the example of a social forestry project in India in which the eleven-year repayment period encouraged farmers to plant fast-growing eucalyptus, which cannot be used for fodder. Rates of return estimations have also been criticized for ignoring environmental impacts outside the project area (such as the drying up of dug wells as a result of the lowering of the water table produced by deep-well construction in irrigation projects).

ALTERNATIVE APPROACHES TO QUANTITATIVE ENVIRONMENTAL IMPACT ASSESSMENT. A number of recent studies have begun to discuss ways to incorporate environmental costs and benefits into project analysis (Ahmad, El Serafy, and Lutz 1989; Winpenny 1991; World Bank 1992e). Winpenny (1991:chap. 3) summarizes some analytical approaches used in industrial nations and assesses the potential applicability of each in developing countries. In addition to cost-benefit analysis and cost-effectiveness analysis he mentions:

- *Environmental benefit estimators.* "Total Economic Value" of environmental impacts is defined as the sum of "user benefits," "existence value" (pleasure derived from knowing that an amenity is available even to someone who does not use it), and "option value" (willingness to pay to conserve or have access to an amenity in the expectation that benefit may be derived from it at a later date).
- *The effect on production (EOP) approach.* An activity may affect the output, costs, or profitability of producers through its effect on the environment (for example, it may reduce the volume of fish caught). These costs are computed as EOP. These methods are intelligible and plausible and are widely used in assessing the costs of environmental degradation.
- *Preventive expenditure and replacement cost.* The value that people attribute to the environment is inferred from the amount they are prepared to pay to conserve or restore it. These methods, too, are intelligible and plausible.
- *Human capital approach.* People are considered units of economic capital, and the costs of environmental deterioration are assessed through

their impacts on labor productivity or educational performance (for example, reduced earnings due to ill health). The approach is used quite widely to assess the potential benefits of preventive or curative health care programs.
- *Hedonic methods.* The value that people place on environmental amenities (or on avoiding environmental problems) is inferred through the additional rent they are prepared to pay to live or work in a good environment. The methods are too sophisticated and complex to be widely usable.
- *The travel cost method.* The value people place on a good environment is inferred from the time and cost they are willing to pay to travel to it. This method is difficult to apply and interpret.
- *The contingent valuation method.* When behavior in response to environmental changes cannot be directly observed, value is inferred by asking people about their "willingness to pay" for environmental benefits or "willingness to accept" compensation for a loss of environmental quality. This approach could be applied in a number of areas such as changes in air and water quality, wildlife, and biodiversity.

THE USE OF A COMPOSITE INDEX. Table 6-2 shows how the twenty indicators can be converted into a simple sustainability index. A five-point rating scale (1 = very poor; 2 = poor; 3 = average; 4 = good, and 5 = very good) is used to assess the degree of sustainability of the project in terms of each indicator. The ratings for each item are added to calculate a sustainability score (maximum of 25) for each of the four components and a total score (maximum of 100) for the project. Table 6-3 illustrates how the indicators for Component A (continued delivery of services and benefits) could be applied to the assessment of the First Bangladesh Integrated Rural Development Project (the project is described later in this chapter).

Box 6-2 shows how the index was used to assess the degree of sustainability of an irrigation project in Viet Nam. Twenty-six senior government officials were asked to rate the project on each of the twenty indicators. The mean scores were Module A, 18.54 points; Module B, 15.0; Module C, 20.86; and Module D, 9.65. The mean total is 64.05 points when the four components are combined.

To use the index, the members of the assessment team must make judgments about how the project should be rated on each indicator. The degree of subjectivity can be reduced in the following ways:

---

**Box 6-2.  Comparing Judges' Ratings to Validate the Sustainability Index: The Tam Phoung Irrigation Project in Viet Nam**

In February-March 1989 the Economic Development Institute of the World Bank organized a seminar for senior officials from Viet Nam and Lao PDR on economic reforms and investment planning. A case study was prepared on the Tam Phoung Irrigation Project in the Mekong Delta in Viet Nam, and following a visit to the project the twenty-six seminar participants assessed the sustainability of the project using the sustainability index. The following indicators were computed: mode (most frequent rating) for each indicator; proportion of respondents selecting the modal indicator, average total score for each of the four components, standard deviation (S.D) for the mean score for each component, and standard deviation as a percentage of the mean score (mean deviation).

| Component | Mode | % Mode | Score (%) | Mean S.D. | S.D./Mean (%) |
|---|---|---|---|---|---|
| A. Service delivery | 3.5 | 50.0 | 18.54 | 2.88 | 15.5 |
| B. Maintenance | 4 | 60.7 | 15.0 | 1.53 | 10.2 |
| C. Institutional capacity | 3.5 | 69.0 | 20.86 | 1.91 | 9.1 |
| D. Political support | 5 | 73.0 | 9.65 | 0.69 | 7.2 |
| Total | 4 | 63.0 | 64.05 | — | — |

The results suggest a satisfactory degree of agreement among the twenty-six evaluators. First, for 15/18 of the indicators more than 50 percent of respondents selected the modal score and in 13/18 cases more than 60 percent selected this score. Second, none of the mean deviations are greater than 15.5 percent of the mean.

The findings suggest that the indicators can be understood and applied with a reasonable degree of reliability. It should be noted, however, that almost all participants gave scores of 3, 4, or 5 to all indicators, thus reducing the variability. The robustness of the index must be tested on projects where some components are operating less satisfactorily.

*Source:* Economic Development Institute Seminar on Project Planning and Implementation for Viet Nam and Lao PDR, February-March 1989, Ho Chi Minh City.

---

- Written guidelines should explain how each of the indicators is to be interpreted. Specific examples should be given showing how to decide which score to give. In some cases quantitative guidelines can be given. For example, where large numbers of units such as wells and pumps are being provided, the guidelines could indicate the percentage of units installed or still in operation, which would fall into each of the five rating categories on indicators A-1 and A-2, respectively. In some cases it is possible to include photographs or drawings to illustrate how the physical condition of roads, buildings, and irrigation channels should be rated.

- The index and guidelines should be tested on a sample of people familiar with the project to ensure the instructions are unambiguous and precise. The testing procedures are similar to those used for the development of attitude scales (see Chapter 10).
- The index should be applied independently by a number of people. Their ratings on each indicator should be compared, and if they differ significantly, the validity of the results should be reassessed. Box 6-2 illustrates how the procedure was applied to an irrigation project in Viet Nam. Two reliability tests were used. First, the proportion of respondents choosing the modal (most common) rating for each indicator was assessed. Second, the mean deviation score (the standard deviation as a proportion of the mean) was computed for the total scores for each of the four components. In both cases a reasonably satisfactory reliability score was obtained.
- Each judge should prepare a written report giving his or her ass ~ sment of each component and explaining how the ratings were arrive l at.

The index can be used to compare the sustainability of projects in two ways. First, arithmetic analysis can be used to compute sustainability scores for each major component (four components are presented in the sustainability index in Table 6-2 and five in the example given in Box 6-1). Projects can then be compared according to their scores on each component, and possibly on their total sustainability score. The arithmetic analysis makes it possible to (a) identify projects that are above or below the average for a component, (b) rank projects in terms of their total sustainability scores, and (c) determine how the performance on one component affects performance on other components.

Second, a *multivariate analysis* can be performed using the kind of model described earlier. Assuming that the dependent variable (an appropriate indicator of project sustainability) can be defined as an interval variable and that the explanatory variables can be adequately defined as interval or dichotomous variables, it is possible to compute regression coefficients to estimate the explanatory power of the independent variables in the equation.[8] In the OED assessment of the sustainability of education projects referred to earlier, it was possible to achieve $R^2$ greater than 0.6 using *output* as the sustainability indicator, up to 0.75 using *efficiency* as the indicator of sustainability, and over 0.85 using an aggregate sustainability index (see World Bank 1989b:Annex I, Tables 3 and 4).

POTENTIAL PROBLEMS IN THE USE AND INTERPRETATION OF THE SUSTAINABILITY INDEX. Despite its possible usefulness in comparing projects and assessing their long-term sustainability, the sustainability index has some methodological problems. To begin with, it is based mainly on the summation of ordinal (rankings on a 4- or 5-point scale in the previous examples) variables. Serious problems arise when such ordinal variables are used as *dependent variables* or as explanatory variables in regression analysis. Other problems arise when ordinal variables are combined to produce summative indices in the simple arithmetic analysis.

A second question concerns the *reliability* of such measures. The ratings are based on personal judgments, and the scale can only be used if there is a high degree of uniformity in how the ratings are applied by different people. Box 6-2 illustrates some of the reliability measures that can be used.

The *validity* of the scores may also be questioned. What does it mean to say that a project was given a score of 62 on the sustainability index? Should this be considered high or low, and how does it relate to the ability of the project to achieve its long-term objectives? To respond to this question, it is necessary to develop an acceptable reference or criterion against which the index score can be compared. Once the index has been applied to a number of projects it becomes possible to compare a particular project with scores obtained on other similar projects.

## Case Study: Sustainability of the First Integrated Rural Development Project in Bangladesh (RD-1)

### The Purpose and Methodology of the Case Study

The RD-1 study was one of three case studies prepared for a seminar on project sustainability in Bangladesh in 1987.[9] The case writers interviewed a sample of farmers (the intended beneficiaries), along with the agencies involved in project implementation and operation and with the officials responsible for the original project design. They also observed meetings of farmers and local government officials and assessed the condition of the pumps, wells, roads, and buildings.

### The Project and Its Objectives

RD-1 was an experimental project, both for the World Bank and for the newly independent nation of Bangladesh. It was appraised in 1974 and was approved as an IDA Credit in 1976. The original five-year implementation period was later extended to June 1984.

The objective was to develop a model of rural development that would focus on (a) investing in low-cost, short-gestation, production-oriented projects aimed at increasing agricultural production; (b) building and strengthening rural institutions to improve agricultural supporting services and to ensure an equitable supply of scarce agricultural inputs to the small farmers; and (c) creating employment for rural landless people. Existing rural institutions would also be improved so as to prevent the more prosperous farmers from dominating farm inputs and credits, promote more rapid expansion of high-yielding varieties of rainfed rice, increase the irrigated area, and create employment opportunities by reactivating the Rural Works Program.

The project covered 1.7 percent of the total area of Bangladesh and was intended to directly benefit 150,000 farm families (about 900,000 people). The project was located in three *upazilas* (districts) with a per capita income (US$70) about 30 percent below the national average. The main project components, which accounted for about 60 percent of the loan were as follows:

- *Rural works program* designed to generate about four million man-days of employment through the rehabilitation and construction of roads, reexcavation of abandoned fish ponds, construction of paved rural markets, and improvement of drainage channels.
- *Minor irrigation* designed to increase irrigated rice area from 39,000 acres to about 97,000 acres. The project provided funds for replacing existing oversized low-lift pumps (LLPs), procuring shallow tubewells (STWs), and hand tubewells (HTWs).
- The provision of short- and medium-term rural credit.

The other financially smaller components consisted of strengthening the operation of rural cooperatives, agricultural extension, livestock improvement, and the excavation of fish ponds.

*Assessing the Sustainability of the Project*

CONTINUED DELIVERY OF INTENDED BENEFITS. Five sets of indicators were used to assess the delivery of benefits. Each set was applied to the three main components: namely, minor irrigation, rural works, and thana facilities. The results for the rural works component are summarized in Table 6-3.

A-1: *Provision of services.* In the case of the *minor irrigation works*, the potential demand for low-lift pumps was overestimated. Furthermore, because of the groundwater conditions, shallow tubewells could not be used everywhere and many had to be replaced. At the same time, almost all the roads provided under the *rural works* program were completed. The only other component not completed was the excavation of fish ponds, which was 70 percent completed.

A-2: *Stability and continuity of services.* There was a rapid decline in the operation of the *minor irrigation* component because the groundwater characteristics had been assessed incorrectly. *Rural works* deteriorated rapidly because of the poor quality of construction and design.

A-3: *Quality of services.* Many locally assembled pumps were of poor quality. The quality of road construction and pond excavation was often poor owing to the lack of supervision.

A-4: *Beneficiary satisfaction* (no information available on this).

A-5: *Accessibility to intended low-income groups.* The project assumed that most of the beneficiaries would be small farmers with incomes below the subsistence level, but in fact the main beneficiaries of the irrigation project were the medium-size farmers (2.5–7.5 acres) and the upper end of the small-farmer group (1.0–2.5 acres). Few small farmers participated because the KSS (the farmers' cooperative society) had difficulty enrolling tenant farmers. Although 20 percent of the land was cultivated by sharecroppers, they operated only 5.2 percent of the project-financed tubewells, and many of the KSS-operated shallow tubewells were privately owned.[10]

Under the fish-pond excavation program, many private landowners were able to get their own private fish ponds excavated, even though the program was only intended for publicly owned fish ponds.

MAINTENANCE OF PHYSICAL INFRASTRUCTURE. There is evidence that much of the physical infrastructure and equipment is deteriorating. The construction and upgrading of roads was inadequately supervised and the quality of work was poor. During the early years, the condition of the roads, drainage channels, and rural markets declined greatly, partly because the thana councils did not have the financial resources to maintain them. Fish ponds also deteriorated, and there was not enough money to have them reexcavated. The number of inoperative STWs increased from 3 to 202. A number of factors contributed to the maintenance problems. First, the resources of the cooperatives were depleted by poor loan recovery rates. The fact that LLPs and DTWs were often privately owned also meant that the cooperatives had no incentive to maintain them. Also in the early years, the thana councils had limited financial resources and were not able to finance maintenance.

LONG-TERM INSTITUTIONAL CAPACITY. The keystone of the institutional framework of RD-1 was the two-tier cooperative system that organized village-based farmers' cooperatives (KSS) into upazila Central Cooperative Associations (UCCAs). Since the launching of RD-1, the number of KSS and membership in the project area have increased considerably. However, the KSS have had severe problems: many were too small to be economically viable; less than half of the project area farmers joined (making it extremely difficult to operate and maintain irrigation systems); the operating performance of most KSS was poor, and an increasing number were virtually inactive; and most of the cooperatives were not able to motivate members to make regular and voluntary savings deposits. Their institutional capacity declined further when they were unable to recover loans and maintain equipment.

The operation and maintenance of the physical infrastructure such as roads, markets, drainage, and buildings were entrusted to a number of agencies. However, the district councils and similar local agencies did not have adequate funds or the technical capacity to ensure maintenance. Originally fish ponds were supposed to be maintained by the pond cooperatives, but most of these ponds were never handed over to the cooperatives, and even those that were had such low yields that cooperatives did not have enough resources to undertake excavation.

A number of operations and maintenance problems were caused by the winding up of the project management unit set up to implement the project. The documents of ownership of certain facilities were not handed over to line agencies, with the result that no agency could make use of them. The residence-cum-office for block supervisors of agricultural extension is a case in point.

FACTORS AFFECTING PROJECT SUSTAINABILITY. Because of the political crisis in Bangladesh at the time the project was initiated, emphasis was placed on achieving numerical targets designed to have a maximum short-term impact on food production and employment. Consequently, there was pressure to expand the number of cooperatives at a pace that made it impossible to institute adequate educational processes and financial controls. As a result, irrigation equipment was distributed without following normal credit procedures, and no attention was paid to the fact that most cooperative members were being recruited from among higher-income farmers.

Design weaknesses, some of which were again due to the pressure to start the project, created further problems. Probably the most serious design problem had to do with the analysis of the water resources.

There were also some problems with the institutional arrangements used to implement and operate the project. The most serious ones related to the poor performance of the two-tier cooperative structure. The extreme economic disparities between the rich and poor was another contributing factor. Because economic and political power was concentrated in the hands of a small number of landowners and the mass of small farmers were virtually powerless, it would have been almost impossible to avoid some distortion of benefits in favor of the politically and economically powerful groups.

The project was also affected by severe flooding, and by the inability of the irrigation works to control the flooding. This caused serious setbacks in certain years.

## Recommended Reading

*General Reviews of Project Sustainability*

Honadle, George, and Gerry VanSant. 1985. *Implementation for Sustainability: Lessons from Integrated Rural Development.* West Hartford, Conn.: Kumarian Press.
Tisdell, Clem. 1988. "Sustainable Development: Differing Perspectives of Ecologists and Economists, and Relevance to LDCs." *World Development* 16(3):373–84.

Uphoff, Norman. 1986. "Improving International Irrigation Management with Farmer Participation: Getting the Process Right."

World Bank. 1990. *Annual Review of Evaluation Results*. Washington, D.C.: Operations Evaluation Department.

————. 1989. *Impact Evaluation Report: Sustainability of the First and Second Education Projects in Indonesia*. Washington, D.C.

### Case Studies

Al-Bazzaz, Mehdi. 1989. *Tunisia Second Urban Development Project*. EDI Case 605/025. Washington, D.C. World Bank.

Bamberger, Michael, and Shabbir Cheema. 1990. *Case Studies of Project Sustainability: Implications for Policy and Operations from Asian Experience*. Economic Development Institute Seminar Paper Series. Washington, D.C.: World Bank.

Centre for Science and Environment. 1985. *The State of India's Environment 1984–85: The Second Citizen's Report*. New Delhi.

Silas, Johan. 1988. "Community Participation and Urban Development: Issues and Experiences in Surabaya," paper presented at APDC/EDI seminar on "Community Participation and Project Management," Kuala Lumpur, July 1988. Summarized in Michael Bamberger and Khalid Shams (editors), 1989, *Community Participation in Project Management: The Asian Experience*. Kuala Lumpur: Asian and Pacific Development Centre.

## Notes

1. Some of the material for this and the following section are taken from Bamberger and Cheema (1990).

2. A project was defined as "sustained" if the reestimated economic rate of return five years after project operation had begun was greater than or equal to the IRR at the time of project completion.

3. It is well established that families at the "tail" of irrigation systems are the first to lose access to water if the system does not operate well (Uphoff 1989). See Cheema (1986) for a discussion of these issues as they relate to urban projects.

4. See Heaver (1988) for a discussion of the links between efficiency and accessibility of health services in India.

5. World Bank (1989b:ii). See Part Four for a detailed discussion of the indicators used to assess the sustainability of the First and Second World Bank Education Projects in Indonesia.

6. Adapted by the present authors. See World Bank (1989b:Sec. 6) for a description of the analytical procedures and a discussion of the principal findings.

7. The principal indicator of sustainability for industrial and commercial enterprises is their ability to remain profitable. This involves indicators such as the maintenance or expansion of markets, competitiveness in terms of prices and quality, and, in many cases, secure access to sources of materials and labor.

8. Ordinal-scale variables (such as a four-point ranking scale) will often be transformed into a set of dichotomous "dummy" variables.

9. This section is based on the case study prepared by Khan and others (1987). The seminar was organized in cooperation with the Bangladesh Public Administration Training Centre (PATC) for senior Bangladesh government officials in July 1987. The other cases covered an Agricultural University and a Universal Primary Education Project. All of the cases are described in Bamberger and Cheema (1990).

10. "The cooperative has little control over KSS irrigation groups who virtually behave like private irrigation groups. Thus in fact the cooperatives are not the owners of the STWs. Unless the village cooperatives succeed in asserting their ownership over irrigation equipment, the benefits of the cooperative irrigation cannot be reaped" (Khan and others 1987:86).

# 7

## Simple, Rapid, and Cost-Effective Ways to Assess Project Impacts

During the past ten years, simple, rapid, and economical (SRE) methods of assessing social programs have gained support in both governmental and nongovernmental organizations. The Agency for International Development, for example, has funded research in more than twelve nations in pursuit of rapid and inexpensive methods of detecting problems in service delivery, identifying their underlying causes, and resolving them. Initially, these methods were used mainly in rural development, where they were known as "rapid rural assessment" (RRA); now they are being applied in other social sectors. At the U.S. National Research Council, the Board on Science and Technology for International Development has funded investigations into rapid epidemiological procedures in several developing countries (Smith 1989). And the World Bank has applied beneficiary assessment to at least thirty projects in housing, education, health, electrification, and the development of small-scale enterprises (Salmen 1992). Evaluators of urban shelter programs have also used simple methods that produce easy-to-interpret information for assessing program impacts (Valadez 1984).

Many researchers prefer these methods to conventional evaluation methods not only because they are more cost-effective, but also because they can strengthen the participation of intended beneficiaries in the planning and management of projects and programs that will affect their lives (Marsden and Oakley 1990; Salmen 1987). Chambers (1991) argues that appraisal and the ownership of information are necessary to the empowerment of rural people. This chapter explains why and when such methods might be used for evaluating social programs.

## Justifying Simple and Rapid Methods

As discussed throughout this book, the duty of an evaluator is to provide managers with information that will help them maintain the quality of social programs and determine whether the programs are achieving their intended impacts. The evaluator must therefore avoid collecting information that is of no practical use, even if it means excluding details of interest to researchers. The evaluator should be goal-oriented and strive to produce analyses in a short period of time that can help managers perform their job. Chambers (1991) notes the importance of "optimal ignorance," which refers to the rigorous elimination of data that are not essential for decisionmaking. Experience has shown that even simple evaluations demand considerable effort. Often, the data collected for research purposes are never analyzed because the work would be costly and time-consuming. Therefore, the temptation to include additional variables in an evaluation instrument because they are of research interest should be resisted unless they are relevant to policymaking.

Chambers (1991:516–17) identifies four major weaknesses of conventional, quantitatively focused evaluation methods that justify a greater use of simpler, more rapid methods. First, project planners, and consequently evaluators, tend to place things before people. Their main concern is usually to construct a particular dam or road. Social scientists are only called in at a later stage to solve any "people problems" that are interfering with the successful completion of the project. Second, most evaluations neglect poorer people. Third, conventional evaluation methods have not been cost-effective. Finally, there is a concern about the ownership of the data. Whereas previously social evaluation was seen as a way to increase the outsider's understanding of the social reality of the project, knowledge is now considered by many researchers as a tool for developing and empowering the affected populations. The more people understand about their own social, economic, and political conditions and how these may be affected by the proposed project, the more power they have to control their own lives.

Evaluators should use methods that are appropriate to the investigation. Shortcuts should not be viewed as a "poor relation" to more "sophisticated methods," nor should they be thought of as expedient. The quality of data is as good as the competence of the evaluator performing the work. One should never assume that because a rapid assessment method has been selected less care or rigor is justified.

By keeping in mind the purpose of an evaluation, one can compare alternative investigation strategies and select the most appropriate ones. Three limiting factors almost always play a role in the selection of evaluation methods: time, money, and complexity. They can affect an evaluation design alone or in various combinations (see Table 7-1).

Time is a limiting factor when management needs an evaluation report within a specific time frame. Donors often require a midterm evaluation, while on other occasions a government administrator may need to report to his chief executive and may have only a small amount of time for preparing a report. And sometimes a condition of additional funding is that an assessment of the program's progress be performed up to that point in time.

Even though money may be plentiful and highly trained personnel may be available, the time constraint may prevent certain methods from being used, such as a large sampling of the population. Large data sets that need to be entered and cleaned also could not be used; nor could anthropological investigations, which can barely get into the field in three weeks, let alone carry out the investigation and analyze the data.

The second limiting factor is one that most investigators are familiar with—the supply of funds. Although there may be no time pressures and no lack of competent local staff, the evaluator will need to develop an evaluation strategy that can be implemented with the available funds. Often a simple, rapid method should be selected so that all work can be performed before the resources are exhausted. Although well-trained people may be available, they may not be affordable, and therefore less skilled individuals will have to be employed. Even if time is not a constraint, the evaluator will consume available funds with salaries and field expenses and not be able to support work beyond a short period of time.

An evaluation strategy calling for several interviewers and a large sample usually cannot be supported. However, a single anthropologist might be able to perform focus-group interviews or observe the participants. Firsthand observation may take a substantially longer period of time. Since there is no time limitation, this may be of no consequence.

**Table 7-1.  Matrix of Seven Constraints Affecting Evaluation Designs**

| *Constraints* | *Solutions* |
|---|---|
| Time | Use large, highly supervised teams; sophisticated support technology; resource-intensive methods; experienced, well-trained, educated personnel; short, highly focused data collection instrument. |
| Time, money | Use smaller data collection teams; minimal supervision; low technology; highly efficient methods with minimal resources requirements; experienced, well-trained, educated personnel; highly focused data collection instrument. |
| Time, complexity | Use small, highly supervised data collection teams; low technology; simple-to-use methods with minimal training requirements; available intelligent personnel; field practice to develop skills of data collectors; highly focused data collection instrument. |
| Time, money, complexity | Use small, minimally supervised data collection teams; low technology; methods that are simple to use with minimal training requirements; available intelligent personnel; minimal training of data collectors; highly focused data collection instrument; critical data only. |
| Money, complexity | Same solutions as in the preceding cell. |
| Complexity | Use small, highly supervised data collection teams; low technology; methods that are simple to use with minimal training requirements; available intelligent personnel; field practice to develop skills of data collectors; highly focused data collection instrument; critical data only. |
| Money | Use small, minimally supervised data collection teams; low technology; methods that are simple to use with minimal training requirements; experienced personnel requiring little additional training; highly focused data collection instrument; critical data only. |

One should also be cautious about trying to obtain additional funding. Extensions are often difficult to procure, either because no funds are available or because the manager has earmarked the funds for other priorities. Sometimes, because evaluations are seen as unnecessary or as being performed only to satisfy the donor's requirements, the work may receive only a small allocation.

The third limiting factor is the complexity of the evaluation design. Without enough well-trained personnel, anything other than a simple investigation is not likely to succeed, even though funds may be available and there are no time pressures. For example, even if the evaluator was to train, say, a team of data collectors in household sampling and interview techniques, it might be difficult to ensure that they will follow directions correctly and gather reliable information. In such circumstances an evaluator is well advised to use as few enumerators (or data collectors) as possible so they can be closely supervised. Although the data collection may take longer, the resulting information may be of much higher quality than what would be produced by a large group of poorly supervised data collectors.

On other occasions the complexity of an evaluation design may be constrained by the terrain of the project site. In dense jungle or mountain areas it may not be possible to provide logistical support for more than a few teams. In difficult logistical conditions the evaluation design should be kept simple and the team small.

The complexity of the evaluation design also affects the "ownership" of the data. The more complex the design and analysis, the more difficult it will be for beneficiaries to understand, control, and use the data. In many cases a more complex design will also reduce the level of involvement of the local evaluation unit in the planning and analysis of the evaluation, and control will pass to the outside consultant or foreign agency.

## Identifying Information Needs

The information collected during evaluations has to do with impacts, processes, diagnostics, and troubleshooting. As discussed in previous chapters, impact assessments determine whether programs have achieved their objectives, and process evaluations determine whether interventions are being performed adequately. Diagnostic evaluations also look at processes but are more concerned with the causes of problems. Troubleshooting helps managers anticipate and avoid problems.

To select an appropriate data collection method, the evaluator must determine both the purpose of the evaluation and the audience. The first ensures that an investigation is pertinent to program administration, and the second ensures that the information is conveyed in a manner that can be understood and used by a manager. These issues were discussed earlier and need not be elaborated further in this chapter.

Since evaluations have different functions, the methodologies will vary with the type of evaluation performed. Methodologies that measure whether an expected impact has occurred often use precise procedures that express results as numbers. The methods appropriate for these investigations are the same as those used in conventional hypothesis testing. After all, an impact assessment is a hypothesis test of whether a program resulted in an expected outcome. For example, programs that are expected to reach or exceed specific objectives such as a reduction in the infant mortality rate, an increase in the literacy rate, a higher proportion of households using potable water, a greater number of educated adults, and the like, are all proposing hypotheses that can be tested with pre- and posttest evaluation designs. The data required for these assessments must be collected by means of precise methods that measure specific variables.

Other evaluations are more concerned with formulating questions and thus have no clear or specific hypotheses to investigate. A manager may try to understand why the program does not function well and determine what action needs to be taken to improve it. In this case, he is looking for guidance and ideas.

## Types of Impact Information

Evaluation is a practical management activity. Although several conventional evaluation methods exist, an evaluator should never assume that they are the only ones available. The method selected should provide the required information within the existing constraints. And the questions investigated should not be chosen simply because the evaluator has a preference for a particular method. As obvious as this point may sound, this mistake is frequently made in the field. Many survey researchers prefer to use structured questionnaires only. Many anthropologists prefer participant observation.

A well-designed evaluation uses methods that address clearly formed and specific questions about a social program. A poorly conceived evaluation is one in which the planner develops questions to suit the methods he or she prefers and thus runs the risk of not investigating the dimensions of the program of vital interest to its managers.

We briefly discuss various types of information that may be considered in an evaluation. In all cases, the information may be either a direct or an indirect measure of a program variable such as an outcome. A direct measure is information that corresponds to the specific object or action under investigation. An indirect measure is information about another variable that is closely related to the variable under investigation and from which the value of the former variable can be inferred. For example, local food consumption in a community can be measured directly by observing food intake. It can also be estimated indirectly by observing food availability in markets or by noting the crops grown locally during a certain period of time. An increase in income can be measured directly by asking people or their employers for salary statistics. In low-income communities, individuals can also be ranked by an indirect indicator of income, such as the quality of their housing or of the building materials.

Whether direct or indirect approaches are used depends to some extent on the purpose of the evaluation and the intended audience. One should not assume that all evaluations require the same degree of rigor or amount of time. During impact assessment, administrators may require thorough, detailed, and precise information about the program. On other occasions— say, during troubleshooting—they may require less precise information for guiding their decisionmaking.

The seven types of information presented below illustrate a variety of styles that can be considered when designing an evaluation.

*Frequencies*

Measuring an impact or process often amounts to counting the number of times an event has occurred. The resulting information can be used to comment on individuals, families, institutions, or some other group. For each level of analysis in the project (that is, individual or group), one can report the frequency of the event. Policymakers are often interested in knowing the average occurrence during some unit of time (week, month, or year), the median value, or the most frequently occurring value (the mode); or they may want to develop some sense of variation among families or communities through a measure of dispersion, such as the standard deviation. For example, an evaluation of a program for controlling diarrheal disease in a community of twenty-three families may produce results of the following kind: after five years of water hygiene education, the average family tended to boil water 16 minutes (± 11 minutes) with a median of 20 minutes and a mode of 0 minutes. These results suggest wide variation in the success of the program. Although a substantial proportion of families took the precaution of boiling their water adequately, a similar proportion did not. In fact, the most frequent response was not to boil it at all.

Frequencies can be measured in several ways, one of which is direct observation. For example, the number of families participating in a self-help housing project can be counted through site visits. This approach can be time-consuming unless the tasks are divided among a team, in which case logistics and management problems will probably increase.

Another possibility would be to review the records of material suppliers for the project and to identify the number of families requesting their share of provisions. As in many systems, the data collector may be able to obtain information from them rapidly and may require little training to carry out this task. However, the accountant or recorder must be reliable. Information systems also have their start-up costs, some of which can be high. They may also be difficult to implement well and may require regular supervision.

A group judgment is yet another possibility. Here, the representatives of various key informant groups are gathered together and asked to reach a consensus on the number of families participating in the project. This approach is neither costly nor time-consuming. However, the coordinator must know something about managing focus groups or similar techniques. A locally respected individual who is able to gather the informants together also needs to be involved. In this format, the frequency of points of view can be tallied.

The frequency of particular responses of community members can also be counted. However, people may not be frank about their participation or they may not be frank about the participation of others. This could be a problem, as discussed in earlier chapters. Furthermore, the counting may be both time-consuming and expensive, depending on the number of individuals to be interviewed. If a representative sample of the community or of the project is required, the interviews could take a long time. In contrast, it may take very little time to interview a small sample of families that the evaluator intends to use for triangulation on other sources of data. In any case, interviews should be performed by trained individuals, but such people may not always be available.

## Measuring Adequacy

Earlier in this chapter we referred to the concept of "optimal ignorance." Often a great deal of effort is put into collecting information that is subsequently never used. Sometimes the data are too detailed for the purposes of the evaluation. Sometimes they can be used for investigating questions of scientific interest, but do not serve management's purposes. In health, population, water, and sanitation projects, for example, evaluators often measure the coverage of a service or intervention in the target communities. Population-based samples are taken to measure the proportion of individuals who have been vaccinated, use family planning methods, use well water, or have a functioning latrine. This information is often unnecessary. What they really need to know is whether a certain threshold of coverage in the population with an intervention has been reached. If coverage in the target population exceeds, say, 70 percent, then one can assume that the project is functioning adequately.

Educational programs may expect to train an adequately performing work force of health workers, agricultural workers, educators, and the like. Adequacy could be defined as "properly performing their technical activities 90 percent of the time." For this type of performance assessment, evaluators need to determine whether a standard has been reached. The degree to which it has exceeded or fallen below that standard may be irrelevant.

Lot quality assurance sampling (LQAS), discussed in Chapter 11, was developed to answer those very questions. The method is based on binomials and classifies communities as either adequately or inadequately covered. The advantage of using LQAS is that it only calls for small samples, which can be collected rapidly. Valadez (1991) used this technique to assess the national primary health care system of Costa Rica. He found that a sample of nineteen children was sufficient to correctly classify communities with coverage below 50 percent and yet keep the misclassification error to 7 percent or less.

Valadez also found that taking six observations of community health workers performing service delivery was sufficient to accurately identify 97 percent of the ones who adequately did their work (Valadez, Vargas, and Rivera 1988). LQAS is also useful for assessing the technical quality of the intervention. Recently, during the midterm evaluation of a public health program in Central America, program administrators needed to know whether the health workers they trained encouraged mothers to have their children vaccinated and whether they taught mothers to properly prepare and use oral rehydration therapy. A rapid three-day assessment using LQAS was carried out to determine whether health workers' performance in households was reaching program goals. The evaluator found that although health workers were well trained, they were not implementing interventions correctly in the households of the client population. They simply could not remember all the steps they had to follow. In this case, time and money were a severe constraint, and so the LQAS method provided the information required for program assessment.

Another way of determining adequacy is to ask the users of a program whether it is addressing their needs. This task can be quite time-consuming if the evaluators decide to interview a representative sample of families. If the objective of the assessment is to identify programmatic problems that concern users, it may be less important to know the exact number of individuals who take that position than to know a group agrees that a problem exists.

Feedback could be solicited from communities in several ways—by organizing a community forum, forming focus groups, balloting communities for their opinions, or conducting exit interviews concerning program facilities. In each case, the objective would be to obtain rapid community feedback rather than perform a conventional measurement.

Judgments based on clear decision rules are rapid and inexpensive, but may require the help of a well-trained person, at least at the beginning, to ensure that data collectors properly understand the information they need to collect and the procedures for doing so.

### Physical Traces

The old adage that "a picture is worth a thousand words" is particularly apt for evaluation activities. A photographic journal of a project site is a rapid means of collecting data that preserves information for depicting progress over time. The resulting data may be useful in any project in which environmental change, attendance, physical quality, or workmanship need to be considered.

At the very least, photographs can demonstrate a conclusion. They can also be used by expert judges who need to participate in the assessment but are unable to make a site visit. When Valadez (1985) asked a group of urban planners to assess an urban development project in thirty neighborhoods of Santiago, Chile, the experts were unable to visit the sites either because they lacked the money or had scheduling conflicts. Valadez took photographs of each site, making sure that he had one snapshot looking out from the center to each point of the compass and from each point of the compass toward the center at all locations. The experts met sometime later as a group and assessed all the photographs.

During a rapid assessment of conditions of health facilities in the Altiplano of Bolivia, one of the authors visited a district hospital to interview the district medical officer. While touring the facility, he noticed that not a single patient was assigned to a bed. In further interviews, he learned that not a single patient had visited the clinic in weeks. Such information is so strong that no other formal measure is necessary.

Webb and his associates (1966) have compiled a compendium of methods for measuring variables using physical traces. It contains additional suggestions on the use of environmental information.

### Community and Individual Response

Many social sectors promote community participation in programs. In health and population programs, in particular, disease cannot be prevented unless individuals change their own behavior and thereby reduce their own risk. In education and regional development, individual participation is also encouraged by having people become the promoters as well as users of services or interventions, or by supplying labor for a task.

As already mentioned, community meetings and focus groups containing key informants can produce valuable information about community attitudes. Other rapid measures may be feasible where local residents and community groups have been encouraged to participate in the construction of health posts, say, knowing that the number of individuals actually participating is less important than knowing whether the health facility exists and is usable. In a sense, all that the evaluator needs to know is that a consensus was reached among a group of people who successfully participated in and finished a task. In Valadez's (1984) regional development project near Santiago, Chile, the evaluators for one part of the study wanted to identify enclaves in which residents were building communally owned plazas. The extent of the participation was less important than determining whether the enclaves had organized themselves to perform the task throughout the city. Therefore, the proportion of finished plazas was a better indicator of the project's success than their number.

In another example, Valadez (Valadez and others 1987) visited a mothers' club in a community on the Haitian border to inquire about the health status of the children. No health facility existed; therefore, health events were not formally recorded. However, the members of the community women's club were excellent reporters of their own health status. As a group, they remembered the deaths of each other's infants and of other women. They were critical of the local health worker, who did not visit their village, and complained about the lack of water and locally available drugs. Since each mother was present to confirm or disagree with the opinions of the others, it was possible to arrive at credible conclusions. The evaluator in this case had to ensure that he developed an open, nonthreatening atmosphere in which he was enthusiastically attempting to solicit the opinions of the people present. The evaluator's objective was to ask the people present the same question and to reinforce disagreement among them as much as he reinforced consensus. In all cases, however, it was vital to preserve a nonthreatening environment.

Another means of systematically acquiring information that also uses the oral responses of individuals has been used in public health programs for several years—the verbal autopsy. Because understanding the determinants of mortality rates is fundamental to many public health programs, obtaining a reliable measure of mortality and causes of death is central to many program evaluations. However, deaths are not always systematically recorded in communities. Therefore, rates can be underestimated or attributed to the wrong causes.

Verbal autopsies assume that mothers or key individuals in the household will remember sentinel events, such as the death of a child or spouse, and will be able to describe the person's basic symptoms up to the time of death. A verbal autopsy is a structured interview in which questions have been developed with yes/no responses. If a response is a yes, then another set of questions, arranged in the form of a tree, is considered in order to eliminate progressively the possible causes of death. The main concern when using verbal autopsies is to classify and count vital events accurately. Detail is less important than the accurate identification of broad categories. This logic may also apply to other social programs in which sentinel events occur (Gray, Smith, and Barss 1990).

## Balancing Time, Cost, and Complexity

Program evaluations are greatly affected by the time, cost, and complexity involved, but the tradeoffs between these factors can be difficult to determine. Table 7-2 contains a matrix of the three basic elements of any evaluation. It shows, first, that evaluations either address questions that have already been developed or identify questions that should be answered. Typically, the former category of questions pertain to whether specific impacts occurred and whether activities are being performed as planned. In the second case, the task is to identify or formulate the proper questions to investigate. This is what happens in a process evaluation in which the manager tries to understand why problems occurred, or tries to perform troubleshooting by identifying any potential problem before it affects the viability of the program.

Second, Table 7-2 shows the methods themselves. Each of the methods has been described at least once in this book.

Third are the constraints themselves: availability of time, money, and trained personnel. Each constraint is sufficient to eliminate a method from consideration. Suppose that a program has adequate funding but that personnel training has only begun. Here the methods selected must be ones that ensure reliable data will be collected. If time is also limited, then the methods must be simple and rapid. If money is yet another constraint, then some thought must be given to appropriate evaluation technology. Each of the constraints, either alone or in combination, has unique effects, as briefly discussed below.

TIME. Many a manager has experienced a need for immediate feedback, If time is the only constraint, then any method that a relatively sophisticated data collector can handle could be an appropriate selection—whether it consists of using archival information and rapid sampling techniques, interviewing key informants, managing focus groups and community fora, taking photographic surveys, looking for physical evidence, performing systems analyses, operating simulations, or reading automatic mechanical counters. Some of these methods are expensive to use, and some demand a fairly high level of education. But if money or personnel are not an issue, this need not be a concern.

COST. When both money and time are in short supply, a few of these methods can be eliminated, automatic counters (water meters, computer information systems) being one. Unless they already exist, such devices are expensive to purchase and to maintain.

## Table 7-2. Matrix of Seven Constraints Affecting Evaluation Designs and Methods to Use

| | Method | |
| --- | --- | --- |
| Constraint | Assessing Impacts and Processes | Problem Identification |
| Time | A, AC, CS, K, L, PS, PT, S, V | A, CF, F, K, S, SA, V |
| Time, money | A, CS, K, L, PS, PT, S, V | A, CF, F, K, S, SA, V |
| Time, complexity | AC, CS, L, PS, PT, S | CF |
| Time, money, complexity | CS, L, PS, PT, S | CF, S |
| Money, complexity | CS, L, PS, PT, S | CF, S |
| Complexity | CS, L, PS, PT, S | CF, S |
| Money | A, C, CS, K, L, PO, PS, PT, V | A, CF, F, PO, S, SA, V |

*Note:* A= archives, AC= automatic counter, C = case study, CF = community forum, CS = cluster sample, F = focus group, K = key informant, L = LQAS, PO = participant observation, PS = photographic survey, PT = physical trace, S = simulation, SA = systems analysis, V = verbal autopsy.

Most of the techniques considered here can only be used by trained personnel. With sufficient time, an anthropologist placed in a community can produce credible participant observational information. Even when time is a constraint, there are many other robust approaches for collecting data. If information systems have been established and maintained, archival information is the first obvious source to consult. Even if record systems are in disarray, an experienced data collector or researcher could sort his or her way through libraries or record rooms to find the information needed to respond to a manager's inquiry.

Most group and interview techniques can also be used, the more complex of which involve key informant interviews and managing focus groups. Although they do not produce quantitative information, they can be useful for assessing consensus in communities and identifying further problems. Focus groups need a trained individual who can handle group dynamics and who has the ability to prevent anyone from dominating the setting in a diplomatic way.

Structured interviews would be desirable, if experienced personnel are available. If they are not, many problems can arise, as already mentioned. The interviewer may not read or deliver the question properly, or may prejudice the response by conveying the impression that there is a preferred response.

COMPLEXITY. The lack of trained or educated personnel is a particularly powerful constraint. It can be risky to ask inexperienced individuals to review existing archives such as record systems, libraries, ledgers, censuses, and the like. Unless data collectors regularly read and write and use numbers, they may search for and record unreliable information. For similar reasons, the evaluator may be unable to ask personnel to interview key informants, to manage focus groups, or to use verbal autopsy techniques.

Cluster samples could still be used since they are relatively easy to collect. The most complex task for a data collector is to select a random starting point for the first observation. The World Health Organization has developed a method of doing so, however, so that even this step can now be reliably performed by a person with little training.

Simulation techniques might also be considered for this task. Simulations create an artificial environment in which participants are likely to behave as though they were in a natural setting. Some project supervisors have used this approach to assess teaching techniques or the performance of local health workers or teachers. Simulations can also be used to determine whether participants are using the proper technique for preparing an oral rehydration solution, constructing sanitation systems, preparing soil, and the like. The great advantage of simulations is that they require few data collectors, and most of the effort consists of developing the simulation itself.

A community forum is another method that can rapidly produce information with high face value. The technical expertise of data collectors may be less important when using this technique than it is to ensure that the person is respected in the community and has certain social skills. If an agenda for a community forum is prepared well in advance by the evaluator, and basic rules are explained to the moderator to ensure that all participants contribute to the forum, this method may yield the information a manager needs to assess the program or to perform troubleshooting. These meetings can take on a momentum of their own to a point where the moderator merely needs to play a note-taking role.

The tradeoffs between these three constraints are not always obvious. As Table 7-2 suggests, however, the availability of personnel can be more constraining than a time limit or the lack of money, which can sometimes be overcome through the efficiency and imagination of the field workers. Without appropriate personnel, even a sophisticated and elegant methodology will lose its force.

## Simplified Evaluation Designs

As already pointed out, it is important to use control groups and to control for confounding variables through evaluation designs, but such control is not always possible. In such cases, the evaluation design may have to be simplified. It may be necessary to eliminate control observations, take information at fewer points in time, or collect information on fewer variables. Although these simplifications may weaken the evaluation design, the information obtained may still ensure rational decisionmaking.

When evaluation designs are too detailed to implement, a careful and thoughtful appraisal should be performed to anticipate the risks of eliminating controls. Often the personnel associated with a program know enough about the conditions that exist in the host country to help the evaluator determine whether the threats to validity discussed in earlier chapters need to be considered in the current evaluation. For example, other programs may interact with one's own program and thereby produce an impact that should not be attributable to that program alone. However, it may not be essential for the manager to know about this interaction at a particular point in the program cycle. He may be more concerned with determining whether outputs are being delivered on schedule and anticipating problems that could undermine the program.

Knowing the impacts that are due to the program alone rather than to such interactions may also be less important to policymakers. The fact that a successful outcome occurred may be the important finding for them. Ultimately, the most important goal for program evaluation may be to promote national development and ensure that well-managed programs are in operation.

## Using Triangulation to Strengthen Reliability and Validity

The degree of confidence in the findings of rapid assessment methods can be greatly increased by comparing estimates obtained from different methods of data collection. The systematic use and comparison of independent data collection methods is known as "triangulation" (Denzin 1978; Ianni and Orr 1979). Here, the evaluator assesses the potential biases in particular methods of data collection and other independent methods that are likely to offset these biases. For example, estimates of household income obtained from direct questions may tend to underestimate income either because respondents do not wish to admit they have illegal or socially disapproved sources of income, or because the respondent may be unaware of, or forget to report, some of the many informal sources of income received by many families. This particular bias could be offset by direct observation (in the street or in the house), by asking families to keep a diary or by more intensive contact with the families through participant observation.

At the same time, one should not rely exclusively on direct observation or on in-depth information from a small number of households because the sample of respondents or observations may be biased. In this case, a small but carefully selected random sample of households could greatly strengthen the reliability and validity of the data.

The effective use of triangulation must satisfy the following conditions. First, the potential biases of each method must be identified. Second, other methods that do not share the same biases must be selected and used. Third, the different methods must be independent of each other so as to provide independent estimates. Fourth, procedures must be established for comparing the estimates obtained through different methods and for explaining any observed differences. To do so, it may be necessary to allocate time and resources to further fieldwork, to help reconcile the differences. While it is interesting to know that participant observation gave a higher estimated household income than did surveys, it is much more useful to be able to explain why this difference occurred and to provide a better estimate of true income that combines both sources of data.

## Recommended Reading

Chambers, Robert. 1991. "Shortcut and Participatory Methods for Gaining Social Information for Projects." In Michael Cernea, ed., *Putting People First: Sociological Variables in Rural Development*. 2d ed. New York: Oxford University Press.

Ianni, Francis, and Margaret Terry Orr. 1979. "Toward a Rapprochement of Quantitative and Qualitative Methodologies," In *Methods in Evaluation Research*. Beverly Hills, Calif.: Sage.

Ingersoll, Jasper. 1990. "Social Analysis in AID and the World Bank." In Kurt Finsterbusch, Jasper Ingersoll, and Lynn Llewellyn, eds., *Methods for Social Analysis in Developing Countries*. Social Impact Assessment Series 17. San Francisco: Westview Press.

Miles, M., and A. M. Huberman, eds. 1984. *Qualitative Data Analysis: A Sourcebook of New Methods*. Beverly Hills, Calif.: Sage.

Scrimshaw, Susan, and Elena Hurtado. 1987. *Rapid Assessment Procedures for Nutrition and Primary Health Care: Anthropological Approaches to Improving Program Effectiveness*. Tokyo: United Nations University.

# 8

## Quasi-Experimental Designs for Estimating the Size of Project Impacts

Despite the fact that most international development assistance has long been committed to improving the *long-term* economic and social conditions of program beneficiaries and that organizations such as the Operations Evaluation Department (OED) of the World Bank have been evaluating project impacts at least since the late 1970s, the primary concern of governments and donor agencies until recently was the *short- and medium-term* aspects of *design* and *implementation* (see Chapter 6). Now, however, more attention is being given to the long-term effects of development assistance: whether the investments have achieved their intended impacts and whether they have benefited the intended target groups. This shift is particularly evident in the growing concern with long-term environmental impacts, the involuntary resettlement that takes place during the construction of power projects and irrigation schemes, the impact of development assistance on the poor in general and on poor women in particular, the decrease in HIV/AIDS prevalence, and the sustainability of development programs. The efficiency of development portfolio management is another focus of attention.[1]

## Assessing the Impacts of Development Projects

To deal with these issues, governments and donor agencies need to know more about the impacts of development assistance, especially where the poor and vulnerable are concerned. Some are already taking measures to collect such information. The World Bank, for example, conducts evaluation studies to assess the extent to which resettled populations are at least as well off after resettlement as they were before.

To respond adequately to concerns about the impacts of development programs it is necessary to determine (a) whether the desired social and economic changes have occurred in the intended target populations, (b) the extent to which these changes can be attributed to the development projects rather than to other independent factors (such as general changes in the economic environment or the effects of other programs or policies), and (c) the direct and indirect impacts on other population groups.

According to much of the evaluation literature, these kinds of assessments should use a *randomized evaluation design* (Boruch and Wothke 1985) or a *quasi-experimental (QE) design* (Cook and Campbell 1979; Rossi and Freeman 1993). In practice, however, few major development projects have followed a "methodologically rigorous" quasi-experimental design. Indeed, a growing body of researchers would argue that these designs are unrealistically complex, slow, and expensive, and that there are more rapid and economical ways of performing such assessments capable of providing all the essential information policymakers, planners, and managers might need.

In this chapter we examine current views about the practical utility of the conventional QE designs for evaluating project impacts. We discuss the rationale for quasi experimentation, the main QE designs, and the way they have been used in developing countries. We examine ten QE designs that the literature would classify as "methodologically robust" and three widely used designs that are simpler and more economical to use, but methodologically "less robust" because they do not control for some of the major factors likely to affect the validity of the findings (Table 8-1).

These simpler and more economical designs offer innovative solutions to the problem of how to integrate quantitative and qualitative techniques so as to provide the greatest degree of methodological rigor possible in real-life situations. In particular, they try to compensate for the lack of baseline data on the characteristics of project beneficiaries and control groups before the project began.

## Table 8-1. Thirteen Impact Evaluation Designs Classified into Methodologically Robust Quasi-Experimental Designs and Simpler and More Economical Designs

---

*Methodologically robust quasi-experimental designs*

1. Pretest and posttest on project and control groups: the basic quasi-experimental (QE) design.
2. Partitioning variations in the intensity of an intervention: basic QE design but with multiple intervention groups.
3. Controlling for the influence of multiple interventions on outcomes: basic QE design but with additional groups to represent nonproject interventions.
4. Nonequivalent control group with multiple pretests: extending basic QE design to include multiple pretest observations.
5. Nonequivalent control group with multiple pretests and posttests.
6. Controlling for test-intervention interactions: adding control and intervention groups to basic QE design.
7. Controlling for selection effects: multiple levels of intervention and control groups.
8. Controlling for historical effects: 2 pre-and posttest measurements on intervention and control groups.
9. Interrupted time-series analysis with a nonequivalent control group.
10. Interrupted time-series analysis without a control group.[a]

*Simpler and more economical designs*

11. Comparison of project group before and after the project intervention without a control group.
12. Ex-post comparison of project and control groups without a pretest.
13. Pretest and posttest on experimental group combined with ex-post comparison of project and control groups.

---

a. This could be considered a less robust design as it does not include a control group. However, if sufficient observation points are included, it is often possible to use econometric or multivariate analysis to provide a reasonable degree of control.

Like other designs, these simpler ones have their strengths and their limitations. They can certainly answer many questions of concern to policymakers and planners, but in some cases a QE design is still more appropriate, especially where information is required about the impacts of projects on nonbeneficiary groups, or about the precise costs and benefits of alternative intervention strategies. Nevertheless, the simpler designs, particularly when they use multiple surveys of different groups and combine quantitative and qualitative methods, can provide most of the information policymakers and planners need for their decisionmaking.

Numerous evaluations are cited to show that quasi-experimental designs are in fact quite widely used, especially for questions concerning education, population, and health. In most cases they are used where the evaluation design is relatively simple, with a limited number of clearly defined treatments, and some easily measurable impact indicators. However, impact evaluations have also been used with more complex projects, three of which are described here: the West Africa River Blindness Control Program, the EDURURAL Primary Education Program in Northeast Brazil, and three components of the Bolivian Social Investment Fund.

As this chapter explains, simpler and more economical evaluation designs are quite satisfactory for most purposes, but in certain situations a more rigorous quasi-experimental design may be the only way to obtain the necessary information. Although it may take some ingenuity to apply the QE designs to many real-life situations, there is evidence to show that they can be used and can produce policy and planning information that justifies the investment of money and time.

## Using Quasi-Experimental Designs in Evaluating Social Development Programs

Quasi-experimental designs assess the impacts of project interventions by measuring the changes that have taken place in the social and economic conditions of project target groups and by systematically isolating the effects of other factors (other projects; changing social, economic, and political conditions; climatic and other natural changes, and so on) that might have contributed to the observed changes. A QE design can be used to assess the overall impact of projects on target groups, identify the groups that have been most and least affected, and identify the inputs that produce the greatest impact at the lowest cost. The QE design can also provide information on the interaction between project interventions, beneficiary characteristics, and external factors, and the part they play in the impact of a project.

QE designs allow the evaluator to observe not only the group in which the intervention has been introduced, but also a control group. Pre- and post observations are taken in both groups. The assumption is that other unknown and unexplained factors, in addition to the interventions, may also contribute to changes in the project area. In a well-designed and executed evaluation, the control group detects and adjusts for changes that are unrelated to the project, while the intervention group detects changes due to the project. Therefore, changes in the intervention group minus those in the control group should reveal impacts attributable only to the intervention.

Of course, in experiments in the natural sciences individuals are randomly assigned to intervention and control groups. In most QE assessments of development projects, individuals are assigned to groups on the basis of operational selection criteria (such as geographical location, low income, malnutrition, female-headed household, or lack of assets). Thus, the two groups will not have the same, or even very similar characteristics. QE designs therefore use additional "controls" to help evaluators distinguish between effects due to an intervention and those that are due to factors unrelated to the project.

THE MAIN DISADVANTAGES OF QE DESIGNS. Whether the QE design is useful when the "intervention" being evaluated is a development project is a subject of considerable debate. First, because observations are taken before and after the intervention, many evaluators complain that QE designs take too much time to arrive at a judgment about the impact of an intervention. Although in some cases, such as population programs, these costs and delays are considered worthwhile, in others, such as agricultural programs, they are sometimes said to be unjustified. Second, QE designs can be quite complex and may require multiple control and intervention groups in order to capture project effects. Therefore, considerable expertise may be needed to design the evaluation and to analyze and interpret the results. Third, even though observations are taken before and after, some QE results may remain open to alternative explanations, because when the client population is nonrandomly assigned to either receive or not receive an intervention, it can be argued that the differences between intervention and control groups, rather than the intervention itself, may explain an impact. The interpretation of results is further complicated by external events such as natural disasters, changing employment opportunities, election campaigns, and projects organized by other agencies—all of which may have different effects in project and control areas. Another complaint of planners is that the results of a project in one location may not be applicable to other locations.

Researchers who have worked in the agriculture and rural development sectors also cite the very expensive, and largely unsuccessful, attempts to introduce large-scale and rigorous impact evaluations in the 1970s. In a number of countries, of which Nigeria is a prime example, large farm-systems research programs were set up to provide a solid empirical basis for evaluating the economic and social impacts of agricultural investments. While huge amounts of data were generated over many years and at great expense, in the opinion of many experts these efforts produced almost no useful results. One of the biggest problems was that it was virtually impossible to obtain reliable estimates of farm income.

In practice, a combination of financial, administrative, technical, and organizational factors have limited the use of the methodologically more robust QE designs in the evaluation of most major social development projects. Recently, a World Bank task force report concluded that owing to data limitations, budgetary constraints, and local research capacity, it is seldom possible to use the more robust (and more expensive and time-consuming) evaluation designs in assessing project impacts.[2] Furthermore, the simpler and more economical designs can usually provide the information required by operational staff and policymakers. In most countries and sectors, there is relatively little demand for the more sophisticated kinds of information generated by the robust evaluation designs. The Operations Evaluation Department of the World Bank has conducted some sixty impact evaluations of Bank-financed projects, mainly in the fields of agriculture, irrigation, and education.[3] All of these studies used one of the three simpler and more economical evaluation designs (Designs 11–13) described below. Three examples are provided to illustrate these evaluations.[4]

The authors of all of these studies were fully aware of the limitations of the existing data sources and made every effort to strengthen the data base through the use of innovative, multimethod designs. Maximum use was made of existing data sets such as national censuses, state or national migration surveys, satellite images, land sale records, and consumer price surveys, specially commissioned tracer studies (on families who did not move or who left the project); and interviews with key informants such as local officials, community leaders, and religious leaders. OED emphasizes the importance of involving beneficiaries in all stages of the evaluation and was one of the first parts of the World Bank to introduce beneficiary assessment techniques.

THE CASE FOR QE DESIGNS. The arguments for and against the use of QE designs are examined in greater detail later in this chapter. The important point to note here is that simpler and more economical designs are usually unable to assess the impact of projects on nonbeneficiary groups (such as families who were not resettled or who did not remain in squatter upgrading housing programs). Because these excluded groups are often the poorest and most vulnerable in society, this lack of information makes it difficult to fully assess project impacts on all affected population groups.

Also, the simpler designs provide little information about the extent to which changes can be attributed to the project, which project components are the most and least effective, and how project components interact with beneficiary characteristics. Without this information, it is more difficult to improve the cost-effectiveness and efficiency of future project design. In many cases, however, these kinds of problems can be overcome in part by in-depth case studies and technical studies.

The extent to which these limitations would justify the additional investments of time, money, and human resources required for a QE design will depend on the individual case.

## Sectoral Differences in the Use of QE Designs

Attitudes toward the use of QE designs vary considerably from one sector to another. Evaluation practitioners in the fields of rural development, agriculture, and to a large extent housing and urban development make little use of QE designs (and often claim that these methods are not applicable in developing countries). The designs are frequently used, however, in the fields of health, nutrition, population, water supply, sanitation, and education.

A case in point is an assessment of a population program in Barbados, which had developed contraceptive counseling strategies to delay second pregnancies (Bertrand and others 1986). In Colombia, QE was used to determine whether a combined delivery of antiparasitic drugs and contraceptives, in comparison with the contraceptive alone, increased contraceptive acceptance (Gomez 1985). And in Peru, the country's Population Council (1986) used QE to identify the optimal number of doctor's visits to forty slum clinics in Lima to insert IUDs, deliver gynecological services, and treat contraceptive side effects.

QE has also been frequently used by educators and public health agencies. During 1979 to 1981, for example, the Mit Abu El Kom rural reconstruction project in Egypt used a QE design to determine whether improved living conditions contributed to increased awareness of the health implications of better sanitation among project recipients, and to assess whether beneficiaries and nonparticipants differed in their final attitudes and behavior toward the health project (Weidner, Nosseir, and Hughes 1985).

In Colombia, QE helped researchers determine whether the earnings of trainees increased after they participated in a national in-service training program (Jimenez, Kugler, and Horn 1989); and in Nicaragua, QE demonstrated that radio-based mathematics instruction was an effective educational method (Searle and others 1978).

Although housing projects are often considered too large and complex for a quasi-experimental approach, it has been successfully used in a number of such cases. In Chile, during the early 1970s, the designers of a new suburb in Santiago used a QE to investigate whether social participation could be enhanced through architectural designs (Valadez 1984). In El Salvador, large-scale QE designs were used to evaluate sites and services housing projects (Bamberger, Gonzalez-Polio, and Sae-Hau 1982), and in the Philippines to evaluate squatter upgrading projects (Philippine National Housing Authority 1979a, 1979b, 1980, 1981).

Health professionals have been among the largest group of QE users, perhaps because of the laboratory training of many health specialists or the large-scale social experiments designed by health professionals, such as the Salk Vaccine Field Test of 1954 (Meier 1978). In a more conventional use of experimental techniques in developing countries, the Egyptian Ministry of Health compared the benefits of three oral rehydration salt protocols to assess their effect on mortality (Kielman and others 1985). Another QE revealed that the repetitive training of mothers, health providers, and pharmacists improves the ability of mothers to manage their children's diarrhea episodes (Goma and others 1988; Kielman, Nagaty, and Ajello 1986).

In the Philippines, the results of a QE demonstrated that four of several interventions in a comprehensive health education program exhibited the greatest community acceptance. These interventions consisted of purifying drinking water, improving kitchen sanitation, consuming food from kitchen gardens, and storing limited quantities of food (Hill, Woods, and Dorsey 1988).

Whenever policymakers want to use QE to compare the benefit of a new technology with that of a traditional one, they need to pay particularly close attention to the timing of the before and after studies. It takes time for users to become accustomed to, and to accept a new technology. Consequently, the ex-post study should not be conducted too soon. At the same time, if the ex-post study is delayed too long, the control group is likely to have begun using the new technology (Loft, Anderson, and Madsen 1989).

## Identifying Intervention and Nonintervention Populations: The Basic Quasi-Experimental Design (Design 1)

As already mentioned, quasi experimentation provides alternative explanations for a program effect and by controlling for them makes it possible to assess whether social change should be attributed to an intervention or to external factors unrelated to the project. In QE designs, individuals are not randomly assigned to intervention and control groups, so there is always a possibility that changes attributed to the project intervention are due (at least in part) to initial differences in the demographic, economic, social, or geographical characteristics of the project and control groups.

Throughout this section we use a shorthand notation to describe quasi-experimental designs (see Campbell and Stanley 1966; Cook and Campbell 1979). $O$ refers to a point in time at which an observation is made. $X$ symbolizes the point at which an intervention is introduced into a group. Subscripts to $O$ indicate the order in which observations or interventions occur. The *intervention* (project) group is identified as $I$, while the *control* group is identified as $C$.

The first step of control is to identify the individuals who receive a program's interventions and those who do not. Ideally, both groups should have as many relevant characteristics in common as possible, beside the fact that one group has the intervention and the other does not.

An important implication of this first principle of control is that program planners must make several decisions early in the development of an intervention about who is exposed to it, how to identify and monitor both intervention and control groups over time, when one group should receive the intervention, and when to expect an outcome.

In Design 1 (which can be considered the basic quasi-experimental design), $O_1$ refers to observations made in both the intervention and control groups before the intervention $X$ has been introduced. These observations form the pretest; $O_2$ is the posttest, since observations occur in both groups at the same time but after the intervention $X$ has been introduced. $O_2$

---

**Design 1.  Quasi-Experimental Nonequivalent Control Group:**
**The Basic Quasi-Experimental Design**

| Intervention: | $O_1$ | X | $O_2$ |
|---|---|---|---|
| Control: | $O_1$ | | $O_2$ |

---

observations are made when sufficient time has elapsed for an impact to be expected from the project. If the intervention group has a similar distribution of characteristics as the control group $C$ and if the values in the first set of observations in both groups are the same ($IO_1 = CO_1$), then a trend can be identified that is independent of the intervention:

$$D_{trend} = CO_2 - CO_1.$$

This relationship can be used to assess changes in the control group that are due to local nonproject influences (such as changing employment opportunities, income variations, availability of water for irrigation, and prices of agricultural inputs). These changes are presumed to have occurred regardless of the intervention. The trend indicates the direction and magnitude of local influences that should not be attributed to the intervention.

Suppose that a campaign promoting extended breast-feeding was introduced into one region of a nation, and that a second region, where no promotional activities took place, was left as a control group. Although managers expect the average length of breast feeding to increase among mothers in the target group, they also need to determine whether the average length of breast-feeding has changed in the control group. Any such change in the control group should be subtracted from the outcome measures of the intervention group in order to identify the net changes due to the program.

An intervention outcome can be measured as

$$\text{Intervention Outcome} = IO_2 - IO_1 - D_{trend}.$$

To exclude local trends, $D_{trend}$ is subtracted from the difference between the pretest and posttest observations of the intervention group. The result therefore indicates the change after influences external to the project have been eliminated. The above formula could be used to assess the impact of a child survival project. Suppose that infant mortality in the project area was initially 106 per 1,000 live births and dropped to 85 per 1,000 at the end of the project. Also assume that $D_{trend}$ in a control area exhibits a decline in infant mortality of 10 per 1,000. Therefore the project impact could be estimated as $85 - 106 - (-10) = -11$, or a decline in the infant mortality rate of 11 points.

*El Salvador: Using the Basic QE Design to Assess the Impact of a Low-Cost Housing Project on Income*

One of the principal objectives of a sites and services housing project in El Salvador during the 1970s was to increase the incomes of participating families. To test this impact, a sample of 196 future project families was randomly selected from among all successful applicants; and a control group of 300 families was selected through a stratified sample drawn from the three main types of low-income settlements. Future project families and the control group were interviewed in 1976, a few months before the project began to obtain baseline information on the social and demographic characteristics and economic conditions of the households. Families were again interviewed in 1978, soon after the project group had moved to their new houses, and again in 1980, when the project was fully established. In order to assess the project impact on household income and employment, average household income was computed for the project and control groups in 1976 and again in 1980 (the estimates made in 1978 will not be used in this example, although having three observation points rather than two greatly strengthens the evaluation design). Table 8-2 shows that in 1976 future project households had an average monthly income of 335 colones compared with 258.3 for the control group. Between 1976 and 1980 the income

Table 8-2. Monthly Average Earned Income for Families Participating in a Housing Project in El Salvador and for a Control Group, 1976–80 (colones)

| Participants | Before project begins (1976) | When project under way for 2–3 years (1980) | Change (1976–80) | |
|---|---|---|---|---|
| | | | Absolute | Percent |
| Participants | 335.0 | 569.6 | 234.5 | 70.0 |
| Control group | 258.3 | 451.0 | 172.7 | 74.6 |

*Source:* Bamberger, Gonzalez-Polio, and Sae-Hau (1982).

of project families had increased by 234.5 colones (70 percent), while the income of control households had increased by 172.7 colones (74.6 percent).

This example clearly demonstrates the importance of a control group. If only the project group had been studied (as is often the case), it might have been assumed that the project produced a very significant impact on household incomes, which increased by 70 percent over a four-year period. Once it is known that the incomes of the control group increased by 74.6 percent over the same period, it becomes clear that the project had no clear positive impact on incomes, and that in fact it may have had a slight negative effect.

## Partitioning Variation in Types of Intervention and Intervention Intensity (Design 2)

The simple quasi-experimental control group design can also be expanded to assess situations in which different kinds and combinations of services are offered or where interventions may be offered at different levels of intensity. This would be useful in a site and service housing project, for example, where it is important to know how much of a house should be built by the project and how much should be left to the participants to finish. This design could also be used to compare different methods of teaching literacy (see the example of a cost-effectiveness analysis of alternative methods of using educational television in the Philippines cited in Chapter 4) or in promoting public health and providing medical services.

When evaluating an intervention with varying intensities, one should evaluate alternatives independently, as in Design 2. This approach is referred to as *partitioning an intervention*.

In Design 2, an intervention has been partitioned into three intensities: $X_1$, $X_2$, and $X_3$. "Intensity" can refer to an intervention with systematic increments in housing construction or in the number of yearly household

---

**Design 2.  Partitioning Variations in the Intensity of an Intervention**

| | | | |
|---|---|---|---|
| Intervention 1: | $O_1$ | $X_1$ | $O_2$ |
| Intervention 2: | $O_1$ | $X_2$ | $O_2$ |
| Intervention 3: | $O_1$ | $X_3$ | $O_2$ |
| Control: | $O_1$ | | $O_2$ |

---

visits by a health worker. For example, $X_1$ could be quarterly visits, $X_2$ biannual visits, and $X_3$ annual visits.

### Egypt: Evaluating a Diarrheal Control Project That Offers Various Levels of Treatment

In Egypt, the impact of different ORS (oral rehydration salt) protocols was recently evaluated in a trial community intervention in diarrheal disease (Kielman and others 1985). The intervention consisted of improved training for health personnel, the distribution of Oralyte rehydration salt, instruction for mothers in the early detection of dehydration and the management of ORS, and the different methods of distributing the salt and sugar to stores and homes. The objective of the study was to determine the way in which different ORS protocols improved case management in diarrheal diseases. The techniques employed were (a) a static-group comparison between treatment levels involving referral and (b) a pretest-posttest control group design for mortality. Measurements were taken before and after the test to assess changes in morbidity and mortality in the treatment and control groups.

The researchers found statistically significant differences in referral and treatment between different methods of service delivery. The results were affected by age, however, and by the general health of each family. It was found that the availability of ORS through "improved" regular services (control 2) had a greater effect on service utilization than other protocols involving mother and staff training.

### Peru and Barbados: Assessing the Appropriate Intensity of Medical Visits

In Lima, Peru, a study was conducted to assess the differential impacts on reduced fertility of one, two, and four medical visits during the first month following the insertion of an intra-uterine device (IUD) and the provision of gynecological services (Peru, Population Council 1986, cited in Dennis and Boruch 1989:294). Clinics were randomly assigned to one, two, and four visits from a doctor during a one-month period, and observations were made on how this affected the behavior of women who had received the IUD and received gynecological services. A similar study was conducted in Barbados (Bertrand and others 1986) to compare the impact on delaying second pregnancies through the provision of one to three follow-up visits by a nurse to provide advice on postnatal care, hygiene, and contraceptive use.

## Creating Protective Barriers to Control for the Influence of External Factors (Design 3)

As discussed earlier, the second principle of "control" ensures that other interventions extraneous to the project do not influence the outcomes. Ideally, a program site should be located in a place where one category of intervention will not affect another. For example, it is difficult to assess the impact of the promotion of community participation on a household's willingness to use its own labor in house construction if at the same time the families are offered subsidized building materials and technical services. The successful completion of housing could be due to these subsidies rather than to the promotion of community participation (see Keare and Parris 1982).

In other words, program planners should ideally avoid locations in which other activities target the same outcome. If this separation is not possible, the evaluator may still be able to isolate external factors and to estimate the influence of project interventions. Design 3 shows four groups that share similar characteristics: two of the groups are exposed to the project (one in isolation and the other is exposed to both the project and another independent intervention); one is exposed to an alternative intervention; and one is not exposed to any project and serves as a control.

A project's intervention effect in the presence of another intervention unrelated to the project can be estimated as follows. Suppose that the independent (not project-related) intervention is a health education project, $X_a$, and the target intervention is a water and sanitation project, $X_b$. Both projects are intended to reduce the frequency of diarrhea. The nonproject's intervention effect can be estimated as the difference in the dependent variable, in this case the frequency of diarrheal disease ($E$) at $t_2$. In its simplest form, Design 3 assumes that the first set of observations, $O_1$, were equal for all groups. In the following notation, $E$ refers to an effect or outcome, $I$ is the intervention, and $C$ is the control. $O$ is a set of observations,

---

**Design 3. Controlling for the Influences of Multiple Interventions on Outcomes**

| | | | |
|---|---|---|---|
| Nonproject intervention: | $O_1$ | $X_a$ | $O_2$ |
| Project intervention: | $O_1$ | $X_b$ | $O_2$ |
| Combined project and nonproject intervention: | $O_1$ | $X_{a+b}$ | $O_2$ |
| Control: | $O_1$ | | $O_2$ |

and the subscript refers to the sequence. The effect of the health education can be estimated as follows:

$$E_a = (I_1O_2 - CO_2).$$

The effect of the water and sanitation project can be estimated in a similar way:

$$E_b = (I_2O_2 - CO_2).$$

The effect produced when both the education and water and sanitation projects are both present ($X_{a+b}$) in the same environment is

$$E_{a+b} = (I_3O_2 - CO_2).$$

In this third intervention, the effect of the target project, $X_b$, can be estimated as follows:

$$E_{b'} = (E_{a+b} - E_a).$$

However, it is difficult to determine whether the influences of two programs are additive, multiplicative, or diminishing. It is not always possible to determine what influence $X_a$ has had on $X_b$. Hence, $E_{b'}$ may be an over- or underestimation of the impact of $X_b$ when it is implemented alone.

If the influence of one project on the other is interactive, so that one intervention enhances the other ($X_{ab}$), then the effect of $X_b$ alone can be estimated as $X_{ab}/X_a$.

For a discussion of statistical procedures for the analysis of interaction terms, the reader should consult one of the standard statistical texts on multiple regression and analysis of variance (see for example, Blalock 1979, for an easily understandable introduction; or Hays 1977, for a more advanced discussion). The examples given above, and in the following sections represent the simplest case in which the characteristics of the control and experimental groups are very similar at the time that the project interventions occur. Frequently, however, significant differences will be found between these groups, particularly where the project is intended for groups with certain clearly defined economic, demographic, or social characteristics. In these cases it will normally be necessary to statistically adjust for these initial differences through the use of multiple regression or other forms of multivariate analysis. These procedures are widely available through statistical packages such as SPSS and SAS. The manuals for both of these programs provide an introduction to the use and interpretation of the statistical procedures.

In addition to these kinds of statistical procedures, useful information on the patterns of interaction between projects and external factors can often be obtained from in-depth case studies conducted on a subsample of subjects covered in the sample surveys. Examples of this application of case studies are provided later in this chapter in connection with the evaluation of the River Blindness Resettlement Programs in West Africa (McMillan 1987, 1993).

## Eliminating Alternative Explanations for Program Results (Designs 4–10)

In international development programs, participants are rarely selected randomly. Candidates for intervention and control groups are most often selected for logistical, economic, or political reasons. Therefore, an evaluator should always assume that extraneous influences will affect participants in both the control and intervention communities. These influences may affect the accuracy of the evaluation and need to be excluded from the analysis. In the following sections we discuss several factors of this kind (see Box 8-1 for a list, which is derived from Valadez 1991).

The principal task of the evaluator is to assess a project's achievement in relation to its objectives. When performing this task, he or she is responsible for the internal validity of the evaluation design. This means the conclusions about the impact of a specific intervention must be free of alternative explanations. Only after *internal validity* has been ensured should the evaluator try to determine whether the conclusions are valid for other program sites. This latter form of validity, as explained earlier, is *external validity*.

### Effects of History on Internal Validity

Two types of historical influences ought to be considered when designing a QE. The first one concerns historical factors shared by both the intervention and control communities; the second concerns local historical influences that affect either the intervention or control communities, but not both. The following are examples of historical events that had to be taken into consideration in the design of a number of the evaluations cited in this chapter:

- In the Polonoreste Resettlement program in Brazil, the planned settlement program was completely overtaken by the interests of state politicians wanting to promote immigration from other regions of

Brazil, and by the deepening depression throughout the country. The combined effect of these factors meant that unplanned settlements grew at three to four times the rate of planned settlements. As a result, the original plan for assessing environmental impacts such as cultivation patterns, land occupancy, and occupancy and deforestation had to be changed (World Bank 1992d).

- In the evaluation of the River Blindness resettlement programs in Burkina Faso, it was found that the impacts on the socioeconomic conditions of the settlers depended more on their patterns of interaction with local communities than it did on the intensive rice cultivation methods introduced by the project. Host communities varied considerably in their degree of hostility or receptivity to settlers. Local history had even more impact on the conditions of women, as little provision was made for them under the project (McMillan 1987, 1993).

- In the Maharashtra Irrigation Resettlement Project in India, the impact of the project was affected by local history as the result of a change in the property legislation affecting the definition of land titles. This significantly changed who was eligible for resettlement. Consequently project impact was significantly affected by whether a community was resettled before or after this new law went into effect (World Bank 1993b).

MEASURING TRENDS. To minimize the influences of shared history, both intervention and control groups should be included in the QE design. If both groups are equally affected, the resulting differences between the control and intervention groups in the posttest should be due to the intervention. As already mentioned, the effect attributable to the historical influence can be measured as follows:

$$D_{trend} = CO_2 - CO_1.$$

$D_{trend}$ is the difference between pre- and posttests of the control group. If the historical influences were not present, presumably the two observations, $CO_1$ and $CO_2$, would not differ.

The impact of the intervention is the difference between $O_1$ and $O_2$ in the intervention group minus the influence of the historical trend. This outcome is presented as follows:

$$Outcome = IO_2 - IO_1 - D_{trend}.$$

### Box 8-1. Factors Affecting the Accuracy of Explanations of Program Results

| Threat to Validity | Measurement Problem |
| --- | --- |
| History | Results attributable to national trends |
| Local history | Local social, economic, political events within either the treatment or control group that explain differences in impact measures |
| Maturation | Results attributable to internally motivated changes in participants |
| Testing: preferred | Response due to perception of testing instrument |
| Testing: test wisdom | Response due to low retest reliability |
| Instrumentation | Results attributable to change in the measuring instrument through interviewer improvement, instrument modification, or instrument deterioration |
| Selection: control versus study group variation | Results attributable to the diverging characteristics of the study populations rather than to the program |
| Selection: inadequate predictor variable variation | Inability to determine whether or not a variable explains program impact |
| Selection bias in epidemiology | Group assignment procedure associated with the impact |
| Regression to the mean | Extreme values of the pre-implementation group gravitate toward the population mean |
| Attrition or mortality | Results attributable to change in the composition of program participants |
| Diffusion | Results due to contamination of control group by program intervention |
| Rivalry | Results attributable to the control group, improving its own condition instigated by competitive rivalry with the treatment group |

In this QE design, as in previous examples, the evaluator should try to ensure that the control and intervention group do not differ in any meaningful way in their pretest scores:

$$CO_1 = IO_1.$$

**Box 8-1 (*continued*)**

| Threat to Validity | Measurement Problem |
| --- | --- |
| Compensatory equalization | Intervention introduced into the control group, thus eliminating potential for comparison with treatment group |
| Resentful demoralization | Conditions worsen among control group participants demoralized from knowing they were not permitted to receive the intervention |
| Political indifference | Managers impede or do not implement a program because it is perceived as irrelevant or deleterious to their own priorities |
| Political interference | Actions of political actors impede program implementation and thereby change the program model in ways that managers cannot control |
| Seasonal cycles | Results attributable to seasonal variation rather then the intervention |
| Interactions: selection maturation | Results attributable to increasingly acute differences between the treatment and control groups |
| Interactions: selection history | Initial differences between participants are obscured because participants enter program at different points in time |
| Interaction between treatments | Program impacts are influenced by the sequence in which activities are implemented |
| Interaction of setting | Program impacts and treatments are influenced by variations in environmental, administrative, and demographic conditions of the site |
| Interaction of selection and treatment | Program impacts associated with the characteristics of local populations |
| Interactions of history and treatment | Program impacts associated with the historical conditions in the site area |

MULTIPLE PRETESTS. When historical trends are expected to have an influence before an intervention occurs, the evaluator should attempt to perform multiple pretests in both the intervention and control groups (Design 4) in order to measure the trends before the beginning of the project. With multiple pretest designs, it is also possible to assess the regularity of

---

**Design 4.  Nonequivalent Control Group with Multiple Pretests**

Intervention:    $O_1$    $O_2$    X    $O_3$

Control:           $O_1$    $O_2$          $O_3$

---

a trend by measuring it in both the intervention and control groups. A trend in the control group may not be replicated in the intervention group. Having the three observations in the control group can provide data for judging whether the trend is stable over the three time points. This information can be important when an apparent trend may in fact be the result of seasonal variations or short-term economic or political events. The evaluator can have much greater confidence in the existence of a trend if the observations are consistent over three or more observation points.

For some projects, the effect of history can be modeled formally and thereby neutralized by including it as a coefficient in the analysis. For example, the rate of increased demand for educated workers or the inflation rate could be reflected as coefficients in statistical equations used for the analysis. Although it is beyond the scope of this chapter to discuss such modeling, the evaluator should be alert to the effects of history and seek expert consultation while planning the evaluation.

*Controlling for the Effects of Maturation on Internal Validity (Design 5)*

Maturation in the target population makes it difficult to evaluate programs accurately whenever the change in an impact indicator can be explained by learning, fatigue, boredom, or any other biological process unrelated to the intervention. If subjects in either the intervention or control groups are more experienced, more cynical, more exhausted than their counterparts, these circumstances could explain the presence or lack of a project's effect.

Maturation can be analyzed by stratifying the data by the suspected maturation factors. Suppose that the results of an evaluation of a health education campaign, which (among other things) encourages child-spacing, have been called into question because the average number of previous births to mothers in the intervention and control groups differ. The problem is that women who have more children may wait longer until they have the next one. This issue could be investigated by stratifying mothers in both the intervention and control groups by the number of children to which they have already given birth. Statistical tests could then examine whether the child-spacing intervention exhibits different effects across the different strata of mothers.

Another type of maturation may explain why some intervention effects are not sustained over time. For example, a project that introduces primary health care facilities into low-income communities may appear to be producing an effect through a continued low diarrhea mortality rate (DMR) in comparison with a control area. Nevertheless, by including additional observations, as in Design 5, it is possible to detect whether either group exhibits a diminishing or increasing trend in diarrhea mortality before the intervention and whether any effect is sustained over time.

The advantage of this design is made clearer in Figure 8-1. Multiple pretests (three in this case) indicate that the control group was already experiencing a declining DMR before the project intervention following time-point 3. This maturation effect would not have been evident with only one pretest. At $O_3$, the intervention and control groups appear to have commensurate disease rates, which suggests that they are comparable.

The multiple pre- and posttests facilitate the interpretation of the diminishing difference in DMR between the two groups. By the sixth observation, no difference exists between them. Figure 8-1 suggests that the reason may be maturation within the control group. Mothers are becoming more skilled at controlling the hygiene of their families.

### Controlling for the Effects of Testing Threats (Design 6)

Whenever the act of measuring affects the variable being measured, an evaluation has a "testing" problem. Such problems occur when the testing instrument itself influences the responses of informants rather than the intervention. Examples include: test wisdom, preferred response, and test-intervention interactions. A dramatic example comes from a child-feeding program in Ghana (visited by one of the authors). Poorly nourished children may have discolored hair, and it was observed that mothers dyed

---

**Design 5. Nonequivalent Control Group with Multiple Pretests and Posttests**

| Intervention: | $O_1$ | $O_2$ | $O_3$ | X | $O_4$ | $O_5$ | $O_6$ |
|---|---|---|---|---|---|---|---|
| Control: | $O_1$ | $O_2$ | $O_3$ | | $O_4$ | $O_5$ | $O_6$ |

**Figure 8-1.  Example of Multiple Pretests Used to Control for Historical Trends**

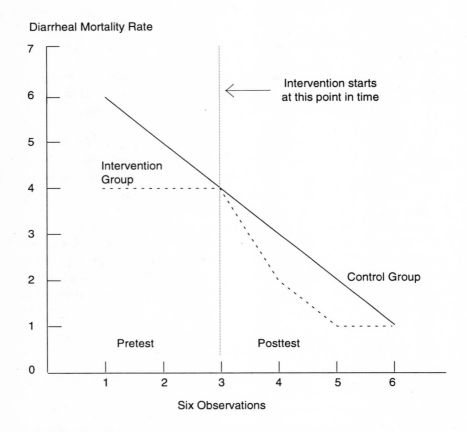

Diarrheal Mortality Rate

Intervention starts at this point in time

Intervention Group

Control Group

Pretest          Posttest

Six Observations

black their children's reddish hair to make them appear well nourished once the nutritional testing program had begun.

Since the third type of testing problem, test/intervention, can be controlled in QE designs, it is discussed here. This testing problem occurs whenever pretesting interacts with the intervention and affects the impact of the intervention. For example, when families in a control group are interviewed, they may think they are being preselected for a housing project, and this may affect their decisions to move or to invest (or not invest) in housing improvements. Similarly, asking mothers what they feed their children may encourage them to change to what they consider socially

---

## Design 6. Controlling for Test/Intervention Interactions

| | | | |
|---|---|---|---|
| Intervention 1: | $O_1$ | $X_a$ | $O_2$ |
| Intervention 2: | | $X_a$ | $O_2$ |
| Control 1: | $O_1$ | | $O_2$ |
| Control 2: | | | $O_2$ |

---

acceptable foods, even before they have received the health educational inputs through the project. Some evaluators use a Solomon design to control for such interactions. In this design a pretest is performed with one set of interventions and control groups and not with a second set. In Design 6, for example, both the intervention and control groups have the necessary pretest. But a second set of intervention and control groups having only a posttest is also studied.

Assuming the four groups are equivalent at the time of the pretest, one can measure the test-intervention interaction as follows:

- The effect of the pretest on posttest observations is $(C_1O_2 - C_2O_2)$.
- The effect of the pretest in interaction with the intervention on posttest observations is $(I_1O_2 - I_2O_2)$.
- The effect of the intervention is assessed by eliminating the effects of intervention in addition to any trends. The following formula takes all these influences into account: $[(I_1O_2 - I_1O_1 -(I_1O_2 - I_2O_2)] - [C_1O_2 - C_1O_1 - (C_2O_2 - C_1O_2)]$.

### Controlling for the Effects of Selection Threats (Design 7)

In QE, selection may become a problem whenever differences in the subjects rather than the intervention can explain the outcomes. In such cases, the difference between the outcomes may be attributed to one group being older, to a different cultural background, to the enriched soil of their land, to more efficient transport, or the like. Such selection problems confound the interpretation of the outcome. In the case of the Maharashtra Irrigation project referred to below, the families who were resettled were those with established land rights, while families who were not resettled either had shared land rights or were landless. It is likely that the project group (resettled families) had a number of significant initial differences from those not resettled, and that these initial differences may have at least partially explained differences in outcomes.

**Design 7.  Controlling for Selection Effects**

Intervention:

| Educational | Level I | $O_1$ | X | $O_2$ |
| | Level II | $O_1$ | X | $O_2$ |
| | Level III | $O_1$ | X | $O_2$ |

Control:

| Educational | Level I | $O_1$ | | $O_2$ |
| | Level II | $O_1$ | | $O_2$ |
| | Level III | $O_1$ | | $O_2$ |

The influence of dissimilar characteristics of the participants and control group could be examined and possibly eliminated by stratifying the data according to the confounding variable. For example, one could assess whether uneducated and educated people in an intervention group display equivalent outcomes in relation to the control group.

Design 7 displays both the intervention and control groups stratified by three levels of education. If the analysis indicates that project effects vary across the educational strata, education would be considered a confounding variable. A variable confounds an analysis when that characteristic as well as the intervention can affect the outcome variable. In this example, the evaluation could report the results for each stratum in order to exhibit the influence of educational level on a project's impact.

Table 8-3 contains hypothetical data for Design 7. Notice that the crude infant mortality rate in the intervention group is about 12 percent lower after the intervention. When the data are stratified by the education of mothers, the improvement changes. The group with the highest level of education (Level III) experiences a 28 percent reduction. The other groups are less affected. In the control group, infant mortality remains stable among individuals at Level III education. Therefore, the reduced infant mortality should not be attributed to the project alone. Education level also plays an important role.

SELECTION-MATURATION INTERACTION. Selection maturation refers to those instances in which initial differences between intervention and control groups continue to increase over time. The presence of selection maturation is not readily detected without multiple pretests. Referring to Figure 8-2, suppose that two communities are selected on the basis of their

Table 8-3.  Stratification of Infant Mortality Rates within Intervention and Control Groups

| Groups | Pretest | Posttest |
|---|---|---|
| *Intervention group* | | |
| Level I (n = 80) | 75 | 73 |
| Level II (n = 100) | 66 | 62 |
| Level III (n = 90) | 60 | 43 |
| Total (n = 270) | 67 | 59 |
| *Control group* | | |
| Level I (n = 50) | 73 | 70 |
| Level II (n = 90) | 69 | 67 |
| Level III (n = 40) | 60 | 60 |
| Total (n = 180) | 68 | 66 |

equivalent educational level at time point 1 ($t_1$). Had an earlier set of observations been taken at $t_0$, it would have been possible to see one of the communities accelerating its educational level faster than the other. This community continues this trend over time. In Figure 8-2, the control community continually increases its educational level from $t_0$ through $t_2$. Therefore, at $t_2$ no significant difference results from a comparison of control and intervention groups. This result is not due to an ineffective intervention. Rather, it is due to "selection maturation," which prevents a conventional evaluation from detecting the improvement.

Design 4 (presented earlier) includes two pretest observations and could be used to inspect the intervention and control groups for the presence of this influence. Design 5 could also be extended to include additional pretests since a simple regression effect could occur at any point in the pretest series. In Design 5, an additional pretest measure could clarify whether $O_1$ is a simple regression effect (that is, whether the community scored unusually or atypically low or high values on an outcome variable and will tend to return to normal levels during the next observation), or whether a selection-maturation effect exists.

Although another set of observations would be valuable, funds are usually difficult to obtain for such pretesting. Data collected by other projects in the area can sometimes be used as a pretest in one's own evaluation. Sometimes it is possible, through interagency cooperation, to

Figure 8-2.  Graph Exhibiting a Selection Maturation Effect

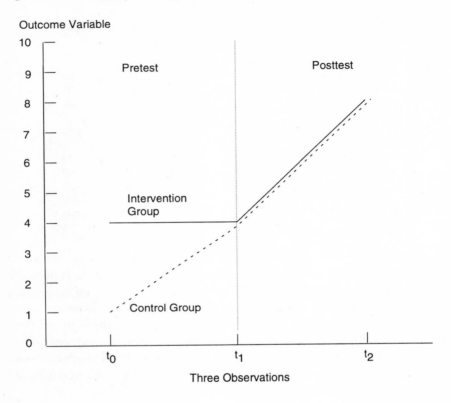

obtain information from another agency. In our experience, managers of other projects are often willing to help a colleague in need.

*Controlling for the Effects of Selection-History Interaction (Design 8)*

The problems produced by a selection-history interaction are similar to those produced by selection maturation. That is, local historical conditions in either the intervention or control group, such as the implementation of another development project, may have a continuing impact on the outcome variable used to assess the project.

The logic followed in the above section can also be applied to design controls for a selection-history effect. Design 8 includes multiple posttest

---

**Design 8. Controlling for Historical Effects**

| | | | | | |
|---|---|---|---|---|---|
| Intervention: | $O_1$ | $O_2$ | X | $O_3$ | $O_4$ |
| Control: | $O_1$ | $O_2$ | | $O_3$ | $O_4$ |

---

observations to assess population characteristics and their trends both before and after program implementation. Such a design not only permits an evaluator to detect and correct such problems before the intervention begins, but allows one to tell whether such selection issues continue after the project starts.

It would be ideal for evaluators to include more than two pretest and posttest observations when feasible since some data can exhibit regression effects and additional time points may be needed to determine whether an increase or decrease in values at $O_2$ in comparison with $O_1$ is stable.

*Interrupted Time-Series Analysis (Designs 9 and 10)*

This section briefly outlines a QE design for identifying regular patterns of behavior in a target population both before and after a program is implemented. The interrupted time-series analysis can be used with or without a control group. The design (Design 9) involves multiple observations *before* the project intervention and also multiple observations after the intervention. The analytical strength of the design will often be determined by the number of observation points (Cook and Campbell 1979:chap. 5; McCain and McCleary 1979). All the threats to internal validity that may arise in the analysis of the nonequivalent control group designs are also applicable to time-series analysis. Hence, each threat should be considered a possible alternative interpretation for an impact. Consequently, the design should ideally include a control group to make clearer the effects of history, local history, maturation, selection maturation, and selection history.

---

**Design 9. Interrupted Time-Series Analysis with a Nonequivalent Control Group**

| | | | | | | | | | | |
|---|---|---|---|---|---|---|---|---|---|---|
| Intervention: | $O_1$ | $O_2$ | $O_3$ | $O_4$ | $O_5$ | X | $O_6$ | $O_7$ | $O_8$ | $O_9$ |
| Control: | $O_1$ | $O_2$ | $O_3$ | $O_4$ | $O_5$ | | $O_6$ | $O_7$ | $O_8$ | $O_9$ |

---

Time-series analyses are used to assess five types of impact evident in longitudinal data. Although it is possible to assess any trend line with respect to any one of these five characteristics, evaluators generally analyze for all of them simultaneously.

1. Interventions can cause the *intercept* or *level* of a time series to shift. In Figure 8-3 the introduction of a project (as indicated by the broken line) shows a downward shift in the level of the trend line. Although the slope of the downward trend is the same as it was before the program, the Y intercept is lower, thus indicating that lower values will be reached sooner than they would have if a downward shift had not occurred. The Y intercept is the location on the y axis where a trend line would connect if an imaginary line were drawn from it to the y axis.

Figure 8-3. Example of a Shift in the Intercept of a Trend at the Point of Project Intervention

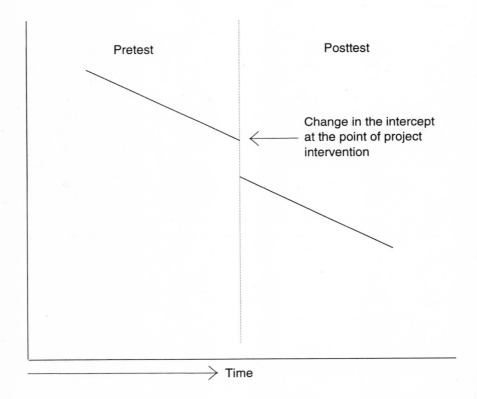

2. A change in the *slope* of the trend line subsequent to program intervention may occur in the postintervention phase of the program. The data
presented in Figure 8-4 could lead one to attribute the decreasing values to
the intervention, since the slope of the postintervention trend line differs
from that of the pre-intervention data.

3. The duration of program effects can also be detected with time series.
In Figure 8-4, a discontinuous effect is suspected since, after an initial
decline in the values, the trend swings upward. Such an analysis assesses
whether an effect is continuous or discontinuous.

4. Seasonal cycles may affect the trend line and erroneously suggest an
intervention effect or a discontinuous effect. Such cycles are suggested by
regular patterns that are replicated over numerous observations. The ef-

Figure 8-4. Example of Change in the Slope of a Trend before
and after an Intervention

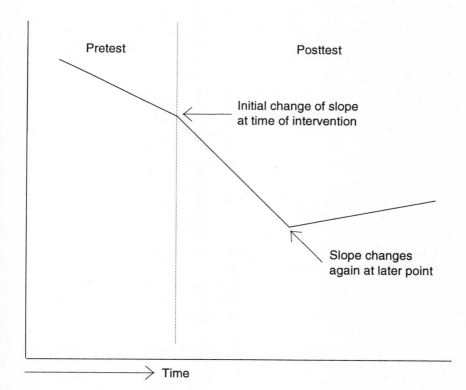

fects may be related to seasons of the year, weeks in a month, days in a week, hours in a day, and the like.

5. An intervention may have either an *immediate* or *delayed* impact, depending on the nature of the phenomenon on which an intervention is focused. Evaluators need to be especially sensitive to delayed effects to ensure that sufficient postintervention observations have been made to allow a program's impacts to occur. One reason given for the apparent failure of some international projects is that they have been evaluated too soon after their implementation.

Although the evaluation design should ideally include a control group, in practice this will frequently not be possible. In addition to questions of cost and access to data, the interrupted time-series analysis is often used to evaluate programs (such as programs to reduce accidents from drunk driving) that cover the total population so that it would be impossible to identify a control group. In this case, Design 10 would be used. As mentioned earlier, the strength of this design will frequently depend on the number of observation points taken before and after the intervention.

*Manila: Using an Interrupted Time Series to Assess the Impact of Investments in Housing Improvements on Food and Other Basic Expenditures*

A squatter upgrading project in Manila required families to invest in improvements to their house as part of a process of "reblocking" sectors of the community to permit the installation of water, sanitation, and roads. A concern of management was that increased housing expenditures might have a negative effect on the capacity of poor families to satisfy their basic nutritional requirements. In order to assess the impacts of housing investments on basic expenditures, 100 families were asked to keep detailed daily records of all income and expenditures during the three-month period before the start of the project, the three months of most intensive housing investments, and the following three months (Reforma and Obusan 1981). Figure 8-5 summarizes the average household expenditures on food and building materials and the average earned income and receipts of inter-household transfers over a period of approximately one year. The expen-

---

**Design 10.  Interrupted Time-Series Analysis: Without Control Group**

| $O_1$ | $O_2$ | $O_3$ | $O_4$ | $O_5$ | X | $O_6$ | $O_7$ | $O_8$ | $O_9$ | $O_{10}$ |
|---|---|---|---|---|---|---|---|---|---|---|

---

## Figure 8-5. Use of an Interrupted Time Series to Assess the Impact of Reblocking Squatter Housing on Food and Other Basic Expenditures and on Interhousehold Transfers, Tondo Foreshore Project, Manila

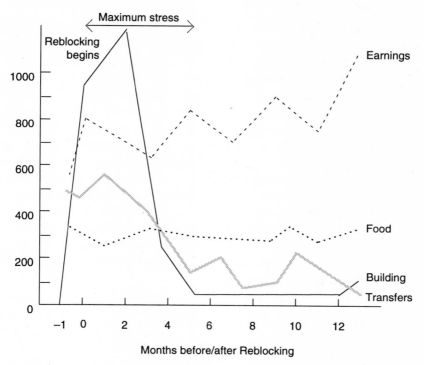

Months before/after Reblocking

diture on building materials increases from almost nothing before the project begins to more than 1,300 pesos per month during the two months after the start of the project. Labor market earnings drop during this same period as family members withdraw from the labor market to work on their houses. Expenditure on food drops slightly but much less than might be expected given the decline in earnings and the sharp increase in housing investments. One of the main reasons for the relatively stable food expenditures is that families received significant support from friends and relatives in the form of income transfers.

This example illustrates the benefits of a longitudinal study with continuous observations for periods before and after the project intervention. Given the fact that all of the income and expenditure items are fluctuating widely from one month to another, it is apparent that twelve monthly observations can provide a much more reliable picture of what is happening than could be obtained from only two or three observations.

## Three Simpler and More Economical Evaluation Designs

Despite a wide variety of relatively powerful quasi-experimental designs, most evaluations in developing country evaluations—for reasons of time, cost, or convenience—use one of the following simpler and more economical designs. One of the important lessons is that impact evaluation requires creativity and flexibility. Researchers must draw on all available data and must often develop supplementary measures to fill in information gaps and to assess effects on nontarget groups.

In several cases the evaluation was not originally planned in the way described here, and the original survey often had more limited objectives. However, the ex-post impact evaluation study was able to use existing baseline data to approximate a pretest posttest comparison on at least part of the affected population. For example, in the Khao Laem Hydroelectric Project in Thailand, the original study was conducted for planning purposes and to obtain beneficiary views on the proposed program design. It was not envisaged that the survey would subsequently be used as the baseline for an impact evaluation.

### Before and After Comparisons of the Project Population without a Control Group (Design 11)

Some future project beneficiaries are interviewed or observed before the project begins to assess their status in terms of the variables that the project is intended to influence (income, literacy, height and weight, housing quality, and the like). The observations are repeated at some interval after exposure to the project. Differences in the key indicators (dependent variables) are assumed to be attributable to the impact of the project. This is illustrated in Design 11.

---

**Design 11.  Comparison of Beneficiaries before and after the Project Intervention**

$$\text{Project group:} \quad O_1 \quad X \quad O_2$$

---

In its simplest form, this is a weak design because no attempt is made to control for the effects of external events or even maturation. It is therefore extremely difficult to attribute observed changes to the project.

### *Philippines: Assessing the Impacts of Nutrition and Health Interventions on Child Morbidity*

An evaluation was conducted to assess the pilot phase of a child health program in the Philippines consisting of nutrition and health interventions offering a variety of services, including water purification, oral rehydration, child growth monitoring, immunizations, breast-feeding, and the treatment of parasitic infections (Hill, Woods, and Dorsey 1988).

Two community sites in metropolitan Manila and twenty additional study groups in rural and suburban areas were selected on the basis of their health needs and family commitment to participate. A questionnaire was administered containing eighty-five items about socioeconomic status, education, health, behavior, and nutrition.

Nineteen groups (237 households) completing six months of continuous enrollment were evaluated with regard to household practice and disease duration. Significant improvements were found with respect to the purification of drinking water (7.1 to 74 percent), kitchen sanitation (1 to 64 percent), food consumption from the household garden (19 to 62 percent), and storage-days of food supply (33 to 50 percent). Diarrheas/fevers over a two-week period among children under the age of six decreased from 1.4 to 0.42 episodes; days of infection also declined, from 5.95 to 2.78.

The problem with this design, however, is that the inclusion criteria shifted household selection toward those willing to participate, who were therefore more likely to achieve the program objectives.

### *Using a Before-and-After Survey of Resettled Households to Evaluate the Impact of a Major Power Project: The Khao Laem Hydroelectric Project in Thailand*

The hydroelectric project called for the involuntary resettlement of forty-one affected villages with a total of 1,800 families and 10,800 people.[5] The project was implemented between 1980 and 1985.

EVALUATION METHODOLOGY. The Operations Evaluation Department of the World Bank used evaluation Design 11 to assess this project. A survey of 50 percent of the intended beneficiaries was conducted by the Chulalongoan University in 1978–79 and was used in project planning. Results were discussed with families and were used in designing the project and planning its implementation. Although this was originally intended as a planning study and was not envisaged as part of an impact evaluation design, the OED team was able to use it as a baseline study of the beneficiary population. It was possible to stratify the sample to also include some groups not eligible for resettlement.

A follow-up survey was conducted in 1989–90 with 200 resettled families who remained in the project. No formal control group was used either before or after movement, although evaluators consulted a number of national surveys on things like income, contribution of agriculture to household income, and migration patterns. One justification for not using a control group is that the criteria used by the World Bank and the Thai government for evaluating forced resettlement projects is that resettled families should be at least as well off as they were before the project.

Quantitative surveys were combined with qualitative interviews in which families were asked to assess whether they considered their conditions were better, the same or worse than before being resettled. While quantitative surveys showed that most families were better off, the majority of families considered they were worse off.

No information is available on families who did not move to resettlement areas or on the 30 percent who did not remain in the project.

ASSESSMENT OF PROJECT IMPACT. The project had a generally positive impact on affected families: that is to say, the economic conditions of most families were better after the project. Income had increased, most communities had access to better social and physical infrastructure, families on average spent a lower percentage of their income on food (50 percent compared with 80 percent before the project). Most families exceeded the Bank of Thailand's recommended daily rice consumption, and fewer families were below the poverty line. Although there were still wide disparities in income in the communities, the situation was no worse than before.

Seventy percent of the settlers were still in the new communities, which is a high proportion when compared with normal internal migration rates in Thailand. Agriculture began to play a much less important role in household income.

Despite the apparent success, a high percentage of beneficiaries felt that they were worse off, in part because families traditionally assessed their well-being on the basis of agricultural output and access to land (which are now less important throughout Thailand), and in part because of the political protests pushing for increased compensation, which may have raised people's expectations about the compensation they could expect.

The resettlement communities, with their substantial infrastructure investments, served as magnets, and by the time of the renewed study the original settlers were in a minority.

*Comparing Participants and Control Groups after Implementation but without Any Pretest (Design 12)*

In many cases, because of the cost or timing, the evaluation does not begin until the project is already operational. A control group is selected when the project is already in operation. It is assumed that this group will represent the situation that would have existed if the project had not taken place (Design 12).

With this model, the trend can be represented by $CO_2$ (the observation of the control group after the project), and that project impact can be represented by

$$IO_2 - CO_2.$$

The problem here is that participants are seldom randomly assigned to project and control groups, so the two groups will almost always be different from the start (in terms of age, income, education, motivation, and so on). As a result, questions will arise concerning the comparability of the control and project groups and how closely $CO_2$ represents what would have been the situation of the project group. The lack of information on the preproject situation also makes it difficult to know the magnitude and direction of change that has occurred in the project and control groups.

---

**Design 12. Ex-Post Comparison of Project and Control Groups without Any Pretest Measure**

|  |  |  |
|---|---|---|
| Project group: | X | $O_2$ |
| Control group: |  | $O_2$ |

---

Unless pretest or other similar data are available, little meaning can be attached to the observed difference between the groups.

*Comparing Planned Resettlement and Spontaneous Settlement to Assess Environmental Impacts of the Polonoreste Program in Brazil*

The purpose of the Polonoreste evaluation was to determine how—and how effectively—the World Bank and the government of Brazil anticipated and dealt with the principal environmental aspects and consequences of the country's major physical infrastructure (highways and regional feeder roads) and productive small-scale agricultural development (and directed colonization) and social service (particularly public health)—activities whose installation, expansion, and improvement were cofinanced by the World Bank in Northwest Brazil.[6] Because many of the project components closed only recently, the present evaluation focuses on the environmental impacts of the Polonoreste strategy in general.

EVALUATION METHODOLOGY. The evaluation was based in large part on an ex-post comparison of the conditions in the planned settlements and in the unplanned, spontaneous settlements. It was not possible to systematically select a control group, so most of the information was obtained from existing secondary data. General information was available on land usage and population densities, but since migrants came from all over Brazil it was not possible to carry out a systematic ex-ante study. Reasonably good data were available on land areas, forestry coverage, and land prices. Satellite imaging provided information on forestry patterns.

EVALUATION FINDINGS. Although the program was designed using sound social project planning, these efforts were overridden by the construction of Highway BR-364; state government efforts to attract migrants and a general depression in much of Brazil made migration to these region very attractive. This put pressure on low-fertile soils and meant that planned migration only accounted for about 25 percent of total migration.

Satellite imaging showed that land clearing had proceeded rapidly since 1975, particularly from 1985 on, and that there was a high correlation with rapid rural settlements and deforestation. Little reforestation was attempted because the prices of timber fell, and thus few farmers had any economic incentive to replant.

It was impossible to isolate the project from macroeconomic events and forces, including pressure from large landowners and from state politicians trying to promote migration.

The World Bank promoted, financed and, legitimized the construction of Highway BR-464 more rapidly than would otherwise have been the case. This accelerated the migration and development and shortened the time available for project preparation and ex-ante studies.

Without access to long-term credit, partly because of a depression, settlers were unable to finance perennial crops and were obliged to cultivate annual crops, which are environmentally more damaging.

*Combining Before-and-After Comparisons of the Project Group with an Ex-post Comparison of the Project Group and a Control Group (Design 13)*

In this design information collected on future project participants before the project begins is compared with information collected after the project has been completed. Information is also obtained on a control group at the time of project completion. In some cases the control data may be obtained from the host communities in areas where families are resettled, whereas in other cases it may be obtained from secondary sources such as the census or state or national migration data, and satellite imaging (see Design 13). As explained further below, this design was used in the Maharashtra Irrigation project.

The design is stronger than the two earlier ones in that it permits two independent estimates of project impact, namely:

$$IO_2 - IO_1 \text{ (changes in the project group following project completion)}$$

and

$$IO_2 - CO_2 \text{ (a comparison of project and control groups after project completion).}$$

---

**Design 13. Combining a Comparison of Beneficiaries before and after the Project with an Ex-Post Comparison of Beneficiaries and a Control Group**

| | | | |
|---|---|---|---|
| Project group: | $O_1$ | X | $O_2$ |
| Control group: | | | $O_2$ |

---

A few basic problems persist, however, that could lead people to draw some wrong conclusions about project impacts. First, the control group is likely to be different from the project group in enough respect, to make it impossible to think that observed differences between the two are due solely to the effects of the project. Second, because no pretest was conducted on the control group, it is not possible to assess how much the members changed over the period of the assessment.

*Combining Before-and-After Measures of Project Beneficiaries
with Ex-post Comparisons of Settlers and Host Communities:
Second Maharashtra Irrigation Project, India*

The Maharashtra Irrigation II was the first project to attempt a statewide attack on the major technical and institutional bottlenecks to improved irrigation and water management in India.[7] The project called for the construction of six extensive irrigation schemes. All had been started five to ten years earlier, but only 8,000 hectares of the potential 620,000 had been provided with irrigation at the time of the evaluation. The project was implemented between 1980 and 1985, and the evaluation was one of several conducted by OED in 1990. The project suffered serious implementation delays, and at the time of the evaluation only two of the seven dams had been completed. The evaluation focused on the Krishna Dam, which was one of the most advanced at the time of project closing in 1985.

EVALUATION DESIGN. The evaluation included the following studies:

- Socioeconomic surveys, stratified by host communities and settlers, were conducted by the Command Area Development Authority in 1978 and 1985.
- OED commissioned a socioeconomic survey to update information on household income and expenditures.
- A sample survey was also conducted of villages which remained in the catchment area. This was not an ideal control group in that many of the host villages also received some families affected by the dam.[8]
- A tracer study was conducted in 1990–91 in eight impounded villages to locate landless and families who had resettled themselves. It also helped the authorities determine what compensation would be given to the approximately 50 percent of families who were not eligible to receive land.

No data were available on the before-settlement incomes of the fully or partly affected villages. As a result, the OED 1990 socioeconomic survey was designed to include four of the host villages covered by the household surveys carried out by the Command Area Development Authority in 1975 and 1987. This enabled the surveyors to compare annual incomes over time. To ensure that the comparison was meaningful, they adjusted the income results from the two previous surveys to reflect 1990 prices, by using regional price indices. The results indicate that real incomes doubled between 1975 and 1987 for three of the host villages and increased fourfold for one of the host villages. Incomes have not increased further since 1987, except in one village, where they doubled again.

A weakness of the original evaluation design was that it shed no light on the situation in families who were not eligible for replacement land or a house-plot and who had resettled out of the catchment area. Even so, the OED impact study had invaluable side effects, among them the tracer studies that were subsequently commissioned to examine these groups. These studies were able to estimate for the first time the magnitude of the group (which proved to be about 45 percent) and to assess how they had been affected by the project. Although it was impossible to carry out pretest and posttest comparisons without preproject data, the design provided valuable information showing that most of the families who were not resettled did not appear to have been too severely affected by the project.

EVALUATION FINDINGS. On a per capita basis, the resettled population was substantially better off than the host populations. Therefore, the income of the resettled population must have gone up since before resettlement. In contrast, those families who chose to stay behind in the catchment area had lower per capita income than the host villages. Although it was assumed that the impact of the project would mainly take the form of increased agricultural income, it was found that families rely on a variety of sources of income and try to diversify these sources to as to reduce risk.

About three out of four resettled families said that they were better off in terms of income and access to services. The 25 percent who claimed to be worse off were mainly landless and "truncated households" that had been split and forced to resettle in different areas.

Only limited information was available on the situation of the approximately 45 percent of families who were not eligible for replacement land or house-plot, and who resettled out of the catchment area. The tracer study shows that 75 percent were joint families and 25 percent were landless. Among joint families, groups of related families bought land with compensation money in cheaper areas. Individual families moved to where they had relatives. Only 8 percent moved to Bombay. Noneligible families indicated that irrigation had generated a demand for labor, and it appears that many moved to the command area on their own initiative. The study also showed that the families who were not resettled included both poor and relatively well-off farmers and that the impacts varied for different subgroups.

The integration turned out to be fairly successful in that distances were not too large and most settlers were of the same tribe as their hosts. In addition to reducing tensions, hosts were able to lobby to help settlers acquire land and other assets.

## Limitations on the Operational Utility of "Less Robust" Evaluation Designs

While fully recognizing the reasons why many project impact evaluations do not use the more robust designs, it is important to ask: *Does it really matter to managers and policymakers when the evaluation designs are methodologically less robust than they could be?* This section considers some of the important operational and policy questions that can be at least partly answered using these less robust designs. We then raise a number of questions that cannot be adequately answered using these designs.

*Operational and Policy Questions to Which These Less Robust Designs Can Contribute*

The following questions can be answered at least in part with less robust evaluation designs:

- These designs can be used to provide a rapid assessment of whether a project has produced any significant effects before investing in more expensive and time-consuming evaluations.
- A before-and-after study of project beneficiaries without a control group can usually provide quite precise information on whether the conditions of resettled families are better or worse than they were before the project. Where adjustments are made for price changes, it is usually possible to obtain good estimates of the changes in household income and sources of employment, expenditure, and consumption.

- Farm systems research can also examine changes in production systems and can determine whether changes and improvements are likely to be sustainable (because they are due to improved production methods that increase productivity on the same land area) or are due to increased land areas brought under cultivation, which may not be sustainable.

Beneficiary assessment, and related techniques such as Participatory Rural Assessment, are becoming widely recognized as effective and economical tools to provide insights into the many different ways in which projects can impact the lives of different groups. The following examples are taken from evaluations conducted by the Operations Evaluation Department (OED) of the World Bank[9]:

- The surveys undertaken for the Malaysia Jenka Triangle projects and for the Indonesia Transmigration projects showed that households valued schools and other opportunities for educational advancement far above increased incomes, land title house or material possessions— the lesson being that the provision of educational infrastructure can play a vital role in successful settlement projects.
- The surveys for cotton projects in West Africa revealed that women who were cotton producers were getting no extension advice, even though in some villages they outnumbered male cotton producers. The lesson is that women need to ensure that they do indeed receive extension visits.
- In four irrigation projects in Mexico and Morocco, the surveys showed that the land tenure system is continually evolving as a result of the increased value and higher productivity of land. Hence the country needs a flexible development strategy, particularly if the irrigation infrastructure has been designed on the basis of a static situation.
- In Morocco, the workload increased when irrigation was introduced and as a result daughters had less access to education than before. Thus it became all the more important to ensure that girls would still have the opportunity to attend school even when land productivity increased.

*Operational and Policy Questions to Which Less Robust Designs Are Not Able to Respond*

A number of major issues are still beyond the scope of these QE designs:

- Most of the designs provide only limited information on the conditions of the families or individuals who were not the main beneficiaries of the project. In the case of involuntary resettlement related to power or irrigation works, many families who were forced to move because of project interventions did not go to the resettlement areas. Some did not move through choice, but many others were not eligible to be resettled because they were landless, did not have clear title, or were joint owners. Without preproject information, it is difficult to make quantitative comparisons of how these people were affected by the project. In the Maharashtra irrigation project in India, the OED evaluation established that no baseline information was available on the 45 percent of households not eligible for resettlement. In the Karnataka Irrigation project, 21 percent of the families did not move to the resettlement areas. Despite the innovative approaches used to obtain data on nonbeneficiary families after resettlement, the studies were hampered by the lack of baseline data on this group, particularly since many of these households may be worse off as a result of the project and have been forced to move, often without adequate compensation, financial or otherwise, for the relocation. This failing should be of concern to policymakers and possibly to program managers.
- Similar problems arise with urban renewal and low-cost housing projects. Although detailed information is usually available to indicate the value of houses and infrastructure, and the economic conditions of families in the project areas, almost nothing is known about families who leave—either through a rational decision to sell their house and make a capital gain or because they are either coerced into doing so or are unable to keep up with rising taxes and service charges.
- A difficulty for many of the designs is how to assess project impact, both positive and negative, on surrounding areas. In many cases the investments in settlement communities and the supporting infrastructure development attracted large numbers of additional migrants, and in several instances (for example Polonoreste and Maharashtra), the project settlers were a minority of all migrants. Most of the above evaluation designs did not collect systematic information on non-project migrants and consequently provided only a partial assessment of total impacts of project investments. This again must be of concern to government policymakers and international agencies who have a say in regional development patterns. Although baseline data were

seldom available, most of the evaluations sought to obtain information on the nonproject populations as they evolved after resettlement (for example, the Polonoreste project in Brazil and the River Blindness Resettlement studies).

- Although without control groups it is possible to assess whether project participants are better off than they were before the project, it is difficult to determine whether they are better off than they would have been if the project had not taken place. In view of the dynamic changes occurring in many regions, some areas would have changed drastically even without the project intervention. Consequently, current evaluation designs give policymakers little information with which to assess the return on their investments.
- Without a control group, some might assume that the observed changes are due to the project, whereas in fact they may be due to external factors (see Table 8-2). In El Salvador, for example, the housing project of 1976–80 might be credited for a 70 percent increase in the earned income of project families over this period until it was learned that the income of the control group increased by 74.69 percent over the same period.
- The lack of control over the evaluation design means that it will often be difficult to disaggregate data so as to determine which groups benefit the most or the least or to evaluate the relative contributions of different project components, or the interactions between these components and characteristics of the target populations.
- These limitations also make it difficult to assess the replicability of different project designs. This concern takes on added dimensions in countries where a number of similar projects are being planned and it would be essential to know how to improve the cost-effectiveness of project designs.

By and large, it appears that the simpler evaluation designs can provide useful information on how projects have affected the direct project beneficiaries. Because this is the information most frequently required by many governments and donor agencies, the designs are usually able to satisfy the information requirements of key policymakers and planners.

These designs are usually ill equipped to assess the impact of projects on sectors that were not eligible for compensation or project benefits, such as resettlement, loans, scholarships, or nutritional supplements, or the impact on those who opted not to participate in the project or not to move to the resettled areas. A notable contribution of many of these studies (for example, the Maharashtra and Karnataka studies) is that they make policymakers aware of the magnitude of the nonproject beneficiary population. Without baseline information, however, they will be unable to assess the quantitative impact on income and other indicators of welfare. Moreover, because these excluded groups contain many of the poorest and most vulnerable members of society, this lack of information makes it difficult to fully assess project impacts on all affected population groups.

Also, the weaker designs make it difficult to judge how far changes can be attributed to the project, which project components are most and least effective, how project components interact with beneficiary characteristics. In turn, this makes it more difficult to improve the cost-effectiveness and efficiency of future project design, although these problems can in many cases can be partly overcome by in-depth case studies and technical analyses.

Whether additional investments of time, money, and human resources would be justified under the circumstances, depends on the individual case. Some guidelines for deciding when to use the more rigorous evaluation designs appear at the end of this chapter.

## Ways to Strengthen Less Robust Designs

Several methods can be used to strengthen these designs and thus to improve the quality and usefulness of the findings. Many of these methods are described in more detail in Chapter 7.

MULTIMETHOD DESIGNS WITH SPECIAL SURVEYS FOR PARTICULAR POPULATIONS. Since projects have different effects on different groups, it is important to design surveys, or other methods of data collection, to target each of the affected population groups.

USING RECALL TO ESTIMATE THE PREPROJECT SITUATION. Respondents can be asked to recall their income, housing conditions, expenditure patterns, birth control practices, or other behavior at one or more points in the past. However, one would have to assess the reliability of the recall data. Accuracy is affected by many factors, including the length of the recall period and the complexity of what is being recalled. It may be easier to recall the type of housing one lives in than to recall income from multiple sources or consumption patterns. The sensitivity of what is being recalled is also important. Mothers may not wish to admit to socially disapproved child-rearing practices or eating habits. The willingness of respondents to provide the correct information can also be an impediment. Families may exaggerate the improvements in their living conditions to please project staff.

If recall is to be used on a regular basis, it is worth assessing its validity. Families can be interviewed at one point in time and asked for information about income, consumption, behavior, and other topics of interest. The same families can then be re-interviewed at different points in the future and asked to recall this information. The differences between recall and the original information can be used to assess the reliability of recall. A more systematic assessment would require a larger sample in order to assess how the reliability of recall is affected by factors such as age, sex, education, and income.

It is sometimes possible to conduct independent checks on recall. For example, information on wage rates could be obtained from employers, housing conditions could be checked with landlords or neighbors, and data on income could be obtained from organizations such as credit unions.

USING SECONDARY DATA. Secondary data can often be used to estimate conditions in the preproject period or used as a control. Potential sources include:

- Public health records on infant mortality, incidence of different infectious diseases, number of women seeking advice on contraception, or condom consumption.
- Household income and expenditure surveys.
- Labor market surveys on employment, labor force participation rates, and wage rates.
- Records of cooperatives, credit unions, and other financial institutions.
- Specialized surveys conducted by universities, consulting groups or NGOs. It is frequently possible to locate studies that were carried out in the particular communities where the evaluation is being conducted.
- School records on attendance, repetition, examination performance, and the like.

- Satellite images can be used to study deforestation, settlement patterns, land areas under cultivation, and other large-scale environmental impacts.

USING MULTIVARIATE ANALYSIS TO STRENGTHEN COMPARABILITY OF INTERVENTION AND CONTROL GROUPS. Multivariate analysis can be used to statistically control for differences between project and control groups on variables such as age, income, education, demographic characteristics of the household, time living in the present residence, or time in employment. In this way it is possible to eliminate alternative explanations of apparent project effects. When used with an ex-post comparison, this analysis can also be used to estimate preproject conditions. For example, in an assessment of job training programs it is possible to calculate how earnings are affected by age and time on the job and hence to assess the likely earnings of job trainees prior to the training.

Jimenez, Kugler, and Horn (1989) conducted an analysis of this kind to assess and compare the effectiveness of long and short courses offered by the Colombian Apprenticeship and Vocational Training Service (SENA). The evaluation compares the overall efficiency of long courses (averaging 2,000 hours or more and including apprenticeships and promotional and complementary courses) with that of short-qualifying ones (200 hours or more per course). The benefits of SENA training were calculated using ordinary least-squares regression with a view to estimating an earnings function. Since the data were not longitudinal, 2,433 individuals (cases and controls working under the same supervisor) were surveyed. SENA and non-SENA trainees were compared to determine differences in pre- and posttraining average earnings. Four independent variables that could affect earnings (formal schooling, job-related experience, SENA training, and socioeconomic status using father's education as a proxy) were incorporated in the four training models.

The apprenticeships and complementary courses produced an incremental differential in earnings between SENA and non-SENA participants at any level of schooling and years of job-related experience (complementary effect between training/formal schooling and training/experience). The earnings differential from promotional courses were also positive, but inversely related to schooling and experience. Low, positive differentials in short qualifying courses were associated with a small number of years of experience (at any schooling level) but turned negative as the job experience expanded.

It was also found that social returns to publicly subsidized job training in Colombia exceeded the rate of return to capital investments in Colombia (10 percent). In all the long-term courses, social returns exceeded 20 percent. Only with the exception of promotional programs, the rates increased with additional years of formal schooling. These results support longer versus shorter modes of training (higher returns for longer ones). Promotional courses oriented to older, experienced workers even exceeded the average return of 29 percent to higher education.

Other examples of the use of multivariate analysis to evaluate educational programs include the evaluation of rural primary education in Brazil (Harbison and Hanushek 1992) which is discussed later in this chapter, and the assessments of diversified secondary education in Colombia and Tanzania (Psacharopoulos and Loxley 1985).

*Panel studies* on small subsamples can be used to observe patterns of change over time. These were used effectively in the River Blindness studies described later in this chapter (McMillan 1987, 1993) to yield information on the adaptation process of new settlers and their interactions with host communities. They also helped assess the development of sources and income and employment (such as trade) not covered by the original project design. Panels can also be used to study the development of new urban settlements. Many evaluations have emphasized the need to assess project impacts over a much longer period of time as short and long term impacts can be quite different—particularly when population densities begin to increase and new settlers have to adapt without the range of services provided to original settlers.

TRIANGULATION AND MULTIMETHOD APPROACHES. The validity of estimates can be tested by comparing them with estimates obtained from independent sources. Qualitative methods such as interviews with key informants, participant observation, in-depth case studies, and direct observation can be used for this purpose. A useful and simple method is to meet informally with a small but diverse group of respondents or families and ask them how their lives and those of their neighbors or workmates have been affected by the project or by other events. It may be found, for example, that even though families are better off with regard to certain quantitative indicators (such as income), households may not believe that they are better off. They may feel more insecure, their expenditures may have increased in ways not recorded in the survey, or the level of community conflict may have increased because they have had to share (supposedly "cost-effective") services such as water and sanitation. Typical findings that would not be detected in formal surveys might be that much of the increased income is lost in bribes or other forced payments, poor families may be forced to leave a project (even though no title change is recorded), or the costs of services such as water may have increased because of payments to community leaders. In other cases, families may be more concerned about the quality of life than about an increase in income.

Secondary data (discussed above) provide another useful means of conducting consistency checks.

RAPID ASSESSMENT METHODS. These methods, discussed in detail in Chapter 7, make it possible to obtain information rapidly and economically. If used properly (that is, in full knowledge of the inherent limits of small samples that are not randomly selected), they offer a means of broadening the coverage of samples. These methods can be extremely useful, for example, in studying populations who are not primary project beneficiaries, but whose lives may be significantly affected by a project and who were not covered by the survey activities of the project agency. The Maharashtra Irrigation Project, cited earlier in this chapter, illustrates the use of these methods. Kumar (1993) provides a useful overview and critique of these methods, together with eight case studies illustrating the main methods.

## Applying More Robust Impact Evaluation Designs in Assessing Major Development Projects: Three Examples

In the following examples, rigorous QE designs have been applied in the evaluation of large and complex development programs. All three evaluations demonstrate the importance of following a multimethod approach and of working within a broad economic, political, and social context so as to gain a better understanding of the way in which the project interacts with the environment in which it is implemented. As the evaluations also show, while such exercises provide useful information about program impacts they can never achieve the methodological rigor that the textbooks suggest.

*Evaluating the Impacts of Water Supply and Sanitation, Primary Health,*
*and Education Programs Financed under the Bolivian Social Investment Fund*

The Bolivian Social Investment Fund (SIF) was a follow-up to the widely publicized Emergency Social Fund (ESF) (Jorgensen, Grosh, and Shacter 1992) started in 1985 with a view to disbursing funds for social and economic projects as rapidly as possible to protect low-income communities during the harsh economic reform programs being introduced at the time.[10] The SIF provides financing for social and economic projects in the areas of health, education, employment, and infrastructure. The evaluation, which is part of a multicountry study of the impacts of World Bank–financed projects, focuses on one geographical region of Bolivia (El Chaco) and seeks to evaluate the impacts of the health, education, and water supply and sanitation projects being financed under SIF. Interestingly, a different research design was used for each of the three subprojects so as to reflect their different characteristics, the proportion of the population to be covered by each project, and the stage of development of each project at the time the evaluation began.

FORMAL EDUCATION: QUASI-EXPERIMENTAL DESIGN. Schools in each of the four supervisory districts were ranked on the basis of indices of "infrastructure," "overcrowding," and "equipment," and schools that would receive high priority in the deliberations over SIF financing were identified on the basis of a composite score derived from these three indices. Because there were not enough resources to extend the project to all schools in the El Chaco region, a randomization procedure was used that made it possible to randomly select a control group in each district.[11]

PRIMARY HEALTH CARE: ECONOMETRIC CONTROL. The health subproject will provide materials and equipment and help rehabilitate the physical infrastructure in at least 90 percent of the ninety-three health centers in the region to bring them up to basic standards. In view of the high intended coverage, it is not possible to use QE design with random assignment and a control group. Because different centers will receive different levels and combinations of services, depending on what they need, econometric analysis will be used to examine the relationships between inputs, exogenous characteristics, and outcomes. A two-stage random sample will be selected with information drawn from a household survey, a community questionnaire, and a health facilities questionnaire.

WATER AND SANITATION: A MATCHED COMPARISON. The SIF supports twelve basic water and sanitation projects to improve the quality of water, quantity of water available, and the proximity of water. Because the projects had already been selected, it was not possible to randomize the selection of project sites. A number of areas not affected by the project will serve as controls. Because the El Chaco region is fairly homogeneous, this should provide a satisfactory basis for comparison. The information for the study will be taken from a household survey and interviews with community leaders to determine the present quality of water and sanitation. Both project and control groups will be studied before the project begins and after services have been introduced.

### Assessing the Resettlement Components of the West Africa River Blindness Control Program

This is a longitudinal impact evaluation that includes many of the elements of a robust evaluation design.[12] It also describes a fairly typical situation in that many of the important elements of the final evaluation design were not included in the original design, since the sponsoring agency had a more limited set of operational objectives. The case is also typical in that the sponsoring agency did not wish control groups to be included in the original evaluation design (a situation that was found in some of the evaluations of involuntary resettlement projects discussed earlier in this chapter).

In 1976 Purdue University received a USAID contract to collect field data in order to document farming systems in several West African countries. In Upper Volta (as Burkina Faso was then called), Purdue provided technical assistance to the Autorité des Aménagements des Vallées des Volta (AVV), the national agency charged with helping farmers settle in land cleared of onchocerciasis under the regional disease control program. The purpose was to help monitor the program at the farm level. Part of the understanding was that Purdue would be able to use the data in a regional comparative analysis, and that some Ph.D. candidates would be able to conduct their dissertation fieldwork in villages where the settlers came from, and in villages close to new settlements.

About 25 AVV staff were trained and the existing survey work done in 1975–76 was expanded into a systematic survey of resettled families in 1977,

1978, and 1979 to show whether they applied the AVV extension recommendations, and with what effects (Murphy and Sprey 1980). *At this point
AVV did not agree to have a sample of control households included.* The survey
was repeated annually for several years and was used by AVV to improve
their settlement, extension, credit, and research programs. The monitoring
unit also kept track of settlers' involvement in local markets, prices, evidence of increases in income and well-being, and any indication of where
surpluses were being invested—whether in the new villages or in the
villages of origin.

From 1978 to 1980 Purdue supported Della McMillan's anthropological
dissertation fieldwork in villages that many of the settlers had come from,
and AVV allowed her to collect data from some of the recently resettled
families. After completing her dissertation, she was able to continue visiting
the villages periodically over the next ten years. The resulting studies are
among those referred to later in this section.

By the late 1980s the World Bank's Onchocerciasis Unit, working with
other donors, decided to document what had happened under the program
with a view to providing some lessons on settlement and institutional
issues to a number of countries becoming involved in river blindness
control. Della McMillan, whose fieldwork had been connected with this
project, was hired by one of the research contractors and this, combined
with the fact that the original technical adviser to AVV was on the research
steering committee, led to a follow-up study using the survey data collected
in 1977–79. If it had not been for the involvement of these two people in the
later study—both of whom were familiar with the original research program
(and had access to the original sample lists through their own personal
files)—the earlier field material would probably never have been used.

EVALUATION DESIGN. The initial research design was built around Farm
Systems Research, which sought to study in detail the impacts of the project
on agricultural production systems and outputs. The research was based
on a set of interrelated longitudinal studies beginning in 1978 (the year
before families moved) and continuing in 1979 (the first year after the
move). As explained above, anthropological field studies were included
during the 1978–80 period because of Della McMillan's thesis work, and
with a follow-up some ten years later. In the later 1980s the World Bank
and other interested donors decided to commission follow-up studies to

assess the long-term impacts of the river blindness control program, and a fortunate coincidence made it possible to include a comparative study over time, using the 1977–80 studies as a reference point.

The original study consisted of three main parts:

- A monitoring questionnaire was applied to a sample of 132 households in 1978 and 313 in 1979 to compare households who moved to new infection-free areas with families from the reception areas into which they were moving. Families were followed through two agricultural seasons with weekly interviews conducted with male household heads. Two key variables in the sample design were *family size* (number of workers and dependents), which determined the amount of land given, and *years in the AVV*, which determined access to animal traction.

- One hundred and forty-one households were reinterviewed in three study sites in 1988 and 1989 (household head and one wife interviewed). The sample was stratified to include tractor owners, farmers using animal traction, and those only using their own labor. The sample was also stratified to represent major ethnic groups. It proved possible to include 60 of the 144 families who had been interviewed in 1979, and 20 of these were selected for intensive longitudinal study.

- Special studies were conducted on household expenditures and revenue (all members of 56 households), pastoral production systems (30 households), all large markets in the affected areas, special issues for women taken from the farming systems sample, and immigration patterns (sample of migrants and interviews with heads of host communities).

More intensive case studies were conducted on a subsample of households from one of the main recruitment zones. The first year of the study was conducted in the village from which settlers were recruited and the next year in the new area to which they had moved. The in-depth case studies revealed a number of areas in which project effects were significantly different from those assessed by the monitoring study. A selection of results follows.

- *Income.* The statistical survey examined net income from the sale of cotton, because it was assumed, on the basis of preliminary findings, that there was no significant income from cattle or off-farm earnings. The case studies, however, indicated significant income from the sale of cattle and also from trade. The estimates of income from these

studies were 8 to 23 percent higher than the statistical estimates and in the fifth year were as much as 40 percent higher.
- *Grain production.* Case studies found much greater increases in production because they monitored the activity of settlers up to the fifth year, by which time they had paid off loans in cereals and were able to increase production. The case studies also covered all land, not just official land, and noted that the increase in income was related to the increase in land area rather than to increased productivity resulting from improved technology. In addition, much of the increase was due to the increased provision of land for women outside the project.

FINDINGS OF THE EVALUATION. The following are some of the main findings of the evaluation.

- The outcome of the resettlement depended largely on positive and negative links to the local social and economic environment, and projects were not independently sustainable.
- The project was designed around the planned and carefully controlled production of cotton and sorghum, in which intensive cultivation of assigned land areas would be developed. In fact, families tended to drop these intensive cultivation methods once they had been in the project for a few years and project supervision was less intense. Increases in output were due more to increases in the area of land than to improved technology. Much greater increases in production occurred after several years, once settlers had paid off their loans (in cereals) and were able to increase production. Much of the increase could be traced to women cultivating land outside the project area.
- Significant income was obtained from the sale of cattle and also from trade, but neither of these activities was covered by the project. Successful projects must promote diversified economic opportunities, including off-farm employment.
- In many project areas, settlers were not able to fully exploit local marketing and nonfarm opportunities because of the resistance from local tribes. This was particularly true in areas where gold was discovered and substantial opportunities for trade had opened up but the areas were monopolized by the local tribes.
- Infrastructure, particularly roads, proved to be a key factor in developing new economic opportunities.

- Economic opportunities for women were the key to the success of many settlements, but this was largely outside the scope of the original program. There was inadequate planning for women, as already discussed. The project thus ignored traditional patterns of giving women land to cultivate. Once families became established, they began to give land to women. They also received traditional gifts of grain, which they both sold and planted. Women also acquired animals, again outside the project and not captured by the statistical surveys.

- Resettlement projects need to have a long time perspective and to plan for what will happen with the arrival of second-generation settlers and increased demand for land and services. A population increase will put greater pressure on the land. If intensive cultivation systems have not been adopted, then the demand for new land, combined with the lack of concern for conservation, can lead to ecological problems.

- Many of the most successful communities were those in which settlers left the planned settlements and moved to new areas where the economic opportunities were greater, the controls were fewer in number, and there were fewer problems with local tribes.

- Projects need to adapt to local customs and land tenure systems. Planning needs to take into account all major stakeholder groups, including local communities—and not just settlers.

- The long-term sustainability of isolated settlements is highly questionable. Success depends on integration into areas with high economic potential.

### *Evaluating the Performance and Impacts of Rural Education in Northeast Brazil: the EDURURAL Program*

Probably the most rigorous evaluation of any large-scale education program in a developing country was the five-year evaluation of major investments to improve access to, and the quality of, primary rural education programs in a number of states in Northeast Brazil (EDURURAL).[13]

It is widely assumed that one of the largest problems facing primary education in most developing countries is that countries lack the resources to provide access to essential educational inputs such as qualified teachers, textbooks, and basic classroom equipment. Since empirical evidence has shown that students who have access to these inputs tend to perform better, it is frequently assumed that more investment in these facilities will lead to improved educational outputs such as a lower dropout rate, higher scores on aptitude tests, and ultimately higher earnings and a better standard of living. However, researchers do not often have the opportunity to examine scientifically collected data to determine whether these theoretical benefits are in fact achieved in real situations in poor countries, particularly in remote rural areas.

The evaluation component of the EDURURAL project took advantage of a program of major and sustained investments in primary education inputs in selected municipalities throughout the nine states of Northeast Brazil to address two evaluation questions:

- Did the specific education interventions accomplish their goals? More specifically, was the package of improved inputs (that is, the better-paid teachers with more years of schooling, better instructional material for the teachers, teaching and curriculum design available to teachers, drinking water and electricity in schools, basic materials such as textbooks, chalk, pencils, and so on) responsible for the improvements?
- What are the implications of the project for education and education policies ? Does the provision of these inputs improve the quality of education by reducing the number of dropouts and repetitions, improving tests schools for mathematics and Portuguese and increasing access to education?

BACKGROUND AND OBJECTIVES. The massive educational investments in primary education in Northeast Brazil in the late 1970s and early 1980s, combined with the desire of the government to assess the effectiveness of these investments in improving the economic conditions of the largely poor population of the region, provided a unique opportunity to conduct a systematic evaluation of a significant education intervention. The World Bank, which was the principal source of funding for this program, cooperated with the national and local governments in the designing and implementing the evaluation.

The size of the investments, the large numbers of children affected, and the willingness of the government to continue the evaluation over a long period of time probably make this the largest and most systematic evaluation of primary education in any developing country.

The evaluation addressed the following policy questions:

- Does a major investment in educational resources actually improve the access of children in poor and remote areas to better educational inputs?
- Does improved access lead to higher academic achievement, as measured on tests in mathematics and Portuguese?
- Does access to a better education actually improve the performance of the educational system as reflected by key indicators such as reduced dropout and repetition, and improved promotion?
- Does improved performance provide greater numbers of students with access to the educational system?

EVALUATION DESIGN. Data were collected at three points in time: 1981, before the project began; 1983 and 1985, during the period in which resources were being distributed and the project was beginning to have an impact; and 1987, after the project was fully implemented.

In each state, schools were selected randomly from among those to receive resources under the project. A control group of schools in the same states was selected on the basis of cluster sampling. For reasons of cost and administration, the study focused on only three of the nine states, but they included one of the poorest (Piaiu), a medium state (Ceara), and a more advanced state (Pernambuco). Table 8-4 describes the characteristics of the sample.

General socioeconomic data were also collected for each region. This included information on the characteristics of the child, the family, and the community. Specific tests of student achievement in mathematics and Portuguese were also developed and used.

Table 8-4. Sample Design for the EDURURAL Evaluation

| | 1981 | | |
|---|---|---|---|
| Item | EDURURAL | Control | 1983, 1985, and 1987 |
| Counties | 30 | 30 | Similar samples |
| Schools | 397 | 189 | were taken in |
| Teachers | 463 | 231 | subsequent years |
| Students | | | |
| Second grade | 3037 | 1681 | |
| Fourth grade | 1075 | 639 | |

*Source:* Harbison and Hanushek (1992), Table 3.6 (adapted by the authors).

A key feature was the separate collection of detailed, disaggregated costs of school inputs. On each occasion samples were taken of second- and fourth- grade students in the same schools, so that it was possible to reinterview many of the students.

ANALYSIS PLAN AND FINDINGS. Multivariate analysis was used to control for socioeconomic characteristics that could explain achievement and promotion rates.

It is not possible to consider educational reform in a simple before-and-after design, as it is a process that must be studied over time and that is greatly influenced by the political and economic environment in which the program is developed. Table 8-5 shows the complexity of the analysis as there are considerable changes in outcome, depending on the comparison years. In this table a series of quality indicators were combined to provide an indication of the direction of change. In the case of Ceara, the state illustrated in this table, when 1983 is compared with 1981 it is found that for the EDURURAL schools, there was a 46 percent improvement in the quality variables, there was no change in 8 percent, and 46 percent declined.

Table 8-5. Distribution of Quality Indicators by Direction of Change for EDURURAL and Control Areas in Ceara, 1981, 1983, and 1985

| Direction of Change | Percentage of Variables | | |
|---|---|---|---|
| | EDURURAL | Control | Total |
| 1983 > 1981 | 46 | 58 | 42 |
| 1983 = 1981 | 8 | 8 | 12 |
| 1983 < 1981 | 46 | 33 | 42 |
| Total | 100 | 100 | 100 |
| 1985 > 1983 | 75 | 63 | 83 |
| 1985 = 1983 | 8 | 0 | 4 |
| 1985 < 1983 | 17 | 38 | 13 |
| Total | 100 | 100 | 100 |
| 1985 > 1981 | 63 | 58 | 67 |
| 1985 = 1981 | 21 | 8 | 21 |
| 1985 < 1981 | 17 | 33 | 13 |
| Total | 100 | 100 | 100 |

*Source:* Harbison and Hanushek (1992), Table 7.3.

These changes were less favorable than they were for control areas: 58 percent of the variables showed signs of an improvement.

In contrast, when 1985 is compared with 1981, the EDURURAL areas experienced an improvement on 63 percent of the variables compared *with* only 58 percent for control regions.

It can be seen that in general EDURURAL quality indices were higher than for the selected control areas in two out of the three comparisons; but in two of three cases they were lower than for all rural schools in the region.

The second question is whether these higher quality indices are reflected in higher educational achievement. Table 8-6 presents achievement scores in EDURURAL schools as a proportion of achievement scores in control schools. It can be seen that in 1981, before the program began, the EDURU-RAL schools had significantly higher achievement scores than did the control schools. For example, second-grade EDURURAL schools performed 13 percent higher in Portuguese and 21 percent higher in math. The EDURURAL schools performed even better in 1983 on both portuguese and math but suffered a significant decline in 1985. For fourth grade there was a significant decline in EDURURAL relative performance throughout the period.

This shows the importance of a control group and of computing the data at as many points of time as possible. If the study had only been conducted in 1983 and 1985, it would have given the impression that the project had a very positive effect, but the inclusion of the 1981 reference points suggests a different conclusion.

Table 8-6. Mean Educational Achievement in EDURURAL Schools as Proportion of Control Schools, Ceara State, 1981–85

| Area of Achievement | 1981 | 1983 | 1985 |
|---|---|---|---|
| *Second grade* | | | |
| Portuguese | 1.13 | 1.21 | 1.05 |
| Mathematics | 1.21 | 1.29 | 1.05 |
| | | | |
| *Fourth grade* | | | |
| Portuguese | 1.12 | 1.04 | 1.01 |
| Mathematics | 1.31 | 1.20 | 1.04 |

*Source:* Harbison and Hanushek (1992), Table 7-7.

Results with respect to program efficiency were even more disappointing and the impact on student promotion was very limited.

## Conclusion

The authors of the EDURURAL study conclude:

> In simplest terms we find very little appeal to a simple quasi-experimental design methodology. Major projects which run over a period of time will always be confounded by outside factors and purposeful behavior of the participants. It is difficult to imagine being able to collect sufficiently large and randomly drawn samples to allow uncomplicated comparisons of mean relationships.

Moreover, simply collecting readily available data on basic resources does not allow assessment of effects. It is necessary to know how to weight any differences in resources. And for this, there is no substitute for investigations into the fundamental educational relationships that lie behind student performance.

Finally, as seen from the previous analyses, accounting for changes in samples of students and schools over time can have important effects on the interpretation of any data. As projects evolve, both schools and students disappear, sometimes to be replaced by new observations. Unless sampling is perfect, these changes can lead to misleading evaluations.

PROBLEMS. A number of difficulties confounded the evaluation process:

- Schools disappear over time as a result of drought, elections and the resulting political changes, and economic changes in a fragile environment. A total of 611 schools closed between 1981 and 1983.
- Even when schools remain open, not all of them continue to have a fourth grade. Between 1983 and 1985 there were 100 schools without a fourth grade.
- There were also significant differences between states with respect to closings.
- Even when schools remained open, it proved harder to match students than had been expected.

- It also proved to be extremely difficult to match general socioeconomic data to particular schools and communities at given time periods because of the fact that different sources of data have to be matched up.

## Keeping Quasi-Experimental Designs in the Evaluation Repertoire: When and How to Use Them

While the immediate concern of most managers, planners, policymakers, and donors is to monitor project implementation and improve performance, there are a number of situations in which policymakers require detailed and precise information on the impacts of development programs on all affected groups. Most development programs are intended to improve the quality of life of beneficiaries in some way (or, as in the case of involuntary resettlement, at least to ensure they are no worse off as a result of the project). Consequently, there are occasions when governments and donor agencies are required (by their own management or by external groups) to provide an assessment of the real impacts of development policies and programs. This may be part of a portfolio review (for example, when a new multiyear lending program is being negotiated) it or may take place when critics are complaining about the potentially negative impacts of development programs in areas such as environment or resettlement, or when there is a need to ensure that development programs are reaching and benefiting the intended target groups.

Under these circumstances, among others, borrowers, executing agencies and financiers may require the best possible information about whether these benefits have been produced, how much they cost, which groups have benefited most and least, and what factors affected the outcomes. When such information is required, a more complex and robust evaluation design than conventional program monitoring is normally needed to obtain it. These more rigorous evaluation designs may be justified in several circumstances.

A recent review of development program evaluations (Dennis and Boruch 1989) concluded that QE designs are justified when decisionmakers perceive the need to improve present practice and settle disagreements about which policy alternative best addresses the need. Field experiments are useful when decisionmakers need to justify new policies and when older ones are imperfect.

Quasi-experimental designs are required when it is necessary to assess the changes that a project or program has produced in the welfare of the affected populations. Most development projects are justified on the grounds that the affected populations will be better off than they would be if the project had not taken place. The purpose of QE designs is to determine precisely what impact has been felt by different groups.

In sum, more rigorous, time-consuming, and expensive impact evaluation designs may be justified under one or more of the following conditions:

- When it is essential to understand the impacts (both positive and negative) of large-scale social investments. In many cases the impacts will be difficult to measure and may affect widely dispersed populations over a long period of time. In such cases a more rigorous evaluation design may be required to ensure that all potential affected groups are identified and the impacts of the project on them studied systematically over a long period of time. Cases in point are irrigation, power, and urban renewal/housing projects that cause major disruptions and important changes in the lives of many people. In situations such as this, a strong case can be made for conducting a broad, longitudinal impact study covering a number of different projects and with a design that takes into account the impacts on all affected groups. The value of such an evaluation would not be judged, as it is now, in terms of the immediate information needs of the policymakers and planners associated with a particular project, but in terms of the information it would provide to the development institutions and all concerned national agencies concerning the costs and benefits of these major investments.
- When large social investments are planned in a country or sector and there are serious disagreements about the benefits of the programs or about the most effective way in which they should be implemented. In these cases a carefully planned impact evaluation may improve one's understanding of potential program benefits and may improve cost-effectiveness by identifying the most efficient delivery systems. The EDURURAL program in Brazil is one example. Others can be found in the fields of population and the delivery of public health and primary health care services.
- When decisions have to be made concerning major new investments in continuing or modifying a program, the cost of the evaluation may be justified in terms of the money saved in selecting the correct

investment alternative. A case in point was the Experimental Housing Allowance Program in the United States, where it has been estimated that the investment of several million dollars in a rigorous evaluation of the merits of different kinds of incentives for families and entrepreneurs to invest in housing improvements, may have saved the government several billion dollars per year.

The key point is that the justification for a rigorous impact evaluation will often depend not only on the benefits to policymakers or planners concerned with a particular project or program, but also on the usefulness of the information to a wider audience. In some cases this may involve other countries and agencies considering similar projects, whereas in other cases it may be of interest to the international development community to assess more carefully the impacts of the policies and programs they are supporting. As we have shown, a number of important developmental questions cannot be fully answered through simpler and more economical evaluations, particularly questions concerning the impact of programs on the groups who are not the primary beneficiaries or clients of the concerned agencies and about whom information is less easily available. We have also shown that experience, although often quite limited, is available to guide the design and implementation of such evaluations.

## Recommended Reading

Cook, Thomas, and Donald Campbell. 1979. *Quasi-Experimentation: Design and Analysis Issues in Field Settings*. Chicago: Rand McNally.

The standard reference text on quasi-experimental designs.

Dennis, Michael, and Robert Boruch. 1989. "Randomized Experiments for Planning and testing Projects in Developing Countries: Threshold Conditions." *Evaluation Review* 13(3):292–309.

Useful compilation of examples in which experimental and quasi-experimental designs have been used in developing countries, together with a discussion of the conditions under which these designs are potentially feasible and useful.

Freeman, Howard, Peter Rossi, and Sonia Wright. 1979. *Evaluating Social Projects in Developing Countries*. Paris: Organization for Economic Cooperation and Development.

Chapter 4 presents examples of impact assessments in developing countries.

Harbison, Ralph, and Eric Hanushek. 1992. *Educational Performance of the Poor: Lessons from Rural Northeast Brazil.* New York. Oxford University Press.

One of the best and most comprehensive descriptions of how rigorous quasi-experimental designs can be applied to large-scale development projects. It shows clearly how policy questions are defined and how a research design can be developed to answer them. It also stressed the many political, economic and technical factors which limit the implementation and interpretation of a large-scale evaluation.

McMillan, Della, Jean-Baptiste Nana, and Kimseyinga Savadogo. 1993 *Settlement and Development in the River Blindness Zone. Case Study: Burkina Faso.* Technical Paper 200. Washington D.C.: World Bank.

Detailed, but easily understandable explanation and assessment of the research methodology. The study is particularly useful for understanding how case studies can complement quantitative survey methods. It also demonstrates that most major development projects require a complex evaluation design with many specially selected subsamples and with longitudinal studies that can observe the processes of change over a long period of time.

World Bank. 1993. *Early Experience with Involuntary Resettlement: Overview.* Operations Evaluation Department. Report No. 12142.

An overview of the findings of the first studies on involuntary resettlement in Thailand, India, and Ghana. This provides a review of the issues arising in these programs and shows how the findings of evaluation studies can be used. References are given to the more detailed countries studies for readers interested in the details of how each evaluation was conducted.

## Notes

1. In the case of the World Bank this latter concern was reflected in the 1992 *Effective Implementation: Key to Development Impact* (the Wappenhans Report).

2. Internal World Bank report. Draft, June 14, 1993.

3. The OED impact evaluation reports are listed in the OED catalogue of publications that is published annually and is available through the World Bank bookstores.

4. The studies cited are the Maharashtra Irrigation Project in India, the Polonoreste Resettlement Project in Brazil, and the Khao Laem Hydroelectric Project in Thailand.

5. For more information on this evaluation see World Bank (1993).

6. For more details on the evaluation see World Bank (1992d).

7. For more information on this evaluation see World Bank (1993).

8. The impact evaluation of the Karnataka Irrigation Project probably had a better control group as it included a sample of households affected and not affected by the dam. A tracer study was also conducted to identify and study families who remained in the area. See Operations Evaluation Department (1993) Report 12132.

9. Personal communication from Dennis Purcell, December 6, 1993.

10. The information for this section was obtained from internal World Bank progress reports as the evaluation is still under way and no formal documentation is yet available.

11. A certain number of schools had already been selected for SIF financing before the evaluation began. These were excluded from the evaluation design and the number was not large enough to have a significant effect on the outcome or interpretation of the evaluation.

12. For more information on this evaluation see McMillan (1987, 1993); and McMillan, Nana, and Savadogo (1993). For a description of the River Blindness Resettlement Program. For a general description of the River Blindness Program, see Wigg (1993). The authors would like to thank Josette Murphy, who was technical adviser to AVV, the national agency during the early years of this study, and who maintained contact throughout the ten-year period in which longitudinal studies were being conducted, for providing important background information and for commenting on the text.

13. For a detailed discussion of this evaluation, see Harbison and Hanushek (1992).

# Part III

## Data Collection
## for Monitoring and Evaluation
### A Guide for Practitioners

# 9

## Quantitative Survey Methods

The purpose of a sample survey is to collect *standardized information* from a *carefully selected sample* of respondents. It is carried out by means of a *structured instrument* such as a questionnaire or observation guide. Sample surveys are appropriate when the research design calls for comparable information about a relatively large number of subjects. The information may be used to compare different groups at a given point in time, to estimate changes over time, to compare actual conditions with the goals established in the project design, or to describe conditions in a particular community or group. Unless all data are collected in a sufficiently uniform and precise way, it will be impossible to make meaningful comparisons between groups or between points in time.

### Definition and Uses of Sample Survey Methods in Evaluation Research

*Definition and Uses*

The required information may be in the form of *interval data* (number of household members, household income, educational level and school attendance, number of vaccinations received by each child in the household); *ordinal data* (ranking of housing quality on a 10-point scale; opinions on whether conditions in the community are better, the same, or worse than five years ago); or *nominal data* (respondents are asked to explain why they migrated to the city, what they think about the main problems facing the community, or what types of illnesses children have had during the past two weeks).

The following studies illustrate some of the ways in which sample surveys are commonly used in evaluation research:

- An observation guide was applied to a sample of plots in a sites and service housing project to measure the progress of house construction and to identify groups whose rate of house construction is falling behind schedule. The enumerator (one data collector) had to indicate, on the basis of direct observation, how many rooms were built, what building materials were used, the total area constructed, and whether there were any building materials on the plot (Senegal Bureau d'Evaluation 1979).
- A questionnaire was administered to a sample of families to determine whether they had received and understood information explaining how to prepare and administer oral rehydration therapy. The questionnaire also included information on the social and economic characteristics of households so as to determine the education, family size, and income of households that were not receiving adequate information (see Valadez, Vargas, and Sell 1989).
- A questionnaire was administered to samples of heads of households who were and were not members of a fishing cooperative to study their opinions of the cooperative and to estimate the impact of the cooperative on household income (Nucleo de Acompanhamento e Avaliacão 1983) and nutritional status.

Sample surveys are often used in experimental or quasi-experimental designs in which the same information must be collected from a sample of project participants and a control group at two or more points in time to estimate changes in a set of indicators of project impacts. For this kind of rigorous analysis, the survey instrument must satisfy a number of conditions. First, the concepts to be measured must be clearly defined. Second, the indicators must be valid measures of the concepts being studied. A mother's report on the number of incidents of diarrhea among her children in the past six months will not be reliable information in areas where diarrhea is common and easily forgotten. Third, the questions must be clear and unambiguous so that the information will be reliable and consistent, and not subject to different interpretations by different respondents or by different interviewers.

Finally, information collecting must be supervised to avoid deliberate or unintentional distortion by the interviewer. Sometimes an interviewer will force certain responses by asking the question in a biased way—for example, "Wouldn't you agree that conditions in this community have gotten worse over the past few years?" In other cases the interviewer may assume certain answers without asking the question. If the family looks very poor, for example, the interviewer may not bother to ask if they own a television set.

Even when less statistical rigor is sought, it is still essential to ensure that the information is collected in a precise and uniform way to permit comparisons between respondents, households, organizations, or communities.

### Appropriate and Inappropriate Uses of Quantitative Survey Methods

For many researchers, evaluation is synonymous with quantitative sample surveys, whether they are considering the impact of a project on the physical environment, the efficiency and effectiveness of community participation, changes in employment and income, or the reasons for high default rates on loan repayments. Not all project evaluations require structured questionnaires to be applied to large samples of subjects for the sake of precision and statistical rigor. In some cases, quantitative survey methods are not even appropriate, and certainly have their drawbacks when used to evaluate community participation and organizational behavior. A questionnaire may inhibit people from speaking frankly about the political tensions and personal rivalries that often occur in community organizations. Also, the activities or processes being studied (how a community decides whether to participate in a donor-sponsored project, the organization of self-help house construction, or the maintenance of handpumps and deep tubewells in an irrigation project) comprise a series of events and involve many different actors. Any attempt to simplify such activities or to classify them in a predetermined category may force the researcher to ignore available evidence. Complex activities cannot easily be dissected into separate and quantifiable events without losing sight of how they function. Each activity is unique and must be described and understood within the particular context in which it occurred. In many group situations it would be difficult to know beforehand what should be described. For many studies of community organizations, the most effective methods will be direct observation, combined with conversations with residents and project field staff.

In an analysis of changes in the quality of the physical environment, the required information (types of improvements made to the house, water supply, quality and cleanliness of the streets) can often be obtained from direct observation without having to ask any questions. Table 9-1 summarizes conditions under which sample surveys are appropriate.

## Developing the Survey Instrument

*Exploratory Work to Understand the Issues to Be Studied*

Before preparing a first draft of the questionnaire, evaluators should conduct an *exploratory study* to identify the communities and the issues

**Table 9-1.  Types of Evaluation Studies in Which Sample Surveys Are and Are Not Appropriate**

| *When Sample Surveys Are Appropriate* | *When Sample Surveys Are Usually Not Appropriate* |
|---|---|
| • A project affects large numbers of beneficiaries.<br>• Policymakers require accurate estimates of project impacts.<br>• Statistical comparisons must be made between groups.<br>• Implementation procedures are thoroughly tested and are expected to operate well, thereby justifying investment in the evaluation of impacts.<br>• The target population is heterogeneous and it is difficult to isolate the influence of factors unrelated to the project. | • A project affects small numbers of beneficiaries.<br>• Policymakers are mainly concerned with project outcomes. (Were houses completed on time and within budget? How many people use the health clinics?)<br>• Implementation procedures are new and untested, and it is likely that the way in which the project is implemented will affect outcomes and impacts.<br>• The purpose of the evaluation is to study and evaluate the operation of community organizations.<br>• The purpose of the evaluation is to assess easily observable changes in the quality of the physical environment. |

to be studied. Patton (1982) calls this process designing "thoughtful questionnaires."

The exploratory study should begin with a review of existing reports and studies relating to the communities and to the project. Frequent visits should also be made to the target communities to become acquainted with the areas and the residents. The aim is to understand attitudes to the project, anticipate potential problems, and estimate impacts on beneficiaries and the surrounding areas. Lawrence Salmen (1987) has pointed out the importance of this kind of preliminary study and some of the problems that can arise when project management is not familiar with the areas or their residents.

On the basis of these contacts, the evaluator should identify all the potential *stakeholders* likely to be affected by, or to have an interest in, the project. They may include the principal socioeconomic groups in the community, community organizations and religious and other outside organizations involved in the community, political parties, local and central government agencies, and the donors. The evaluation design should assess how each of these groups will be affected by the project.

Information useful for developing evaluation designs can often be collected through informal meetings with the agencies involved in the project and with interest groups involved in the project or the community (such as university researchers, business, political, and religious groups). Other useful sources of information may include journalists, police, storekeepers, and door-to-door salesmen. Group discussion can often be enlightening.

It may also be helpful to select a small sample of families and to prepare short, descriptive case studies relating to the main concepts to be investigated in the project. Box 9-1 illustrates how case studies were used to evaluate the impacts of one housing project on household income. An important conceptual issue was to understand how to define a "household," as this was to be the basic unit of analysis. The study concluded that many community residents had quite different concepts of the household than did the evaluators. These preliminary interviews helped the evaluators clarify the basic concepts and avoid what could have been serious confusion during later stages of the study.

There is more agreement on the definitions of other basic concepts. For example, the World Bank Living Standards Measurement Study (Chander, Grootaert, and Pyatt 1980) spent several years developing the concepts and analytic instruments needed to collect comparable data on living standards

Box 9-1.  Using Informal Case Studies to Understand the Key
Concepts to Be Used in an Evaluation Survey: Understanding
the Concept of "Household" in Cartagena, Colombia

"We interviewed a man living in a poorly built shack. He had arrived in
Cartagena not long ago, was not interested in creating or using a social
network; instead he considered his most precious asset to be a large machete,
which he proudly retrieved from under his bed. In that house he lived with
his female companion, his brother and sister-in-law, and with their respective
children. However, no meaningful socioeconomic interaction seemed to exist
between the two brothers. Aside from the large machete, the only possessions
in the house were two old beds and two kitchen stoves, one for each brother
and his family. The patterns of food preparation and consumption therefore
appeared to be better indicators of the boundaries of each household than the
housing structure itself. After repeated field experiences it became clear that
sharing food from the same *olla* (pot) is an important factor in the definition
of the household group. For poor families, eating is a basic survival strategy
and great importance is placed on who pools resources. Households are clear
in their own mind about who does and does not use the *olla* and this seemed
to be a good indicator of membership in the primary economic resource
pooling group."

*Source:* Bamberger, Kaufmann, and Velez (1984).

in a large number of developing countries. In another example, Grootaert
(1982) defined three approaches for measuring welfare, each of which
implied different data and analytical requirements:

- *A true index of welfare* can be developed that incorporates measures of
  the consumption of goods, leisure, household composition, and access
  to public services. These data permit an analysis of the allocation of
  time between work and leisure; domestic work and paid work outside
  the home; and study, work, and leisure. The data and analytical
  requirements make this an expensive and complex tool, with the result
  that few developing countries make much use of it.
- *Total household expenditure* can be estimated. Here, welfare is assumed
  to be equivalent to the total value of the consumption of goods and
  services by the household. This means the true market price of all
  goods and services consumed by the household must be estimated and

then adjusted for differences in household size and age composition. This is an analytically simpler approach.

- *Full household income* can be estimated by calculating the true market value of all goods and services consumed by the household as well as the value of services obtained from household capital goods (such as a house or a car). One problem with this approach is that it is not easy to estimate the full value of publicly provided services, nonmarket services, and leisure.

## The Choice of Survey Instrument

Although the most widely used survey instrument for most kinds of evaluation studies is the questionnaire, a number of other tools are available, some of which are more appropriate for particular kinds of studies, as explained below (also see Table 9-2).

A *questionnaire* is a set of questions administered by an interviewer to a sample of respondents. The responses are recorded by the interviewer for subsequent analysis. Although questions can be formulated in many ways, a drawback of the questionnaire is that the analysis and interpretation are based solely on the written record made by the interviewer. Often the persons doing the coding and analysis have not been involved in the interview process and may never even have visited the areas where the study was conducted.

An *attitude scale* is a specialized form of questionnaire designed to measure the strength of the respondent's feelings or opinions about a certain topic. The two most common forms of attitude scale ask respondents how strongly they feel about a particular subject (Thurstone scale) or whether they agree or disagree with a series of statements that have been selected to measure different strengths of opinion on a particular subject (Lickert scale). These two methods are described later in the chapter.

A well-designed attitude scale permits more rigorous statistical comparisons between groups or between the same people at different points in time. Questions can be carefully tested to ensure that they are *reliable* (the same response will be given if the question is repeated or if it is asked by different interviewers) and *valid*; that is, they are good indicators of the characteristics being studied. Attitude scales have practical and theoretical drawbacks. On the practical side, they are expensive and take time to construct, which makes them inappropriate for most small-scale studies or

**Table 9-2.  Main Kinds of Survey Instruments and Their Strengths and Weaknesses**

| Instrument | Advantages | Disadvantages |
|---|---|---|
| Questionnaire | Flexible and can be applied in most surveys. Easy to use by inexperienced interviewers. | Analysis relies on written record only. |
| Attitude scale | Assess intensity and extremeness of opinions. Rigorous comparisons of attitudes between groups and over time. | Expensive and complex to develop. Only measure unidimensional variables. Agree-disagree formula produces bias. |
| Observation guide | Study variables on which subjects are unable or unwilling to answer questions. Consistency check on questionnaire responses. Observe behavior as well as verbal responses. | Observation can be misleading if not combined with questions. Difficult to interpret meaning of what is observed. |
| Telephone and mail surveys | Cheap and rapid way to obtain information. Can prepare respondents for written survey or interview. Obtain access to people too busy for personal interview. Cheapness permits wider geographical coverage. | Most people in developing countries do not have telephones. Sampling bias, because only covers telephone owners/users. |
| Written test | Gives respondents time to provide more detailed data. Ensure respondents read and understand questions. | Difficult to use where literacy is low. |

even for quite large studies that are only to be conducted once. When, as often happens, attitude scales are constructed without following the required procedures, the data are of questionable value. Attitude data can be useful in the health sector, however, where studies of knowledge, attitudes, and practices may be essential to managers trying to determine whether public health interventions have altered a population's perceptions of essential hygiene or preventive practices that reduce their risk of illness. Many AIDS programs are designed to influence the attitudes and practices of people with regard to both the disease and the people who are infected.

As for the methodological difficulties, most scales can only measure a unidimensional variable where all respondents can be given a single score reflecting the strength of opinion for or against a particular subject. In reality, people often have complex, multidimensional opinions. For example, most people would not simply rate a housing project "good" or "bad" but would respond favorably to some aspects and unfavorably to others. There is a danger that the statistical procedures for selecting scale items may eliminate many of the most interesting questions and create a scale that is statistically reliable but that has limited utility.[1]

An *observation guide* consists of information to be gathered by the researcher through observation rather than questions. For example, the data collector may note the building materials used in a sample of dwellings, assess the cleanliness of the streets, or evaluate how well playgrounds and community centers are maintained. He may also observe health workers delivering services to their community in order to assess the adequacy of their technical competence (Valadez and others 1989). An observation guide can also be used to record the frequency of certain activities, such as the number of people entering a community center or the number who speak in a meeting, or to describe how a meeting or work group is organized, the decisionmaking procedures, leadership styles, the efficiency with which labor is used in a community construction project, the number of children vaccinated by health workers, or the proportion of mothers who know how to prepare and administer oral rehydration therapy. The utility of an observation guide depends on how clearly the observational categories are defined. Some instruments leave too much to the judgment of the observer, with the result that different observers may classify the same phenomenon differently (Valadez, DiPrete, and Weld 1990).

*Telephone interviews* and *mail surveys* are widely used in industrial countries but have more limited applications in developing countries (see Babbie 1973; Nachmias and Nachmias 1981). The obvious limitation of the telephone interview is the smaller number of telephones in these countries— particularly among the groups of interest in most evaluations. The advantage of the telephone survey is the speed and low cost with which data can be obtained, particularly when respondents reside in different cities and a personal interview would cost too much in money or in time to carry out.

One of the advantages of the mail survey is that it permits respondents to provide more detailed information, some of which they themselves may be called upon to collect and organize. For example, banks might be asked about the number and size of small business credits, businesses about how credits have been used, and cooperatives about the kinds of loans they have given. In countries with poor mail service, messengers could deliver and collect the surveys. One drawback of mail surveys is that they depend on the goodwill of potential respondents to fill out the questionnaire and return it. Since no interviewer is present, there is often no incentive to complete them. Therefore, the return rate of mail surveys is generally quite low.

Telephone and mail surveys can be effectively combined with personal interviews. For example, the respondent could be contacted by phone to explain the purpose of the study and agreement obtained to complete the mail survey. Once the information from the mail survey is obtained, there could be a follow-up telephone or personal interview.

*Written tests* can be used to assess the effects of a project on skills or knowledge. Such tests are used to measure changes in literacy or knowledge of subjects taught in school (see Fairweather and Tornatsky 1977). In the Philippines, tests of reading skills and of knowledge of mathematics and science were used to compare the effectiveness of educational television with increased access to textbooks and improved teacher training.

Participants can also be asked to keep *diaries* or *written accounts* of income and expenditures, persons contacted during the day or week, or use of time (see Grootaert and Chung 1980). Reforma and Obusan (1981) asked a sample of 100 households in Manila to keep daily records of all income and expenditures over a period of two years when families were upgrading their housing.

### Defining the Content of the Survey Instrument

A questionnaire should only include those questions that are specifically required for the purposes of the evaluation. Any questions that sound "interesting" but have no specific purpose should be eliminated. Four kinds of information are normally required for an impact evaluation (Table 9-3).

Table 9-3.  Typical Questions Required for an Impact Evaluation

| Kind of Question | Purpose | Examples |
|---|---|---|
| Classification | To assign the interview data to the correct group in the analysis | Participant or control group<br>Services received<br>First or repeat interview |
| Exposure to treatment variables | To measure the intensity with which subjects were exposed to the project services | Which services were received (attends school, piped water in house, vaccinated)<br>Amount of services received (volume of water, size of loan) |
| Outcome variables | To measure the immediate *products* produced by the project; the *sustained* outputs after a certain number of years and; the *impacts* produced as a consequence of the project | *Immediate products*<br>Number of houses constructed<br>Number of loans approved<br>Number of patients treated<br>*Sustained outputs*<br>Condition of roads, houses, etc. after (say) five years.<br>Number of farmers receiving irrigated water after (say) five years<br>Socioeconomic profiles of actual and intended users<br>*Impacts*<br>Changes in income, school attendance, health etc. |
| Intervening variables | To identify and evaluate the effects of other interventions and of social and economic characteristics of the target and control groups on participation in the project and the direction and intensity of changes produced | Income, education, sex of participant or household head, household size and composition, and assets of household or enterprise |

CLASSIFICATION OF NOMINAL DATA. Respondents may be classified according to whether they are project participants or belong to the control group; or by the types and levels of services (shallow or deep tubewells, clinics, water supply, credit) they received before and after entering the project. Where a longitudinal design is being used, it is also important to know whether the respondent is being interviewed for the first time or whether it is a repeat interview. Frequently the analysis of the results is impeded by the omission of some of these seemingly obvious classification questions.

EXPOSURE TO TREATMENT VARIABLES. Not all project beneficiaries receive exactly the same package of services. A family living close to a paved road, having piped water, and sending their children to the community kindergarten will obviously receive more benefits from a project than a family that lives half a mile from the nearest paved road, has to queue up to get water from a communal standpipe, and still has children on the waiting list for kindergarten. It would be misleading to put both families in the same category of "project beneficiaries." Therefore it is important to record the services received and the frequency or amount of services (how much credit, how many visits by the community promotor, how much water, and so on).

A more difficult task is to assess the *quality* of the services. One possibility would be to ask a panel of experts or the project participants to rank the quality of the services. For some services—for example, potable water—there are well-established testing procedures for measuring quality. Lot quality assurance sampling (Valadez 1991) is a rapid method based on industrial quality-control procedures.

OUTCOME VARIABLES. Projects are intended to produce a certain set of outcomes or effects. These outcomes can be classified into three broad categories:

- *Immediate products, such as houses constructed, small business loans approved, deep tubewells completed, or the number of children receiving measle vaccinations each week.* Normally, these products are clearly defined in the loan agreement or the project documents.
- *Sustained outputs or continued delivery of services over a long period of time.* The questions to ask here are whether the houses are well maintained and still occupied; whether the tubewells are maintained and operating and user charges being paid; whether the clinics are well maintained and staffed; what proportion of children under three years of age are covered by preventive services; and how many patients they are treating. It may be important to know who is using the services because many projects are coopted by certain wealthier or more influential groups.

• *Project impacts.* The design of most projects assumes that the sustained delivery of outputs will generate certain benefits or impacts, such as improved income, health, or employment, or cheaper and faster transportation of goods. These assumptions must be evaluated.

Table 9-4 illustrates indicators used to measure six common impacts. For example, many projects seek to increase employment or the income of beneficiary households. One indicator of project impact would be the changes in total household income. Other general indicators include the number of people working and the labor force participation rate of certain groups, such as women or young adults.

INTERVENING VARIABLES. Intervening variables are factors (such as characteristics of households, communities, small businesses, or farms) that affect participation in the project or the level or kinds of products, outputs, or impacts produced. For example, the level of education will often affect participation in a community improvement or a small business credit program. Similarly, household characteristics such as income, number of household members, length of time living in the community, and religion tend to affect participation and outcomes. Maternal education is known to be associated with infant mortality.

The evaluation design should take into consideration the influence of intervening variables. The choice of intervening variables to be included in the questionnaire should be determined by a review of previous studies and by the results of the preparatory studies referred to earlier.

*Translating the Content Areas into Measurable Indicators*

The questions to be included in the survey instrument are derived directly from the concepts being studied. If the *concept* to be studied is project impact, it can be defined in terms of a number of *content areas* such as income, expenditures and consumption, health, and attitudes to the project. The concept of income is disaggregated into a series of *elements*: labor income, profits from own business, rental income, and transfers or gifts from relatives and friends.

In addition, each element must be translated into a set of *measurable indicators* or *questions*. Earned income, for example, might be estimated through questions on hours worked, wage rates (per hour, day, or week), overtime rates, and other bonuses. One of the main impacts of many urban

**Table 9-4. Examples of Six Microeconomic Project Impacts and Some Indicators That Could Be Used to Measure Them**

| *Type of Impact* | *Quantifiable Indicators* |
|---|---|
| Employment and income | Total family income |
| | Sources of income |
| | Income stability |
| | Type of employment |
| | Number of people working |
| | Labor force participation rate of particular groups |
| | Proportion of self-employed |
| | Proportion working in formal and informal sectors |
| Demographic characteristics of the family | Family size and stability |
| | Age composition |
| | Education of household head and of mothers |
| | Proportion of children attending school |
| | Civil status of household head |
| | Geographical mobility |
| Housing costs, quality, and value | Sale or rental value of house |
| | Construction quality (ranked on scale) |
| | House size |
| | Access to services |
| Health | Infant and maternal mortality rates |
| | Cause specific mortality rates and leading causes of death |
| | Time lost from work or school due to illness |
| | Access to medical services |
| | Amount spent on medical services |
| | Anthropometric measures of weight and height |
| Consumption patterns | Amount spent on housing |
| | Amount spent on food |
| | Amount spent on clothing |
| | Amount spent on transportation |
| | Amount spent on health |
| | Amount saved |
| Community participation and attitudes | Number of community organizations in which family participates |
| | Number of friends in the community or project |
| | Political, social, and religious organizations |
| | Participation in mutual help programs |
| | Satisfaction with the community |
| | Satisfaction with social, economic, and political situation |

projects is increased rental income. If the questionnaire included only earned income, the evaluation would have completely missed this important effect.

Table 9-5 illustrates how the conceptual framework for the World Bank Living Standards Measurement Study (discussed above) was translated into a set of measurable indicators. Three alternative models had been proposed for estimating welfare, and the table shows the information requirements for each model. The table identifies the variables, states the level of data collection (individual, household, community, district, region), and explains the analytical purpose.

A survey instrument could fail to validly assess project impacts for any one of the following reasons:

- The wrong content areas were selected: perhaps the project did not affect income, although it may have had other impacts not covered by the survey.
- The elements selected were not good measures of the content areas: perhaps wages are not a major source of income in areas where most people are self-employed.
- The indicators did not adequately measure the principal elements: hourly wage rates may not be a good estimator of labor market earnings in situations where bonus payments are large in relation to basic hourly wage rates.
- If respondents are unable or unwilling to respond accurately to the questions, the data obtained will be biased or incomplete.

The above example shows that the design of a survey instrument must follow a precise logic and that each question must be directly related to a particular element of a carefully thought out content area. Care must be taken not to include several questions for each element in an effort to collect all the potentially important information. There is a limit to the patience of the respondent and to the time he or she is prepared to give to the interviewer. Every additional question increases the risk of tiring or annoying the respondent or of having something interrupt the interview before it is completed.

## Ways of Asking Questions

There are many ways to ask a question, and an important function of the *pilot study* (see following sections) is to help find the best way to obtain the information.

Table 9-5.  Data Needed to Measure Welfare: The World Bank's Living Standards Measurement Study

| Variable | Level of Collection | Analytical Purpose |
|---|---|---|
| *Basic welfare measures* | | |
| Expenditures | Household | Basic welfare measures to be deflated with price index and equivalence scale |
| Household composition (age, sex) | Individual | Equivalence scales, general analysis |
| Prices | Community | Price index (by region, urban/rural or socioeconomic group |
| *Sources of welfare* | | |
| Income by source | Individual and household | Causal analysis of welfare; earnings functions; labor force participation in the household context |
| Costs/outputs of the household enterprise | Household | Causal analysis of welfare; farm production functions |
| Opportunity wage rates | Community | Imputation of value of time for construction of income variables; analysis of labor force participation decisions |
| Time use: Which tasks | Individual | Imputation of value of time for construction of income variables |
| Average duration | Community | |
| Asset holdings and purchases | Household | Accumulation and potential for income growth; earnings functions; separation of short-term variations; definition of socioeconomic groups |
| Changes in asset holdings over time | Household (retrospective questioning) | Trends in accumulation |
| Gifts, remittances (donor location, relation to recipient, income level, recipient motivation, stability) | Household, community | Vulnerability; modeling of networks of social support |

308

| Variable | Level of Collection | Analytical Purpose |
|---|---|---|
| *Labor market* | | |
| Schooling, work experience | Individual (retrospective questioning) | Earnings functions; separation of short-term and long-term variations |
| Employment status, sector, occupation, hours worked, formal and informal sector identifiers | Individual, household | Earnings functions; labor market segmentation; labor force participation decision analysis; definition of socioeconomic groups |
| Demand for labor | Community, district, region | Identification of work opportunities; modeling labor force participation decision |
| Perception of labor demand | Household | Information bottlenecks (contrast with objective data); modeling labor force participation decision |
| *Other* | | |
| Housing physical characteristics, amenities, type of tenure, location | Household | Hedonic rent equations; construction of income variables; short-/long-term variations; definition of socioeconomic groups |
| Changes in housing conditions | Household retrospective questioning | Trends in quality of housing |
| Entitlements | Household | Flagging high risk groups; identification of potentially poor |
| Changes of location | Household (retrospective questioning) | Studying migration decision |
| Other demographic and socioeconomic characteristics | Individual, household | Definition of socioeconomic groups; miscellaneous analysis |

ASKING VERSUS OBSERVING. Many kinds of information concerning the size of the house, quality of construction materials, number of rooms, the existence of certain services, and so on, can be obtained by direct observation. However, observation can be misleading. For one thing, it cannot be assumed that the house belongs entirely to the family being interviewed. Similarly, it should not be assumed that services do not exist simply because they are not where the observer expected to find them—the water tap may be located at the rear of the plot, or it may be locked in a box to prevent other people from taking the water without paying. (Observation techniques are discussed more fully in Chapter 10.)

OPEN VERSUS CLOSED QUESTIONS. "If every time it rains the streets are flooded for several days, causing health problems, what do you think should be done?" This is an *open question*, since no answer is suggested and the interviewer will carefully note what the respondent says. It could also be formulated as a closed question, with the respondent being asked to select from among a number of predetermined alternatives:

"If every time it rains the streets are flooded for several days, causing health problems, which of the following do you think should be done?"

- Organize a community meeting to develop solutions.
- Ask the community leader to solve the problem.
- Write the Ministry of Health.
- Organize local families to dig a drainage ditch.

Open questions allow the respondent to answer in his or her own words, rather than being forced to choose among alternatives that may not include his or her true opinion. There are advantages in using open questions when asking about social behavior that is disapproved of. Bradburn and Sudman (1979) found that respondents reported higher levels of drinking and sexual activity in response to an open question than when they were asked to rate the level of activity on a scale that included the categories "never," "once a year or less," "once a month," "once a week," "several times a week," and "daily." The multiple-choice question makes it easier for respondents to choose the "never" or "once-a-year" categories, whereas the open question permits them to admit to a higher (and hopefully more accurate) level of activity.

A disadvantage of the open question is that the results are harder to analyze than are standardized responses, and the interviewer's way of recording responses may introduce unanticipated and therefore uncontrolled biases. There is also the danger that some of the responses may be too general and therefore difficult to interpret. Converse and Presser (1986) cite a study on work satisfaction in which a frequent response to the question, "People look for different things in a job; what would you most prefer in a job?" was "the pay." This response leaves it unclear as to whether respondents were concerned with "high pay" or "steady pay." This ambiguity could have been resolved through the use of a closed question that included both "high pay" and "steady pay" as options.

Closed questions are relatively easy to analyze and have the advantage of making the respondent choose among the alternatives of interest to the researcher. For example, if a researcher wants to know whether the expectation of a better job was a primary reason for migration, this can be included as one of the alternative responses. With an open question, on the other hand, the fact that the respondent does not mention employment does not necessarily mean it was not a factor in the decision to migrate.

There is always the danger with closed questions that important responses may be left out, and that the respondent will then be forced to choose among meaningless or unimportant alternatives. This risk can be reduced by a follow-up question in which the respondent is asked, Are there any other reasons (factors, points) you would like to mention that were not included in the list?" The interviewer should always ask follow-up questions or use probes whenever the answers are not clear or it is felt that the respondent has other things to add.

THE IMPORTANCE OF THE "NO OPINION" OPTION. Whenever closed questions are being used, the response options should include a "no opinion" category. Earlier studies have shown that when respondents are encouraged to admit that they do not have an opinion, this can reduce by as much as one-third the number of respondents who will give their opinion on the topic being studied . Many people seem to feel that they should have an opinion, so it is important to show respondents that it is quite legitimate not have an opinion. Rather than simply including "no opinion" as one of the options on the list, it is better to have a screening question such as

- "Here is a question about another country. Not everyone has an opinion on this. If you do not have an opinion just say so."
- "Could you tell me whether there is any kind of cooperative organization to which families living in this community can belong?"

- "There have been a number of articles in the local newspapers on the problem of teenager alcoholism. Could you tell me whether you have thought about this issue?"

Another point of some concern is whether a question that asks respondents to rate how strongly they agree or disagree with a particular statement should include a neutral position ("neither agree nor disagree"). Some researchers look upon "no opinion" as wasted data and prefer to force people to choose. Others feel that the data are meaningless when respondents are forced to have an opinion on a topic they know or care nothing about. The "don't know" category is more complex. One could argue both for including and excluding it as a response option. The reasons for including it are identical to those stated for listing "no opinion." However, the reasons for excluding it are also compelling. In surveys that are intended to test people's knowledge, it is often important to have the respondents themselves conclude that they don't know the answer to a question rather than give them an easy way to avoid responding. For example, answers to open-ended questions such as "How many polio vaccinations should your child have before his first birthday?" lead to different policy conclusions, depending on whether mothers overestimate or underestimate. Children are more at risk to polio if their mothers underestimate.

Sometimes impatient interviewers will mark a response as "don't know" rather than give a mother the time to collect her thoughts and try to answer to the best of her knowledge. In the experience of one of the authors, it is better to instruct interviewers to write "don't know" next to a question when the interviewee concludes that he or she does not know the requested information. This simple step has tended to reduce the number of "don't know" responses.

SELF-ADMINISTERED QUESTIONNAIRES. Sometimes, the respondent is asked to complete all or part of the questionnaire himself. When literacy is not a barrier, the self-administered questionnaire can be useful for collecting detailed information, particularly when the information has to be obtained over a period of time, say, when families are asked to keep records of their dietary intake, incomes, and expenditures or the way they use their time. Self-administered questionnaires are also often used in attitude studies.

## Measuring Attitudes

Many evaluation studies need to assess respondents' opinions about the way they have been affected by a project and also the *intensity* of those feelings. Such assessments are particularly useful for projects designed to *change attitudes* toward the efficacy of community organization, for example, as a way to resolve problems. These attitudes may include the willingness to cooperate with people from other cultural groups; the willingness to accept responsibility for maintenance of infrastructure; and views about how conditions of life will change over the next few years.

There is considerable disagreement about the utility of measuring attitudes. Most economists do not attempt to measure attitudes directly but instead use indicators such as increased rental value of properties to assess satisfaction with improved services. Some sociologists and social psychologists who study attitudes argue that it is essential to understand how people feel about a project or other major change in their environment in order to understand and perhaps predict how they will react. Information on attitudes may help managers and policymakers understand why certain groups have been less enthusiastic than expected and how to modify the project design or implementation to make it more attractive.

An attitude scale is a specialized form of questionnaire designed to measure the direction and intensity of feelings or opinions about a certain topic. The two most common attitude scales (Thurstone and Lickert) ask respondents either how strongly they feel about a particular subject or whether they agree or disagree with a series of statements selected to measure the degree of intensity of feelings.

A *Thurstone scale* consists of a series of statements relating to the attitude being measured (for example, opinion of the utility of cooperatives). A group of judges might be asked to rank each statement to indicate its degree of favorableness (to cooperatives). A rank of 1 might indicate the statement was extremely favorable to cooperatives and a score of 11 might mean the statement was extremely unfavorable. An average score would then be computed for each statement and a set of low-, medium-, and high-ranked statements would be selected for the scale. Respondents would be asked to indicate the items with which they agree and disagree, and the score of each respondent would be calculated as the mean of the items with which he or she agreed.

A number of studies have challenged the validity of "agree-disagree" questions of the kind used in the Thurstone scales. Lenski and Leggett (1960) found that about 10 percent of their sample agreed with both of two mutually contradictory statements. Many researchers believe that a proportion of respondents tend to agree with whatever statement is presented in the survey. Schuman and Presser (1981) found that the lower the educational level of a subject, the more likely he/she is to agree with statements given to them by the interviewer.

To construct a *Lickert scale*, the interviewer again selects statements that represent different degrees of favorableness to the subject being studied, but the respondent is now asked to indicate how strongly he or she agrees or disagrees with each statement. Sometimes a 5-point scale is used ("agree strongly," "agree," "neither agree nor disagree," "disagree," and "disagree strongly"). Other researchers prefer a 7- or 11-point scale in which one extreme represents "strongly agree" and the other extreme represents "strongly disagree." A score is then computed for each respondent by multiplying the rank score for each item by its degree of favorableness.

It takes careful preparation to construct an attitude scale, particularly for test items that are to be administered to a large number of respondents. The final items are then selected using rigorous statistical criteria. If these procedures are not used, the validity and reliability of the scales are likely to be low and the results misleading.

An alternative approach is to show the respondent a picture (for example, a group of people in a meeting) and to ask what he or she sees:

- "Who are the people in the picture?"
- "If these were people in a community meeting, what do you think they might be discussing?"
- "Do you think the people listening agree with what the speaker is saying?"

Despite the methodological difficulties, attitude measurement is an important area of research. Participants often judge the impact of a project in a different way from the outside observer. Because the primary objective of the project is to improve the quality of life of the project beneficiaries, it is important to know what they feel about what has happened.

THE ORDER OF QUESTIONS. Respondents tend to interpret a particular question in the context of the questions that preceded it. Turner and Krauss

(1978) have found that respondents are less likely to say their taxes are too high after being asked about a number of items on which government spending should be increased; and Cowan, Murphy, and Weiner (1978) report that subjects previously asked about their attitude toward crime are more likely to tell whether they have been victims of crimes. Similarly, if respondents have been asked a number of questions about the problems of finding jobs, and are then asked to identify the most serious problems facing the community, they tend to refer more frequently to problems of employment.

Although there are no well-defined guidelines, it is clear that the researcher must think carefully about the order of questions and must avoid introducing earlier questions that might prompt respondents to answer in a certain way.

## Selecting and Training the Interviewers

Regardless of how well the questionnaire has been designed, it may fail to collect accurate and complete information if it is administered by poorly selected or trained interviewers. Problems may arise if the interviewers are not motivated, if they are not well trained, if they do not have the necessary professional training or experience to understand the subject of the study, or if they are unable to establish rapport with the respondents. The following are some of the points to consider in selecting interviewers:

- *Is it better to use students or rather older and more mature people?* It is often easier to locate and contract students, they are also more flexible in their working hours and may be more willing to work in difficult areas. At the same time, community leaders, businessmen, or older community residents may be reluctant to discuss personal or business affairs with someone much younger than themselves.
- *Is it better to use male or female interviewers, or a combination of both?* Mothers may be reluctant to discuss child rearing or family affairs with a male interviewer, and male respondents may be unwilling to discuss politics or other assumed masculine subjects with a woman. In many kinds of studies, a team consisting of a man and a woman can be effective. Community residents usually discuss different things with male and female interviewers, so this approach could produce a more detailed response. Care should be taken not to make too many assumptions about how people will respond to male and female interviewers.

In some cases, males may speak about their problems more freely with a woman because they may not feel the need to keep up a "macho" image with a woman. This is not always the case, however. One public health study found that mothers in rural Costa Rica preferred a male interviewer since they had grown accustomed to speaking with men about their own health.

- *Are interviewers required to have any specialized skills or knowledge?* It is often necessary or useful to contract interviewers with certain technical or professional backgrounds. For example, nurses may be useful for studies on health or child rearing, architects or engineers for studies on housing, and accountants or economists for studies on small businesses or employment generation programs. In other cases, it may be necessary to contract people with special research or interviewing skills, such as sociologists, psychologists, or anthropologists. However, the personality and motivation of the interviewer often seem more important than professional training. According to Salmen (1987), professional training does not seem to affect a person's ability to conduct participant observation studies, and an economist, architect, or social worker could do equally well. The most important factor is their interest in living in a community they are not familiar with and getting to know the people living there.

Interviewer training is an important, but often ignored aspect of the research process. A common problem is that different interviewers use different criteria for deciding who to interview and how to treat nonresponse or for interpreting some of the questions. This kind of confusion can drastically reduce the reliability and comparability of the survey responses.

Training should normally cover the following points:

- The purposes of the study and how the results will be used.
- The procedures for selecting respondents and for dealing with situations where the respondent cannot be located or cannot be interviewed.
- The concepts being used in the study (such as the household, household member, income, employment).
- The way to ask each question, to classify replies, to handle those who fail to respond, and to determine what kinds of follow-up questions are required.

- The fact that interviewers should practice administering the questionnaire to each other and should then conduct some practice interviews with the kinds of subjects included in the survey.
- How interviewers can be selected on the basis of their performance during training.

It is important to prepare a complete interviewer's guide explaining in detail how each question should be asked, how responses should be recorded, and what kinds of follow-up questions are required.

## Testing and Administering the Questionnaire

Once a list of questions has been developed, a draft questionnaire should be prepared. This draft is tested in a *pilot survey* or *pretest* to determine whether the questions are clear, what length of interview is appropriate, whether respondents would be willing to reply, which questions are awkwardly phrased and difficult for interviewers to ask, and which are difficult for respondents to understand. A long questionnaire will sometimes take at least three months to compile from the time the first draft is completed to the actual interviews. It is also a good idea for pilot interviewers to work in pairs, with one conducting the interview and the other observing. Interviewers should meet at the end of each day to exchange experiences and to assess the strengths and weaknesses of the questionnaire.

Before the formal survey begins, it is often necessary to establish contacts in the community. In some cases the research director may be required to meet with community leaders or local government authorities to explain the purposes of the study and to seek their permission and support. In some communities in El Salvador, residents had been advised not to respond to interviews if the study did not have the approval of community organizations. Although contact with community organizations may cause some methodological problems, it is important to be aware that many "interesting" communities are continually invaded by interviewers, most of whom take up a great deal of residents' time without offering anything in return. The researchers have an obligation to explain the purposes of the study to the community and to try to ensure that the results will be used to help the community. A good practice, but one that is rarely followed, is to meet with the community leaders to discuss the results of the study once it is completed. It is also wise to cite the reasons for the interview in any introductory remark at the beginning of each questionnaire.

Procedures must also be set up for supervising and guiding the interviewers. In the early stages of the study, the interviewers are bound to make a number of mistakes and will need constant assistance. Supervisors should therefore meet with interviewers every evening or morning to discuss their experiences and to advise on how to solve problems. In a complex survey, it may be necessary to have one supervisor for as few as every five interviewers. The supervisor should, among other things:

- Revisit a sample of households to ensure that the interview was conducted with the right person and to reconfirm some of the basic information. There will always be a few interviewers who are lazy, who make up some of the information or in extreme cases who falsify the entire interview. This can only be detected by spot checks of this kind.
- Be in the community most of the time to provide advice.
- Accompany the interviewers during a few interviews to discuss interviewing techniques and problems.
- Carefully review all completed interviews and provide immediate feedback the next day.

A careful record must be kept of what happens during each scheduled interview. The record must indicate whether the respondent was located and interviewed, what procedures were used if he or she could not be found or interviewed, and what problems arose in the interview. An accepted convention is to visit a household where no one is currently at home at least twice before selecting an alternative. Neighbors often know the whereabouts of a resident and when he or she will return home.

## The Importance of a Multimethod Approach

To avoid the problems that can arise from a mono-method bias, the questionnaire should be complemented by other data collecting procedures, which can help to check the reliability of the information and to interpret its meaning. Unstructured interviews should be conducted during the pilot study to identify the key issues and to determine how respondents perceive them (see Box 9-1). During the application of the survey, informal contacts should be maintained with the community to obtain feedback on how well the community understands and responds to the questions (see Box 9-2). Intensive unstructured follow-up interviews can also be used with a small

Box 9-2. Using Qualitative Data to Complement Survey Findings:
Survey of a Fishing Cooperative in Natal, Brazil

A rapid evaluation of a fishing cooperative in Brazil not only presented a statistical analysis, but also included the following verbatim comments of fishermen to help the reader understand the meaning of the statistical findings.

"The majority of the fishermen here don't own their boats, but are hired by a boat owner. He gives us everything we need, and when we return everything is for him."

"When the cooperative arrived they said that they were going to help us by providing materials and buying our fish, but this hasn't happened. We go on suffering and have to buy smaller quantities of everything elsewhere at higher prices and we still have to sell our fish at lower prices."

"The cooperative has to offer us something more attractive if we are going to believe in it. This cooperative decides things without consulting with us fishermen. They even close the doors of the room where the fish are washed and we are not allowed to enter."

*Source:* Nucleo de Acompanhamento e Avaliacao (Natal, Brazil) (1983).

number of respondents to check the consistency of the survey responses and to help interpret the results. Case studies can be prepared on a few respondents to explain the survey findings in more detail.

Direct observation should also be used to provide an independent check on some of the information being obtained (see Box 9-3).

Once the results of the analysis are available, informal interviews should be conducted with key respondents to discuss the findings and to help interpret them. The following are typical examples of issues that might be covered in the follow-up interviews:

- When families received financial support to build their houses, where did this money come from? Was it a loan to be repaid? What did the giver expect to receive in return for his or her support?
- Why did households headed by females make less use of building material loans than households headed by males?
- Many families claim that they are better off living in the project than they were before. However, their health status does not seem to be any better than that of families in the control areas. Why do participants believe they are better off? Has their quality of life increased in ways

---

**Box 9-3. Examples of the Use of Indicators That Can Be Obtained by Direct Observation**

In their classic study, Webb and his colleagues suggested a wide range of "unobtrusive measures" that could be used as indicators of more complex processes or events. Examples of such indicators might include

- The amount of wear on steps as an indicator of the use made of a community facility.
- Analysis of garbage dumps as a source of information on consumption patterns.
- The number of tin roofs or tin utensils as an indicator of wealth.
- The quality of clothing washed and left out to dry as an indicator of consumption patterns and wealth.
- Types of commodities on sale in local stores as an indicator of the economic level of the community.

---

that were not captured by the survey, or is their satisfaction experienced in ways unrelated to health?

## Measurement Issues in Sample Surveys

Given the practical difficulties of returning to the field once survey data have been collected, the validity and practical utility of a quantitative evaluation will be determined to a large degree by the way in which the data were collected. If concepts were badly defined or if the indicators were measured incorrectly, the results of the study will be by and large invalid. The analysts, report writers, or policymakers may not always realize this when they are using the results to plan future projects. This section discusses some of the methodological and conceptual issues that arise in defining and measuring some of the most common indicators used in social sector evaluations.

### Measurement Issues Related to Employment, Income, and Consumption

Changes in employment, income, and consumption are widely used as indicators of the economic impact of projects. Problems of comparability frequently arise from the considerable variation in the way that concepts such as employment are defined.[2] Analysts sometimes collect employment data only on the household head (however that is defined), on the assumption that this person is the principal earner.[3] There are also differences with respect to the minimum age at which household members are included in the labor force, the kinds of economic activities that are defined as employment, and the number of hours or months that someone must work to be classified as a part-time employee (Mehran 1980). The reference period over which employment data are collected may also vary. If the reference period (day, week, or month) is short, the data may be more accurate, but seasonal employment, particularly in agriculture, will be a problem. If a longer reference period is used (for example, a year), it then becomes difficult to estimate rates of labor force participation. It will also be difficult to decide how to treat unpaid household labor, traditional forms of marginal labor (such as scaring away birds from growing crops), and unpaid apprentices.

Some of the most serious biases relate to female employment and women's contribution to household income and to gross national product. Women's household labor and much of their contribution to farm management and agricultural production are frequently undervalued because it is not remunerated. This has had serious implications for the way in which projects are designed. That is to say, the role women play in farm management or in small businesses is often underestimated, with the result that credit and technical assistance programs are often designed on the assumption that they will be used mainly by men.

Similar problems arise in estimating household income and expenditures. The average household income in a community is subject to both short-term and long-term fluctuations. Therefore, the estimation of project impact through the comparison of income at two points in time can be misleading. Figure 9-1 illustrates the difficulties of comparing two time periods to assess the impacts of a housing project on income. Income is subject to both regular seasonal trends (in Figure 9-1, income tends to be higher around December, perhaps because of the coffee harvest or an influx of tourists, and lower around June) and also to annual fluctuations related perhaps to the climate or to fluctuations in the international economy. For example, incomes were generally higher in year 3 than in years 4 and 5. Thus, depending on the time periods selected for the comparison, a project may appear to have had either a positive or a negative impact.

The income of individual households is also subject to considerable fluctuations from month to month, and even from day to day. The problem is further compounded by the fact that many households receive income from several wage-earners, all of whose incomes are subject to the kinds of fluctuation described earlier.

Many low-income households receive a significant proportion of their household income in the form of transfers from relatives or friends. Transfers have been found to account for up to 50 percent of the total household income of certain groups of families (Kaufmann and Bamberger 1984). Transfers are either ignored or not well measured in many household surveys, which therefore significantly underestimate total income. Transfers are difficult to measure because families tend to consider them a form of social rather than economic exchange and may not mention them in response to questions about income (Bamberger, Kaufmann, and Velez 1984).

Often, the respondent may wish to deliberately provide false information on income. In some cultures, the husband may not wish his wife to know how much he earns, and he may understate his true income if the interview is conducted in his home. In other cases, the respondent may deliberately distort the household income in order to fall within the income eligibility

**Figure 9-1. Long-Term Trends and Short-Term and Seasonal Fluctuations in Household Income in the Years Following the Start of a Housing Project**

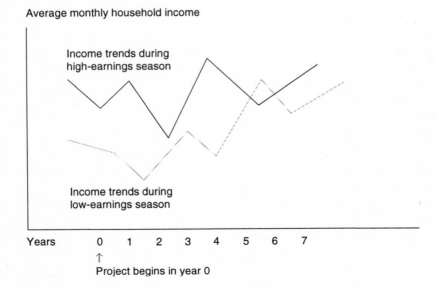

limits established for a certain type of project. In addition, families may not wish to mention certain sources of income that are either illegal or socially unacceptable. Illegal beer brewing, prostitution, illegal fishing, and operating a business without a license are all common examples of sources of income that are not reported. It is also difficult to obtain reliable information on rural landholdings in countries that restrict the amount of land a family can own. Chambers (1983) cites Panse's law, which states that "the average size of landholding in a village increases with the length of residence of the investigator." In other words, when the investigator first visits the community, it is easy for farmers to convince him or her that they own relatively little land and consequently merit special consideration. Once the researcher has spent more time in the community, however, it becomes possible to piece together the information on the ownership of different parcels of land and to find out who the biggest landowners are.

## Measurement Issues Related to Basic Demographic Data

Evaluation studies frequently collect basic demographic information on the household and community. Such variables may be used as indicators of project impacts (for example, better housing may affect geographical mobility or school attendance) or to explain variations in project outcomes (for example, projects may have different impacts on households headed by males and those headed by females, on large and small families, and on families with different educational levels).

Considerable confusion has arisen about how to define a household and a household head.[4] Most countries make some reference to food sharing, but vary greatly when it comes to defining where household members live. In many countries, household members must "live together in a single room or group of rooms" (as in Bangladesh) or "use the same kitchen or cookery pot" (as in Mexico). But in many African countries the geographical definition is more complex, as in the case of Botswana: "Living together means living at any one of the customary living places of the household. This frequently includes a set of huts in a village, another set of huts at a separate land area where crops are grown and a third set of huts at a separate cattle post" (Wahab 1980:22).

Low-income households have been described as "fluctuating coalitions" in which members constantly join and leave in response to changes in their economic conditions. In Cartagena, Colombia (Kaufmann and Bamberger 1984), more than 10 percent of household members have been classified as "temporary," and in El Salvador (Nieves 1979) and Kenya (Nelson 1978) children are transferred from one household group to another either to leave mothers free to work or to transfer the children to an economically more stable family group. Such factors can make it difficult to decide who is a household member and even how the household unit should be defined.

Households in many countries experience regular seasonal fluctuations as members return to the rural areas for harvesting or special ceremonies, or as men return to the city during the months when the demand for labor goes up (for example, during the dry season, when most construction work takes place, or during the tourist season). Care must be taken when making comparisons over time to ensure that measurements are made in the same month of each year.

It is often difficult to establish who is the household head because a woman may be reluctant to admit she has been abandoned by her spouse and prefers to state that her husband is temporarily working elsewhere, as a truck driver, for example. Care must be taken not to count someone who has permanently left the household as a permanent household member, let alone the household head. Wahab (1980) cites similar definitional problems from a number of countries. In Botswana, for example, a widowed mother who builds her hut close to her daughter and who receives food from the daughter may be classified either as forming an independent household or as part of her daughter's household, depending on how the mother classifies herself. Similar ambiguities may arise in situations where a man is supporting one or more women and their children.

Many households contain people who are living there illegally and who will not be reported in the survey. A common example is a subtenant who is there without the permission of the landlord. In other cases, relatives or friends may be living in the city illegally without a work or residence permit.

Cultural factors, too, may affect the reporting of who lives in the household. In some cultures a child is not considered to have been born until it has reached a certain age and has been named. Until then it will not be reported. During the testing of a questionnaire in Mombasa, a male household head was asked how many of his children were living in the house. He named four, all of them boys. Since a number of young girls had been observed in the house, he was asked if he had any other children. "Do you want me to include the girls as well?" he asked!

*Attitudes toward Projects and Their Organization*

See Chapters 4 and 5 for a discussion of measurement techniques and issues.

*Measuring Project Impact on Health*

Poor health and nutrition affect employment, income, education, and also the achievement of other objectives. Matorell (1982) identifies eight sets of indicators that between them provide a comprehensive assessment of the health status of a particular community:

*Anthropometric* measures of height and weight for children of a particular age are sensitive indicators of malnutrition and can indicate wasting and stunting. Growth charts are available in most nations of the world for assessing infant growth and development. These indicators can also be used to identify malnourished women who may have risky births. Although the measurements may seem easy to carry out and reasonably valid, the work needs to be carefully supervised (Valadez and others 1989). These measures can provide an indication of health and nutritional improvements in areas affected by projects, but they must be adjusted for seasonal fluctuations.

*Birth weight* is a good indicator of the health status of both child and mother and is also a good predictor of infant mortality.

*Vaccination status* can indicate the risk of the population to diseases that can be prevented through vaccination, such as polio, diphtheria, tetanus, measles, and tuberculosis.

*Measures of food and nutrient intake* are often required to assess access to adequate food supplies and nutritional status. This is an important indicator for evaluating nutrition programs or any program that seeks to raise disposable income. Various estimation procedures can be used. On the national level, it is possible to use national or regional data on food production, sales, or purchases. At the local and project levels it is usually necessary to conduct studies of household food purchases or consumption by particular individuals. The latter are important when the purpose is to study food consumption by particular groups, such as women or young children.

*Breast-feeding* is another important indicator of nutritional status. The age at which breast-feeding ceases is also the time at which the infant becomes exposed to many kinds of infections.

*Biochemical analysis* can be used to study nutritional status, to assess health, and to identify the incidence of viral and parasitic infections. Unfortunately, these methods can only be used to a limited extent because of their cost, the difficulty of collecting the samples, and the scarcity of trained personnel. The simple analysis of stool samples can be one of the best indicators of the impact of sanitation and water supply projects on the transmission of parasites. Sometimes sophisticated analyses may not be essential. For example, blood in the urine may be used as an indicator to assess the proportion of residents with schistosomiasis.

*Information on illness* is a useful indicator of health status, but the information may be difficult to obtain from a sample of the population being studied. Most families in developing countries are unable to provide reliable information on their illnesses, the treatment they have received, or even on basic facts, such as the incidence of diarrhea. Absence from work or school due to illness is sometimes used as an indicator of health status, but that information can be misleading. For example, someone who is self-employed is much less likely to take time off work when he or she is sick than a person who is working for a large company that pays sickness benefits.

*Community information* can be useful in assessing changes in health practices as a result of projects (for example, whether drinking water is taken from the new well; how garbage is disposed of).

The health impacts of some development projects may be almost impossible to assess, particularly in new housing or water and sanitation projects. First, health status is affected by so many different factors (climate, income, food supply, employment, public health policies, and education) that it is often well-nigh impossible to say which observed changes in health status are the result of the project.

Second, the cost of collecting reliable health data on sufficiently large samples is often prohibitive. Yet large samples may be required to estimate changes in infant mortality or to compare anthropometric indices for different subgroups.[4]

Third, data collection will often require the cooperation of the families being studied (children have to be brought to a health center to be weighed or stool samples have to be collected). Although such cooperation may be feasible in the project areas, it may be impractical in the control areas.

Fourth, a number of problems affect the collection of stool samples. In a community with a high level of illiteracy, it is quite difficult to ensure that the samples are being collected from the right child. One health worker reported in El Salvador that if the child being studied did not have a bowel movement, the mother would collect a sample from another of her children "to help the doctor with the study." Another problem is the poor quality of the analysis in understaffed laboratories.

## Recommended Reading

*Questionnaire Design and Methods of Asking Questions*

Converse, Jean, and Stanley Presser. 1986. *Survey Questions: Handcrafting the Standardized Questionnaire.* Quantitative Applications in the Social Sciences 63. Beverly Hills, Calif.: Sage.

This summarizes many of the findings from the longer work by Schuman and Presser (1981).

Patton, Michael Q. 1982. *Practical Evaluation.* Beverly Hills, Calif.: Sage.

Chapter 5 is particularly helpful.

Payne, Stanley. 1951. *The Art of Asking Questions.*

The classic work on this topic.

*Attitude Measurement*

Blalock, Hubert, and Ann Blalock. 1968. *Methodology in Social Research.* New York: McGraw-Hill.

Robinson, John, Robert Athanasiou, and Robert Head. 1969. *Measures of Occupational Attitudes and Occupational Characteristics.* Ann Arbor: Institute for Social Research, University of Michigan.

See Chapter 3 in particular.

## Notes

1. Many statistical procedures are designed to select scale items that have a strong statistical correlation with a single criterion variable. For example, the frequency of attending community meetings may be used as a criterion variable indicating degree of community participation. A question would be considered an acceptable scale item if it has a strong negative or positive correlation with the frequency of

attending community meetings. However, people may turn out to have various attitudes toward community participation. For example, they may have certain attitudes about the importance of attending community meetings; others about the effectiveness of community organization in producing different kinds of social, economic, and physical improvements in the community; and still others about whether community organizations should be organized along political party lines. Many questions that are not highly correlated with attendance at community meetings may be good indicators of people's attitudes toward the efficacy of community organizations in achieving certain kinds of community improvements. If all items were assessed in terms of their correlation with attendance at meetings, many potentially good indicators of other dimensions of community participation might be rejected. Statistical procedures do of course exist for the construction of multidimensional scales, but these make the process of scale construction even more complex, time-consuming, and costly.

2. Visaria (1980) describes the way in which these concepts are defined in household surveys in Asia, and Wahab (1980) describes how the concepts of income and expenditure have been defined in household surveys in a sample of twenty-three countries around the world.

3. In fact, Mehran (1980) cites studies to show that the earnings of the household head represented only 26 percent of total household income in urban Iran in 1976 and 33 percent in Trinidad and Tobago in the same year.

4. See Clark (1993) for a review of the literature on Kenya; and Buvonic, Youssef, and Elm (1978) for a more general discussion of issues related to female headed households. Wahab (1980) describes the way in which households have been defined in surveys in twenty-three developing countries.

5. Sullivan, Cochrane, and Kalsbeek (1982) show that the size of sample required to estimate infant mortality rates for particular education or income subgroups where birth rates and infant mortality rates are very low (crude birth rate = 30/1,000 and infant mortality = 75/1,000) could be as high as 41,160. At the same time, the required sample size could be as low as 1,267 where the crude birth rate is 50/1,000 and the infant mortality rate is 150/1,000.

# 10

## Qualitative Methods for Collecting Data

As mentioned earlier, quantitative surveys, with their links to positivist-behaviorist paradigms, have come under increasing scrutiny in recent years. Much of the criticism comes from researchers who believe that greater weight should be given to qualitative methods. This chapter examines qualitative methods and the ways in which they complement quantitative methods in most kinds of evaluation research.

### Comparing Quantitative and Qualitative Methods

Qualitative methods have been described as "a particular tradition in social science that fundamentally depends on watching people in their own territory and interacting with them in their own language, on their own terms" (Kirk and Miller 1986:9). They differ from quantitative methods in at least two respects. First, their goal is to *understand* reality as it is construed by the persons being studied. Second, they encourage researchers to try to understand the *meaning* of particular activities or beliefs in the context of the culture being considered. Qualitative methodologists are strongly opposed to isolating a particular event (or "social fact") and studying it apart from the context in which the action occurs.

Qualitative methodology has its origins in the *ethnographic* branches of anthropology and urban sociology. Some of the founding fathers are Franz Boas, Margaret Mead, and members of the Chicago school of sociology

(Burgess, Park, Whyte, and Anderson). For the purposes of this discussion, ethnographic techniques are considered part of qualitative methodology, and there is no need for a separate discussion of ethnographic methods of collecting data.[1] A distinction that could be drawn is that the *unit of analysis* of anthropological ethnography is society or culture, whereas most qualitative evaluation studies focus on a much smaller unit such as the community, family, or individual. However, many urban ethnographic studies have also focused on small groups such as a gang or even a category of person. Therefore, no firm distinction can be made between these disciplines.

Although some writers have recommended that quantitative survey methods be virtually abandoned, our position is that evaluators should use both quantitative and qualitative methods. The deciding factor is the question being asked. Many qualitative researchers say that the goal of the social sciences should be to understand the world as it is perceived by the individuals or groups being studied.[2] The *verstehen* approach, which has always emphasized living with, and seeking to understand, the patterns of thought and feelings of the populations being studied, has wide support in anthropology (Gans 1967; Lewis 1961; Liebow 1967; Lomnitz 1977; Nelson 1978; Peattie 1968; Stack 1974; Whyte 1955).

Lofland (1971:1–2) observes:

> To live in the modern world is to know about very many more categories of human beings than one knows directly. . . . But in only knowing about—rather than directly knowing—them, a fuller portrait constructed from such a distance is likely to contain significant oversimplifications, distortions, errors and omissions. In being constructed from a distance these portraits more easily serve the particular purposes of the people constructing them. If a measure of dislike and distrust exists, portraits of people only known about are likely to reflect these feelings. The less known about an object, the more inventive one can be—and must be—in constructing an image of it. . . .
>
> [E]ven the most cynical and exploitative of us, surely recognizes that to know about—to know through stereotypes and typifications—is not enough. We want a more direct sense of what other people are about and what their lives are like than is provided by casual and unexamined typifications.
>
> In order to feel that one understands what is "going on" with others, most people try to put themselves in the other person's shoes.

The fullest condition of participating in the mind of another human being is face-to-face interaction. Face-to-faceness has the irreplaceable character of nonreflectivity and immediacy that furnishes the fullest possibility of truly entering the life, mind, and definitions of the other as this other conceives it.

Although many social scientists agree that an anthropologist requires intimate face-to-face contact to understand a community's customs and beliefs, few of the studies designed to evaluate development programs have made use of participant observation or related qualitative techniques. On the whole, economists and sociologists rely on quantitative analysis of information from sample surveys and from secondary data in their program evaluation and policy research. By doing so, however, they overlook many important insights of direct interest to planners and project managers. Salmen's (1983, 1987) work in Bolivia and Ecuador showed that house ownership (which housing economists frequently use as a dichotomous variable in regression analysis) had a positive effect on a person's self-respect, dress code, and willingness to invite outsiders to visit. These turn out to be important topics that should be considered in a survey evaluating the impact of a housing project. Furthermore, these kinds of findings from qualitative studies can play an important role both in the formulation of the hypotheses to be tested in the quantitative surveys and in the interpretation of their findings.

Qualitative methods can also be justified on ethical grounds. Development programs are intended to have an impact on the lives of large numbers of people. The programs are based on a set of explicit or implicit assumptions about the needs of the population, about how they will respond to certain types of interventions, and about how their lives will be affected. Because many programs produce major changes in the lives of the population (not all of which are positive), planners have a moral obligation to understand how the population feels about these programs and how it is affected by them. Not to try to understand the point of view of a community resident (who will perhaps suffer if the project does not go as expected) is tantamount to ignoring democratic principles of social participation. Although quantitative methods can describe some of the behavioral changes that occur, they usually cannot reveal how people feel about these changes. Direct face-to-face contact with the affected population may often be the best way to find out. In other words, in order to understand the ways in which people respond to and modify a project, one must also understand the ways in which they experience it.

From a purely methodological point of view, qualitative methods can also be used to cross-check information obtained from quantitative surveys. Many types of surveys have a tendency to produce information biases

and systematic errors of measurement, or to use a restrictive set of predetermined responses. The response categories may be too narrow and may
not reveal the answers respondents would have given if they had greater
room for choice. The former type of problem may be traced to the inherent
"reactivity" of some surveys. For example, an informant may be reluctant
to confide in a stranger (the evaluator) and be unwilling to offer frank
responses to structured questions.

Such reluctance may also be rooted in local cultural factors. In the town
of Posadas, Argentina, an important nutritional supplement for the squatter population is the fish from the Rio Parana, which is a source of protein.
Even so, local laws do not allow people to fish for it without a license. This
ordinance was passed because the fishery is a tourist attraction and hence
an important part of the regional economy. But the impoverished squatters
are unable to afford licensing.

Before 1978 field researchers interviewed squatters about their source of
food using structured questionnaires. The variety of answers obtained did
not mention fish. In an attempt to cross-validate this conclusion, Valadez
(1978) went to the barrios of Posadas and watched the people. He then
approached one of several people he saw carrying a line of fish. First, he
introduced himself in the manner of an interviewer or survey researcher.
Then, he asked the man whether or not he fished. The squatter said he never
did and never ate fish. He then disappeared into his house with the fish.
Clearly, this individual had no intention of telling a perfect stranger that he
had just broken the law and that he intended to continue breaking the law.
This incident demonstrates the problems that can arise with questionnaires
that do not take into account cultural factors and thus could bias the results.

## Participant Observation

A Malay proverb states,

> The onlooker may be in his most sympathetic state
> But the shoulder 'neath the burden is the one to feel the weight.

### The Method and Its Objectives

Participant observation requires the field researcher to become a member
of the subpopulation being studied. He or she participates in its activities,
observes how people behave and interact with each other and with outside
organizations, and tries to become accepted as a neighbor or participant

rather than as an outsider. Although some social scientists suggest that such observers can collect information unobtrusively and systematically (Bogdan 1972), this activity is likely to alter the behavior that is being observed. This phenomenon is called reactivity. Many investigators consider participant observation to be more of an art than a science since there are no hard and fast rules about how it should be performed. Nevertheless, there are principles that can reduce "reactivity" or other biases.

In a standard scenario for participant observation, a field worker examines various local conditions (for example, diet, sanitation, water supply) by participating in the daily activities of the community in which he or she is living. These activities enable the evaluator to study a habitat firsthand. Typically, a day is divided into several observing and note-taking sessions. During the former, the researcher participates in the life of the community. During the latter, observations from the preceding session are recorded. Information should be as detailed and as precise as memory allows. Direct quotations should be recorded extensively. In the early stages, selective recording should be of less concern so that everything potentially relevant to the goal of the study can be collected.

The three main components of participant observation are pre-fieldwork, fieldwork, and analysis. Pre-fieldwork involves choosing the site and, depending on the approach adopted, contacting local authorities and community leaders. In some studies permission is obtained, whereas in others the researcher remains anonymous. During the fieldwork stage the evaluator gains acceptance in the community, establishes rapport, and gradually accumulates information. A crucial step here is to develop and describe a systematic method for obtaining and recording data. In the analysis phase the collected information is integrated into a logical framework in order to shed light on specific aspects of the population. Although these three phases occur in a logical sequence, preliminary analysis should begin as soon as the researcher starts living in the community. This early synthesizing of information helps focus the research on key issues and ensures that data are systematically collected to investigate a number of alternative hypotheses about the community.

Many participant observer and ethnographic studies fail to collect and analyze data systematically. Ethnographers typically work alone, and although they may make copious notes, these are usually not included in the research reports and are not readily accessible to other researchers. Regrettably, many times the researcher does not even list the questions that were asked. Hence, the reader is asked to trust that the conclusions were based on a systematic study and not on the researcher's personal opinions, which were supported by a few carefully selected quotations or events.

Many qualitative researchers are either defensive about this point or dismiss the issue as another example of the narrow-mindedness of quantitative researchers. Although one can appreciate the arguments on both sides of the debate, all methods should be stated explicitly so they can stand up to scrutiny. The following is a recommended set of questions that researchers should pose in participant observer studies used in program evaluation:

- What questions were asked and how were they asked?
- Who was asked each question? (It is helpful to include tables indicating who was asked each question.)
- How were respondents selected? Was the sample considered representative?
- How was the information recorded (tape recorder, notes taken during the interview, notes written from memory)? How long after the interview were the notes written up?
- In the opinion of the researcher, were replies honest and reliable? Which questions were respondents reticent about? Which questions did they find difficult to answer?
- How were the data analyzed?
- What procedures were used to test the *reliability* of responses and the *validity* of the data (Kirk and Miller 1986)?[3] Was systematic use made of triangulation (that is, were data for the same variable collected with different methods and then compared)?

Miles and Huberman's (1984) comprehensive discussion of qualitative data analysis stresses that preliminary analyses should be conducted throughout the study to redirect the data collection and to identify categories of information still lacking. Such an approach also exposes the researcher to continuous peer review.

*Levels of Analysis*

Qualitative methods tend to focus on a circumscribed field, particularly on the behavior of a single person or family. The question often raised here is how can a detailed description of a small unit of analysis be generalized to a much larger unit such as a community or city. Lisa Peattie (1968:1) would respond that it is important to describe what is going on in urban neigh-borhoods. She focuses on La Laja, a rapidly growing, planned city in the interior of Venezuela: "Supposing that what is happening in La Laja is neither unique nor isolated, and trying to understand what is to be seen in terms of the connections which seem to appear between La Laja's life processes and elements of the surrounding environment, the attempt is made to come to some understanding of the surrounding environment, as a new city, as Venezuela, or as one of the typical developing countries."

Lofland (1971), in his guide to qualitative research, suggests that quali-tative analysis can deal with at least six levels of generality:

- *Acts* refer to a situation that is brief and lasts only a few minutes or hours (for example, participation in a meeting).
- *Activities* take a longer period of time (days or weeks), involve a significant amount of the actor's time, and normally involve interac-tions with other people (for example, during the organization and implementation of a self-help construction project).
- *Meanings* refer to the ways in which actors interpret and structure their actions. Lofland (1971) calls them "focal concerns." He found that teenagers define everyday happenings with the aid of six such con-cerns: trouble, toughness, smartness, excitement, fate, and autonomy.
- *Participation* refers to the patterns of involvement in different social settings (the categories can be defined by the subjects or the re-searcher). For example, Lofland (1966) has classified users of public space into newcomers, customers, patrons, and residents. A similar classification could be used in an analysis of community behavior in meetings and in the use of public facilities. Community facilities such as a multipurpose center are often taken over by a particular group such as women or teenagers, who could be considered the "residents" since they control the conditions under which other community groups ("newcomers," "customers," and "patrons") are "permitted" to use the facility.
- *Relationships* refer to the patterns of interaction between persons or groups in an organization or community. Whyte (1955) used these relationships to study the organization and activities of a Chicago teenage gang. He showed that the gang had a well-defined internal structure and that a person's position therein strongly influenced his or her behavior in the group (see Suttles 1968 for another example). Similarly, Lomnitz (1977) describes the organizational structure of a

Mexican shantytown through the relationships between various networks, the economic conditions of households, and their survival strategies. The following kinds of analyses of relationships can be useful in program planning and evaluation: interhousehold networks may be considered a way of mobilizing financial and human resources for projects such as housing and small business development; community organizations can be seen as a vehicle representing the entire community or special interest groups; and the efficacy of networks can be studied as a community communication mechanism (see Chapter 5).

- The *setting* in which key individuals live or work (such as an organization, group, community, or development project) may prove useful to project planners and evaluators. Numerous studies have been done on the determinants of organizational structure and the behavior of its members, (Festinger, Reicken, and Schachter 1964; Goffman 1961; Lomnitz 1977; Roberts 1969; Valadez 1984). These studies suggest that the structure of an organization can explain the delivery of outputs and other behavior.

Azad (1986) described a new economic setting provided by a project affecting social and economic development programs for women in Madras, India. The following excerpt focuses on a day in the life of a vegetable vendor.

Before dawn breaks, at 3 a.m in the morning, the vegetable vendor rises. At an unearthly hour when the city sleeps, no vehicles ply, except autorickshaws known personally to the vendors. While traffic rules state that the number of passengers of autorickshaws should be a maximum of 2, drivers often cover the meter with a cloth and carry even 7 vendors. The fare to the market is thus minimized for the vendor. Furthermore, the Kotaval Chavadi area (wholesale market) has of late been the spot of knifing, waylaying, looting and petty crime and is safely traversed only in a known rickshaw by these women. Finally, vendors unarmed yet protected by their numbers can choose and buy fresh vegetables at their leisure till about 5 a.m. until the first busful of prospective buyers arrive.

At the vegetable stalls, mounds of red, green, orange and deep purple vegetables glimmer through the dew and water droplets sprinkled on them. The women decide the price by experienced, shrewd glances as well as by testing the flesh of vegetables. Once decided, the haggling begins between the experienced buyers and sellers. . . . The retail vendor carries her stock and moves to the next stall to begin the bargaining all over again. She continues to drag and carry her purchases for fear of their being stolen, as it sometimes happens. Pinched, pushed, stamped upon, harangued and harassed by male buyers and sellers, she finally spots a coolie and engages him to carry her purchases in a gunny bag to the bus stand. Now she has to follow the coolie swiftly who might otherwise bolt away with the vegetables into one of the numerous alleys of the area. The vendor still faces the risk of her vegetables and coolie being run over by a moving truck, bullock cart, autorickshaw. Finally she reaches the bus stand at 5:30 and sips her first cup of tea. A banana, a bun, and some betel nuts are consumed at the tea shop on the bus stand.

The setting should be analyzed whenever it is important to throw some light on the structure of the society as a whole. In one urban shelter project, an ethnographer identified three distinct low-income subpopulations (Bartolome 1978): (a) a labor force living near the city center that provided the principal support for day-labor activities in the business district of the city, (b) part-time laborers living on the western outskirts of the town who also cultivated subsistence gardens, and (c) an "underground" of smugglers, prostitutes, and gangsters on the eastern outskirts. This finding had distinct implications for program planning, delivery, and evaluation. The first population relied on local markets for food and was most likely to be informed about the goings-on in the city. The second one had small gardens to supplement their diet, and their economic and medical problems were less likely to be known because they lived outside of town. The third population had specific health problems related to the reported high incidence of sexually transmitted diseases. Once these three sectors in the target population were identified, it was possible to examine them individually in order to assess the relative impact of the urban shelter project across these three subcultures. This is but one example of how ethnomethodology can contribute to evaluating urban shelter programs.

A comprehensive review of how ethnographic approaches can be used to plan and evaluate agricultural and rural development projects is found in Cernea (1985). Cernea examines social and cultural factors underlying the organization of forestry, pastoralism, fishing, and farming and demonstrates the importance of understanding these factors in the planning and implementation of development projects.

*Static and Dynamic Analysis*

A study conducted at one point in time would be called static or cross-sectional analysis, and one continued over time would be called dynamic, longitudinal, or phased analysis. Examples of static analysis include a description of one community meeting or one workday in a community construction project. Dynamic analysis would involve repeated observations of community meetings or workdays over a period of time. Dynamic analysis leads to a better understanding of group processes because it sheds light on the following kinds of questions:

- Which aspects of the situation remain constant and which are transitory? Is a conflict observed in the first meeting a regular feature of the group and does it occur again in later meetings?
- How do external events affect the community (such as a local election, or economic or by seasonal variations)?
- How do relationships change between community members or subgroups? Does the group learn by experience? Does the composition of the group change?

Depending on the nature of the activities being studied, dynamic analysis can be completed in several weeks, or it can continue for several years. In El Salvador, the communal house construction phase lasted between six and nine months; one study continued over this period, and another, concerned with evaluating whether group performance improved from one project to another, continued over several years.

*The Role of the Observer*

At the outset, the participant observer must decide what role he or she is to play in the community. The decision raises a number of ethical issues.

SHOULD HE OR SHE BE IDENTIFIED AS A RESEARCHER? In some studies, researchers present themselves as someone interested in conducting a study of the community. They will either make a point of introducing themselves to the community leaders on this basis (Salmen 1983) or will be willing to explain to anyone who asks. At other times, the researcher may enter and live in a project community as a normal resident without arousing the curiosity of other residents. In a study of life in a low-income tenement in San Salvador (Herrera and Baro 1978), the researchers simply rented a room and conducted their observations while participating in normal residential activities such as queuing for water and buying things in a local store. They behaved in the same way as other residents, and no one ever asked why they were living there. A much more controversial approach is that of the researcher who gains entry by deliberately misleading other members of the group. One researcher posed as a mental patient; others joined a group of religious mystics by pretending to share their beliefs (Festinger and others 1964); and another joined Alcoholics Anonymous, pretending to be an alcoholic (Lofland and Lejeune 1960). Many of the ethnomethodologists also make a point of not informing the subjects that they are being observed, because such knowledge can affect the situation, especially if the subject feels self-conscious as a result. Still another option is to conduct the study in the community one is already living in. For example, Lisa Peattie was working as an urban planner in southern Venezuela and studied the community she was living in with her family.

IDENTIFICATION WITH THE PROJECT AGENCIES. In some projects, if the researcher is thought to be closely involved with the implementing agency, community residents may be reluctant to discuss their feelings about the project. Where community-agency relations are tense, the community may even seek to avoid the researcher or force him to leave. It is sometimes more advisable to work through a high-level agency that is not directly involved in the project (for example, the Ministry of Planning, a university, or research institution). Such an association not only provides legitimacy, but the remoteness of this agency could make local individuals feel less threatened by the researcher. Whatever the affiliation, it is useful to carry documentary proof (such as a letter) since community leaders or local authorities may ask for credentials.

Where the researcher is contracted by a local agency, what type of relationship should the evaluator maintain with the sponsoring agency? The researcher may discover information that could be of immediate use to the agency (for example, dissatisfaction with aspects of the project, criticism of agency staff, or actions the community is planning to take that might affect the agency). Although the researcher must maintain the trust of the community, it may be unethical not to pass on to the agency information that could help avert problems or improve the operation of the project. There is no standard solution to this dilemma (see Salmen 1987).

PASSIVE OR ACTIVE INVOLVEMENT IN THE COMMUNITY. Another issue concerns the extent to which the observer should become involved in community activities. Although taking sides in community conflicts or becoming emotionally involved with one community group could jeopardize the researcher's objectivity, there are many situations in which it is difficult not to become involved. For example, Carol Stack (1974) needed to be accepted by the group of low-income black women she was studying. To gain their confidence she participated in family quarrels and crises. Similarly, Lisa Peattie became actively involved in a controversy over the contamination of the community water supply as a result of the construction of a sewer outlet. In both of these cases the most valuable insights came as a result of being emotionally and organizationally involved.

It may even be possible to objectively observe one's own involvement in community activities. Herbert Gans (1967) has described such a dual role. At some points he specifically adopted the role of researcher (attending community meetings and conducting a survey); at other points he described his own experiences as a new community resident. For example, he, like the other residents, peered from behind his curtains to observe neighbors before going out to meet them.

*Entering the Community*

One of the first questions to deal with is whether the researcher should live in the community or just maintain close contact with it. In general, it is preferable to live in the community since many aspects of community life should be experienced rather than observed. The researcher who uses informants to learn about the time wasted queuing for water or the problems of getting to sleep because of quarreling neighbors and street fights will not see these events in the same way as someone who has experienced them personally while living in the community. Similarly, the community members will usually feel differently about someone who lives in the community than about a frequent visitor. In some cases, however, it is neither practical nor advisable to live in the community. In a study of a slum community in Bangkok that was about to be relocated to a new residential area, it would have been impossible to enter into the community during the last weeks preceding its move.

Assuming the decision is made to live in the community, it is important to choose a residence that does not identify the researcher too strongly with a particular faction. Also, it may not be advisable to ask the community leader to arrange a residence as this will inevitably lead people to identify the researcher with the leader's faction. It is usually preferable for a researcher who is working alone to live with a family rather than by himself. Salmen (1987) shared his rented house in Guayaquil, Ecuador, when he was evaluating a housing project there. The renters helped him gain entrance into the community through their relatives and friends.

As a rule, researchers should avoid becoming too involved with the first people they meet until they know how these individuals are related to the social structure of the community. Community residents will tend to associate the researcher with these people. Thus, it is important not to inadvertently become identified with, for example, a local political group. For similar reasons the researcher may wish to make the first visits to the community alone rather than accompanied by someone from the project agency.

In general, observers should plan and control their own activities and not let informants tell them what to observe. When one researcher working in southern Patagonia wanted to make an appointment with the chief of a local agricultural group, the chief's assistant suggested that another day would be better because more people would be in the office, and consequently the context would be more interesting. In order to not offend the assistant, the researcher accepted the advice. However, he also visited the agricultural station several days before and after the appointment to see what standard activities were like in comparison with those specially planned for him. On the day of his appointment, several dignitaries were visiting that the assistant assumed the researcher would like to meet. This visit would have been misleading if it had been used as the sole example of typical office activities.

The field worker would also be wise to be "unassuming" and to play down his or her own knowledge so as not to inhibit local people from sharing their ideas. The researcher should become closely involved with co-workers so that they will have something to tell informants, who will undoubtedly want to know all about the field worker. Casual exchanges can provide the basis for deeper trust. Holding oneself aloof can isolate the researcher from informants and inhibit them from open communication. The field worker should indicate he has nothing to hide.

*Methods of Collecting Data*

Lofland (1971) provides the following guidelines on the collection and analysis of data.

STRUCTURING THE STUDY. It is always advisable to spend time settling down in a community before addressing specific research issues and hypotheses. In the second phase, the researcher should begin to organize discussion around a specific issue expressed in terms of particular topics: economic, political, or social. Each topic should be discussed separately before seeing how they interact. There are several other ways of categorizing information—for example, by examining individuals, families, neighborhoods, and the community at large. Analyses should be divided into topics before examining patterns of interaction.

The evaluation should also attempt to compare the situations of several groups with respect to the general properties of the phenomenon being studied. It is equally important to contrast different groups to show how the phenomenon is specific to each one of them. For example, the evaluation might compare and contrast the household economic system of several families to assess how family finances are managed. Such a discussion should show the diverse range of systems as well as the average or most typical system.

SELECTING CASES. Qualitative studies often involve the intensive study of a small number of observations (individuals or households). A frequent criticism of participant observation studies is that the cases are selected randomly, and thus the findings may be biased or unrepresentative. The choice of subjects depends in part on who is willing to spend time talking to the researcher. Carol Stack (1974), in her study of poor black families, spent a long time visiting families before one woman finally confided in her. The decision to confide was made by the woman and not by Carol Stack. Informants are chosen in this way with a much higher frequency than many researchers would like to admit. Because most researchers want to generalize (at least to a limited extent) from their cases, it is extremely important to report how the cases were selected and how representative they might be.

One way to select informants is to apply the principles of sampling and to define categories of respondents to be covered by the study. For example, an evaluation of a fishing cooperative in Brazil identified the following groups as likely to be affected by the project: owners of large fishing boats, owners of small fishing boats, crew foreman, crew members, fishermen (in all of the above categories) who did not join the cooperative, and middlemen who buy fish from the fishermen.

RECORDING DATA. The dilemma for the participant observer is that although she would like to record detailed information, she must also act in as natural a way as possible with the respondents. For this reason, note taking may inhibit the respondent. There are a number of ways to record data.

A tape recorder can be used without apparently affecting the informality of the interview situation. Once the confidence of the respondent has been gained, he or she will often not be inconvenienced by the tape recorder. A tape recorder should *never* be used without first asking permission from the respondent. A tape recorder also raises a number of practical problems. It can be difficult to decipher the tape if there is background noise or if more than one person was involved in the interview, and the transcription of long interviews can be quite expensive.

Brief notes can be taken. It is particularly important to record dates, numbers, and names. With practice, notes can be taken inconspicuously. Normally, however, notes will be written up after the interview. Inevitably some bias will be introduced, and some parts of the interview will be omitted. The interviews should be written up as soon as possible. This method is particularly problematic if more than one interview has to be written up by memory.

A unique method used by Carlos Cabarrus, a Central American anthropologist, was to take a portable typewriter to the interviewer and to type his notes while the interview was being conducted! In these days of laptop computers, this option should be explored further.

### The Subject as Informant/Observer

A number of studies have attempted to train members of the community as informants in order to gain access to data that may not be available to the outsider. Oscar Lewis (1961) made extensive use of recorded case histories. His subjects dictated their histories or their opinions onto a tape recorder. The responses were subsequently reviewed by Lewis and discussed with the subjects. Respondents were also asked to relate everything they had done the previous day.

Similar techniques have been used in network research. For example, Epstein (1969) asked an informant in Zambia to recall everybody he had met during the previous few days and the types of interaction with each person; Boswell (1971) asked an informant to provide information on all the types of assistance that his family received in the organization of a funeral; and Kapferer (1973) and Muller (1975) asked both spouses to separately provide information on everyone who formed part of their personal networks.

One of the present authors asked a number of community leaders in Venezuela to record their versions of the history of a community junta. Although each leader sought to present himself in a good light, the comparison of different histories provided valuable perspectives on some of the key events.

## Other Qualitative Methods

### Unobtrusive Measurement

An unobtrusive method is a *nonreactive measurement* of a phenomenon, such as a physical trace or an existing record, that is intended to exclude or reduce as far as possible biases introduced by the observer. It is sometimes difficult to ascertain whether information obtained through interviews is truthful or is a response influenced by the informant's perception of the data-gathering context. In the previous example of the Posada fisherman, the answer that he did not eat fish caught illegally was a reaction to the interviewer. Being unfamiliar with the stranger, the squatter was unable to assess his motives; therefore he was reticent. Thus, that particular interview technique was a reactive measure.

An unobtrusive way to estimate the contribution of the fishery resource to the squatter diet might be to count the number of fish and to note their sizes. In this specific case, the evaluator developed a friendship with an aquatic ecologist studying the Rio Parana who had the confidence of the local people. Together, the evaluator and his ally counted the catch in the boats of all the local fishermen over several days. In order to estimate the percentage of those fish that were transported from the squatter settlement for sale in local markets, the ecologist interviewed fishermen and noted the number of fish loaded onto the trucks of merchants. Counting the fish was an unobtrusive measure; contacting the aquatic ecologist and interviewing the fishermen were examples of using "key informants." The latter technique is discussed in the next section. Noting the number and size of fish sold to merchants was another example of an unobtrusive measure.

Unobtrusive measures are nonreactive since they do not require interaction between the data collector and the people being researched. Thus, there is no respondent bias, although, of course, the researcher may be biased in his or her perception of the phenomenon.

There are several types of unobtrusive measures. A *physical trace* is environmental evidence. Most people use this type of information in everyday life. For example, when someone finds himself in a strange city, he might walk through the streets in order to assess the quality of housing (for example, the relative number of derelict houses), the status of its residents (for example, the numbers and types of automobiles), and the cleanliness of the neighborhood (for example, the quantity of exposed garbage). Similarly, one could appraise food marts on the freshness of the produce and the manner in which it is displayed. Photography can also be used to develop a record unobtrusively. A researcher could systematically record the different types of toilet facilities or water sources in a town with photography. Such techniques, used together with systematic sampling procedures for selecting the number of houses, streets, and neighborhoods to inspect, could yield valuable insights into the various phenomena under scrutiny.

There are two types of *running record*: informal and formal. *Informal* or noninstitutional records consist of diaries, journals, and the like. A family testament found at the back of an old Bible can be useful for tracing lineages and estimating mortality and fertility rates, age at death, and other such family data. *Formal* running records are kept by institutions such as political, economic, social, medical, or religious organizations.

Such records may be subject to selective-deposit or selective-survival bias, however (Webb and others 1966:54–57). The former problem often arises when a fee is charged for birth registration, which may discourage people at the lower end of the social scale from registering their infants. In such cases, the data registered in the formal record would refer to middle- and upper-class citizens. Selective survival may be demonstrated with an anecdote from anthropology. A research team tracing mortality rates might refer to information recorded on tombstones, that is, dates of birth and death. The material with which the marker is made may reflect social status; individuals of greater means could afford the more labor- intensive material (that is, stone), whereas the poor might use wood. Since wood deteriorates more quickly than stone, the surviving record would consist predominantly of information for the middle and upper class.

The third form of unobtrusive measure, *simple observation*, consists of observing a target population without them being aware they are being watched. In the earlier example concerning the Argentinean fisherman, it was possible to watch and see whether people brought fresh fish into their homes or unloaded them from boats.

When using these techniques, the researcher must assess how "unobtrusive" and "nonreactive" the measures are. Tax collectors in many rural areas have found that there is no unobtrusive way to observe the number of cattle or chickens that a family owns as many of these will vanish as soon as it is known that a stranger is approaching the village. Similarly, anyone who has tried to take photographs of a community unobtrusively will know how the presence of a camera (however discretely concealed) will change behavior. In many low-income urban areas in Latin America, as soon as a foreigner with a camera appears, children are whisked into their houses, only to reappear a few minutes later in their best clothes in case they are in any of the photographs!

### Direct Observation

Direct observation can often be a rapid and economical way of obtaining basic information on the social and economic conditions of a household or community. Observation can also provide valuable consistency checks on data obtained from surveys, key informants, or secondary sources.

We will illustrate some of the ways in which direct observation can be used to study household income. Much economic activity occurs in the street or in public places where it can be easily observed. Most businesses operating from a private dwelling will advertise their services by a sign or by a display of goods or raw materials in the street. By walking along a randomly selected sample of streets and by noting all signs of businesses it is possible to obtain a quantifiable estimate of the minimum number of businesses. If the same sample of streets is revisited at different points in the future, it is possible to estimate changes occurring over time. This method is likely to underestimate the number of businesses because some may not be easy to detect from the street. Some of the businesses that may be missed are those that are illegal (beer brewing, selling drugs, prostitution) or those that are conducted on a casual basis and that do not advertise. The observer should be on the lookout both for businesses that are conducted in a fixed place (in the house, a stall in the street) and those that are ambulatory and do not have a fixed site. The following categories of business are among those that can often be observed: services provided in the home (hairdressing, baby sitting, repair of electrical and other small devices), informal schools and other educational activities (typing classes), retail stores in private houses, stalls in the street, entertainment services (beer, gambling, prostitution), ambulatory services (clothing, plastic goods, catalog sales, lottery tickets), transport services for people (taxi, rickshaw) and goods (water seller, help carrying goods home from the bus stop), building materials and construction services.

Another source of information is advertisements put up in local stores or on walls. These indicate the kinds of services offered in the community.

Other kinds of observation can only be made inside the house of the respondent. During a formal survey, an interviewer can be trained to look for signs of economic activity that may provide a consistency check for the responses to the direct questions. Because most low-income houses are small, any type of business will either be conducted in an area observable from the living room or kitchen in which the interviews are normally conducted. Some of the indicators of economic activity include raw materials (cloth, leather, wool), tools or machinery (sewing machines), items apparently for sale (large quantities of clothes, shoes), customers visiting the house (children coming to make payments or to pick up goods), receipts or sales catalogs, and noise (hammering) or smell (beer brewing, curing leather, gluing wood).

Interviewers should be careful not to make inferences directly from what is observed. They should use observations to guide the conversation. Eventually, the respondent may explain his business, especially if he is proud of his work.

## Secondary Data

During the preparatory stage of any study, a search should be made to identify the sources of published data. Secondary data may include government reports, theses, and other university research projects, newspaper and magazine articles, records kept by cooperatives, and other local organizations. Careful investigation will usually reveal useful sources of unpublished government information such as the reports of public health inspectors, credit information on small business loan programs, records of land purchases, and the price paid for land.[4]

## Photography

Photographs are a useful way to document physical changes in a community such as improved housing or roads, or the recent development of squatter housing. If carefully planned, the photographs can also illustrate concomitant changes in the social and economic life of the community. Photographs provide a more dramatic and vivid record of the physical condition of houses or streets or the style of dress than can statistical tables and verbal description.

One frequently used technique is to take photographs from exactly the same place and angle at different points in time to illustrate the progress of a project or to show the patterns of activity at different times of day or seasons of the year.

Because photographs are usually used to "illustrate" points made in the text, their validity is seldom questioned, and they, too, can be instruments of bias (Becker 1979). Authors may select the most dramatic photograph and refer to it in the text as though it were typical. Photographs can make a house, community, or workplace look exceptionally poor or prosperous. The validity of photographs should be treated with the same caution as issues that arise when other ways are used to select and present the data collected.

## Key Informants

A key informant is an individual who, as a result of his or her education, experience, or physical or social position in a community, has access to information about the functioning of society, the habits of its people, or their problems and requirements. It is not necessary for these informants to be professionals. A storekeeper, policeman, or long-established resident can be a valuable source of information.

According to Kumar (1989:2–3), key informant interviews are particularly useful in program evaluation when

- General, descriptive information is sufficient for decisionmaking.

- Understanding of the underlying motivations and attitudes of a target population is required.
- Quantitative data collected through other methods need to be interpreted.
- The primary purpose of the study is to generate suggestions and recommendations.
- Preliminary studies are needed for the design of a comprehensive quantitative study.

With nonreactive techniques, however, informants are not questioned about the meaning of what is observed; hence, there is a danger that the researcher will misinterpret what he or she sees. Earlier, it was mentioned that housing quality could be measured in terms of the materials used for construction. It would not be immediately apparent how to assign value to a particular material. Thatch, metal, clay, wood, or cardboard may all be used as roofing material; yet, their relative status may vary from one culture to another. To analyze such data, one must first determine their meaning within the local community, for example, through consultation with a "key informant." Such people, whose status affords them access to intimate knowledge about needs, attitudes, and requirements of the local population could include citizen leaders, clergy, and traditional doctors. Shopkeepers and pharmacies could also be useful informants because of their familiarity with the consumption habits in the community.

At the same time, these people should not perform the role of the evaluator. Their role is to act as a source of information which can assist in the measurement of the variables for a particular study. A key informant clarifies issues or defines problems from their point of view only. Each key informant interviewed may have a different perspective. An evaluator can triangulate on salient issues or problems by determining where the opinions of key informants tend to overlap. These opinions should be used merely as another way of gaining some insight into the complexities of the research context. Such data contain the respondents' biases; the difficult chore is to separate them from reliable information.

Key informants have been used in international development projects for some time. Wyon and Gordon (1971) and Cassell (1974) sought out key members of the Indian and African villages in which they worked to help them identify the magnitude and extent of health problems there and the causes of these problems. This source of data is now a basic component of a "community diagnosis" approach to preventive health care. Through key community leaders it is possible to identify environmental problems (for example, the condition of water and sanitation systems, house quality, garbage disposal), life-styles, and the location of newborns or children under five years of age. The type of information obtained from a particular informant depends on the area of community life to which she or he has special access. For example, community health volunteers who visit the households to provide health education should be able to identify the location of young children. Priests or prominent local women in a community who are privileged to local gossip or confidences could be other "experts" with whom to cross-validate such information.

There are several points to consider in selecting key informants. According to Campbell and Levine (1970), the idea is not to identify cross-sectional representatives of the community. Rather, the researcher should look for experts on certain aspects of community life who have special access to information. In the area of health care, certain individuals are typically well known in the community and rapidly identified: voluntary health collaborators, midwives, health promoters, nurses, and others associated with the extension of coverage of primary care, water, and sanitation. If key informants are used, their area of knowledge must be clearly identified. Key informants on health matters may be ill-informed about agriculture or small businesses.

The image of key informants in the community and the degree to which they are accepted should be verified by asking local leaders or a sample of the population about their status. Verification can also be done through a standard social science technique—the sociogram. Here, the field worker records who speaks to whom and how frequently. Those individuals with whom the greatest number of people communicate and most frequently are indeed the preferred sources of information and are often recognized as leaders. The sociogram is particularly useful where community leaders do not have highly visible social roles. For example, there may be only one or two people (usually women in the case of information on health-related topics) who are inquisitive and know about the private lives of people. Such women may be the first to know about pregnancies and births. Through sociograms it may be possible to identify the persons who have most access to these kinds of information.

The sociogram can be constructed in a variety of ways. Through systematic and unobtrusive observation the evaluator can construct a partial social network. An alternative is to ask individuals to list people who form their social networks and then the amount and kinds of contact they have with each person. A comparison of these lists could reveal overlapping communication networks and thereby identify key community informants or leaders.

As with all techniques, using key informants has both its advantages and disadvantages. The information can only be as accurate as the key informants that are chosen. Also, it may take a long time to develop their confidence. It may be equally difficult to defend one's eventual choices of informants. The evaluator should include a record of the criteria used to select informants in his or her research reports.

An important, and frequently ignored, issue concerns potential biases in the selection of key informants and in obtaining reliable information from them. Kumar (1989:33–34) suggests that key informants should be assessed in terms of their knowledge (of the subject under study), credibility (thoughtfulness and candor of responses), impartiality, and willingness to respond and outside constraints (were the interviews affected by the presence of outsiders or other factors that might affect the willingness of the respondent to reply fully and impartially?).

## Community Forum

A logical extension of the key informant is the community forum, which means the community as a whole is consulted. This method is often quite complicated owing to the number of people who are brought together and to the problems of controlling the interactions between them.

Interviewing the local community as a whole can provide valuable insights into why a project does not work or how it could perform better. Indeed, what may be an obvious programmatic problem to a local resident may be overlooked by a program manager. For example, the delivery of health services may be inadequate because the user population finds the terrain difficult to traverse or the division of household labor affects when, where, and how often a mother can bring her child to a facility. The low participation of residents in self-help housing projects may be due to the fact that they assign higher priority to other activities in their community than to the project. A properly managed method of regular feedback from the community could identify or anticipate many of these problems. In short, there are many managerial, political, and cultural reasons why local communities should be considered both valuable and essential sources of information and therefore should be included within monitoring and evaluation systems.

A community forum can be organized in many ways (see Kumar 1987). The following is one suggestion:

- Before the forum, the evaluator should use ethnographic and other techniques to understand social, political, economic, and cultural characteristics of the community that affect the manner in which the forum is organized. These factors may determine whether the community should meet as a whole, or in separate groups (for example, men and women) and how the meeting is organized and publicized, the places in which it is held, who attends it, and who runs it. Political factors may determine the critical individuals who need to be contacted. A meeting can be either boycotted or canceled by a respected or powerful community resident who has been inadvertently slighted by an uninformed evaluator.
- Local voluntary organizations or community organizations should be contacted. For example, Village Health Committees often exist in public health projects. If such committees or groups do not exist, the help of local leaders should be sought to identify who should participate.
- The committees or groups who will participate in the forum are first interviewed about their activities and concerns in order to obtain a comprehensive view of the community's status and priorities.
- With their collaboration, the evaluator advertises a community-wide meeting to which everyone is invited (insofar as cultural norms permit universal attendance). In the event that the community is either too large or diverse to be accommodated in a single meeting, the community should be divided into several groups or subpopulations with separate meetings for each group.
- The forum should be advertised using traditional communication methods (newspapers, radio, churches, informal communication networks). Key members of the community should also be invited individually.
- A moderator should be appointed. He or she must be a respected person in the community and informed on the subject being studied. It is important to select a moderator who is perceived as impartial and who will encourage open discussion.

- A successful forum can obtain information on the following topics: whether programs are being organized and implemented as planned, and if not, why in the view of the community; whether problems that the projects were supposed to combat still exist; and additional local needs that should be incorporated into future projects.

A community forum has some drawbacks, however. In many cultures, community meetings are not used to discuss ideas; rather, leaders use them to seek consensus on decisions that have already been made. In other cases, only members of high-status groups are expected to speak in public, and it is extremely difficult to obtain the participation of lower-status groups. In low-income urban communities, the tenants and squatters who do not have the security of land tenure are not likely to express their views (Salmen 1987). Similarly, in rural areas it will often be the landowners or the wealthier farmers who speak. Under these circumstances, it will usually be necessary to use other techniques such as participant observation or informal individual meetings) to understand the opinions and concerns of the "silent majority."

## Self-Monitoring

Self-monitoring means that informants monitor their own activity by recording pertinent variables (such as hours worked, incomes and expenditures, use of fertilizers, participation in community activities, diet, medical regimes, growth, and health status) in a diary or by tape-recording their reports. Nurses are among those who have been encouraged to record problems at their health posts and to categorize such problems by the order of their severity. Physicians may perform the same function for indicating problems hospitals. Mothers, at the local level, have been trained to keep infant growth charts. Diaries have also been used extensively for recording information on income and expenditures.

Another self-monitoring technique consists of supplying an informant with a camera and asking him or her to photograph the community. If the water supply or sewerage was being studied, the informant could be asked to photograph the various types of pertinent technology. With such instructions, the informant would have to rely on his own understanding of the community for choosing what to photograph. Once the film was developed, he and several other key informants could be asked about the relative prevalence of each system.

*Mapping*

Mapping social networks can be valuable for studying how information flows through a community informally and also for defining the parameters of a neighborhood, such as who knows who, who people talk to or visit. By carefully recording such information, one can often determine which individuals are the most frequent transmitters of community information. Some theories of organizations suggest that power can be defined in terms of networks. Individuals with the most numerous contacts and the most information are considered powerful.

Another type of mapping concerns the residents' images of and knowledge about their habitat. Participants could be asked to point out on a map of the target city (or a section of it) the limits of their own community or the areas they most frequently use. The researcher could also ask direct questions while pointing at the map: "How many people in this area do you know?" or "How often do you shop in this area?" or "Identify the households in which you provide services."

Mapping techniques were used by the Bangladesh Rural Advancement Committee in a study of the power structure in ten villages. The first stage of the research was to "record carefully all the examples of oppressive, exploitative and illegal activities we could find" (BRAC 1983:3). Information that could be checked from at least four sources was used to construct a chart indicating the relationships between individuals and groups within the power structure. Profiles were then prepared on each individual in the power structure covering their background, political, business, and other activities, and their landholding. Thus, it was possible to identify the power factions within each village and how they were interconnected.

## Applications of Qualitative Data

Qualitative methods can be used in many ways in the planning, control, and evaluation of projects.

*Understanding the Actual and Potential Impacts of Large-Scale Development Plans on the Target Population*

Lisa Peattie, in the introduction to "A View from the Barrio," writes:

> The conceptualizers and planners have to operate on a large scale; the scale of maps of regional economic flows, of migration statistics, of predictions on

labor force need and supply. But in the end, all these generalizations and plans are summaries of what individual human beings are doing with themselves or will be doing in the future. It sometimes helps, even for the general planner, to look at what his plans and generalizations mean on a small scale, the scale of the individual human being or the single neighborhood. The planner may also find it most useful to look at what is happening outside, inside and around his plans and his control. This is an attempt to take such a look at some large-scale social processes from the bottom, working out from a single small case.

Planners often have little direct personal contact with the population whose lives they will deeply affect. Qualitative methods and particularly participant observation can provide insight into the ways in which households and local communities perceive the projects and how they are affected by them. They can also identify projects in which the community is interested. For example,

- Families in various regions of El Salvador differed in the levels of priority they assigned to higher levels of services, as opposed to more land area (FSDVM 1978).
- In Mombasa, Kenya, it was found that Swahili households would not accept the more economical communal water and sanitation services that would be shared by households from more than one compound. Since the traditional family organization did not permit women to leave the compound after dark, it was impossible for them to use the communal facilities at night.
- In the Tondo project in Manila, a participant observer study revealed that many low-income households would have preferred a lower (and more economical) level of services than had been indicated in community meetings. Many of these families said they had felt pressured by community leaders (Barangay captains) to vote for a higher level of service (Philippines Housing Authority 1979a).

### Initial Community Diagnosis

Many projects run into trouble because no effort is made to understand the social and political organization of the target areas. Salmen (1983) showed, for example, that an upgrading project in Guayaquil, Ecuador, was never able to start because the implementing agency was not aware the community junta was controlled by a political group opposed to physical improvement projects. Bamberger (1968) showed that development agencies in Venezuela tended to have limited and oversimplified perceptions of the internal organization of urban barrios. Internal conflicts frequently made it logistically impossible to implement the types of community-wide projects being proposed by the outside agencies.

## Evaluating Project Implementation

Observational and qualitative studies can be conducted either on a routine basis or when rapid feedback is needed on problems that have arisen. These studies are particularly useful for identifying the following types of problems:

- Implementing agencies often rely on one or a limited number of community organizations as their communication intermediaries. Frequently these organizations represent particular interest groups or have very limited community contacts. It is common to find that the implementing agency is completely unaware of the limited or inaccurate information that residents have received about a project.
- Projects often become a focal point of community conflicts. In some cases the project will be supported by house-owners but not by renters; in other cases, a fishing cooperative may benefit boat owners but not their crews. Again it is common for the implementing agency not to be fully aware of these conflicts.
- Rapid studies are also useful for troubleshooting. In Lusaka, Zambia, it was found that the attempt to improve cost recovery in a water project through the use of community pressures was ineffective because of opposition from the local political organization (Bamberger, Sanyal, and Valverde 1982). In Florianopolis, Brazil, the main reason a washerwomen's cooperative was not expanding membership was that the founding members discouraged new members in order to keep their own incomes high. Similar restrictive practices were identified in cooperatives in El Salvador (World Bank 1978b).

## Monitoring Project Accessibility

An objective of many projects is to ensure that benefits are accessible to particular target groups, usually the poorest or most disadvantaged groups. Because these groups are not very vocal and often difficult to locate, project managers may find it difficult to monitor their access to the project and may not be aware they are being excluded from benefits. The following examples show how qualitative methods can be used:

- In La Paz, Bolivia, many of the poorest renters did not have access to the project's benefits, particularly water connections. Because most of these families had not been covered by planning surveys, the project managers were not aware of the problems being encountered (Salmen 1987).
- A fishing cooperative project in Recife, Brazil (Nucleo de Acompanhamento 1983), was more likely to benefit owners of large boats than it was to benefit crews and the owners of smaller boats.
- In El Salvador, a study of the way in which the housing construction groups were organized showed that some of the poorest families and households headed by females were being forced out by having to participate every weekend in the construction groups (World Bank 1978a).

*Complementing Quantitative Studies*

An exploratory qualitative study can identify issues that should be covered in a quantitative survey. Simple observations can help the evaluator understand the issues of concern to the community and the ways in which these issues are perceived and expressed. In Cartagena, Colombia (Bamberger, Kaufmann, and Velez 1984), participant observation was used to shed light on the concept of the "household" and to examine the functions of inter-household transfers. In Chile, Valadez (1984) found that when residents were assigned to one of three experimental variations of plazas, those in the most private and enclosed plazas tended to develop and maintain their units in a newly planned city, whereas the residents who lived in the most public and least-defined plazas neglected these public spaces.

Quantitative studies frequently produce statistical findings without being able to explain or interpret them. For example, a study in an upgrading project in Manila found that the rate of turnover of low-income renters in the project area was significantly higher than the turnover rate for middle-income renters. The survey did not permit the researchers to explain why this difference existed and whether the poorer renters were being forced to leave as a result of the project.

In cases such as this, observation is particularly helpful because respondents may not be fully aware of their reasons or might have difficulty in expressing them in an interview. An observer could study the relations between tenants and landlords. In some communities strong social pressures discourage landlords from evicting families, particularly the poorest. These social pressures are usually subtle and can only be perceived once the observer has been sufficiently accepted by the community for the pressures to be exercised in his presence. On the other hand, landlords often use indirect or direct pressures to force families to leave. In a project in El Salvador, landlords would not admit to using these pressures, and it was necessary to directly observe how toilets were locked and water turned off to encourage families to leave (Fernandez and Bamberger 1984).

## Rapid Impact Studies

Participant observation, direct observation, and contacts with key informants can often provide a rapid and economical alternative to a full-scale longitudinal impact study. Although lacking the statistical rigor of a large survey, such techniques can provide general insights into the types of impacts that a project produces in a community.

## Case Studies

Case studies of individuals or groups can often be informative about life in a community. Such portraits can be approached from many directions and levels of generality, for example: "Food Supplementation in Northern Thailand," "Sanitation and Water Supply in Barrio Norte," "Self-Help Housing in Cali," "Seasons and Sickness," and "Health Education in the Family."

The basic purpose of such studies is to thoroughly explore a single case as an archetypal example of a situation that may be prevalent throughout a population. A case study can provide rich information because the intricacies of a phenomenon can be explored in ways that show how they relate to the patterns of everyday life. Case studies must be critically scrutinized and complemented by other systematic methods. Yin (1984) states that a good case study must address an important issue, be complete, consider alternative perspectives, display sufficient evidence, and be composed in an engaging manner.

## Comparison of Pitfalls

Each nonsurvey technique has its drawbacks. For one thing, unobtrusive measures have temporal and geographical selectivity problems, as discussed above. For another, residents may respond negatively to unskilled investigators stalking around and poking into backyards. A suspicious population could restructure their environment by withdrawing artifacts and evidence and thus neutralize the effectiveness of unobtrusive measuring.

Participant observation is inherently reactive since a field worker is the filter for evidence about a target population. Thus, personal biases, predilections, and selection problems can prejudice the results. Ethnography, as already mentioned, has disadvantages similar to those of participant observation. It is inherently reactive and is thus susceptible to informant as well as researcher bias. There are unavoidable selection problems. Another concern is whether the researcher is able to distinguish between salient and marginal information. This problem is particularly common when the field worker is unfamiliar with the culture under discussion and has been in the field a short time.

## Recommended Reading

Gans, Herbert. 1967. *The Levittowners: Ways of Life and Politics in a New Suburban Community.* London: Allen Lane.

> Detailed description of both qualitative and survey methodologies. Useful discussion of the role of the observer.

Kumar, Krishna. 1987. *Conducting Group Interviews in Developing Countries.* Program Design and Evaluation Methodology Report 8. Washington, D.C.: U.S. Agency for International Development.
_____. 1989. *Conducting Key Informant Interviews in Developing Countries.* Program Design and Methodology Report 13. Washington, D.C.: U.S. Agency for International Development.

> These two reports provide a guide to the uses and methods of implementation of group interviews and key informant interviews, together with a discussion of the strengths and weaknesses of each approach. They also include useful guidelines on how to analyze and interpret the results and procedures for increasing the reliability and validity of the information.

Lewis, Oscar. 1961. *The Children of Sanchez.* New York: Random House.

A classic description of a broad range of ethnographic techniques, including participant observation, case histories, and other qualitative and survey techniques. Useful description of the use of tape recorders.

Miles, Mathhew, and Michael Huberman. 1984. *Qualitative Data Analysis: A Sourcebook of New Methods*. Beverly Hills, Calif.: Sage.

Clear and comprehensive discussion of how to conceptualize and analyze qualitative studies.

Peattie, Lisa. 1968. *The View from the Barrio*. Ann Arbor: University of Michigan Press.

Readable description of the application of participant observation and action research in an urban squatter settlement in Venezuela.

Salmen, Lawrence. 1987. *Listen to the People*. New York: Oxford University Press.

Readable description of how to apply participant observation and other beneficiary assessment techniques to the evaluation of urban housing projects; and how to use them to improve project design and implementation. Useful discussion of the limitation of conventional approaches to evaluation.

## Notes

1. It should be noted, however, that not all ethnologists apply qualitative methods. Some, such as Murdock (1967) in his *Ethnographic Atlas*, seek to identify observable social regularities and statistical uniformities.

2. See, for example, phenomenologists such as Husserl (1960) and Schutz (1967) and ethnomethodologists such as Garfinkle (1967) and Cicourel (1981).

3. Kirk and Miller (1986) distinguish three kinds of reliability: *Quixotic reliability* occurs when a method always yields the same response, even though it may not be valid. An example in many cultures is a positive response to the question "How are you?" *Diachronic reliability* occurs when a method elicits the same response over time. And *synchronic reliability* refers to the similarity in observations using different methods within the same period (Kirk and Miller 1986:41–42).

4. Information on land prices will frequently be required for cost-benefit analysis and cost-effectiveness analysis.

# 11

## Principles of Sample Design

A sample consists of a number of people, households, communities, or other units of a population that have been selected in a systematic way and will be used to evaluate the characteristics of that population. A well-designed sample will include enough interviews to ensure that the estimates *are precise to a specific degree* a certain percentage of the time. When researchers use a sample of children to measure polio vaccine coverage, for example, they try to make certain that the estimate is within 10 percent of true coverage at least 95 percent of the time.

### Why Are Samples Used?

Samples are widely used in evaluation research for several reasons. One is to determine whether it is technically possible to obtain statistically valid answers to the questions posed in an evaluation proposal. If a *statistical evaluability analysis* shows that the questions being posed are impossible to answer, then it can safely be concluded that the evaluation being planned should not be conducted. Suppose that researchers need a sample of several thousand cases to obtain statistically valid estimates of changes in crude birth rates but find that it is not be feasible to collect a sample of this size. By discovering that it is technically impossible to demonstrate a statistically significant change in birth rates before their proposed study begins, they can avoid pursuing what is likely to be a costly but fruitless endeavor.

Second, a carefully designed sample will help clarify the objectives of a study and will clarify the categories of information to be collected from the appropriate number of subjects, at the required points in time. Carefully prepared designs can also optimize the likelihood that the statistical questions posed by the evaluation will be answered with the available data.

Third, a well-designed sample will obtain the required information at the least cost. By using the correct procedures for estimating sample size, the evaluation can avoid collecting more information than necessary yet obtain sufficient information to attain the required degree of precision. These objectives can only be achieved if manager and researchers alike understand the basic logic of sample design.

## Confidence Intervals and Sample Precision

The kinds of information to be collected should be determined through a close collaboration of the project manager and the evaluation team. As already pointed out in other chapters, it is vital to define the indicators needed to measure dependent, independent, and intervening variables. This chapter concentrates on the procedures used to decide how *precise* the estimates should be. It also explains the meaning of *significant differences* and how large a difference must be to be considered "significant."

Unless every household or person in a population (or community, city, or small business sector) is interviewed, the results of a survey can only provide *estimates* of the true values of a population. If a survey is repeated and a new sample selected, the estimates of average income, family size, crop yield, vaccination coverage, and so on, will be different.

When researchers use sampling procedures properly, they have better control over the *precision* of their estimates. The precision depends in large part on the sample size. By increasing the number of interviews, researchers can usually improve the precision of an estimate. To achieve a significant improvement, however, they may have to increase the number of interviews substantially. Suppose that a sample of 400 families will be adequate to estimate average household income with a *confidence interval* (defined below) of plus or minus (written as ± ) 100 pesos. Let us further assume that to bring the confidence interval to ± 50 pesos, the sample size would have to be increased by 1,600 families. If it costs $10 to conduct and analyze each interview, the manager must decide whether it is worth paying an additional $1,600 to reduce the confidence interval by half.

The concept of confidence level cannot be understood without first defining *standard deviation*, since the former concept derives from the latter. Suppose we wish to estimate the average income of a community consisting of approximately 5,000 families. Suppose further that after interviewing a carefully selected sample of 100 families, we find their mean income is 525 pesos, and that incomes around the mean vary by an average of 75 pesos. This average variation from the mean is called the *standard deviation*, and here it is expressed as 525 ± 75 pesos. The standard deviation is calculated as follows:

(11-1)          $$\text{Standard deviation} = \frac{\sqrt{\sum (x_i - \overline{X})^2}}{n}$$

where $x$ = the income of an individual household, $\overline{X}$ = mean household income, and $n$ = number of interviews (for example, individuals sampled).

(11-2)   *Standard deviation is also calculated as:*    $\dfrac{\sqrt{\sum (x_i - \overline{X})^2}}{n - 1}$ .

This more conservative (and more typical) calculation controls for a potential underestimation that can result from rounding the square root and the average. This is said to be a more mathematically sound way of making statistical inferences.

The standard deviation is a convenient way to describe the dispersion of observations around the mean. For most distributions, approximately 65 percent of the observations lie within 1 standard deviation of the mean; and about 95 percent lie within 2 standard deviations. In the present example, where the standard deviation is 75 pesos, approximately 95 percent of the families would be expected to have an income between 375 pesos (that is, 2 standard deviations below the mean of 525 pesos or 525 − (75 × 2)) and 675 pesos (that is, 2 standard deviations above the mean, or 525 + (75 × 2)). Note that if a family is selected at random, its income will be within 2 standard deviations of the mean 95 percent of the time. The range between 375 pesos and 675 pesos is referred to as the *95 percent confidence interval*. Some investigators call this the 0.05 level because there is only a 5 percent chance of the income of a given subject falling outside this range.

The range between 375 pesos and 675 pesos is referred to as the *confidence interval* at the 95 percent *confidence level*. These concepts are illustrated as follows:

| Confidence Level (%) | Number of Standard Deviations | Confidence Interval | Range |
|---|---|---|---|
| 65 | 1 | 450–600 | ± 75 |
| 95 | 2 | 375–675 | ± 150 |
| 99 | 3 | 300–750 | ± 225 |

*Precision*—another important objective of sample evaluation—relates to sampling error and sample size. Precision is represented as a range of values above and below an estimate. The true value of the variable being estimated is said to lie within that range. Suppose that researchers using a sample survey estimate that 80 percent of the children in a particular have received polio vaccine and that this figure is within 10 percent of the true value. Given a confidence level of 95 percent, we could be 95 percent sure the true level of coverage was in the range of 70 to 90 percent. In formal terms, precision is defined as

$$(11\text{-}3) \qquad\qquad d = \sqrt{\dfrac{C^2 pq}{n}}$$

where $d$ = precision of an estimate for a particular confidence interval, $C$ = the Z score for the selected level of confidence, $n$ = sample size, $p$ = the probability at which the event being measured is expected to occur, and $q$ = the probability that the event will not occur ($= 1 - p$).

As this equation suggests, precision, sample size, and the estimate of the variable under study are closely interrelated. If the sample size increases, the value of $d$ decreases because of the increased precision. If the value of $p$ varies, the value of $d$ will also vary. Frequently, the value of $p$ is set at 0.5 because the highest possible value of $d$ results. If $pq = 0.5 \times 0.5$, the product is higher than for any other combination of $pq$. This can be verified by experimenting with alternative values of $p$ and $q$ in the following equation. Remember that $p + q$ is always equal to 1.

Let us assume that we are assessing a health program's effectiveness in covering a population with polio vaccine. The coverage is estimated through a sample survey of 96 randomly selected children to be vaccinated. At a 95 percent confidence level, $C$ is equal to 1.96. The precision of the estimate is calculated as follows:

$$d = \sqrt{\frac{1.96^2 \,(0.5)\,(0.5)}{96}} = 0.1$$

which is $\pm 10$ percent of the estimated coverage.

One can be 95 percent sure that true coverage was in the range of 40 to 60 percent. Precision could be increased by increasing the sample size. If project funds permitted 200 observations, then the precision of that sample would be calculated as follows:

$$d = \sqrt{\frac{1.96^2 \,(0.5)\,(0.5)}{200}} = 0.069$$

which is $\pm 6.9$ percent of the estimated coverage.

Because precision depends on sample size, one could calculate the sample size required in order to obtain estimates with a desired level of precision. Precision can be exchanged with the sample size term $n$. Thus, if a precision of 5 percent was required, the sample size would have to be:

$$n = \frac{1.96^2 \, p\, q}{d^2}$$

$$n = \frac{1.96^2 \,(0.5)\,(0.5)}{0.5^2} = 384.$$

Precision can also be calculated for a sample of a population already collected. In our previous example where mean household income was 525 pesos and the confidence interval was $\pm 150$ pesos at the 95 percent confidence interval, we could conclude that the measure was very precise. However, as the confidence interval increases, the measure becomes less precise. Therefore, the precision of a measure is an expression of the confidence interval in terms of the sample mean. In formal terms:

(11-4) $$d = \frac{(\overline{X}+I)-(\overline{X}-I)}{X}$$

where $d$ = the precision, $I$ = the range of values in the confidence interval, and = the sample mean.

Using the values from the previous discussion, the confidence level, $I$ was ± 150 pesos of the mean (525 pesos) at the 95 percent level of confidence. The precision of the sample is

$$d = \frac{675\ pesos\ -\ 375\ pesos}{525\ pesos} = 57\%\ .$$

The measure is not very precise since it has such a broad range, namely, 57 percent of the mean. As the confidence interval drops, the precision increases. For example, assume that the confidence interval is ± 75 pesos. The precision would be improved:

$$d = \frac{600 - 450}{525} = 29\%\ .$$

*Standard Error*

So far we have been discussing the distribution of individual household incomes around the mean income of a sample. But how accurate is this estimate produced from a sample in comparison with the true average income of the entire population? If another sample of 100 families was selected, the mean income of the second sample would almost certainly be different from the figure of 525 pesos found in the first sample; and if a third sample was drawn, the mean would again be different. If enough samples were selected, it would be possible to calculate the mean value of all of the means produced by each sample, and the standard deviation of these individual sample means from the overall mean for all samples. If an infinite number of samples were taken, the mean of all the samples would equal the true average income of the population from which it was drawn. Moreover, the standard deviation of that sampling distribution would equal the true standard deviation of income of the population.

Obviously, it is not practical to continue drawing new samples. As a result, researchers have devised a method of estimating the standard deviation of the population mean from a single sample. If $s$ is the standard deviation of household incomes from the mean of a particular sample, then the standard deviation from the mean of all samples, or the entire population, can be estimated as

(11-5)                                      $S = \dfrac{s}{\sqrt{n}}$

where $S$ = estimated standard deviation from the population mean, $s$ = standard deviation of income from a single sample's mean, and $n$ = number of interviews (that is, the sample size).

In the present example, if $s = 75$ and $n = 100$, then the estimated standard deviation of the mean for all samples is 7.5 = (75/10). At the 95 percent confidence level, the confidence interval for the estimation of the population mean can be expressed in the following way:

Estimated monthly income = 525 pesos ± (7.5 × 2).

This signifies that we are 95 percent confident that the true value of the *population mean* lies between 510 pesos (525 minus 2 standard deviations) and 540 pesos (525 plus 2 standard deviations). It is important to understand that sampling theory is always based on probabilities and never on certainties. In this example, since we are 95 percent confident, there is a 5 percent chance that the true value of the mean is less than 510 or greater than 540. If we wanted to increase the level of confidence, we could select a range of 3 standard deviations instead of 2. At that level, there is a 99 percent probability that the true value of the mean lies between 502.5 pesos and 547.5 pesos (that is, 525 ± (7.5 × 3). To attain a higher level of confidence it is necessary to increase the confidence interval of the estimate.

*Selecting the Parameters of a Study*

Most evaluations find the 95 percent confidence level adequate, but if lower risk is required, the 99 percent level may be used. Some medical or engineering research—where the consequences of wrong inferences can be very serious (for example, as to whether a new treatment is effective)—may require even higher confidence levels.

The parameters of a particular evaluation study should be selected on the basis of criteria defined by the users of the study—namely, the managers, planners, and policymakers. The criteria, in turn, will depend on how the findings are to be used. In most cases, these parameters should satisfy several criteria, such as the following:

- The results of the study should determine what percentage of households are eligible for housing allowances. A family must have an income below 350 pesos to be eligible; therefore the study should be able to estimate the approximate proportion of households with incomes below 350 pesos. The research report must demonstrate that "normally acceptable sample survey procedures have been followed." In other words, the 95 percent confidence level should be used.

- The 95 percent confidence interval must not be greater than 20 pesos.
- The precision of the estimate of the mean household income must be less than 15 percent at the 95 percent confidence level.
- The study will test the hypothesis that average household income has increased following the implementation two years ago of a housing materials loan program. When the program began, mean income was estimated at 310 pesos with a standard deviation of 6 pesos. The 95 percent confidence level will be used to test this hypothesis.
- No more than 200 interviews can be conducted because of a limited budget. Therefore the study should aim for the best possible estimate of household income. Because this is a preliminary study, the budgetary constraint could be used to reassess whether any of the above parameters should be altered (for example, confidence level or precision).

All of the above criteria would help the researcher determine what size of sample would be appropriate. As explained later in the chapter, other criteria govern sample design (whether it a simple random, stratified, cluster, systematic, or lot quality assurance type). Whatever kind of sample is used, it will always be necessary to specify the required precision of the estimates. In most cases, the choice of precision level depends largely on how the results are to be used. In the last item of the above list, a preliminary study is being planned, so a lower confidence level might be acceptable.In other cases, a numerical value may be required, as in the first item of the list. (A later section explains how this information is used to estimate sample size for typical impact evaluations.)

## Statistical Significance

One of the main purposes of an impact evaluation is to determine whether a project has produced the intended change to an identified or targeted population. This can be done by comparing certain indicators in the targeted group (which receives the programmed intervention) with those in a control group (which does not receive the intervention) and calculating whether the difference is statistically significant. "Significant difference" is calculated as follows.

Assume that between time points $T_1$ and $T_2$ the proportion of self-employment among the previously unemployed adults in the project area (that is, those who had access to the necessary credit and technical assistance to become self-employed) increased from 20 percent to 45 percent after a certain project had been implemented, whereas the proportion in the control group remained at 20 percent. This difference would seem to suggest that the project had affected the probability that participants would become self-employed. But what if only five families had been interviewed in the intervention group and five in the control group? This would mean that between $T_1$ and $T_2$ the actual number of self-employed families in the experimental group increased from 1 to 2. A sample of this size is usually too small to draw any meaningful conclusions from the difference in the two groups. If the sample consisted of 1,000 families in each group, however, we would probably be fairly confident that the difference was "significant." In other words, a difference within a large sample entitles us to be more confident of its significance than the same difference within a small sample. But how large is "large," and what do we mean by "significant"?

"Significant" has two possible meanings in the present context, which are based on general usage, on the one hand, and technical usage on the other. In its general sense, "significant" means "important" or "meaningful." If incomes increased from $400 to $402 over a one-year period, this is not usually considered an *important*, or notable, difference. If incomes increased from $400 to $500, the increase would probably be considered important. What minimum increase is considered important will be decided by project managers and researchers before the study is designed. The amount of the increase could be expressed as a percentage. For example, project managers and researchers may decide that if the incomes of those participating in the study increase 10 percent more than those of the control group, they will assume that the project has had a significant (important) effect. The degree of difference considered *important* is decided on policy rather than statistical grounds.

In its technical sense, "significant" means there is a very low probability that a difference—say, between control and intervention groups in a properly conducted survey—could have occurred by chance. Table 11-1 shows a section from a hypothetical map of control and intervention households and the number of family members in each. The typical household in the control group contains one, two, or three individuals, whereas the typical one in the experimental group consists of six, seven, and eight. Thus if a random sample was drawn from each group, one would expect family size to be much smaller in the control sample. In this case, the control group has only a small number of families with seven, eight, or nine members, and the experimental group has only a few with one or two members. If we

**Table 11-1.  Map Showing Family Size in Control and Experimental Areas**

| Control Area | Experimental Area |
|---|---|
| 2 3 4 2 2 1 7 3 | 6 5 7 8 6 5 6 6 |
| 2 1 9 3 2 1 1 1 | 1 7 2 9 8 5 6 2 |
| 1 2 1 1 3 2 1 9 | 8 7 7 7 8 4 9 6 |
| 2 1 1 1 1 2 2 2 | 7 1 8 7 8 8 5 2 |
| 4 3 2 1 1 8 1 1 | 1 7 6 9 5 4 5 6 |
| 2 2 3 1 3 4 2 2 | |

*Note:* Each number is the size of a household.

were to draw a large number of samples, we would expect, purely on the basis of chance, to occasionally draw large control families or small intervention families. But if we were to do so, we might erroneously conclude that the control group had larger families than the intervention group.

To avoid such an error, sampling theory has devised a way of estimating the probability of finding by chance an observed difference between two samples when there really is no difference between the populations from which they are drawn. If the probability of finding a difference by chance is very small, we can reject the hypothesis that the two samples were drawn from groups that are ostensibly the same population. In other words, the two groups differ with respect to the variable being studied (for example, income, fertility, mortality). The results of drawing a sample from these control and experimental populations are given in Table 11-2.

The estimated mean family size for the control group is 2.7, and for the experimental group it is 8.1. The mean difference between them is 5.4. A *t*-test evaluating this difference suggests there is only 1 chance in 100 that such a difference would occur by chance. Therefore it can be safely concluded that the average household of intervention families is significantly (in the statistical sense) larger than the average control family.

In many kinds of social research the probability of a result occurring by chance must be less than 0.05 for it to be accepted as significant. This is only a convention, however, and where the chance of error has to be smaller, as in the testing of new drugs, a much more stringent significance level (say, 0.01 or 0.001) could be used. Conversely, in exploratory studies of new hypotheses in which concepts are still at an early stage of development, less stringent significance levels can be used (for example, less than 0.10).

Table 11-2. Average Household Size in Hypothetical Experimental and Control Communities

| Group | Sample Size | Mean | Difference of Means | Test of Difference | t-Score | Probability |
|---|---|---|---|---|---|---|
| Control | 80 | 2.7 | | | | |
| | | | 5.4 | t-test | 2.26 | 0.01 |
| Intervention | 90 | 8.1 | | | | |

In the following example taken from another hypothetical community (Table 11-3), the mean difference in family size is 2.6, and the project families again seem to be larger. In this case, the t-test indicates there is a 1 in 10 chance of a difference as large as this occurring, even if the two samples are drawn from the same population. Although the difference is large, it is not statistically significant by the more conservative convention. Note that the test does not say there is no difference between the two groups. Rather, a difference of this magnitude has a 1 in 10 chance of occurring when the two samples come from the same population. In other words, there is no meaningful difference between the two, according to this standard. If it is important to decide whether the two groups really are different, the investigator may (in cases where the difference is "almost significant") repeat the survey with a new sample or may increase the sample size. Similarly, if the t-score had been a little higher, say 1.98, so that it just reached the 0.05 level, the researcher would have to exercise caution in concluding there is a meaningful difference. It is good research practice to present the results of statistical tests so that readers can assess their meaning for themselves.

Significant differences are not always programmatically meaningful. As already mentioned, the precision of a sample is related to its size. If a large, precise sample is taken, a small difference in means may produce a sig-

Table 11-3. Hypothetical Example in Which a Relatively Large Difference between Means Is Not Statistically Significant (at the 0.05 level)

| Group | Sample Size | Mean | Difference of Means | Test of Difference | t-Score | Probability |
|---|---|---|---|---|---|---|
| Control | 95 | 4.7 | | | | |
| | | | 2.6 | t-test | 1.80 | 0.1 |
| Experimental | 85 | 7.3 | | | | |

nificant result. Conversely, a small sample with a large difference may not be statistically significant. In order to judge a difference in means, one must always determine the confidence interval. The method of calculating a confidence interval will vary with the test. A statistical text should be consulted for the calculation (see the references at the end of the chapter).

If the difference between the household incomes of two large samples is 5 pesos, with a confidence interval of 2 pesos, and this difference is statistically significant at the 0.01 level of confidence, the question would still remain, is this difference meaningful? The difference could range from 3 to 7 pesos. But does this monetary difference signify a qualitative difference in the two groups under study, or does their quality of life remain the same? This question cannot be answered without a careful study of what those few pesos can buy.

In summary, the meaning of "significant differences" depends on the size of the difference considered important and the confidence level used to show the difference has not come about by chance. The following sections explain how these concepts can be used to estimate the sample size required for typical evaluation studies.

## The Importance of Control Groups

The objective of an impact evaluation is to estimate the effects of the project on the persons who have been exposed to it. These impacts are estimated by comparing scores from a set of indicators representing the impact (for example, changes in household income) on participants after the project had been implemented with scores from indicators representing the impact on participants if the project had not taken place. In such comparisons, the control group usually consists of subjects who are as similar as possible to the participants but who are not exposed to the project. The income (employment, housing quality, health status) of the control group after the project has been implemented provides an indication of what participant income (employment, or some other factor) would have been if the project had not taken place.

To understand why a control group must be included, consider what would happen if a study only collected information on participants. Suppose that the income of participants increases by 27 percent in the three-year period after the start of the project. This increase cannot automatically be attributed to the project because there are a number of other plausible explanations: the increase may be due to inflation; government legislation might have decreed a general wage increase for all workers; income may have gone up as a result of the general economic situation; or new sources of employment may have opened up in the sector of the city where the project is located.

For all these reasons, it would clearly not be possible to make assumptions about the impacts of the project without having information on the economic conditions of other similar families in the city. That is to say, a well-selected control group is an essential component of the evaluation design since the alternative explanations would affect them as well as the group receiving the intervention.

## Methods of Selecting a Sample

A sample can be selected in many ways. Three classic and useful approaches are discussed below: simple random sampling, cluster sampling, and stratified random sampling. A few other sample designs are also explained.

### Simple Random Sampling

In a simple random sample, each unit of the population (household, person) has an equal chance of being selected. This type of sample is simple to design and is usually quite adequate when the population to be studied is relatively small and concentrated in a small geographical area. However, selecting individuals for a simple random sample can be expensive, complex, and time-consuming when the population units are difficult to identify or are scattered. Many cities or rural areas have no list or map showing where all households are located. Even if such a list did exist, the costs of interviewing would increase considerably if the sample was scattered throughout a city, province, or region. The interviewers would have to spend a great amount of time traveling and their interviewing rate would drop considerably (while transport costs would skyrocket).

## Cluster Sampling

In cluster sampling, the population is divided into clusters, such as blocks, neighborhoods, communities, villages, or other small and easily definable units, and interviews are conducted in a relatively small number of randomly selected clusters. If maps are needed, they can be prepared only for those selected units. Even where maps do exist, it is common to cluster the interviews so as to reduce travel time and costs. The estimates obtained from a cluster sample are usually thought to be less precise than those obtained from a simple random sample because the characteristics of the small number of clusters selected are likely to be less varied than those of the total population (see Kish 1965:chap. 5). Yet, as already mentioned, precision can be increased by increasing the sample size.

In summary, the smaller the number of clusters, the greater the potential bias in the estimates. Conversely, the greater the number of clusters, the more precise the estimates. The researcher will have to decide whether precision is more or less important than the cost of the interview.

## Stratified Random Sampling

Some of the groups of special interest in an evaluation frequently represent a small proportion of the total population (for example, the urban poor, children under three, small businesses). In such cases, a simple random sample would be a costly and inefficient way to evaluate these groups. If recent migrants represent only 5 percent of the population, for example, a simple random sample of 1,000 households would probably include only about 50 recent migrants. If statistical analysis required that the sample include a minimum of 100 recent migrants and 100 established residents (which also make up 5 percent of the population), it would be necessary to conduct a total of 2,000 randomly selected interviews in order to locate about 100 recent and 100 established migrants.

The cost of sampling can sometimes be reduced by dividing the population into strata (see Kish 1965:chap. 4). In the present example, recent migrants and established residents form two strata. The required number of interviews for each stratum are then selected from among all households in that stratum. Stratification would *theoretically* make it possible to obtain the required 100 interviews in each category with a total sample of only 200, instead of the 2,000 that would be required in simple random sampling.

A stratified sample can usually provide more precise estimates of a population's characteristics. Yet, considerable costs may be incurred in constructing the strata. In the present case, it would be expensive to identify all recent migrants from which the sample would be drawn if such a list did not already exist. To determine whether to use a stratified sample, it might be necessary to compare the costs of constructing the strata and the expected benefits of doing so.

Sudman and Kalton (1986) present a useful review of methods for sampling special populations that are difficult to locate, such as racial or ethnic groups, special types of households or individuals, certain income groups, and users of particular services. They suggest using partial or multiple lists to identify or screen subjects (if, for example, the available list of farm owners is several years out of date and may have excluded some farmers), mail or telephone interviews for screening, and snowball samples in which one interviewee identifies other people who share his or her own characteristics (such as a migrant in his group of acquaintances). A snowball sample is one in which subjects are asked to identify people they know who fall into a certain category. The people identified are interviewed and they in their turn mention other people. For example, users of certain kinds of birth control devices might be asked to identify other users, members of a political or religious group might be asked to identify other members, and HIV-positive individuals could be asked who else in the community is HIV-positive.

## Related (Panel), Independent, and Mixed Samples

Many evaluation textbooks assume that a panel of the same subjects will be interviewed before and after the project. A panel design may not always be practical, however. Many low-income communities have a high population turnover. Indeed, it is not unusual to find that one-quarter or more of the households have moved away in the two or three years between the first and second interviews. Consequently, the evaluation researcher must choose from among (a) a *panel* of related samples, in which the same subjects are reinterviewed; (b) *independent* samples, in which a new sample is selected for the second interview ($T_2$); and (c) a *mixed* sample, which combines some of the elements of the previous two approaches.

PANEL SAMPLE. If the same households or subjects are reinterviewed in a second survey, they are treated as a panel sample. To use a panel sample it is necessary to prepare maps of the precise location of houses or to use some other similar device to ensure that the original households or subjects can be relocated. At times, it will be difficult to identify the same households two years later since the area may have new houses, street names may be different, and even numbers and street directions may have been changed.[1] In many developing countries, houses do not have addresses; hence, landmarks are used to refer people to a particular location. Another problem is that household composition and the name of the household head can also change. In a first interview, for example, a woman may declare that she is the head of the household. By the time of the second interview, she may have a male companion who is now considered the household head.

Another factor to take into account is the estimated dropout rate and its impact on sample size. Suppose that a sample has to consist of 200 households before estimates can be considered valid. Suppose also that 25 percent of households move before the second survey. Hence, the sample size at $T_1$ must be increased to 250 households to keep the final sample at $T_2$ (after 25 percent of the households have moved) close to 200. If the dropout rate is expected to be high, it is also necessary to consider the effects that this decrease will have on the representativeness of the final sample. Therefore it is advisable to analyze the $T_1$ data at the end of the second survey and to compare the characteristics of households that have moved with those that have remained in the community to determine whether the study has retained individuals of a particular ilk. This can be referred to as selective retention, since the program has tended to retain individuals with particular characteristics and to exclude others. For example, if higher-income families had tended to leave a community, the incomes of the remaining original families would underestimate the average income of all families at the time of the first survey. Thus, changes in the distribution of characteristics must be taken into account when interpreting the findings of an analysis that deals only with households remaining in the community.

INDEPENDENT SAMPLES. In this design, a second random sample is selected for the second survey at $T_2$. No additional sampling problems exist beyond those facing simple random samples.

MIXED SAMPLE DESIGN. This design is the most complicated to administer. It follows the same procedures as the panel study except that replacements are found for original families or subjects who can no longer be interviewed. The simplest option is to replace the household with the new family living in the same structure. This means, however, that families living in new structures built since the time of the previous survey will be excluded from the sample, and the procedure therefore introduces a bias against new households. Moreover, it is difficult to define the population to which new occupants belong. Although many of them are probably new to the community, others may have moved from other houses in the same community.

A better approach is to select a new sample for the replacements. The sample should be selected from all households or subjects who have moved to the community (or to their present dwelling) since the time of the previous survey. This procedure can be somewhat cumbersome since a large number of screening interviews may be required to identify new families. In practice, it is relatively simple to identify new households in sites and services shelter projects; local project managers will usually have records of new arrivals. New participants in control areas may be difficult to select, however, since the evaluator will want to include individuals with characteristics similar to those of the participants who left.

The drawbacks of a mixed sample are related to the estimation of sample size. To make full use of the analytical potential of this sample, the evaluator should conduct a separate analysis of the original households (panel) and new arrivals. Separate estimates of the required sample size for both groups would be necessary since one would have to be sure that each sample was representative of its own group.

## Sampling Units

To design a sample, one must first define a *universe* consisting of a number of *sampling units*. The units are the entities of primary interest. They may consist of the individual, the household head, children, the family, the building. It is extremely important to define the sampling unit precisely. The primary focus of the evaluation may be an administrative unit (such as a school district), a physical structure (such as a primary irrigation system), an apartment building, an economic or social group occupying or owning the physical structure, or both the structure and the users.

When several sampling units are used, the sampling may take place in multiple stages. In a housing survey, the first stage may deal with the structure (apartment building or individual housing unit), the second stage may deal with the family group, and a third stage with particular kinds of individuals in selected families (household head, mother, or wage earners).

In the evaluation of a primary school system, the first stage may concentrate on the school district, the second stage on a particular school, and the third stage on the families with children in that school.

The *physical or administrative unit* is often studied to evaluate the costs or the efficiency of service delivery. Studies of the organization of social or economic units usually focus on the *household* or *production unit*. The *individuals* would be studied if the researcher needs information on the social and economic conditions of the total population (for example, income and employment, or education and employment stratified by age and sex).

## Determining Sample Size

### The Effect of Sample Size on the Evaluation Budget

Interviews are normally among the costliest components of evaluation research. Since the decision about what kind of sample to use can affect the sample size, it is essential to select the smallest, but most economical, sample consistent with the desired level of precision. The effect of a sample design on costs becomes even more important in longitudinal studies where two or more waves of interviews are required. Although budgetary constraints may force interviewers to reduce the size of a sample, if it is too small, it may not provide reliable answers to the questions they are studying.

The main determinants of sample size are the variance of the variables being estimated, the precision required of the sample estimates, and the number of subgroups for which information is needed. In the following sections we show how these factors affect the estimation of sample size in typical evaluation studies.

Many statistical textbooks describe procedures for estimating sample size when a single parameter has to be estimated, but the situation is usually more complicated in evaluation research because a large number of variables must be studied. Furthermore, the main concern is not to estimate confidence intervals for variables at one point in time, but to estimate the significance of changes between two or more points in time. The sampling design problems can be even more complex in projects concerned with squatter upgrading or with providing credit to small businesses, because the researcher may not know which subjects will form part of the intervention group. Thus it may be necessary to start with a larger initial sample to ensure that sufficient project beneficiaries are included. In squatter upgrading projects, many of the decisions about which households to relocate and where to place the roads, water pipes, and other services are based on discussions with community residents. In a large project, this process may take place over a period of several years. Consequently, when the evaluation baseline study is being conducted at the start of the project, there is no way to know exactly which families will be affected. (For a discussion of how community consultation operated in upgrading projects in Lusaka, Zambia, see Bamberger, Sanyal, and Valverde 1982:chap. 7).

Similarly, sample designs may have to compensate for the fact that many subjects drop out of a sample between the first and second interviews. In some cases subjects move, and in other cases it is not possible to identify some of the original households at the time of the second interview. The original families may be difficult to identify because the people have changed their names, families have merged or split up, buildings are divided or combined, or a whole block has been completely redesigned. Households are identified in the survey by name and street address, but if both of these change it can be difficult to determine whether the same family is still there at the time of the second visit. Moreover, at the time the sample is being designed the interviewer may not know which subgroups of the population will be of particular interest and therefore need more intensive study.

### Some Determinants of Sample Size for Social Sector Projects

Several factors affect sample size in the evaluation of typical social sector projects. Where a project is relatively *small* or *concentrated in a small number of locations*, the sample can be small and the costs of interviewing quite low. For these reasons it is usually possible to use much smaller samples for evaluating urban projects located in a small number of sites than for agricultural and rural development projects, where there are large numbers of widely dispersed project sites.

When the *marginal cost of additional interviews is low*, the researcher can use a larger sample size. If the project has a permanent team of interviewers, the expense of additional interviews may be relatively low. The Research and Analysis Division (RAD) of the National Housing Authority in Manila has a large team of permanent interviewers and thus is able to conduct follow-up interviews or to expand the size of an interesting subgroup at almost no cost or delay. In contrast, interviewers in El Salvador are normally contracted and paid for each completed interview. Once the interview budget is exhausted, no more interviews can be conducted for a particular study.

*Projects involving a larger number of options or services* require larger samples to ensure that subjects who have received each option are included. If all children receive the same vaccine and nothing else, the sample can be much smaller than it would be if a number of additional services are provided, such as wells, food supplements, and classes in child care for mothers. When a number of different services are offered, it is usually wise to use a *factorial design*, which means that a certain minimum number of subjects are covered for each "cell" or combination of services. If a rural development project provided two kinds of tubewells (shallow and deep) and if each kind could be financed in three ways, the samples in a factorial design would consist of six cells (three for the methods of financing shallow tubewells and three for the methods of financing deep tubewells) and each cell would cover a certain minimum number of subjects (in this case villages).

A much larger sample is required to assess *the impact of the project on different population groups* than to estimate the global impact on the whole population.

When a panel design is used, the researcher also has to look at the *expected dropout rate* in the intervention and control groups. The higher the dropout rate, the larger the initial sample must be to ensure that there will be an adequate number of subjects for the second and third surveys.

*The smaller the proportion of the population* that is expected to be substantially affected by the project (for example, proportion of families who will be relocated, proportion of artisans likely to receive loans), the larger the sample required to ensure that sufficient beneficiaries are included.

In cases where it is difficult to identify project beneficiaries, it may be necessary to *screen* through a sample first, in order to identify interview subjects with the desired characteristics. Such a procedure might be necessary to identify children who have received a certain kind of medical treatment, people who have a particular occupation, families who are subletting part of their house, or families who are receiving remittances from relatives outside the country. If the proportion of the population with this particular attribute is quite small, it might be necessary to conduct large numbers of screening interviews to identify the group of interest. Resourceful researchers can often find ways to simplify the selection procedure. For example, they might find that hospitals have records of families who have received a certain treatment, or that they can identify rented rooms by direct observation.

The *way the project is organized* may also affect sample size. If everyone receives the same package of services, the sample can be smaller than it needs to be when the services are distributed randomly or unevenly. If the available records indicate how services were allocated, this can also simplify the sample design and reduce the sample size.

### Effect of Turnover Rate on Sample Size

Suppose that a *panel sample* is being used and that a sample of 400 people is considered necessary to ensure that the estimates attain the required level of precision. Because of the nature of the panel design, the same individuals will have to be compared in each interview, and therefore the original sample will have to be large enough to guarantee that at least 400 of the respondents interviewed in the first survey $T_1$ can be reinterviewed in the second $T_2$ and third $T_3$ sessions. Suppose also that previous studies suggest a 25 percent annual dropout rate should be anticipated. Assuming the interview in $T_3$ is conducted two years after the $T_1$ interview, how many families would have to be interviewed in $T_1$ to ensure that after a 25 percent annual dropout there will still be at least 400 families in $T_3$? The answer is given by the equation:

$$(11\text{-}6) \qquad Y = \frac{X}{(1-p)^t}$$

where $Y$ = the required interviews in $T_1$, $X$ = interviews in $T_3$, $p$ = the annual sample dropout rate, and $t$ = the number of time intervals (years) to which the dropout rate applies.

In a panel study, 711 interviews would have to be conducted in $T_1$ to ensure that 400 of the original families are still living in the same house community in $T_3$. Table 11-4 indicates that the original 711 families in $T_1$ will be reduced to 533 in $T_2$, and to 400 in $T_3$. If we were using a *simple panel design*, we would accept the reduced sample size and would only reinterview the remaining 533 original families in $T_2$ and the remaining 400 in $T_3$. The largest number of interviews would be required for a *mixed sample*. In

**Table 11-4. Number of Interviews Required in $T_1$, $T_2$, and $T_3$ with Each Sample Design to Ensure a Sample of 400 in $T_3$**
(assuming a 25 percent annual turnover)

| Sample Design | $T_1$ | $T_2$ | $T_3$ | Total |
|---|---|---|---|---|
| Mixed sample | 711 | 711 | 711 | 2,133 |
| Panel sample | 711 | 533 | 400 | 1,644 |
| Independent random samples | 400 | 400 | 400 | 1,200 |

Note: The required sample size to estimate the difference of differences of proportions is 400.

this case, we include replacements for the dropouts, so that in $T_3$ we still have 711 families, although only 400 of them were in the original sample.

Table 11-6 shows that for both the mixed and the panel sample designs, the higher the estimated dropout rate, the greater the number of interviews required in $T_1$. If the dropout rate had been 10 percent, instead of 25 percent, the number of interviews required in $T_1$ to guarantee a final sample of 400 would have been 494, instead of 711.

## Estimating Sample Sizes for Typical Impact Studies

This section provides guidelines for estimating sample sizes in typical impact studies. It covers the procedures used to determine what size of sample is required to estimate differences between proportions and differences between means. It also explains what happens when separate estimates are made for subgroups or strata and indicates the typical sample sizes for common kinds of evaluation.

### Estimating Sample Size to Evaluate the Difference between Proportions

One of the basic questions in sample design is how large must a sample be to determine whether there is a statistically significant difference between two groups? In the present case, the two groups being studied are the intervention and control groups. To begin with the simplest situation, consider the differences between proportions.

If we wished to test the hypothesis that the project will increase the proportion of self-employed heads of households, our hypothesis could be

$$H: I_2 - I_1 \quad C_2 - C_1$$

where $I_2$ and $I_1$ are the proportions of self-employed in the intervention group at $T_2$ and $T_1$, respectively, and $C_2$ and $C_1$ are the proportions of self-employed in the control group.

Table 11-5 shows the number of interviews that the researcher would have to conduct in each group to be 95 percent confident that the observed difference was not due to chance. In this example, the policymaker has indicated how large a sample must be before the project can be considered to have a "significant" impact. In one case, a 20 percent difference between the groups is expected from the project. In another case, a 5 percent difference is considered significant. As the table indicates, the smaller the required difference to judge an impact, the larger the sample required.

Table 11-5 shows the sample sizes that would be required to establish statistical significance at a 95 percent level of confidence when the observed difference between two groups is 5, 7.5, 10, 15, and 20 percent. The table can be applied to any study in which changes in proportions are compared and the figures represent the minimum differences that might be considered important in various contexts. The equation used to estimate the required sample size ($n$) for the project and control groups is

(11-7)
$$n = \frac{4\,(0.75 + p_2\,q_2)}{(p_1 - p_2)^2}$$

where $n$ = required sample size in project and control groups, $p_1$; $p_2$ = the proportions of project families with the attribute (self-employed) in $T_1$ and

Table 11-5.  Sample Size Required to be 95 Percent Confident
That an Observed Difference in the Change of Proportions
between Project and Control Groups Is Not Due to Chance

| *Minimum difference (%) between project and control groups to judge an impact* | *Required Sample Size* | | *Total Sample Size* |
|---|---|---|---|
| | *Project Group* | *Control Group* | |
| 5 | 1,596 | 1,596 | 3,192 |
| 7.5 | 707 | 707 | 1,414 |
| 10 | 396 | 396 | 792 |
| 15 | 174 | 174 | 348 |
| 20 | 96 | 96 | 192 |

$T_2$; and $q_2$ = the proportion of project families who do not have the attribute in $T_2$, or $1 - p_2 = q_2$.

Table 11-5 indicates that in order to test whether a difference of only 10 percent in the change between the project and control groups was statistically significant at the 95 percent level, samples should contain 396 individuals in each of the two groups. To evaluate a 5 percent difference, it would be necessary to use samples of 1,596 for each group.

### Estimating the Sample Size to Test for Differences between Means

The above discussion is based on the assumption that we wish to evaluate *differences of proportion*. Many studies are more interested in the difference between means (for example, differences in average income, value of houses, years of education). To estimate the sample size required to test for the significance of a difference between two sample means, such as the difference in the mean income of project and control families, the researcher needs to examine the standard deviations of the two samples being compared. If this information is available, then the following equation can be used to estimate the required sample size to test for a specified difference between means:

$$(11\text{-}8) \qquad\qquad n = \frac{4\,(s_1^2 + s_2^2)}{p^2} + 1$$

where $n$ = the required sample size, $s_1$ and $s_2$ = the standard deviations of the two means, and $p$ = the minimum difference between the means being tested.

A number of simplifying assumptions have been made. Normally, these assumptions will not affect the sample size except when small samples of less than 50 are used. This qualification is necessary because some of the assumptions may affect how the degrees of freedom are calculated.

The following example illustrates how the equation is used. Assume a baseline survey was conducted in 1985 and mean family income was found to be 300 pesos per month with a standard deviation of 45 ($s_1 = 45$). A second survey is conducted two years later to determine if there has been a significant change in income. We assume that evidence from other recent surveys suggests that the standard deviation of income is likely to increase to 55 pesos ($s_2 = 55$). The project manager says that income must change by at least 5 percent (15 pesos) to be considered operationally significant. How many interviews must be conducted to detect a statistically significant change of as little as 15 pesos? Using equation (11-8),

$$n = \frac{4\,(45^2 + 55^2)}{15^2} + 1 = 90$$

which means that the sample size should be 90 in both the experimental and the control groups. If the manager had stated that he or she wished to consider 10 pesos as the minimum difference, the sample size would have increased to 202 for each group.

Remember, too, that the sample size *cannot* be estimated without first estimating the standard deviations of the pre- and postintervention samples. If the second survey has yet to be designed, then, of course, no information will be available. Nevertheless, the standard deviation of the first sample will be available since it is calculated at an earlier time. If no other information is available, the evaluation can assume that the standard deviation of the second sample will be the same as it was for the first survey. If the first survey is also being designed, an estimated standard deviation can be obtained from other similar studies. If this is not possible, a small pilot study can be performed and the standard deviation estimated from it.

## The Effect of Subgroup Analysis on Sample Size

In many cases, it will also be necessary to compare different subgroups, such as families that have received different types of services (credit, credit combined with technical assistance), or female- and male-headed households. Before such comparisons can be made, each subgroup has to be large enough for real differences to be detected using statistical criteria.

To evaluate a difference of proportions in two subgroups of approximately equal size, the same rules would apply as presented in Table 11-5. Thus, for a difference of 10 percent to be detected, 396 observations are needed in each group; for a difference of 15 percent, the figure drops to 174 per group; and for 20 percent, 96 observations per group are required.

## Typical Sample Sizes

Table 11-6 shows how sample size is affected when an interviewer is estimating the proportions of some of the variables discussed earlier. As the table makes clear, the characteristics of the population and the required

**Table 11-6.  The Estimation of Sample Size for Impact Evaluation with Mixed Samples under Different Assumptions**

| Assumption | Intervention Group 1 | Intervention Group 2 | Control Group | Total Sample Size in $T_3$ | 10% Drop-out | 25% Drop-out |
|---|---|---|---|---|---|---|
| To test for minimum difference of 10% between intervention and control groups | 396 | 0 | 396 | 792 | 978 | 1,408 |
| To test as in (1) and also test for 15% differences between 3 control group strata | 396 | 0 | 522 | 918 | 1,133 | 1,632 |
| To test as in (1) and also test for 10% difference between two equal size intervention groups | 396 | 396 | 396 | 1,188 | 1,467 | 2,112 |
| To test as in (1) and also test for 10% difference between intervention groups with 25% and 75% of families, respectively | 396 | 1,188 | 396 | 1,980 | 2,444 | 3,520 |
| To test as in 1 but when it is not known in $T_1$ which families will be participating. It is expected that 20% will participate | 1,980 | 0 | 396 | 2,376 | 2,933 | 4,224 |
| To test as in 3 but testing for 15% difference | 174 | 174 | 396 | 744 | 919 | 1,323 |

Header grouping: "Sample Size at $T_3$" spans Intervention Group 1, Intervention Group 2, Control Group, Total Sample Size in $T_3$. "Total $T_1$ Sample Size" spans 10% Drop-out and 25% Drop-out.

*Note:* Sample sizes are for estimating proportions. As a rough guideline, sample sizes should be at least doubled for estimating differences between means.

level of precision can substantially increase or decrease the required numbers of interviews. Following are some typical sample sizes used in estimating proportions.

EXAMPLE 1. The task here is to estimate sample sizes for a longitudinal study in which some of the interviewees are expected to drop out. Some

396 interviews would be required in each study group to estimate a 10 percent difference in proportions between the control and intervention groups at $T_3$. Therefore, the sample size $T_1$ should be 978 or 1,408, depending on whether a dropout rate of 10 percent or 25 percent was expected. This calculation was performed using the following formula:

(11-9)
$$n_1 = \frac{n_3}{(1-d)^t}$$

where $n_1$ = the sample size to start with at $T_1$, $n_3$ = the expected sample size at $T_3$, $d$ = the dropout rate, and $t$ = the number of time intervals for which the dropout rate applies.

In the present case, the result is as follows:

$$n_1 = \frac{792}{(1 - 10\%)^2} = 978.$$

Some rounding does occur, and so the sample size calculations at $T_1$ and $T_2$ are not always symmetrical. In the preceding example, if $T_1$ has a sample of 978, given a 10 percent dropout rate (a 90 percent retention rate), one would expect 792 to remain at $T_3$:

$$n_3 = 978 \, (0.90)^2 = 792.$$

Yet, if one knew in advance that a minimum of 800 observations was required at $T_3$ and asked how many should be selected at $T_1$, the answer would be slightly different:

$$n_1 = \frac{800}{0.90^2} = 987.65 (\approx) 988.$$

EXAMPLE 2. If each of the three strata in the control group is also to be analyzed separately, the sample should be further increased to ensure a sufficient number of interviews in each stratum. If we can accept a minimum difference of 15 percent as significant, then only 174 interviews would be required in each stratum of the control group (see Table 11-5), and the total sample size would increase by only 126 in $T_3$, to 918 (i.e., 396 + 174 × 3)). Thus, the total sample in $T_1$ would increase to 1,133 or 1,632, depending on the assumed dropout rate of 10 percent or 15 percent, respectively. This design makes it possible to compare all intervention and control groups to test for a minimum 10 percent difference between the experimental and control group, and for a 15 percent difference between the strata in the control group.

EXAMPLE 3. Now let us assume that, in addition to the evaluation described in example 1, it is also necessary to compare two intervention groups and a control group. If a minimum 10 percent difference is considered necessary, then 396 interviews will be required in each of the three groups, increasing the total number of interviews in $T_3$ to 1,188. If a minimum difference of 15 percent instead of 10 percent could be accepted, the sample size could be reduced to 174 for each stratum, and the total number of interviews in $T_3$ would not be any larger than 744.

EXAMPLE 4. Suppose that all the assessments performed in example 3 are also performed here, but that only 25 percent of all families in the second intervention group will participate in the intervention. In this case, it will be necessary to increase the sample size in the second intervention group to 1,188 to ensure finding the 396 families required for the smallest stratum (second intervention group). A considerable reduction in sample size could be achieved if the minimum acceptable difference was 15 percent instead of 10 percent.

EXAMPLE 5. Now suppose that all the evaluations are the same as in example 1, but that the intervention is an upgrading project in which only about 20 percent of families will be affected by the project. If the future project participants cannot be identified before the project begins, the intervention sample will have to consist of 1,980 families to ensure that at least 396 future participants are included. This number could be cut by more than half if a 15 percent difference could be accepted as the minimum.

## Defining the Time Period for the Study

In experimental and quasi-experimental designs, impact indicators must be measured "before" and "after" the project has been implemented. Unlike a laboratory experiment, which has a clearly defined beginning and end, most social projects continue over a long period, say, five years or more, with participants entering at different points in time and with new inputs continuing to be provided throughout this period. Several issues should be considered in designing the evaluation.

*At what point in the project cycle should baseline or pretest data be collected?* In a slum upgrading project, topographical surveys may start several years before the project is announced to community residents. Once households are aware that a project is being considered, however, land values may increase as speculators start to buy up properties.

*Should a baseline evaluation survey be conducted at the time of the topographical survey (which may be two years or more before any infrastructure investments begin)?* In many housing projects a preliminary list of interested candidates may be drawn up years before the first houses are offered for sale (in fact, the lending agency may require this list as evidence that there is sufficient interest to justify the project). The evaluator must consider the implications of these preparatory activities and how they could affect the result in order to decide whether the first survey should be taken at the time when families register, or two or three years later when houses are allocated to applicants.

*Should the "before" measurement be conducted at one point in time or should data be collected for each group at similar points of their own evolution?* Projects do not usually begin at the same time for all participants. Infrastructure such as water and roads may benefit some sectors of a community several years before others. Similarly, families may be selected for a housing project in several waves over a period of years.

*When should the "after" measurement be made?* Projects do not end at the same time for all participants. Some families may have been living in their new house for several years before others occupy theirs.

*Should the "after" measurement be delayed until all of these services are operating (which could mean a delay of several years)?* Most projects cannot be considered finished the day that the installation of infrastructure is completed. The design of many projects includes complementary work such as parks, sidewalks, or community centers to be completed by residents. Some of these may take years to complete. Other projects reserve sites for stores and other types of businesses, many of which will not begin their activities until all or most families have moved into the community. In addition, services such as transport, garbage collection, police, and health centers will have to be provided by other agencies and may not begin to operate for some time. From a certain perspective, the project is not really completed until all of these services are fully operational.

*At what point should an impact be measured?* The time it takes for impacts to be felt varies. Families may not begin to make major housing investments until the community is well established. Some of the health effects may not occur until children born in the new community have reached a certain age, whereas others may be evident as soon as the water and sanitation services are operational. In extreme cases, impacts on migration, household size, female labor force participation, and educational performance may not take place for a decade or more. This suggests that studies may be required at different points in time in order to measure different types of impacts. Although such studies are theoretically possible, in practice it would be difficult to continue the evaluation over a period of many years because of the increase in costs and the organizational difficulties in continuing a study over so many years.

## Lot Quality Acceptance Sampling

The most sought-after methods of project monitoring and evaluation are those that use small sample sizes and that can be carried out rapidly. Lot quality acceptance sampling (LQAS) is one such method. It can be applied wherever the evaluator is interested in determining whether a service or product is being produced in an acceptable quantity or with acceptable quality. The following discussion of LQAS uses public health examples since these programs frequently entail services to large numbers of people in many different locations. In a typical monitoring problem, the evaluator might have to determine whether 700 health posts are adequately vaccinating children under three years of age against polio. With LQAS, a sample of no more than fourteen to twenty-eight children from each area would be sufficient to classify any single health post (HP) as adequately delivering services such as vaccinations. The small sample from each area can then be aggregated to calculate regional or national coverage proportions (Valadez 1991).

Three criteria of quality can be used to assess a program (Valadez 1991). The first one is "adequacy," which determines whether risk groups in a community are receiving services at the appropriate age (i.e., as defined by government institutions such as the Ministry of Health). For example, programs such as an expanded program of immunization (EPI) require that infants be vaccinated with three doses of polio within the first year of life, beginning at two months of age, with at least a one-month interval between doses.

The second criterion is "coverage," which measures whether a minimum proportion of individuals in a community regardless of their age have received a service. For example, mothers of all children under the age of three should be educated in the preparation and administration of oral rehydration therapy (ORT), or children should have an up-to-date vaccination status even if doses were received at ages older then specified by Ministry of Health norms.

The third criterion is the "technical quality" of the health workers. It is used to determine whether critical tasks of a health service (for example, maintains the cold chain or the supply of oral rehydration salts, health worker hygiene, education of mothers) were implemented correctly.

The following discussion briefly demonstrates how to use LQAS to control the quality of interventions such as primary health care (PHC) by identifying which ones operate below a performance standard and therefore require special attention. The basic principle of LQAS is that it measures whether minimum performance standards have been reached.

## LQAS Principles

Local managers find that most sampling designs require large numbers of observations and therefore are often too burdensome to handle. LQAS, on the other hand, can be applied either to small or large populations using a small sample. Although the statistical principles on which LQAS is based may seem complex, it is quite simple to use once program managers acquire minimal training. When first developed about fifty years ago, LQAS was used in industrial settings by inspectors who had little skill and education (Dodge and Romig 1959).

LQAS uses binomials to classify program workers by their performance, which is judged according to three levels of performance: adequate service delivery, somewhat inadequate, and very inadequate. This is known as a triage system and has been used in Costa Rica and Nairobi, Kenya, to assess EPI service delivery. In these countries it took the following form:

- Adequate = 100 to 80 percent of children under three years of age vaccinated
- Somewhat inadequate = 79 to 51 percent vaccinated
- Very inadequate = 50 to 0 percent vaccinated.

LQAS identifies workers whose performance is at either end of the continuum, namely, adequate or very inadequate. It is less sensitive to the health workers in the middle category. However, this is not a serious limitation, since the closer the quality of the health worker is to either end of the continuum, the greater the likelihood that it will be classified as adequate or very inadequate. These two extreme categories of health workers are the most important ones to identify correctly. Health system managers need to identify very inadequate health workers so that resources can be directed to improving the quality of interventions in the communities being served. Conversely, adequately performing health workers need to be identified so that additional resources are not needlessly spent on them.

LQAS differs from conventional sampling methods that measure the proportion of a population covered with a service. Typically, the manager compares an estimated proportion of coverage with a standard set by a Ministry of Health (for example, 80 percent) to judge whether service provision is adequate. Samples as large as 396 can be required. In such cases, substantial resources are invested to produce a measure that is merely compared to an existing standard. Whether the estimated coverage is 81.5 percent, 79.4 percent, or whatever, is less important than whether the 80 percent performance standard has been reached.

The measure produced by LQAS is a probability estimating whether the health worker under assessment has reached the ministry standard. The exact coverage of a given health worker is less important than determining whether the service was adequate with respect to a reference.

## Using LQAS

In most instances of day-to-day project management, a supervisor or manager needs to detect extremes of performance in order to make rational decisions about how to allocate resources. These decisions ought to be made on a regular basis as part of a quality control system. Several steps must be taken before LQAS can be used:

- Define performance standards. These standards ought to be expressed in terms of the triage system discussed earlier.
- Determine the permissible classification errors of the LQAS screening. For example, 5 percent of all health workers could be misclassified (Valadez 1991).
- Decide how many individuals who have not received the intervention should be included in the LQAS sample, at a maximum. This is known as a decision rule. For any number greater than this, the health

worker's performance will be judged inadequate. In the first reported LQAS study in Costa Rica during 1987, the LQAS sample consisted of 28 children under three years of age and their mothers, who were selected from the catchment area of each of 60 health workers. The decision rule was to classify the health worker as inadequate if more than 9 of the 28 children (or their mothers) had not received the intervention under assessment.

All three of these decisions are interrelated. The size of the LQAS sample is a function of all three. For example, in an assessment of vaccination in Costa Rica (Valadez 1991)—where the performance standards were 80 percent = adequate, and 50 percent = very inadequate—precision was set at 95 percent for classifying either adequate or very inadequate health workers. This level of precision was achieved by (a) selecting a sample of 28 children under the age of three and their mothers and (b) deciding that no more than 9 of these were to be individuals who had not received the intervention.

This decision was made as follows. For the sample size of 28, the total classification error that results when no more than 9 individuals without the intervention are permitted is 8 percent. This total error (reported in column 5 of Table 11-7) is calculated from columns three and four in the table—namely (1 minus the probability of detecting adequate areas) + (1 minus the probability of detecting very inadequate areas). As can be seen in Table 11-7, the smallest classification error occurs with a rule of 28:9. It increases or decreases as the threshold number of individuals who have not received the intervention increases or decreases. For this particular size, the classification error is the same (that is, 4 percent), whether detecting adequate or very inadequate areas.

If a sample of 14 individuals was selected, as shown in Table 11-7, the other parameters would change. If 3 individuals had not received the intervention permitted in the sample, 97 percent of the very inadequate performances would be detected. However, the precision is 70 percent for identifying adequate health workers. The total classification error is 33 percent for the 14:3 decision rule. If a 14:4 rule is adopted, then the precision of each judgment shifts. The LQAS would identify at least 87 percent of the adequate areas and at least 91 percent of the very inadequate ones. The total classification error would be less than the preceding option (that is, 22 percent). Therefore, a 14:4 decision rule would be preferable to a 14:3 rule, if the minimizing total classification error is the guiding principle. Similar decisions can be made for any type of LQAS. Several other examples are given in Table 11-7, which points out the propitious decision rule for each sample size.

Table 11-7.  Example of the Application of LQAS Statistics to Detect the Probability of 80 or 50 Percent Coverage of Health Area Residents with Respect to a PHC Vaccination Program

| Sample Size of Appropriate Residents | Number in the Sample not Receiving the Intervention | Probability of Detecting Health Areas with 80% Coverage (a) | Probability of Detecting Health Areas with 50% Coverage (b) | Total Classification Error, $(1 - a) + (1 - b)$ |
|---|---|---|---|---|
| 8 | 0 | 0.17 | 1 | 0.83 |
| | 1 | 0.50 | 0.96 | 0.54 |
| | 2 | 0.79 | 0.83 | 0.38* |
| | 3 | 0.94 | 0.64 | 0.42 |
| 10 | 0 | 0.11 | 1 | 0.89 |
| | 1 | 0.38 | 0.99 | 0.63 |
| | 2 | 0.68 | 0.94 | 0.38 |
| | 3 | 0.88 | 0.83 | 0.29* |
| | 4 | 0.97 | 0.62 | 0.41 |
| 14 | 0 | 0.04 | 1 | 0.96 |
| | 1 | 0.20 | 1 | 0.80 |
| | 2 | 0.45 | 0.99 | 0.56 |
| | 3 | 0.70 | 0.97 | 0.33 |
| | 4 | 0.87 | 0.91 | 0.22* |
| | 5 | 0.96 | 0.79 | 0.25 |
| 19 | 0 | 0.01 | 1 | 0.99 |
| | 1 | 0.08 | 1 | 0.92 |
| | 2 | 0.24 | 1 | 0.76 |
| | 3 | 0.46 | 1 | 0.55 |
| | 4 | 0.67 | 0.99 | 0.34 |
| | 5 | 0.84 | 0.97 | 0.20 |
| | 6 | 0.93 | 0.92 | 0.15* |
| | 7 | 0.98 | 0.82 | 0.20 |
| 28 | 5 | 0.50 | 1 | 0.50 |
| | 6 | 0.68 | 1 | 0.32 |
| | 7 | 0.81 | 0.99 | 0.20 |
| | 8 | 0.91 | 0.98 | 0.11 |
| | 9 | 0.96 | 0.96 | 0.08* |
| | 10 | 0.99 | 0.90 | 0.11 |

*Note:* All probabilities have been rounded. Asterisks indicate the minimum total classification error for a sample size. Sample sizes of health area residents range from 8 to 28, and numbers of cases not receiving a hypothetical intervention range from 0 to 10.

Two labels are given to the probabilities obtained from LQAS. One of these probabilities (1 – the probability of detecting adequate areas) is called the provider risk. This name derives from the fact that providers are at risk whenever they classify an adequate area as inadequate. The risk arises from using resources to improve areas unnecessarily, and inaccurately concluding that a health worker is not performing adequately, and thereby affecting the worker's self-esteem and his/her relationship with the manager. The other probability (1 – the probability of detecting very inadequate areas) is called the consumer risk. Consumers at risk to health problems are those in the care of a health worker who is performing inadequately. Consumers are at risk precisely because the quality of care they receive is poor.

Experience has shown that a sample of 19 individuals is adequate for most assessments. A sample of 28 households in a depressed rural area would take about 8.2 person days of interviewing. A sample of 19 individuals, with 6 uncovered individuals, saves about 2.7 person days of work with an inconsequential increase in provider and consumer risks (0.07 versus 0.04, 0.08 versus 0.04, respectively). Assuming that exactly half of the 60 health areas studied have 80 percent and half have 50 percent coverage, a 28:9 rule will misclassify 1.2 + 1.2 health areas; when these fractions of health areas are rounded to integers, the misclassification is 1 + 1 health areas. With a 19:6 rule, the misclassification would be 2.1 + 2.4 health areas (or 2 + 2 health areas with rounding; see Table 11-1). The difference in misclassification is 2 health areas. The 2.7 days of costs that are saved by selecting the 19:6 LQAS design would more than offset the maximum costs resulting from the two misclassified health areas.

In recent years, Ministries of Health in various countries have defined triage systems for acceptable consumer and provider risks. Bolivia's work team selected an upper threshold of 50 percent coverage and a lower threshold of 20 percent. A sample size of 19 with 12 uncovered individuals was an appropriate LQAS design. In Uganda, a 60–40 percent triage was selected.

The way to use the 19:6 LQAS sample is as follows. The probability of finding 6 or fewer mothers who prepare ORT incorrectly in a sample of 19 mothers taken from a community in which 80 percent of the mothers know how to prepare and administer ORT is 0.93. Therefore, 93 times out of 100, these communities will be classified correctly as having received an adequately performed intervention.

In communities in which 50 percent of the mothers are competent in ORT usage, the probability of finding 6 or fewer mothers who prepare ORT incorrectly in a sample of 19 mothers is 0.08. Therefore, 92 times out of 100 (that is, 1.00 – 0.08), these communities will be correctly classified.

The cost for low provider risk is high consumer risk. In our experience, this tradeoff is worthwhile. This point becomes clear when LQAS is used by supervisors to assess technical quality of health workers. A 6:1 rule is used in this situation. Ninety-seven percent of the workers who perform their tasks correctly 95 percent of the time are correctly identified. All those who make more than 1 error in 6 performances of a task are inadequate performers. The tradeoff is that not all inadequate performers are detected. Provider risk is low while consumer risk is high. During a single round of supervision, numerous performance errors are detected. Typically, because a large number of problems are identified during the first round, the health system is overwhelmed with resolving them, and cannot deal with additional problems at that moment. Therefore, it is desirable to have a lower provider risk than a lower consumer risk.

Once the problems in the substandard health areas are addressed, the Ministry of Health can be ready for a second batch of health areas with an inadequate assessment. A second round of supervision will identify more of them because a large proportion of false negatives occurred in the first round. Since supervision is performed frequently during the year, the sensitivity of the method improves during the longitudinal applications. The likelihood of misclassifying the same health worker for the same task, regardless of the performance level, continuously decreases over time. Within one year most of the problem activities should be detected. Regular use of LQAS supervision continues to reduce classification errors. Eventually, most health workers with problematic technique will be identified.

The continuous reduction in consumer risk with regular use of LQAS is presented in Figure 11-1.

EXAMPLE. LQAS SAMPLING USES THE BINOMIAL FORMULA. In an infinitely large population the probability $P$ of $a$ successes occurring (where $a$ is the number of adequately vaccinated individuals) in $n$ trials is calculated as

(11-10)
$$P_a = \frac{n!}{[a!(n-a)!]} p^a q^{n-a}$$

where $p$ = the proportion of successful coverage, $q$ = the proportion of substandard coverage = $1 - p$, $n$ = the sample size, $a$ = the number in the

**Figure 11-1. Decreasing Classification Error with Each Additional Supervisor Visit**

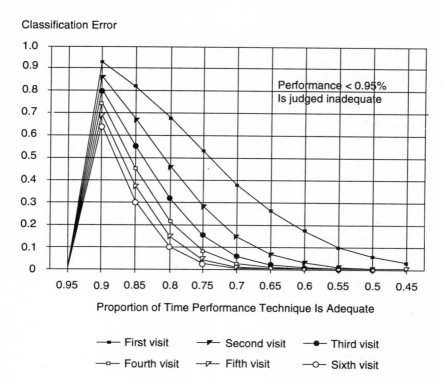

Classification Error

Performance < 0.95%
Is judged inadequate

Proportion of Time Performance Technique Is Adequate

—■— First visit     —▸— Second visit     —●— Third visit
—□— Fourth visit     —▽— Fifth visit     —○— Sixth visit

sample with adequate coverage, and $n - a$ = the number of detectives in a sample (in LQAS, this expression is referred to as $d$).

The above formula was used to calculate all the probabilities in Table 11-7. In each case, the expected value (80 percent or 50 percent) is the value of $p$. These percentages are used because 80 percent coverage is considered adequate in this example, and 50 percent is considered necessary for improvement. Several sample sizes are presented. Each one has its advantages and disadvantages.

For purposes of clarification, we consider momentarily a separate example of a sample size of 12; 3 or fewer uncovered people are permitted before considering the HP as substandard. With such a design the evaluator would identify 79.5 percent of the HPs that have achieved 80 percent coverage of their communities. Similarly, this design ($n = 12$, $d = 3$) would misclassify 7 percent of those HPs that actually had poor coverage. Therefore, 93 percent of the poor HPs would be accurately identified.

These calculations were performed as follows. The probability of correctly identifying an HP in which zero unimmunized individuals were permitted in a sample of 12 individuals, assuming the true level of coverage was 80 percent of the population is

$$P_a = p^n = 0.80^{12} = 0.0687.$$

The probability of identifying an HP in which 1 unimmunized person was permitted in the sample is

$$P_a = (n! \ / \ [a! \ (n-a)!]) \ p^a q^{(n-a)}$$
$$= (12) \ 0.80^{11} \times 0.20^1 = 0.2062.$$

The probability of identifying an HP in which two unimmunized persons were permitted in the sample is

$$P_a = (66) \ p^{10} q^{12-10} = (66) \ 0.80^{10} \times 0.20^2 = 0.2835.$$

And, the probability of identifying an HP in which three unimmunized persons were permitted in the sample is

$$P_a = (220) \ p^9 \ q^{12-9} = (220) \ 0.80^9 \times 0.20^3 = 0.2362.$$

Therefore, the probability of properly identifying an HP in which three or fewer unimmunized persons were permitted in the sample is

$$(0.0687 + 0.2062 + 0.2835 + 0.2362) = 0.7946 = 79.5 \text{ percent.}$$

Similarly, the probability of properly identifying an HP in which two or fewer unimmunized persons were permitted in the sample is

$$(0.0687 + 0.2062 + 0.2835) = 0.5584 = 56 \text{ percent.}$$

The binomial formula was applied to calculate the probability of correctly identifying an HP whose true coverage was 50 percent by permitting three or fewer unimmunized individuals in the sample. This calculation is

$$(0.0002 + 0.0029 + 0.0161 + 0.0537) = 0.0729 = 7 \text{ percent.}$$

Hence, the probability is 93 percent that an HP in which coverage was 50 percent would be correctly classified as below standard.

## Table 11-8. Weighting LQAS Results to Estimate Immunization Coverage for Target Areas

| HP | $n$ | $d$ | $(n-d)/n$ | $N$ | $wt$ | $wt(n-d)/n$ |
|----|-----|-----|-----------|-----|------|-------------|
| 1 | 12 | 2 | 0.83 | 23 | 23/105 | 0.18 |
| 2 | 12 | 3 | 0.75 | 15 | 15/105 | 0.11 |
| 3 | 12 | 0 | 1.00 | 29 | 29/105 | 0.28 |
| 4 | 12 | 6 | 0.50 | 17 | 17/105 | 0.08 |
| 5 | 12 | 5 | 0.58 | 21 | 21/105 | 0.12 |
| Total | 60 | 16 | | 105 | | 0.77 |

Thus, with the design of $n = 12$, $d = 3$ in communities in which the expected coverage is 80 percent, some 79.5 percent of all the successful HPs would be correctly identified, as would some 93 percent of those HPs whose coverage was 50 percent or lower. There remains a grey area of those HPs whose coverage is between 80 percent and 50 percent. The binomial could be used to calculate the probabilities of their classification.

*Weighting LQAS Results to Calculate Coverage*

Table 11-8 shows how to use the LQAS results from several health areas to measure the level of immunizational coverage for a target area. In this example, five HPs are assumed. An estimate of coverage in the area of these five HPs is therefore 77 percent. The 95 percent confidence level for this result could be calculated as follows:

$$1.96 \times \sqrt{\sum \frac{wt^2_i \, (p_i \, q_i)}{n_i}}$$

where $n$ = sample size, $wt$ = weight of $i^{th}$ HP in total sample, $p$ = proportion of successful coverage; and $q$ = proportion of substandard coverage.

## Recommended Reading

Casley, Dennis, and Krishna Kumar. 1988. *The Collection, Analysis and Use of Monitoring and Evaluation Data.* Baltimore, Md.: Johns Hopkins University Press.

Useful and easily understandable reference on both sampling and data analysis. Although it focuses on agriculture, most of the discussion has broader application.

Cochran, W. C. 1963. *Sampling Techniques.* New York: John Wiley.

Standard reference on sampling theory.

Kish, Leslie. 1965. *Survey Sampling.* New York: John Wiley.

A standard reference.

Valadez, Joseph. 1991. *Assessing Child Survival Programs in Developing Countries: Testing Lot Quality Assurance Sampling.* Cambridge, Mass.: Harvard University Press.

## Note

1. For a discussion of experiences in the use of panel samples in housing surveys in El Salvador, see Bamberger, Gonzalez-Polio, and Sae-Hau (1982). These authors even found that the entrances of some houses had moved from one street to another as a result of remodeling.

# Part IV

## Organizational and Management Issues in Program Evaluation
### A Guide for Policymakers, Planners, and Managers

# 12

## Organizational and Management Issues in Program Evaluation

The usefulness of the information produced by monitoring and evaluation (M/E) systems depends in part on the way in which the systems are organized and managed. In view of the rapid increase in the number of development projects and the wide range of information requested by different agencies, it is not surprising that many monitoring and evaluation agencies are unable to provide all the data, analysis, and recommendations required of them. This chapter examines the major organizational and management issues affecting evaluation.

### Issues Affecting the Utility of Monitoring and Evaluation

First, difficulties may arise in *identifying the intended users* of the M/E studies and their information needs. M/E systems are usually developed by a central agency, often with the help of foreign consultants, and are frequently designed to serve the information needs of central planning and finance agencies, with little thought to the information needs of line ministries and project implementation agencies.

Second, even when the users have been identified, *the information may not be available when it is needed*, or may not be in a usable form. Often the fault lies with the quality of the information collected, but many M/E agencies have few resources for field supervision and consequently tend to ignore or play down the problems relating to data quality. Also, project managers have little incentive to use their scarce staff resources to ensure that the information included in their monitoring reports is complete and accurate. Managers soon realize that as long as the required monitoring information is submitted on time to the central agencies, they will receive little feedback and will hardly ever be questioned about the accuracy of the data. Managers also prefer to avoid creating problems and consequently tend not to mention some of the difficulties their projects are facing.

Third, the utility of many evaluation systems is affected by *the way the evaluations are organized* at the project, sectoral, or national levels. The effectiveness of the M/E studies and who uses them depends on where the monitoring and evaluation units are located. Since monitoring systems are centralized, studies often respond more to the needs of central agencies than to those of implementing agencies and project managers. The way the evaluation is organized may also exclude project beneficiaries from the planning and use of the studies. Nongovernment organizations (NGOs) may also be excluded. Furthermore, many M/E systems limit themselves to the monitoring of project implementation and give little attention to the operational phase, the assessment of project sustainability, or the evaluation of project impacts.

Evaluations also suffer from *problems of coordination* between the many different agencies involved in a project and from the *logistical problems* involved in ensuring rapid transmission, processing, and dissemination of monitoring information. These delays create a vicious circle. Because project managers and local agencies receive little feedback on the monitoring information they prepare, they have little incentive to provide prompt and accurate information for central agencies. As a result, the information finally produced is even less timely or useful.

Monitoring is a source of power to those who control the system and a threat to agencies that do not have this control (Bamberger 1988b; Chelimsky 1988; Palumbo 1987). The potentially threatening nature of evaluation has had a destabilizing effect on M/E systems, since those agencies being evaluated have sought to limit the use of any data that affect their budgets and programs. Furthermore, central agencies may compete among themselves to control the systems. As a result of these pressures and conflicts, national M/E systems in South Asia had been unable to operate in their current form for more than three years (Ahmed and Bamberger 1989).

A fifth and pervasive problem is that *the agencies and individuals whose support is essential for conducting the studies or using the results may have little incentive to cooperate.* Monitoring and evaluation are often seen as threats because poor evaluation results may lead to budget cuts, staff reductions, or criticism from higher levels. New projects or inquiries may thus find it difficult to win approval. There are also those who believe that nothing positive will come from a favorable evaluation. In other cases, agencies may object to the additional work involved in collecting monitoring data—none of which they believe will be of any practical use to them.

The lack of incentives, on the part of potential clients, to use evaluation is further complicated by the short time perspective of most policymakers and managers. With a few exceptions (for a discussion of how evaluation data has been used by some policy analysts in Asia, see Lamb and Weaving 1992), they tend to be more concerned with immediate results than with long-term benefits and impacts. Yet, one of the areas in which evaluation can make a substantial contribution is assessing the long term. Consequently, there is a limited demand for many of evaluation's potential products. For the same reason, there is often greater demand for studies which monitor *inputs* than for those which evaluate *outputs*. Earlier, we mentioned that there is some evidence of a growing interest in impact studies, but this still continues to be the exception in most countries.

A final complicating factor has been the lack of coordination between donor agencies. As a result, line ministries such as Agriculture, Irrigation, or Urban Development, which have received assistance from different donor agencies, may be required to operate several independent monitoring systems for projects that are technically similar but are funded by different international agencies.[1]

Fourth, many M/E programs suffer from resource constraints. Sometimes problems arise because M/E was given low priority during project appraisal and resources were not specifically assigned to it. In other cases, resources may have been used inappropriately, leaving many studies of high priority without funding. For example, substantial resources may have been invested in long-term impact studies that provide no useful feedback for managers, and thus little support may be available for short-term monitoring studies that could have been useful to managers. For various administrative reasons, it may also not be possible to hire qualified professional staff, even though resources have been allocated for this purpose.

## Defining the Content and Objectives of M/E Programs

### *Defining Stakeholders and Their Information Requirements*

As mentioned elsewhere in this volume, development projects involve many kinds of agencies: international (donors, NGOs, and foundations); national and sectoral (central government ministries, financial agencies, line ministries, NGOs, and national consulting and research groups); project implementing agencies; and intended beneficiaries. These groups are often referred to as *stakeholders,* for they all have an interest in the outcome of the project and in the orientation and use of the M/E studies. One of the biggest problems for the evaluation team is to reconcile the conflicting demands of these groups.

Stakeholders are concerned about whether there should be an evaluation, what should be studied, and how the results should be interpreted and disseminated. The evaluator must identify the principal stakeholders and understand their information needs to ensure the evaluation is *focused on utilization.* Different users have different perspectives, and the evaluator must often negotiate with stakeholders to reach a consensus on what is to be studied and must try to fairly reflect some of these different points of view. Some writers believe the evaluator should be an objective and impartial outsider who applies rigorous (and value-free) research methods to provide objective answers to questions about how well a program has performed; others argue that the search for objective truth is meaningless and the role of the evaluator is to fairly represent the perspectives of each of the major stakeholders.

Stakeholder analysis raises other questions about the role of the evaluator. Is it acceptable for the evaluator to pass judgment on programs or their underlying assumptions, or should he or she be ethically neutral? A related question refers to the extent to which evaluators should try to control how the information is used. Patton (1978, 1982) believes that the evaluator should try to ensure that the results of the evaluation are properly used and discusses in considerable detail how this can be done. Chelimsky (1987) stresses the importance of understanding how information will be used in different stages of the policy cycle but does not discuss how evaluators can control its use (beyond ensuring that the right kinds of questions are asked and the right kinds of information collected). Weiss (1987) believes the evaluator has little control over how the information will be used.

The orientation and information needs of some of the major stakeholders are summarized in Table 12-1.

## *Successful Strategies for Working with Stakeholders*

The success of many evaluations is largely dependent on the preevaluation strategies that are used to ensure the active involvement of stakeholders. Newcomer and Wholey (1989) recommend the following strategies:

- Evaluators should serve as advocates who convince potential clients of the benefits of the evaluation.
- Evaluators should educate program managers about the great variety of evaluation techniques available.

Barkdoll and Sporn (1989) also stress the importance of "demystifying evaluation." This is important for several reasons. First, a manager who understands the potential benefits of an evaluation is more likely to commission it. Second, managers who have a better understanding of resource requirements are likely to facilitate the process of identifying potential data sources and getting access to them. Third, the evaluation is more likely to help improve the program studied. Finally, a better understanding is likely to promote a better working relationship between managers and evaluators.

- The sensitivity of evaluators to timing, particularly to the deadlines imposed on program managers, is critical to the success of evaluation.
- Program managers attracted by the prospect of a quick turnaround evaluation would be well advised to assign staff to determine information needs before evaluators are brought in.

## *Defining the Scope and Objectives of the Evaluation and the Principal Types of Information to Be Generated*

M/E studies can produce four main kinds of information, each of which serves different objectives: indicators of project implementation, indicators of project effectiveness, indicators of project efficiency, and general planning information (Table 12-2). The collection of each type of information has a cost, and it is essential for management to establish priorities in terms of time and resource allocation between the different kinds of studies.

## Table 12-1.  Information Needs of the Major Stakeholders

*International Organizations*

The *project divisions* of donor agencies require periodic information on physical and financial progress, as specified in the loan agreement. *Program* or *policy divisions* may require broader economic or social data to evaluate project impacts and to help in the selection of future projects. *Donors and foundations* also sponsor broader studies to assess how projects affect, and are affected by, sectoral and national policies.

*National Institutions*

*Planning Ministries* require summary indicators on project implementation and how this affects loan disbursements. Some agencies also compare alternative projects in terms of their cost-effectiveness or their economic rates of return.

The *Ministry of Finance* monitors the *financial performance* of all projects. Monitoring is often limited to standard auditing, but in some cases cost-effectiveness techniques (see Chapter 4) are used. In a number of developing countries the legislative branch is beginning to create its own watchdog agencies such as the Programme Evaluation Organization in India.

*Line ministries* such as Housing, Irrigation, and Health coordinate and supervise projects, and prepare information required by central planning and financial agencies. Ministries vary greatly with respect to the kinds of M/E information they require—which may range from basic monitoring tables to sophisticated research projects.

The *research community* may pressure their colleagues in the evaluation units to make studies more sophisticated or academically "interesting" or to ensure that the evaluation follows a particular ideological line.

*Local Implementing and Coordination Agencies*

*Project implementing agencies* require short- and medium-term information to monitor progress and to detect and help resolve problems when they arise. The agencies also produce monitoring data for national agencies. Different divisions within implementing agencies have different information needs and different expectations from a monitoring unit.

*Project Beneficiaries*

Many projects involve very little consultation with project beneficiaries in the design or review of monitoring studies. However, there is an increasing awareness of the important role that beneficiaries should play in all stages of the evaluation. Many community development organizations encourage beneficiaries to develop their own monitoring systems, particularly to ensure that benefits reach the intended population groups.

## Table 12-2.  The Main Types of Information M/E Programs Can Produce

*Indicators of project progress*
- Selection of participants
- Progress of construction and physical implementation
- Utilization of project services
- Consolidation and follow-on projects
- Dropouts
- Maintenance
- Cost recovery

*Indicators of project effectiveness*
- Accessibility/affordability of services
- Impact on target population
- Multiplier effects
- Impacts on sectoral and national policies

*Indicators of project efficiency*
- Performance of individual project components
- General efficiency in terms of design, finance, implementation, cost recovery
- Comparison with alternative projects in terms of costs, quality, and replicability

*General planning information*
- Socioeconomic characteristics of the target population
- Current living conditions and access to services
- Human development indicators
- Community organization

DEFINING THE LEVEL OF COMPLEXITY AND THE COVERAGE OF THE EVALUA-
TION. Organizations vary considerably in the size and complexity of their
programs and information needs, as well as in the professional and financial resources available for the evaluation. The program manager must
reconcile information needs with available resources. If the monitoring and
evaluation program is too complex, there is a danger of overloading the
capacity of the organization to conduct and absorb the studies. Dissemination will then be delayed, the quality of the studies will decline, and the
program will cost far more in money and staff time than intended.

When the studies begin, they should be kept as simple and economical as possible, so the evaluation team can gradually gain experience and avoid the danger of overloading the capacity of the organization to review and use the results. The volume and complexity of the studies can be increased at a later point, if necessary. It is usually advisable not to include complex longitudinal impact studies in the evaluation of a first project, but to focus on developing an effective system of performance and process monitoring to help management assess how well the basic operating systems are functioning. Impact studies become more important for later projects once the basic operational model has been tested. The manager should define the minimum information requirements for the evaluation and ensure that no unnecessary studies are included.

DEFINING THE DURATION OF THE EVALUATION. It is important to stipulate the points at which the evaluation begins and ends. Many changes will start to take effect as soon as it is known that a project is being planned. For example, as soon as it is known that an urban community is to be upgraded, speculative purchases of land will begin, and squatters who do not have tenure rights may start to leave the community. Many of these changes will be missed if the evaluation does not begin until the project has formally been initiated.

At the other extreme, many impacts will not take place until several years after the physical implementation of the project has been completed. If, as frequently happens, the evaluation ends with the completion of the physical implementation of the project, then it will not be possible to measure many of the most important impacts.

## Deciding How the M/E Program Should Be Organized

### *Organizational Framework for a Typical Project/Program Evaluation*

Most development projects involve a number of different agencies at the international, national, project, and community levels, each requiring different kinds of information on how the project is performing. Every project is supervised by a central or local government agency (Ministry of Housing, Ministry of Education, and the like), often coordinated by a local agency such as a city housing or health authority. Many projects include various subcomponents (health, small business development, transport), each requiring the participation of different agencies at the national, state, or local level.

One or more central agencies will also be responsible for controlling project finances, auditing projects (Ministry of Finance, Auditor General's Office, and the like), and possibly for integrating projects with national or regional development strategies (Ministry of Planning, State Economic Commission). Where projects receive funding from one or more international donors each of these will have its own project supervision and auditing departments.

One or more agencies will also be involved in executing and analyzing the monitoring and evaluation studies. In multicomponent projects, each sectoral agency (health, housing, small business development, and so on) will be concerned with monitoring and evaluation activities. The executing or local coordination agencies may have their own M/E unit(s) or may subcontract studies to local, national, or international consultants.

Since each of these agencies will have different information requirements, the monitoring and evaluation systems can become quite complex. Most of these organizations operate quite independently of each other. Consequently, the work they do may be unnecessarily duplicated. During a single year in one integrated urban development project in Brazil, the local monitoring and evaluation unit (responsible to the city project coordinating agency) was asked to conduct studies by eight agencies, most of which were unaware of the numbers and types of studies being requested by the other agencies.

Sectoral agencies such as a national housing bank, or small business development agency, which are responsible for designing new projects and for monitoring the performance and impacts of ongoing projects, may have their own research staff to conduct M/E and other kinds of studies. In other cases, these sectoral agencies may subcontract studies to national or local research and consulting groups.

## Alternative Ways to Organize M/E at the Project/Program Level

The way M/E is organized at the project/program level will have a significant impact on the kinds of studies that are conducted and how they are used. Following are some of the issues to be considered here:

- Should monitoring and evaluation both be conducted by the same unit or should they be conducted separately?

- Should a special monitoring (and evaluation) unit(s) be created, or should these functions be assigned to an existing division?
- To whom should the monitoring (and evaluation) units report?
- Should monitoring (and evaluation) be conducted in-house or should it be subcontracted?
- Should outside consultants be used, and if so in what capacity?
- Can some or all of the M/E functions be conducted by a central agency?

Figure 12-1 illustrates one organizational option in which two separate units have been created: an evaluation unit reporting directly to the general

**Figure 12-1. Organizational Options for Project Monitoring and Evaluation**

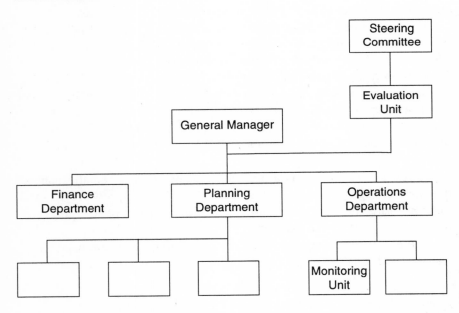

*Note:* In this option the monitoring and evaluation functions are separated: the evaluation unit reports directly to the general manager, while the monitoring unit reports to the chief of operations. Another common option is to combine monitoring and evaluation in the same unit, which may report to the general manager, or the chief of the planning or operations department. A third option is to subcontract the evaluation function to an outside group such as a university, with monitoring being conducted internally and reporting to either the general manager or one of the department heads.

manager and a monitoring unit under the Operations Department. The advantage of this arrangement is that the monitoring unit can respond directly to operational needs, while the evaluation unit can conduct more general and long-term studies. A potential danger is that the separation of functions may lead to a lack of coordination, with either a duplication of functions or certain important types of study not being conducted.

A second option is to have a single monitoring and evaluation unit (MEU) reporting to the Operations Department. This has the advantage of keeping the MEU in close contact with operational activities and project beneficiaries and thus makes it easier to identify operationally useful studies and ensure rapid feedback to the people who can use the findings. A potential problem here is that the choice of studies may be determined by the interests of the department, and so it may be difficult to examine broader issues affecting other departments or which influence the general policy of the organization.

A third option is to have a single monitoring and evaluation unit reporting to the general manager of the project-implementing agency. This permits the MEU to conduct general studies of project efficiency and impact and to have direct access to senior management. A potential problem here is that the studies may become too remote from the operating divisions.

There is no ideal organizational structure, and any decision about how to organize the M/E program must take into account the size, internal dynamics, and level of professional expertise of the project implementing agency. The following guidelines should be kept in mind:

- For the evaluation to be operationally useful, senior management must be involved in the planning and review of the evaluation program. If the evaluation is located in one of the operating departments, it will automatically lose some of its effectiveness.
- In a small organization, the evaluation unit should probably report directly to the general manager.
- In a larger organization that is responsible for a number of different projects, the decision is more difficult. If the evaluation unit reports to the general manager (or executive staff), it may be too far removed from the project. If, on the other hand, it reports to a project manager or department head, then access to senior staff is reduced.
- A balance must be achieved between the requirement of objectivity (and, hence, a certain distance from the day-to-day activities) and the need to maintain close contact with operational activities.

- The evaluation unit should be given sufficient autonomy to be able to contract high grade staff. At the same time it is essential to avoid forming an elite group receiving higher salaries and better working conditions, which creates resentment and makes it difficult to reintegrate evaluation staff into the organization.

SHOULD A SPECIAL EVALUATION UNIT BE CREATED? It is sound organizational procedure to avoid creating additional units that increase overhead and produce bureaucratic delays and problems of control. In addition, if a special evaluation unit is created with outside funding and special employment conditions, it may prove difficult to reintegrate unit staff into the organization when the pilot project ends. Furthermore, an independent unit with some autonomy may not have a strong financial base, since it may not have direct access to normal government funding. These special units can experience long delays in paying staff and meeting other expenses while waiting for authorization to disburse the special funds.

If the evaluation program is very large, however, it is almost essential to create a special unit. Being autonomous, it can provide greater independence and objectivity because the evaluation is not controlled by any one department and may have greater flexibility in hiring staff (and in offering more attractive salaries). Although this may create problems in the long run for reintegrating the unit, in many countries it would be impossible to attract good research staff if only civil service salaries could be offered.

THE ROLE OF THE STEERING COMMITTEE. A steering committee, with representatives of participating agencies as well as planning and research institutions, could oversee the monitoring and evaluation program. It could provide technical guidance in the design and review of studies and could ensure active cooperation from key participating agencies. The steering committee could also ensure a certain degree of objectivity and credibility for the evaluation. It is important not to make the steering committee so large that it is ineffective; nor should it put unnecessary barriers in the way of issuing reports.

CAN MONITORING AND EVALUATION FUNCTIONS BE CENTRALIZED? Some may wonder whether it would be more cost-effective to centralize M/E activities in one specialized agency. This is neither practical nor effective for several reasons. First, it is not possible to conduct a comprehensive study covering all the issues of interest to each agency. A study must be designed for a specific purpose if it is to provide the information needed by a particular client.

Second, each agency needs information that it can trust and that has been collected to respond to its own particular needs. The cooperation required to study delicate issues such as interagency conflicts, poor organizational performance, and lack of community support, will only be given if the agency is able to control how the information will be used and disseminated. Third, there are many areas of potential conflict between agencies because of competition for resources or different political allegiances. Under these circumstances, agencies would not be willing to make information on the performance and problems of their programs available to their potential competitors.

Evaluations must also be fast enough and flexible enough to respond rapidly to the information needs of the organization it serves. In practice, this can only be achieved when the evaluation unit reports directly to the project manager.

THE ROLE OF CONSULTANTS. The use of consultants brings a number of advantages, including access to specialized research skills, a greater degree of objectivity, and greater flexibility in the employment of staff and the use of financial resources. From an administrative point of view, when consultants are used, it is unnecessary to create new permanent staff positions. The disadvantage of consultants is that outsiders are often perceived as a threat and may not be able to establish the rapport with project staff that can be achieved by an internal unit (see Box 12-1). Furthermore, an external evaluation is usually much more expensive and may not help develop an internal research capability. Because the scope and duration of their work is usually precisely defined, consultants may not have the flexibility to adapt to changing management information needs.

Even so, consultants can be used in a number of ways in developing a general in-house evaluation capability. First, an adviser may be contracted, often as part of a donor technical assistance package. The adviser must not become the de facto director of the evaluation unit, imposing a research scheme that may not respond to the needs of the organization or the technical capabilities of the evaluation unit. The ability and willingness to train local staff should be an important factor in the selection of the adviser.

---

**Box 12-1.  Typical Problems When Monitoring and Evaluation Are Subcontracted to Outside Consultants**

In one of the early World Bank urban projects, the design and implementation of the monitoring and evaluation system was subcontracted to a newly formed group of local consultants. The quality of many of the reports was technically very good, but in most cases they had little operational impact for the following reasons:

- The executing and coordinating agencies had no mechanisms for reviewing the reports, with the result that long delays occurred before the recommendations were acted on.
- The government agencies did not have an experienced researcher who could coordinate with the consultants and interpret their work for the executing agencies.
- To avoid controversy, the consultants avoided making direct recommendations or drawing attention to delicate issues. For example, they left it to the reader to assess the policy implications of the high level of illegal subletting that was detected.
- The reports were not presented in a useful way and contained more detail than the average manager was able to absorb.
- The consulting group, which was quite small, encountered personal and financial problems that caused them to lose some of their key staff. As a result, they were unable to complete their contractual obligations or to prepare a final report.
- None of the staff of the executing or planning agencies received any training or guidance in evaluation techniques from the consultants, and five years after the consulting contract began, it was still necessary to look to private consultants to conduct even the most basic evaluation studies.

---

Second, consultants can assist in the design of the instruments and the systems for data analysis, or provide technical assistance on specific topics such as sample design, data analysis or report writing. Third, consultants may be contracted to conduct specific studies requiring special methodologies or the use of large and complex sample surveys.

The use of consultants should be kept to a minimum until the evaluation unit has had time to establish itself. If new and inexperienced evaluation directors have advisers constantly looking over their shoulders, they may never gain sufficient confidence to develop their own research programs and priorities. In the early stages, consultants should provide assistance through periodic visits, perhaps monthly visits from a national consultant or quarterly ones from an expatriate. Ideally, the consultant should help the evaluation team develop their own evaluation program rather than be the person who actually develops the program.

Consultants can also be used when an "independent and objective" perspective is required. Organizations tend to perceive the world in terms of their own objectives, and although they may conduct a rigorous analysis of how well their objectives are being achieved, they may never question the validity of the objectives themselves. For example, a housing project may evaluate the speed and cost of producing shelter units, but may never question whether these units are an effective way to improve the welfare of low-income households. An important function of outside consultants is to evaluate these objectives and underlying assumptions, as well as the way in which they are implemented.

Furthermore, a consultant can serve as a communication link between implementing agencies and project beneficiaries. Managers frequently receive limited and distorted feedback on beneficiary reactions through the members of a small and unrepresentative community junta, or from project technical staff who see their job as "selling" the project to the community rather than listening to the community. The consultant is not subject to these organizational constraints and is able to listen to the point of view of all the main sectors of the affected populations and communicate these views to management (Salmen 1987).

INVOLVING PROJECT BENEFICIARIES. The evaluation should be organized in such a way as to ensure that intended project beneficiaries and potential "victims" are adequately involved at all stages. Unfortunately, beneficiary involvement is rarely built into the evaluation of government projects even though participatory techniques are well known and not difficult to apply (see Chapter 5). How can participatory approaches be built into the management and organization of the evaluation?

National and international funding agencies can make an important contribution by requiring that beneficiary assessment or social impact analysis be conducted during project appraisal and that indicators of social impact be included in monitoring reports and in the project completion reports.

It is also important to ensure that the evaluation team includes staff with the experience to conduct beneficiary assessment, or that consultants are contracted to conduct the initial analyses and to train in-house staff in the use of these techniques. Often this expertise can be obtained through cooperation with NGOs (see following section).

The most important factor, however, is the attitude of project management. Although the techniques for beneficiary assessment are now well established, many project evaluations make little use of them. It is essential for project managers to fully understand the importance of constant dialogue with the groups affected by their projects, and their M/E staff and consultants should be encouraged to use these techniques.

ENSURING CONTINUITY OF THE EVALUATION BEYOND THE PROJECT IMPLEMENTATION PHASE. As already mentioned, most M/E programs focus on monitoring the project implementation phase, and systematic monitoring ceases once the project implementation phase is completed. The reason for this is organizational rather than methodological. It has to do with the fact—among others—that the evaluation is funded under a project loan (so that funding stops when project implementation is completed) or that government agencies want to implement capital investment projects as quickly as possible, but attach a much lower priority to assessing the operation or sustainability of these projects or to evaluating their impacts.

One important step is to decide the appropriate organizational arrangements for longer-term studies. A special project implementation unit, which will be disbanded after project implementation is completed, may be well suited to monitor project implementation, but is obviously not the appropriate agency for conducting long-term studies.

One option is to develop an evaluation capacity in the line ministry or sectoral agency responsible for project design and supervision. This agency (for example, the Ministry of Agriculture or Ministry of Housing and Urban Development) is usually in charge of designing and managing all sectoral projects as well as formulating and reviewing sectoral policies, and thus is a logical place to develop this longer-term sectoral evaluation capacity.

A second option is to contract an agency such as an NGO, university, or consulting group to design and implement long-term monitoring and evaluation systems for certain high-priority projects. This approach could also be used to develop a methodology that could later be applied on a wider basis for sectoral agencies.

A third option is for a central agency, such as the Ministry of Planning, to assume responsibility for conducting (directly or through consultants) these studies.

As discussed below, these organizational arrangements must be complemented by an institution-building strategy to ensure that qualified monitoring and evaluation staff are adequately prepared.

*Organization of Monitoring and Evaluation at the National Level*

Box 12-2 summarizes the key issues in designing and managing a national M/E system. The interested reader is referred to Rist (1990:esp. chap. 1) for a description of how OECD member countries have approached these questions. Countries differ considerably on issues such as the degree of centralization, whether the central evaluation agency reports to the legis-

---

**Box 12-2. Key Issues to Consider in Designing and Operating a National Monitoring and Evaluation System**

- Where should the central M/E unit (agency) be located?
- To what extent should M/E be centralized or decentralized?
- Does the central evaluation agency report to the executive or the legislative branch of government?
- How closely is evaluation integrated with traditional auditing functions?
- How can M/E information be used in the selection and design of future projects?
- Who are the principal stakeholders at the international, national, regional, project, and local levels?
- What are the information needs of stakeholders and how can this information be made available to them?
- Who has access to the findings of the evaluations?
- How should responsibilities for collection, analysis and use of M/E information be divided between central, line, and project-executing agencies?
- Can the information needs of donors be standardized to permit the development of uniform M/E procedures?
- How can the need to rapidly process and summarize information on large numbers of projects be combined with an in-depth understanding of projects?
- How can the appropriate set of M/E indicators be developed?
- How can M/E information be effectively disseminated and built into planning and management procedures at the project and national levels?
- How can the quality of M/E information be controlled?
- How can the benefits of the new computer technologies be most effectively used for M/E?

lative or executive branch of government, and who has access to the evaluation results. Decisions on how evaluation is organized can have a large impact on the kinds of studies conducted.

STRUCTURE OF A NATIONAL M/E SYSTEM. Monitoring and evaluation systems can be classified according to their level of vertical integration and the range of M/E activities they carry out. There are three main levels of vertical integration (United Nations ACC Task Force 1984):

- Monitoring is only conducted at the project level: projects are monitored on an ad hoc basis (usually at the request of donor agencies).
- Monitoring is conducted at both the project and the sectoral (ministerial or agency) levels. There is some degree of standardization of procedures, the scope of the studies is often expanded (to include evaluation as well as monitoring), and the findings from different projects are synthesized to some degree.
- Monitoring and evaluation are coordinated through a central M/E agency. This agency (usually located in the Ministry of Planning, Finance, or Program/Plan Implementation) develops standardized reporting formats that line agencies are required to complete, is responsible for summarizing the status of all major ongoing projects to the cabinet or prime minister's office, and has some responsibility for detecting and helping resolve problems affecting the implementation of projects.
- A fourth level must be introduced for federal systems where state or provincial planning agencies also have significant M/E functions.

The central coordination may also be divided between two or more agencies. The level of integration and complexity of the M/E system tends to be related to the size of the country, its level of economic development, the numbers of projects supported by foreign aid, and its research experience and resources. In countries heavily dependent on foreign aid, monitoring usually begins at the project level. Once a significant number of projects are being monitored, a central monitoring unit, usually in the Ministry of Planning or Finance, may be created—with primary responsibility for monitoring the use of foreign aid.

The efficient planning and management of national development requires timely and accurate information on the progress of projects, the extent to which projects are achieving their objectives in a cost-effective and

**Figure 12-2. Structure of a Typical National Monitoring and Evaluation System**

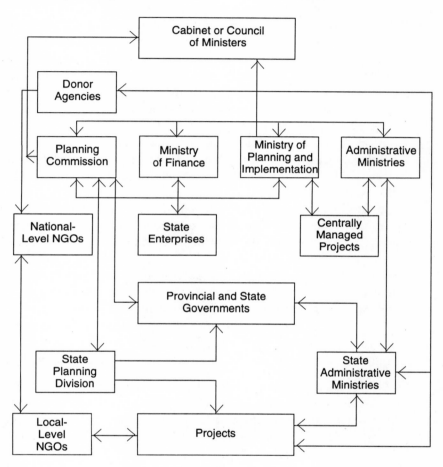

timely manner, and the contribution of individual projects to the achievement of sectoral and national development objectives. Much of this information can be obtained through a national monitoring and evaluation system that provides the information required by policymakers and managers at the national, sectoral, provincial/state, and local levels.

Figure 12-2 illustrates the structure of a typical national M/E system. It will normally have the following components:

- A central agency responsible for defining and coordinating the national *monitoring and evaluation strategy*. This will normally be the Ministry of Planning.
- A central agency responsible for implementing and coordinating the *monitoring* of development projects. This may be the Ministry of Planning, the Ministry of Plan or Program Implementation or, less commonly, the Ministry of Finance.
- A central agency responsible for implementing and coordinating the *evaluation* of development projects and programs. This should normally be the Ministry of Planning.
- A central agency responsible for monitoring resource utilization and aid *disbursements*, for assessing capacity of agencies to implement projects and for defining future resource allocation. This will normally be the Ministry of Finance.
- One or more agencies responsible for ensuring *accountability* to donors and to the national legislature and executive for the use of project funds. This will normally be the Ministry of Planning in coordination with the Auditor General.
- A monitoring and evaluation cell in each development agency and line ministry.
- In federal systems there should be a monitoring and evaluation cell in each state or province. This will normally be located in the planning department of the state or provincial government.
- Monitoring (and possibly evaluation) cells in each major project.

Most developing countries will also have a large number of international agencies (bilateral, multilateral, and nongovernment) monitoring the projects they are financing. The situation of NGOs varies considerably from one country to another, but as discussed below, most governments fail to use the potential evaluation capacity of NGOs to its full advantage.

The responsibilities of each of these agencies and the coordination and communication between them can be defined in many ways, but normally the central planning ministry should be responsible for developing and coordinating the operation of the overall monitoring and evaluation system. Without an overall framework and adequate coordination, certain kinds of essential information may not be collected or analyzed, available information may not be accessible to intended users, information may be incomplete or inaccurate, and potentially useful information may not be collected in a form that is usable.

The M/E functions of these agencies were described in Chapter 2 and their information needs were summarized in Table 12-1.

*Why Most M/E Systems Focus on Monitoring Project Implementation*
*and Ignore Project Sustainability or Impacts*

Although many countries have established, or are in the process of establishing, central agencies responsible for both monitoring and evaluating the performance of projects, until recently almost all of the resources of these central M/E agencies were used to monitor project implementation.[2] A small but growing number of countries are now placing greater emphasis on ex-post evaluations,[3] but in general little attention is paid to whether the projects continue to operate and whether the intended impacts are produced. This situation can be attributed to a number of factors.

First, both donors and borrowers are more concerned with capital investment than with operations and maintenance. Building a new road or school is much more attractive to governments than investing money in repairs and maintenance. Donors have been equally reluctant to include funds for recurrent expenditures in their loans or grants, although in recent years they have been more willing to fund rehabilitation projects.

A second, related factor is that M/E activities are often funded as part of a loan or grant from an international agency. Typically, the loan covers only the period of project implementation, and the funding for M/E studies ends when implementation is completed. A whole generation of urban development projects has stipulated that project impacts must be evaluated, but the funds to conduct these evaluations have dried up and many M/E units were disbanded just as the first families were settling into their new houses.[4]

Third, during the 1970s a number of attempts were made to extend to developing countries the kinds of sophisticated quasi-experimental designs that were being used in the War on Poverty programs such as Head Start, Experimental Housing Allowance Programs, and Negative Income Tax (see Rossi and Wright 1984). Few if any of the attempts to replicate these large-scale evaluations in developing countries proved cost-effective or useful, and by the 1980s most of these ambitious impact evaluation designs were being abandoned in favor of more modest monitoring systems. Casley and Lury (1982) report that large evaluation studies in the 1970s to estimate agricultural project impacts and to construct farm production and household consumption models proved extremely expensive and produced limited results, so that now donors and governments are mainly concerned with collecting basic monitoring information on agricultural inputs and outputs. Similarly ambitious evaluation designs were developed for urban projects (Keare and Parris 1982). USAID and other agencies also funded sophisticated evaluations of water supply and health programs, among others, again with only limited success.

As a result of these negative experiences, many analysts continue to question the usefulness of such broadly based impact evaluations, and many government planners, policymakers, and project managers argue that impact evaluation should either be abandoned or considered academically oriented research—which should not be financed with project funds. In recent years, however, donors and some governments have expressed renewed interest in developing less ambitious and more cost-effective evaluation methods (see Chapters 5 and 7).

### The Role of Donor Agencies in Strengthening National M/E Systems

Donors are the major source of development finance in many developing countries. Because of their concern about accountability in the use of their funds, they have had a strong influence on the development of many national M/E systems. Donor involvement has produced both positive and negative results. On the positive side, they have been instrumental in introducing the concepts of monitoring, have trained local staff in the design and implementation of monitoring studies, and have provided the equipment and logistical support required to conduct the studies. Donors have also supported innovative work in areas such as beneficiary assessment monitoring, sustainability assessment, and alternative methodologies for evaluating project impacts.

However, donor agencies have also hindered the development of national M/E systems because their primary concern has been to monitor the performance of their own projects. As a result, they have shown little interest in helping the government develop M/E systems that can be applied to all projects. Governments are often required to apply different monitoring methodologies in a particular sector simply because projects are funded by different international agencies.

Bilateral agencies are required to account to their governments for the use of funds, and most conduct their own project evaluations with the limited involvement of national agencies. For example, both USAID and Canadian CIDA projects are normally evaluated by agency staff in cooperation with consultants—who may be nationals but who are frequently brought in from outside. Although the *AID Evaluation Handbook* (1987:10) states that "the Agency places considerable importance on making monitoring and evaluation a collaborative activity involving A.I.D's counterparts to the fullest extent possible," in most cases their projects are evaluated by AID staff and consultants, and if counterparts are involved it is to help execute the AID evaluation design.

CIDA's *Practical Guide for Conducting Project Evaluations* (1985) is written exclusively for CIDA staff and makes no reference to the involvement of national evaluation agencies.

The Organization for Economic Cooperation and Development publication "Methods and Procedures in Aid Evaluation" (OECD 1986) documents the procedures used by the major aid donors to evaluate their programs. Each of the three systems described (centralized and independent; centralized, integrated; and dual) are implemented by the donor, with virtually no formal involvement of the recipient country. The report (OECD 1986:50) states:

> There has been little official commitment within the bilateral donor community to provide support for the development of the evaluation capacity of the recipient countries. Only a few donors report explicit policies on this issue. Several, however, have been engaged in activities which in effect do involve recipients either to improve the evaluation or to develop their institutional capacity.

Stokke (1991b) confirms that this situation did not change greatly over the succeeding five years.

The World Bank and the regional development banks require monitoring reports to be prepared by the national project executing agency. Funds for this purpose are normally included in the loan or credit. Some guidelines have been prepared (both general and some sector specific), and technical assistance may be provided by the lending agency.[5] With the exception of the Africa Agriculture Department and the Africa Region Poverty and Social Policy Division (the latter for programs to mitigate the social costs of adjust), however, the World Bank has no monitoring or evaluation units that could provide technical assistance to borrowers in the design and implementation of M/E systems for ongoing projects.

The Operations Evaluation Department (OED) of the World Bank does assist some governments in the preparation of project completion reports and in the development of an evaluation capability to conduct ex-post evaluations.

Although the development banks have helped national agencies develop a project monitoring capacity, the international agencies have made almost no effort to standardize approaches. Second, the studies normally cover only the implementation phase of a project and do not continue during project operation. Thus, no attempt is made to assess sustainability or impacts. Third, the terms of reference and the scope of the monitoring tend to be determined more by the concerns of the donor than by the interests of the borrower. And fourth, the focus is normally restricted to the project level, and no attempts are made to assess the sectoral impacts of a particular project.

While recognizing that donor agencies have responsibilities to their own governments, and must inevitably be primarily concerned to ensure the satisfactory performance of the projects they are funding, Box 12-3 suggests some concrete ways in which international agencies could help strengthen national monitoring and evaluation capacity.

*The Role of Donors in the Evaluation of Poverty Alleviation:*
*The Social Dimensions of Adjustment in Africa*

The Social Dimensions of Adjustment (SDA) Program for Africa is an example of an area in which international agencies have tried to help countries strengthen their capacity for designing, implementing, and interpreting policy and program evaluation. The SDA program (which was discussed in Chapter 3) was a collaborative program of the African Development Bank, the UNDP, and the World Bank. One of its principal tasks was to help countries develop a capacity to generate and analyze the kinds of data required to identify the groups most severely affected by structural adjustment programs and to monitor the implementation of poverty alleviation policies and programs. The principal data collection instruments and the methods of analysis are described in Grootaert and Marchant (1991). Grootaert and Kanbur (1990) and Boateng and his colleagues (1990) illustrate how the methodology was applied in Côte d'Ivoire and Ghana, respectively.

## Box 12-3.  Ways in Which Donors Can Help Strengthen National M/E Systems

Design and Implementation of Project Monitoring

*Where the evaluation must be conducted by the donor agency:*
- Select national consultants and involve national research agencies.
- Identify and review existing national studies.
- Involve national experts at an early stage so that their views can be taken into consideration in the evaluation design.

*Where the evaluation will be conducted by a national agency:*
- Ensure that the M/E system is discussed at an early stage of the loan discussions.
- Ensure that persons technically qualified to design the M/E component are involved in the discussions to avoid having unrealistic terms of reference approved during loan negotiations.
- Provide technical assistance to help the borrower prepare useful and realistic terms of reference for the M/E component.
- Review carefully the proposed organizational and staffing proposals for M/E and ensure that any potential problems are discussed and resolved before the loan agreement is finalized.
- Ensure that adequate arrangements are made for the M/E studies to continue after the closure of the loan or credit.

Strengthening the National M/E System

- Improve coordination between international agencies to help develop standardized M/E information requirements in each sector.
- Help national agencies develop a standardized methodology and upgrade the capacity of their staff to implement this methodology.
- Provide technical assistance for the design and management of national M/E systems, where possible by resource persons from the same region.
- Promote regional or interregional seminars and study tours and provide opportunities for the exchange of experiences.
- Help introduce new evaluation methodologies in areas such as rapid appraisal methods, the assessment of project sustainability, and more cost-effective methods for assessing project impacts.
- Help national agencies assume responsibility for the preparation of project completion reports and for developing data bases to permit the use of this information in the selection and design of new projects.

## The Role of Nongovernmental Organizations

Many NGOs have considerable experience in project evaluation—particularly for local projects that focus on social development goals or on generating employment. In recent years, donors and governments have become increasingly interested in the project execution capabilities of NGOs, and they have been offered a larger role in the implementation and to some extent the design of public sector projects. However, much less interest has been shown in the possibility of involving NGOs in the monitoring and evaluation of government projects.

There are a number of areas in which NGOs could make an important contribution to program evaluation. First, many NGOs have an in-depth knowledge of areas affected by government projects and consequently could provide insight into project implementation, the attitudes of the communities to the projects, the accessibility of project benefits to different groups, and the likely project impacts. Second, many NGOs are concerned about the broader economic, social, and political impacts of development projects and could provide insight into the way such projects affect these broader issues. An example of this kind of study is "The Net: Power Structure in Ten Villages" (BRAC 1983), in which a Bangladesh NGO documented how development resources were being diverted by influential groups at the village level. Another example, "Law and Order in a San Salvador tenement" (Herrera and Baro 1978), describes life in a tenement (*meson*) and shows how the social structure is likely to affect the success of the housing programs being developed by the Salvador Foundation for Low-Cost Housing.

NGOs rely much more heavily on qualitative evaluation methods than do most government agencies and could help introduce these methods into the evaluation of public sector programs. Many NGOs have also developed innovative evaluation methods that could be adapted and used by governments and donor agencies alike. Following are three examples.

- To overcome the difficulties farmers in Indonesia experience in expressing themselves verbally, Bina Swadya suggested that farmers make pictures out of flannel-board to express their ideas on the factors affecting the success of the development projects that have been implemented in their villages.[6]

- To understand the reasons why small entrepreneurs in Peru are not willing to legalize their enterprises, the Foundation for Liberty and Democracy sought to legalize two fictitious companies. They carefully documented the time and cost of complying with each stage of the required legal and administrative procedures and showed that more than one person/year of time would be required to establish even the smallest business venture (de Soto 1989).
- To assess the effectiveness of oral-rehydration therapy (ORT) programs, and at the same time motivate the health promoters to take their work seriously, the Bangladesh Rural Advancement Committee (BRAC) developed an innovative evaluation procedure. The health promoters worked on a piece-rate basis. They received half of their payment on visiting a family and explaining to the mother the principles of ORT. A few days later, the family would be visited by an evaluator from BRAC and would be tested on their knowledge of the ORT program. If the mother had successfully understood the program, the health promotor would receive the other half of his or her payment.

Many more innovative evaluation methods have been developed and could be incorporated into the evaluation of public sector programs. Governments have not made more use of the evaluation expertise of NGOs in part because many NGOs are critical of government development programs, believing them to be expensive, influenced by political considerations, or unavailable to many of the groups that most need them. Consequently, many governments would not wish to open themselves to what they would expect to be a negative evaluation. Many NGOs are not anxious to become too closely involved with the government and the donors. For one thing, they do not wish to lose their independence of action and their freedom to criticize. For another, they are afraid of becoming bogged down in bureaucratic procedures. A third factor is that governments have their own M/E systems and for both administrative reasons and professional pride often do not wish to ask the help of NGOs.

Despite the administrative difficulties and in some cases mutual suspicion, there is a growing interest on the part of both governments and NGOs in seeking closer cooperation. Thus, it is likely that in the future NGOs will play a larger role in the evaluation of public sector programs.

## Implementation, Dissemination, and Use of the Evaluation

*Integrating the Evaluation into the Project Implementation Cycle*

An evaluation will not be useful unless it is able to respond in a timely manner to the changing information needs of management. We saw earlier that most projects go through the following stages: identification and appraisal, planning and design, implementation, evaluation, operations and maintenance, and the identification of new projects. At each of these stages, management requires different types of information. A successful M/E system should be able to respond to the different information needs at each stage. Project managers must decide which kinds of reports are to be produced, when they should be produced, and what they should contain and the level of detail. At least six main types of M/E studies can be identified, each corresponding to one or more of the stages of the project cycle.

PLANNING STUDIES. When a project is being planned, management requires information on factors such as affordability, characteristics of artisans, access to health services, and factors determining project location. Some of this information may not be available when the first project is being planned, but the studies produced during the first project can contribute to the identification, appraisal, planning, and design of future projects. Newcomer and Wholey (1989) recommend the following strategies for ensuring that evaluations are successfully planned:

- Program stakeholders must be involved throughout evaluation planning, implementation and reporting.
- Program managers must question evaluator's choices of evaluation design strategies and techniques to ensure their appropriateness.
- Evaluators should warn their clients against drawing inappropriate conclusions.
- Evaluators should justify their choice of data collection techniques to their clients.
- Prior to evaluations, evaluators should devise a strategy for testing the validity of the data they collect.
- Prior to an evaluation evaluators and program managers should work together to define the ideal final product.

DESIGN STUDIES. Design studies relate to matters such as project layout, choice of materials, and amount of artisan credit.

PERFORMANCE MONITORING. When project implementation begins, regular reports will be required on the progress of physical implementation, financial status, and the causes and possible solutions to problems arising during the implementation process.

ACCOUNTABILITY TO LENDING AGENCIES. Most lending agencies, whether national or international, require regular reporting on the progress of the projects, particularly on their financial status.

QUALITY CONTROL. Management will require regular information on the efficiency with which the project is implemented and the quality of work performed by contractors.

PROJECT EFFECTIVENESS AND IMPACT. Project management and government planning agencies will also require information on how well the project is achieving its more general objectives and its impacts on participants, the city, and national housing policies.

### Deciding Which Information to Present

Even when appropriate M/E information is collected, it frequently proves difficult to process and to apply. A first issue relates to the volume of information collected. In 1987 the government of India financed more than 3,000 projects with a further 6,000–7,000 sponsored by the states; while in Pakistan the Federal Annual Development Plan contained some 3,800 projects (see Ahmed and Bamberger 1989:chaps. 3 and 5). With such large numbers of projects to supervise, the national agencies must restrict their monitoring to a few key indicators of physical and financial performance. Although these indicators may provide a reasonably satisfactory description of the status of an infrastructure project (such as the construction of a road or dam), they are inadequate for assessing the performance of a social sector project such as integrated rural development, community health, or squatter upgrading. An important question is how to combine these quantitative indicators with more qualitative studies designed to understand the operation of a project, its accessibility to different groups, the impacts it is producing and the attitudes of intended beneficiaries. Salmen (1987) illustrates how the World Bank is beginning to use participant observation and related methods of beneficiary assessment to obtain a deeper understanding of how beneficiaries perceive, and are affected by, development projects.

### Defining the Main Kinds of Reports to Be Prepared

A typical monitoring and evaluation system will produce the following kinds of reports, the contents of which are described in Chapters 4–8.

- Monthly or quarterly progress reports on the status of project implementation (see Chapter 4).
- Financial monitoring reports (Chapter 4).
- Process monitoring reports and special diagnostic studies (Chapters 4, 5).
- Interim report on project performance (Chapter 4).
- Project completion report (Chapters 4–6).
- Project audit report (Chapter 4).
- Assessment of project sustainability (Chapter 6).
- Evaluating project impacts (Chapters 7 and 8).

Management must define the priority to be given to each kind of report, the frequency with which they will be prepared, their content, and their audiences.

### Integrating the M/E Reports into the Project Planning and Review Cycles

If monitoring and evaluation are to be operationally useful, reports must be produced in time to assist management with planning and control decisions. This means that the calendar of M/E studies must correspond to the project's planning cycles. Every project has its monthly, quarterly, or yearly planning cycles. Management normally meets at the end of each cycle to review progress and to plan for the next cycle. The production of M/E reports should correspond to these cycles so that the findings are available in time to help management review progress and make future decisions.

It is particularly important to ensure that both monitoring and evaluation are linked into national and project budget cycles as evaluations are coming to be used in some countries (for example Brazil and Colombia) to determine future resource allocation for projects and programs.

Procedures must also be developed to ensure that all M/E reports are reviewed and that feedback is provided for the research team on the strengths and weaknesses of the reports. Approximately once a year there should be an independent outside review of the progress of the evaluation. This can either be done by a consultant or through technical assistance from one of the international donors or lending organizations. Arrangements for this review should be built into the evaluation program.

Dissemination within and outside the organization is an important way to ensure that the results of the evaluation are known and acted upon. A publication plan should be developed.

## Controlling the Quality of the M/E Data

Many central M/E agencies recognize that data quality needs to be improved, but because of staff constraints these agencies have few resources for field supervision and consequently tend to ignore or play down the importance of these problems. Project managers have limited staff resources and little incentive to use these resources to ensure that all data included in the monitoring progress reports are complete and accurate. Managers soon realize that as long as the required monitoring information is submitted on time to the central agencies, they receive little feedback and are hardly ever questioned about the accuracy of the data. There is also a tendency to avoid reporting information that may create problems. Consequently, many organizations tend to avoid mentioning difficulties and to report that everything is progressing as planned.

For many kinds of projects, there are also substantive problems in ensuring the accuracy of the data. Farmers may have an incentive to underreport their crop yields or the amount of water used; entrepreneurs may underreport their income; and residents in housing projects may conceal income earned from subletting part of their house or from other sources prohibited by project authorities. In other cases, families may find it difficult to estimate their total earnings, or mothers may not recall which children have been vaccinated or have been absent from school due to illness.

A useful way to improve the quality of M/E studies is to have evaluation researchers produce an "audit trail" in the same way that accountants are required to do so (Schwandt and Halpern 1988). Following this procedure, evaluators would be required to prepare a complete documentation of all studies, describing how questions were developed, samples were selected, interviews were conducted, and so on. From time to time an "evaluation audit" would be conducted by an outside expert who would attest to the fact that the evaluation had been conducted following normally accepted evaluation research standards (Evaluation Research Society Standards Committee 1982).

### Deciding How the Information Should Be Processed

The first question in this area relates to who processes the information. In many countries information that is collected at the project level is then sent to a central M/E agency for processing and analysis. Although centralization permits economies of scale and makes it possible to use more sophisticated data processing equipment and software and to create a critical mass of professional data analysts, there may be a long delay before the information becomes available to project management and can be used to correct problems or improve project performance. Furthermore, centralization makes it more difficult to use knowledge of the conditions of an area to detect and correct obvious errors in the information. While it may be obvious to project staff that the earnings claimed by fishermen or farmers are far too low or too high, this will probably not be noticed by a data analyst in a central M/E unit who is located several thousand kilometers from the project and probably has no knowledge of the economic characteristics of the project area.

Another question pertains to the way information is analyzed. Because such a large number of projects are being processed, the system of "Management by Exception" is often used. Essentially, this system identifies projects that deviate from the planned target by more than a certain percentage or amount. These projects are then examined in more detail to determine what corrective measures are required. Although this is a logical way to economize on the time of senior government officials, there is a danger that much of the information on projects not classified as problems may be completely ignored.

### Presenting Data

A frequent complaint of project management is that the monitoring and evaluation reports are of limited utility. Reports are often considered to be too long or too technical and said to arrive too late or to be about issues of no importance to the project manager. Frequently the staff of the M/E units will have a background in social research rather than project management and consequently may have difficulty in adapting their research strategies to the operational needs of the project manager. For their part, researchers complain that project managers do not take the trouble to read the reports, do not explain to the researchers what information they want, do not appreciate the complexities and time requirements for conducting research, and are so tied up in their day-to-day concerns of running the project that they ignore the broader issues that affect its long-term success.

A principal complaint is that there are delays in the use of the data. Owing to the logistical problems discussed earlier and further delays that might arise during data processing and analysis, several months may elapse between data collection and the communication and discussion of the results with managers and policymakers. In many cases, the conditions will have changed so much during this period that the information and recommendations are no longer valid. Box 12-4 describes recently developed procedures in India intended to ensure that monitoring information for all major projects is processed and acted upon rapidly.

---

**Box 12-4.  Ensuring the Rapid Utilization of Monitoring Information: The Flash Report and Capsule Reporting System for Priority Projects in India**

The recently created Ministry of Programme Implementation (MOPI) in India is responsible for delivering to the Prime Minister's Office a monthly capsule report on the progress and problems of every major (over one billion rupees) government-financed project. Each concerned ministry must submit to MOPI a status report on their major project by the 14th of the month. These may be preceded by "Flash Reports" from project managers on those projects that are experiencing actual or anticipated problems. MOPI is responsible for checking back with ministries with respect to the causes of the problems or the actions required to resolve them, and for organizing any necessary follow-up meetings. The capsule report, summarizing the status of all major projects, their potential problems, and the recommended actions, must be delivered to the prime minister's office by the 20th of each month. The report is then discussed by the Cabinet and appropriate actions agreed upon.

*Source:* Basu (1988).

---

**Box 12-5.  Providing Users with Direct Access to Information on the Status of Projects through Computer Networks: The SETIA System in Malaysia**

The Implementation Coordination Unit (ICU) of the prime minister's office in Malaysia recently introduced an integrated computer-based network system known as SETIA (System, Economic Planning Unit, Treasury, Implementation Coordination Unit, Auditor General), which coordinates separate systems previously operated by the above agencies and provides all the participating agencies with direct access through computer terminals to the following information on all development projects: data relating to project approval, yearly budget allocations, monthly progress reports (including a summary of major problems or causes of delay), and information on all payments made and authorized on each project.

The information can be aggregated by sector or by geographical region. It is also possible to project onto a large screen so that the information can be used directly for presentations or discussion in meetings. The information on each project is entered directly into the system by the responsible ministries or agencies, thus significantly reducing delays in access to the latest data.

*Source:* Khan (1989).

---

A number of countries are now developing computer networks that permit direct access to information on project status and problems through computer terminals. Malaysia recently introduced the SETIA (System, Economic Planning Unit, Treasury, Implementation Coordination Unit, Auditor General), which gives all the above agencies direct access to information on the nature, budget status, progress, and expenditure status of all development projects (See Box 12-5). Similar direct access systems are being introduced in a number of other countries, including India and Jordan. Box 12-6 presents guidelines on the preparation of M/E reports.

## Resource Requirements for a Project M/E Unit

### Staff Requirements

When preparing the M/E program, it is essential to define staff requirements so that necessary financial and administrative arrangements can be made. A small project monitoring system can be organized so that it

---

**Box 12-6. Guidelines for Preparing and Disseminating M/E Reports**

- Ensure that the information needs of the intended audience are fully understood before the study begins. Know when the report is needed, the level of detail, and the decisions to which the report will contribute.
- Reports should be kept short, leaving out all tables and details that are not strictly necessary. Include reference material in a separate annex.
- Reports should be prepared as quickly as possible. An excellent report that arrives too late will be of no use to management.
- Present an outline of the report *before* the study begins. This should include the main topics to be covered, the number of pages devoted to each topic, and the layout of the main tables. This outline should be discussed and approved by management before the study begins.
- All reports should begin with a short executive summary. Avoid the academic tendency to hide recommendations and conclusions at the end.
- The report should make specific recommendations as to possible actions. Present both what is considered to be the best course and also a number of more modest alternatives that take into account resource and other kinds of constraints.
- Discuss the findings informally with project management before the report is distributed. In this way, the information will reach management more quickly, and their comments and suggestions can be incorporated into the report.
- The basic findings can even be communicated by telephone. *The value of information decreases rapidly over time, so essential findings should be communicated as quickly as possible.*
- Clear the report with all key parties before it is formally presented. This will help to eliminate errors and will also ensure that many points are clarified informally without the embarrassment of confrontations in a management committee meeting.
- Decide who should receive each report. Although information should be disseminated as widely as possible, it may not be possible to speak frankly on delicate issues if the report is circulated too widely.

---

employs as few as one half-time professional and one part-time research assistant, together with a secretary. In addition, several interviewers, some of whom may be borrowed from another department within the organization, will be required periodically. With this level of staffing it will usually be possible to produce a quarterly progress report, to conduct occasional special studies, and to prepare an interim and final report on the evaluation. It should be feasible to obtain this minimum level of staffing within almost every major project. It is important, however, to ensure that these staff members are permitted to work their assigned time on the evaluation, and that they are not constantly diverted to other activities within the organization.

Where more reports or more detailed analysis are required, it will be necessary to increase the staff level. Table 12-3 presents the recommended staffing level, qualifications, and functions for a more comprehensive monitoring and evaluation program for a typical component of a social sector project in one city. With this level of staffing, it will be possible to

Table 12-3. Typical Staffing Level for an M/E Unit for a Project Operating in One City or Geographical Area

| Position | Functions | Qualifications |
|---|---|---|
| Director of Monitoring and Evaluation Unit | Coordination with management<br>Supervision of evaluation design<br>Report preparation<br>Supervision of implementation and dissemination | Preferably a Master's degree<br>Minimum of B.A. with some research experience<br>Experience with survey design and data analysis required for the more complex evaluations |
| Assistant director | Coordination with other divisions of the executing agency<br>Interviews with project staff and community leaders<br>Supervision of data analysis and report preparation<br>Participant observation<br>Training and supervision of interviewers | B.A. degree with some background in research and data analysis |
| Clerical assistant | Revision and tabulation of data from project records<br>Basic data processing | Completed high school |
| Secretary | Normal secretarial activities | Completed high school |
| 2–5 interviewers | Interviewing project participants<br>Application of observation guide<br>Coding/analyzing interviews | Attending or completed high school |
| Driver | Taking staff to and from project sites | |

prepare detailed quarterly progress reports, to conduct regular special studies, and to carry out at least a simple longitudinal impact study.

## Fitting Staff into Civil Service Categories

Many evaluation positions are difficult to classify in terms of existing civil service grade levels. Therefore, it may be difficult to offer competitive salaries to well-qualified staff. If M/E salary scales do not correspond to current salaries being paid to this type of person elsewhere in the civil service or in the private sector or academia, it may be necessary to consider special procedures. Because these personnel problems can take time to resolve, the discussions with the Personnel Management Department should begin early in the project cycle.

Another related problem is that personnel departments are usually reluctant (with good reason) to create new permanent positions for a program that only lasts a few years. Again, this should be discussed early enough to arrive at an appropriate solution.

## Temporary Assignment of Other Project Staff to the Evaluation

An effective way to reduce the evaluation budget is to make maximum use of the staff already in the organization. For example, community promoters can be used as interviewers. In addition to reducing costs, this also has the advantage of integrating the evaluation into ongoing project activities.

## Using Consultants to Overcome Salary and Other Constraints

Staff recruitment is a problem in many countries because civil service salaries are not attractive to well-qualified researchers. University research-ers, for example, often earn part of their salary through outside consult-ing, which may not be permitted if one is working full-time for the government.

One possibility is to use a consultant to fill the position of research director or a senior staff member, since there are usually not the same types of constraints on consultant salaries. This is not an ideal solution, however, because the long-term staff-development problem has not been resolved.

*Training Needs for Monitoring and Evaluation*

Evaluation research is a relatively new field, and because training programs in this area are frequently not offered in local universities, the question is how to provide staff with the necessary training. Monitoring normally does not require as much technical training as evaluation, so the problem there is less severe. If the general upgrading of staff is a project objective, however, it may be useful to consider a scholarship program. Under such a program, evaluation staff (as well as other staff) could participate either in short three- to four-month courses, or study for an advanced degree in a field related to the evaluation.

# Recommended Reading

*The Organization of M/E Systems at the National Level*

Ahmed, Viqar, and Michael Bamberger. 1989. *Monitoring and Evaluating Development Projects: The Experience from South Asia.* Economic Development Institute Seminar Report Series. Washington, D.C.: World Bank.

Khan, Adil. 1990. *Monitoring and Evaluation of Development Projects in South East Asia: the Experience of Indonesia, Malaysia, the Philippines and Thailand.* Washington, D.C.: World Bank, Economic Development Institute.

*Evaluation Guidelines Prepared by Donor Agencies*

Canadian International Development Agency (CIDA). 1985. *A Practical Guide for Conducting Project Evaluations.* Program Evaluation Division, Policy Branch. Hull: Canadian Agency for International Development.

German Development Agency (GTZ). 1987. *ZOPP: An Introduction to the Method.* Frankfurt am Main.

Marsden, David, and Peter, Oakley, eds.1990. *Evaluating Social Development Projects.* Development Guidelines 5. Oxford: OXFAM.

Organization for Economic Cooperation and Development. 1986. *Methods and Procedures in Aid Evaluation.* Paris.

United Nations ACC Task Force. 1984. *Guiding Principles for the Design and Use of Monitoring and Evaluation in Rural Development Projects and Programmes.* Rome: United Nations Administrative Committee on Coordination.

U.S. Agency for International Development (USAID). 1987. *A.I.D. Evaluation Handbook.* AID Program Design and Evaluation Methodology. Report 7. Washington D.C.

## Sector Guidelines

Bamberger, Michael, and Eleanor Hewitt. 1986. *Monitoring and Evaluating Urban Development Programs: A Handbook for Managers and Researchers.* World Bank Technical Paper 53. Washington, D.C.

Casley, Dennis, and Krishna Kumar. 1987. *Project Monitoring and Evaluation in Agriculture.* Baltimore: Johns Hopkins University Press.

## Sector Reviews and Data Synthesis

Chelimsky, Eleanor. 1988. *Evaluation and Public Policy: The Use of Evaluation Products in the Executive and Legislative Branches of the United States.* Washington, D.C.: World Bank, Economic Development Institute.

World Bank. 1987. *The Twelfth Annual Review of Project Performance Results.* Washington, D.C.: Operations Evaluation Department.

———. 1988. *Rural Development: World Bank Experience 1965–86.* Washington, D.C.: Operations Evaluation Department.

———. 1991. *Forestry: The World Bank's Experience* Washington D.C.: Operations Evaluation Department.

———. 1992. *Population and the World Bank: Implications from Eight Case Studies.* Washington D.C.: Operations Evaluation Department.

# Notes

1. At one point, the Mahaweli Irrigation Authority in Sri Lanka had to provide information for fifteen agencies, each of which required a different monitoring format (see Ahmed and Bamberger 1989:chap. 6).

2. This section is based on a paper presented at the American Evaluation Association annual meeting in 1987 and subsequently published in *Evaluation Review* (Bamberger 1989).

3. For example, Brazil, Colombia, Malaysia, Pakistan, India, and the Philippines.

4. See Bamberger, Gonzalez-Polio, and Sae-Hau (1982) for a discussion of this with respect to a World Bank housing project in El Salvador, and Keare and Parris (1982) for a more general discussion of World Bank experience with M/E of urban development programs.

5. For example, the World Bank has prepared the following monitoring and evaluation guidelines (among others): R. H. Slade and R. Noronha, "An Operational Guide to the Monitoring and Evaluation of Social Forestry in India" (1984); Heli Perrett "Monitoring and Evaluation of Communication Support Activities in Low-

Cost Sanitation Projects" (1984); Edilberto Segura, *Guidelines for Evaluating the Management Information Systems of Industrial Enterprises* (1985); Michael Cernea and Benjamin Tepping, *A System for Monitoring and Evaluating Agricultural Extension Projects* (1977); Dennis Casley and Krishna Kumar, *Project Monitoring and Evaluation in Agriculture* (1987); and Michael Bamberger and Eleanor Hewitt, "Monitoring and Evaluating Urban Development Programs" (1986).

6. Presentation by Russ Dilts and E. Moning during a seminar on community participation, project management, and sustainability organized by the Asian and Pacific Development Centre and the Economic Development Institute of the World Bank in Kuala Lumpur in July 1988.

# Part V

## Teaching Monitoring and Evaluation
### A Guide for Training Institutions

# 13

## The Organization of Monitoring and Evaluation Training in Developing Countries

This chapter explains how to teach monitoring and evaluation. It opens with a review of current approaches and points out some of their weaknesses.

### Current Status of Monitoring and Evaluation Training

Training programs have yet to catch up with the growing needs of the numerous public officials whose task is to design, implement, or use monitoring and evaluation studies.[1] Table 13-1 summarizes the findings of a 1988 review of monitoring and evaluation training offered by eleven leading public training institutions in Malaysia, the Philippines, Thailand, and Indonesia (Selvaraj, Mordisi, and Lee 1988).[2] These countries had four main kinds of training programs, which included at least a module on monitoring and evaluation:

- Courses on project planning and management (either general or sector-specific) were offered by many of these institutions. Although some courses were longer, a typical course lasted for two to three weeks and was offered for middle- or senior-level managers and planners. All courses included at least a few lectures on monitoring

Table 13-1.  Monitoring and Evaluation Training Offered by Leading
Public Sector Training Institutions in Southeast Asia, 1988

| Course | Number of Courses Offered | Typical Length | M/E Components | Length of M/E Module |
|---|---|---|---|---|
| Project planning and management/ resource management, and public administration | 10 | 1–6 weeks; 2-3 weeks most common | M/E and project cycle Network planning Implementation monitoring Reporting Uses of evaluation Information requirements at the national, district and local levels | 2–3 days maximum; often only several hours |
| Project development and appraisal | 6 | 2 weeks to 9 months; 2–3 weeks most common | M/E and project cycle | Normally only 1–2 days |
| Planning and management of rural development | 3 | 2–4 weeks | M/E and project cycle Implementation monitoring Reporting procedures | 1–2 days |
| M/E for rural development projects | 2 | 3–11 days | M/E and the project cycle Techniques Implementation monitoring Reporting procedures Uses of evaluation | 3–11 days |

*Note:* Institutions covered by the study are *Thailand,* National Institute of Development Administration, Department of Technical and Economic Cooperation, Community Development Department, Office of Accelerated Rural Development; *Philippines,* Development Academy of the Philippines, Ateneo, Asian Institute of Management; *Indonesia,* Institute of Public Administration, Department of Public Works, Department of Agriculture; *Malaysia,* Institute of Public Administration.

*Source:* Selvaraj, Morsidi, and Lee (1988).

and evaluation and some devoted up to two to three days to these topics. Monitoring and evaluation were normally discussed within the framework of the project cycle, often concentrating on the monitoring of project implementation and the principal reporting requirements. Monitoring was often presented as an output of a planning system, such as logical framework analysis or networking. A few courses also discussed monitoring requirements at the national, provincial, and local levels.

- Project development and appraisal courses were offered for officials in charge of preparing and appraising internationally funded projects. Most courses were multisectoral, although a few were sector-specific. Typical courses lasted for two to three weeks, although some nine-month diploma courses were also offered. Whereas economic analysis was covered in considerable detail as a principal element of project appraisal, in most cases no more than one to two days (and often less) were devoted to monitoring and evaluating projects once the loan or grant was approved.

- Two- to three-week courses on the planning and management of rural development were offered for field staff and middle-level managers. Monitoring and evaluation are treated in much the same way as in general project planning, and two-day management courses were devoted to these issues.

- The only seminars devoted exclusively to monitoring and evaluation were for field staff and middle-level managers working in agriculture and rural development. A number of monitoring and evaluation courses, lasting from three to eleven days were offered. Topics included M/E and the project cycle, techniques of data collection, implementation monitoring, report preparation, and the application of evaluation studies. The main purpose of many of these courses was to instruct officials in the correct procedures for collecting data and preparing reports. Any discussion of methodological components was usually limited.

The training situation in South Asia was somewhat similar (Ahmed and Bamberger 1989), although India provided a number of more technical courses on monitoring and evaluation on a regular basis. The coverage in the Mahgreb, Africa, and the English-speaking Arab countries appears even more limited.[3]

M/E training for public sector officials has its problems in all these countries. First, no country seems to have an M/E training strategy, and the subject is covered in an ad hoc manner as a component of courses with a different focus.

Second, so few courses are offered in this area that they cannot meet the needs of the increasing number of people whose work involves M/E in one form or another. M/E is normally part of the courses on project planning and management. Since most of the participants in these courses are not M/E specialists, the topics tend to be covered in a general way with little discussion of technical issues.

Third, the courses are not designed specifically for planners and managers. Although middle-level and senior officials are given a brief overview of the main concepts, the courses for operational staff are mainly concerned with the correct administrative procedures for data collection and reporting. Following are the main targeting problems:

- Practically no seminars or orientation on M/E are offered for the senior officials whose job is to decide how much importance will be given to monitoring and evaluation. Consequently, project M/E tends to be weakly coordinated with, and integrated into, national planning systems and policy dialogue.
- Project managers receive little training in the design, management, and utilization of M/E systems.
- Little technical training is offered for the M/E specialists who must design, implement, and interpret the M/E studies and systems.
- Most public sector training institutions provide training only for public sector institutions and do not include NGOs. This reinforces the already existing separation between project management and M/E procedures used by government agencies and by NGOs.

Fourth, many courses have a narrow focus. Their central objective is to teach officials how to implement M/E procedures. There is usually little discussion of the procedures for defining the objectives of M/E studies or of the various evaluation designs that can be used to achieve these objectives. Instead, training is by and large oriented to the project cycle, and the staff of line agencies are taught how to implement monitoring and evaluation systems designed to respond to the information needs of donors or central government agencies—rather than to the needs of project managers.

Fifth, as a consequence of the top-down way in which many M/E systems are designed, courses make little or no mention of techniques such as stakeholder analysis and beneficiary assessment, which focus on the needs and interests of the intended beneficiaries.

Sixth, little thought is put into the way the courses are organized. Course participants are usually selected on the basis of seniority, equal distribution between agencies or regions, or who can most easily be spared at the time of the course. Thus, it is difficult to ensure that the officials most directly involved in M/E will be selected. Also, much of the technical M/E material is taught by invited speakers from universities or central government agencies, with the result that the course directors have little control over the material to be presented and find it almost impossible to ensure the speakers will use similar conceptual frameworks or will integrate their material with other modules of the courses. Sometimes it is not even possible to find specialists to deliver the material. Thus, the level of material may be very basic or the quality uneven.

Seventh, many courses have limited *focus* and *coverage*. For example, when courses include an introduction to the methods of collecting data, they often concentrate on quantitative methods and bypass qualitative techniques such as participant observation, rapid assessment, focus group interviews, or direct observation. There is also little discussion of *data quality control*.

Many courses are conducted exclusively in the classroom with little practical experience in evaluation design or data collection. There is normally no discussion of data analysis or the presentation of findings. Most courses focus on monitoring project implementation, and there is no discussion of evaluating the efficiency of project implementation, monitoring project operations, or assessing sustainability or evaluating project impacts. There is almost no discussion of management problems relating to the organization of M/E units, data collection, analysis, dissemination, or use of the data.

Needless to say, training programs inevitably reflect the strengths and weaknesses of their national planning and economic management systems. In a country with a highly centralized planning system, it is obviously not feasible for training programs to teach decentralized monitoring and evaluation to officials from line agencies that are required to follow national planning systems. Similarly, in countries that are major recipients of foreign assistance, M/E training will inevitably address many of the concerns of these international donor agencies. But this does not preclude the advocacy of beneficiary assessment and decentralized evaluation in the seminars and workshops for senior policymakers.

## The Target Audiences and Their M/E Training Needs

At least nine distinct audiences should be taken into consideration in the design of a national M/E training strategy (see Table 13-2).

1. *Policymakers* need to understand the potential usefulness of M/E in providing inputs for policy analysis and in monitoring the performance of national development policies and programs. In particular, policymakers need to understand that a national M/E program can respond to national information needs, as well as donor information requirements.

2. *Planners* at the national, provincial/state, and line agency levels require training in the uses of M/E at the different stages of the project cycle. They also need to learn how information from ongoing and completed projects can be used to improve the selection and design of new projects, and how *meta-analysis* and *prospective evaluation* (see Chapter 2) make it possible to glean valuable lessons from earlier evaluations. Planners should also be concerned with the organization and management of M/E at the national and sectoral levels and with the coordination and information flows between these levels.

3. *Project managers* and *project staff* (who are not directly involved in the implementation of the M/E studies) are primarily concerned with the design, management, and utilization of M/E at the project level. They also need to understand how project evaluation fits into the national M/E system and how the information they generate will be used. The project manager may also be concerned with some of the more substantive issues relating to the design and use of particular kinds of studies. Of particular interest will be the design of *diagnostic studies,* since these are intended to be management tools. The manager and staff should also be familiar with the concepts of stakeholder analysis and beneficiary assessment if they are to understand the information needs of the many different groups likely to be interested in the evaluations.

Courses should demonstrate the potential utility of M/E studies to their particular division as well as to the organization in general. Courses should also familiarize staff with the kinds of information and assistance they will be asked to provide and teach them how this information will be used. One effective teaching method is to involve staff in ongoing evaluations as a form of on-the-job training. They can act as interviewers or information collectors, or can attend informal workshops to discuss operational problems and to work on the design of evaluation studies.

**Table 13-2.  The Main Target Audiences for Monitoring
and Evaluation Training in Developing Countries**

| Target Group | M/E Training Needs |
|---|---|
| Policymakers | Potential utility of M/E in providing inputs for policy analysis and in monitoring the performance of national development policies and programs. Ensuring that M/E systems are designed to respond to national information needs as well as those of donors. |
| Planners | Uses of M/E at the different stages of the project cycle. Using information from completed and ongoing projects to improve the selection and design of future projects (meta-analysis and prospective evaluation). The organization and management of M/E at the national and sector levels. |
| Project managers and staff | Design, management, and use of M/E at the project level. Links between project and national evaluation systems. Diagnostic studies. Stakeholder analysis and beneficiary assessment. |
| Central M/E agencies | Uses of M/E in project planning and management and in policy analysis. Links between central, sectoral, and project-level M/E. Technical issues relating to design, implementation, and analysis. Quality control and the importance of multimethod approaches. Stakeholder analysis. Creating national data bases and utilization of meta-analysis and prospective evaluation. |
| Project M/E units | Integration of M/E into project management and linkages with national M/E system. Technical issues relating to design, implementation and analysis. Stakeholder analysis and beneficiary assessment. Diagnostic studies and rapid feedback methods. |
| Training institutions | Most of the above topics plus discussion of design and delivery of training. Emphasis on use of case studies and the importance of field visits and practical exercises. |
| Nongovernmental organizations | Similar to preceding courses. In addition discussion of more rigorous methods for evaluating the performance of NGOs. Cost-effectiveness analysis and institutional assessment. |
| International agencies | In addition to their own internal training they may participate as observers in some of the above courses. |

4. *Central M/E agencies* refer not only to the M/E divisions of core ministries such as Planning, Finance, and in some cases Plan or Program Implementation, but also to the M/E cells of line ministries and autonomous bodies. Training should cover the use of M/E in project planning and management, and in national and sectoral policymaking. Emphasis should also be placed on understanding the links between M/E systems at the central, provincial, ministerial, and project levels. Training should cover all the technical issues relating to the design, implementation, interpretation, and use of the main kinds of studies. Some of the important topics include data quality control, rapid analysis and feedback, how to identify and respond to the information needs of stakeholders, and how to develop data bases to synthesize the findings of all studies on continuing and completed projects.

5. *Project M/E units* need to be oriented toward the way M/E links into the planning, implementation, and management of the project, as well the way information is used by central government agencies and donors. Technical training should stress the wide variety of evaluation and data collection methods and should emphasize the importance of a multi-method approach. Diagnostic and rapid feedback studies should receive particular attention.

6. The *training institutions* responsible for M/E training will require training on all of the above topics, as well as on issues relating to the development of an integrated training strategy, curricula development, and the organization and delivery of courses. Emphasis will also be placed on the preparation and use of case studies and review papers. It is important to discuss the integration of M/E training with other major training areas such as project appraisal, planning, and management; public expenditure management; and macroeconomic planning and management. The coordination and integration of training for public officials and NGOs should also be discussed. In many countries, it will also be important to encourage more dynamic training methods, such as small group discussions, field visits, the use of case studies, and management games.

7. *NGOs* not only require training, but are an important training resource with respect to the previously mentioned topics, among others. It is important to develop rigorous methods for evaluating the performance of NGOs, as they become more involved in the execution of public sector projects. One topic that should be emphasized is the methodology for assessing the cost-effectiveness of NGOs in project implementation and service delivery.

8. *The staff of international agencies* also require training. Although much of this is provided by their own agencies, it is often useful for donor agencies to participate in some of the M/E-related training activities for government and NGOs. Because donors have a strong influence on the kinds of M/E studies conducted in many countries, and even on how the national M/E systems are organized, it can be beneficial for them to participate in seminars and workshops in which the strengths and weaknesses of current M/E practices are discussed.

## The Elements of an Integrated National M/E Training Program

A national M/E training strategy should include four basic kinds of training activities, the outlines of which are given in Tables 13-3 through 13-6. As both demand and the level of professional expertise increase, a number of more specialized courses can be developed around these four. Most of the reading material and the outline curricula can be obtained from the appropriate chapters of this volume. Tables 13-3 to 13-6 indicate the most appropriate chapters for each kind of course. An article by Al-Bazzaz and Bamberger (1990) provides detailed recommendations on readings and curricula for a monitoring and evaluation seminar, and a similar article by Bamberger (1992) provides similar recommendations for a seminar on the design and management of sustainable poverty alleviation projects.[4]

The first activity should be a series of *short seminars and workshops for senior policymakers and planners* (Table 13-3). It is essential for key officials in the national and provincial/state governments to fully understand the role that monitoring and evaluation can play in the formulation and achievement of national development goals. It is equally important for them to understand what is required of M/E systems if they are to make their full contribution. The main objective of the seminars should be to indicate that M/E is important at the national level, since it is usually regarded as no more than a routine administrative activity or a requirement of international agencies. Once this has been established, the second objective should be to stress that a standardized system needs to be developed for all (both national and internationally funded) projects and that this responds to national information needs in addition to providing information required by donor agencies.

A third objective is to emphasize that a system needs to provide feedback on projects and programs throughout their economic life rather than simply during their implementation phase. Systems must therefore be designed to

**Table 13-3.  Outline of Seminars/Workshops for Senior Policymakers and Planners**

| | |
|---|---|
| *Audience* | Senior policymakers and planners. |
| *Duration* | Series of short half-day to two-day seminars and workshops. |
| *Objectives* | Familiarization with the important contributions M/E can make to policy analysis and planning at the national and sectoral level; and understanding of the organizational and resource requirements to ensure maximum effectiveness of the M/E systems. |
| *Content* | • The contributions of M/E to policy analysis.<br>• Using M/E as a tool for national and sectoral planning.<br>• Assessment of the strengths and weaknesses of how M/E is currently organized and used.<br>• Review of how M/E is organized and used in other countries.<br>• Discussion and recommendations on how to strengthen the organization and utilization of M/E.<br>• Case studies on how M/E has been of practical utility to policymakers and planners.<br>• Identification of key policy and planning areas where M/E could contribute. |
| *Methodology* | Short presentations, brief case studies and review papers, small group discussions, definition of an action plan. Follow-up meeting to review progress. |
| *Readings and curricula* | See Chapters 1–3 and selected sections of Chapters 4–8 of the present publication. See also recommended reading at the end of each chapter. See Al-Bazzaz and Bamberger (1990) for a recommended curriculum and selected readings. Bamberger (1992) recommends a curriculum for a seminar on the design and management of sustainable poverty alleviation projects which also addresses evaluation issues. |

provide regular feedback on project sustainability and to assess, for selected projects, the extent to which they have produced their intended benefits and impacts. The organizational structure needed to achieve these objectives must also be discussed. Often this will involve creating or strengthening M/E cells in line ministries and provincial or state governments rather than just relying on ad hoc monitoring units in each project. Training courses should also discuss the appropriate division of responsibilities between central, ministerial, and local M/E units. Many countries have overcentralized M/E, with the result that its benefit as a management tool has not been fully realized.

Given the senior level of participants, the maximum duration of these seminars and workshops will normally be two days, and many will last only half a day. The strategy is to make them short but to hold them relatively frequently (perhaps two or three times a year).

The second component should be an *M/E module to be included in longer courses and seminars on project planning and management* (Table 13-4), which are organized for planners and project managers. The first objective of these modules (which can also be offered as a stand-alone seminar) should be to inform project managers and planners how M/E can help them achieve project objectives and integrate projects into national development programs and policies. The second objective should be to discuss the design and management of M/E systems and to point out that they are an effective management tool rather than simply an administrative reporting unit.

The module should stress careful planning and design of the M/E program at the time the project itself is being designed. Frequently, M/E is ignored until the project is already operational. If impact studies are to be conducted later, it is also important to ensure that necessary baseline data have been collected for before and after comparisons.

Emphasis should be placed on the design and utilization of diagnostic studies and stakeholder analysis.

The third component should be *seminars and workshops for central monitoring and evaluation agencies* (Table 13-5). The principal objective should be to provide these agencies and cells with the necessary technical skills to select, design, implement, analyze, and use the different kinds of M/E studies. Table 13-5 lists some of the main course components, although they will vary greatly, depending on the extent of the national M/E system and the development priorities of each country.

M/E practitioners must be made aware of the actual and potential contributions of M/E to national, sectoral, and project policymaking, planning, and management. They must also understand the importance of coordinating the elements of the M/E system, which has different, equally important functions at the project and provincial levels. As already mentioned, many national M/E systems are overcentralized. Therefore central M/E agencies should support the local agencies and help them carry out their own responsibilities—rather than simply act as a data-collecting service for national agencies.

**Table 13-4.  Monitoring and Evaluation Module to Be Included
in Courses on Project Planning and Management or to Be Offered
as a Stand-Alone Course**

| | |
|---|---|
| *Audience* | Project managers from government and possibly NGOs. Donor agencies might also participate. |
| *Duration* | One- to two-week module in a three- to five-week course. Module could also be offered separately as a stand-alone course. Regular follow-up workshops should be organized as the projects progress. |
| *Objectives* | • To familiarize project managers with the contributions of M/E as a tool of project management and as a feedback mechanism for ensuring the integration of projects into national development strategies.<br>• To help project managers to understand how to organize, manage and utilize M/E studies. |
| *Content* | • The contributions of M/E to project management.<br>• Linking project M/E into national, sectoral and donor information requirements.<br>• Designing a project M/E system, defining the organizational structure and resource requirements.<br>• Managing the project M/E system.<br>• Defining stakeholders and designing the M/E system to respond to their information requirements.<br>• M/E and the project cycle.<br>• Designing and using diagnostic studies.<br>• Ensuring the effective utilization of M/E studies. |
| *Methodology* | • Short presentations followed by discussions.<br>• Use of short case studies and review papers.<br>• Group discussions, case studies, and management games.<br>• Field exercises.<br>• Preparation of action plans with follow-up review sessions. |
| *Reading material and curricula* | See appropriate sections of Chapters 3-7 and 11 of the present publication and the recommended readings at the end of each chapter. See also Al-Bazzaz and Bamberger (1990) for recommended readings and a suggested curriculum, and Bamberger (1992) for the application of the evaluation methods to poverty alleviation projects. |

## Table 13-5. Seminars/Workshops for Central Monitoring and Evaluation Agencies

| | |
|---|---|
| *Audience* | Staff from central agencies (core ministries and M/E cells of line ministries) plus M/E staff from major NGOs. Donor agencies may also be invited to participate. |
| *Duration* | Three to five-week basic course followed by shorter more specialized workshops. |
| *Objectives* | To provide M/E staff with the technical skills to carry out their work and to help them understand how the work of their central agencies is integrated into M/E activities at the provincial and project levels. The role of M/E in overall development planning and management is also explained. |
| *Content* | • The organization and functions of the different elements of the national M/E system. |
| | • The importance of close cooperation with government and NGO M/E activities. |
| | • The contribution of M/E to national development planning and management. |
| | • M/E and the project cycles for nationally and donor funded projects. |
| | • The design and utilization of different kinds of studies. |
| | • Methods of data collection and analysis. |
| | • Principles of sample design. |
| | • Research designs for the estimation of project impacts. |
| | • Creation and utilization of M/E data bases (meta-analysis, sectoral reviews, and prospective evaluation). |
| | • Management of data bases: quality control, ensuring rapid utilization and feedback. |
| *Methodology* | • Reading assignments followed by lectures and discussion. |
| | • Small group exercises and discussions. |
| | • Preparation and use of case studies. |
| | • Field exercises to test different data collection methods and to conduct rapid assessments of ongoing or completed projects. |
| *Reading material and curricula* | See Chapters 1–4, 10–12, and selected sections of Chapters 6–9 of the present publication and the recommended readings at the end of each chapter. |

In addition, more emphasis should be put on controlling the quality of data. Because of a lack of time or resources, many central agencies accept uncritically all the data they receive from lower-level agencies, even though the data are likely to contain errors and inconsistencies, or in some cases may even have been fabricated. *Regular field visits* are essential for quality control. In addition to providing an opportunity to check the validity of data, these visits help build rapport with local M/E agencies, because it allows them to see that the information they collect is actually being used and gives them an opportunity to discuss and make suggestions for improving the studies and systems being used. Visits also help central agency staff better understand the projects being studied and hence to better interpret the data they receive.

Second, *multimethod* evaluation designs and data collection and interpretation should be emphasized. There is still a strong bias toward quantitative methods in many agencies, and the vital role of qualitative evaluation is not well understood.

Third, *stakeholder analysis* should be discussed. Trainees should be taught how to identify stakeholders, how to assess their interests in the evaluation, how to reconcile these various interests in the evaluation design. In many countries, project beneficiaries will be one of the most important stakeholders.

Fourth, M/E studies must continue throughout the life of a project and program and must not end when the physical implementation of the project is completed. Therefore, planners must also discuss the organization of M/E and the need to develop a permanent M/E capacity in the main line agencies.

Fifth, some attention should be devoted to the lessons of completed projects and programs. This topic would cover data management, synthesis and review studies, prospective evaluation, and possibly meta-analysis.

The final component of the integrated training program should be *seminars and workshops for project monitoring and evaluation units* (see Table 13-6). The objectives would be to provide M/E staff with the technical skills required to carry out their work and to help them understand how the work of their units is integrated into M/E activities at the ministerial, provincial, and national levels. The contribution of M/E to project management and the overall achievement of project goals should also be emphasized. These seminars should cover stakeholder analysis (including the importance of consultation with beneficiaries), multimethod approaches, diagnostic studies, and the effective utilization of studies.

## Table 13-6. Seminars/Workshops for Project Monitoring and Evaluation Units

| | |
|---|---|
| *Audience* | Staff from project level M/E units, local consultants, and researchers involved in the evaluations; evaluation staff from concerned NGOs; and possibly donor agencies involved with the projects. Where concerned ministries have M/E cells, they may also be invited. |
| *Duration* | Three- to five-week basic course followed by shorter more specialized workshops. |
| *Objectives* | To provide M/E staff with the technical skills to carry out their work and to help them understand how the work of their units is integrated into M/E activities at the ministerial, provincial, and national levels. The contribution of M/E to project management and the overall achievement of project goals will also be emphasized. |
| *Content* | • The organization and functions of the different elements of the national M/E system and their links with project M/E units.<br>• The importance of close cooperation with NGO M/E activities.<br>• M/E and the project cycles for nationally and donor-funded projects.<br>• The kinds of studies and reporting requirements called for under the project agreements, together with an explanation of how each kind of information will be used.<br>• The design and implementation of different kinds of studies.<br>• Methods of data collection and analysis.<br>• The importance of a multimethod approach and the need for checks on the reliability and validity of data.<br>• The importance of participant observation and other qualitative methods to understand the project from the perspective of the intended beneficiaries.<br>• The design and utilization of diagnostic studies.<br>• Stakeholder analysis.<br>• Principles of sample design.<br>• Research designs for the estimation of project impacts. |
| *Methodology* | • Reading assignments followed by lectures and discussion.<br>• Small group exercises and discussions.<br>• Preparation and use of case studies.<br>• Field exercises to test different data collection methods and to conduct rapid assessments of ongoing or completed projects. |
| *Reading material and curricula* | See Chapters 2–3, 4–8, and 10–12 of this volume and the recommended readings at the end of each chapter. |

## Training Methods and Materials

### Country and Sector Review Papers

To fully understand the operation of national and sectoral M/E systems, it may be necessary to commission a review paper comparing the organization of national M/E systems in different countries (Khan 1989, 1990). Attention should also be given to the particular kinds of studies (for example, impact evaluation) performed in individual countries. These studies could describe and illustrate the various systems used.

A comparative review of M/E systems may take three to six months because the researcher may have to visit a number of countries. Often two visits are required, the first to identify a local collaborator and to agree on how the information is to be collected, and the second (possibly one or two months later) to review the information that has been collected. National reviews can usually be completed in two to three months, depending on how much fieldwork is required.

### Case Studies

Case studies describe in much more detail how a monitoring and evaluation system was designed and implemented for a particular project. Normally, the case will describe the evaluation *process* as well as the system's organization and methodology. Many cases will also discuss the implementation problems and attempt to show how the original evaluation design had to be adapted to changing circumstances. A well-prepared case will help inexperienced evaluation researchers better understand the complex political, administrative, social, and cultural environment in which the evaluation is designed and conducted.

Case studies may be commissioned before the course or seminar, or participants can be asked to prepare a case on their own projects, which they will then present in the seminar. For a discussion of how to prepare and present a case study, see Yin (1984).

Cases can be used in several ways in an M/E seminar. First, the lecturer can use them to illustrate the lecture, and students may subsequently use them as reference material to illustrate the ways in which M/E was organized and the kinds of problems that arose. (For a typical example of how monitoring and evaluation were used at the sectoral level in the countries of South Asia, see Ahmed and Bamberger 1989.)

Cases also provide material for group discussions. The case describes the context in which an M/E study or program was undertaken and provides information on a study that has either been conducted or is about to be conducted. The members of the group are asked to discuss the evaluation and to suggest how it should be organized or analyzed.

In addition, the case is a useful tool in role-playing exercises. One group may be assigned the role of the evaluation team, another project management, and a third the agency funding the project. The task may be to agree on the objectives and organization of the evaluation program or to present and discuss the findings of a study. The purpose is to help participants understand the political dimensions of evaluation and the perspectives of various stakeholders.

*Field Visits*

Because monitoring and evaluation are both operational activities that take place mainly in the field, it is essential to include field visits in the training programs. This is not normally done because of the time and money involved. Various kinds of activities can take place in the field. Different M/E organizations can simply meet to exchange views on how they conduct and use studies, or participants can be given some practical experience in executing a monitoring or evaluation study. If there is enough time, participants can be asked to conduct a rapid appraisal or diagnostic study combining direct observation with interviews with key informants, discussions with project staff, a review of secondary material, or the like. A field visit of this kind can be conducted in one day but must be preceded by a thorough briefing, with adequate background material.

If more time is available, participants may spend several days in a project area to conduct a more thorough study. Chapter 6 explained how a sustainability assessment study can be organized. The Economic Development Institute has organized two- to three-day field studies of this kind as part of seminars in Jordan, Tunis, Malaysia, and Viet Nam.

*Panel Discussions*

Panel discussions, in which a number of different speakers exchange views, can be an effective teaching technique. At times, speakers will describe and compare the way evaluation studies are conducted by their respective agencies; in other cases, they will present different perspectives on an evaluation that has been conducted by the seminar participants.

## Recommended Reading

Al-Bazzaz, Mehdi, and Michael Bamberger. 1990. "Seminar on Monitoring and Evaluation of Development Projects and Project Sustainability." *EDI Review.* January 1990.

Presentation of a curriculum and reading list for a typical monitoring and evaluation seminar for planners and project managers.

Bamberger, Michael, and Shabbir Cheema. 1990. *Project Sustainability: Case Studies from Bangladesh and a Review of Asian Experience.*

Example of case studies on project sustainability that have been used for teaching purposes in a number of countries.

Davis, Barbara Gross, ed. 1986. "Teaching Evaluation across Disciplines." *New Directions for Program Evaluation* 29. San Francisco: Jossey-Bass.

Review of evaluation training programs available in the United States.

Economic Development Institute. 1991. *Catalog of Training Materials.* Washington, D.C.

Lists all of the training materials that can be obtained free of charge on request from EDI. Many of these deal with issues relating to monitoring and evaluation at the sectoral or national levels.

Khan, Adil. 1989. *A Review of Current Monitoring and Evaluation Thoughts and Practices in South Asia.* Washington, D.C.: World Bank, Economic Development Institute.

Example of a comparative country review of how monitoring and evaluation are organized at the national level.

Yin, Robert K. 1984. *Case Study Research: Design and Methods.* Beverly Hills, Calif.: Sage.

Explains the different ways in which case studies can be designed, analyzed, and used.

# Notes

1. This chapter draws heavily on one author's experience in organizing monitoring and evaluation training programs in Asia and to a lesser extent North Africa and the English-speaking Arab countries. The lack of direct experience of the M/E training situation in Latin America and Africa is acknowledged.

2. The study covered only public sector training programs and consequently does not include the training programs of nongovernment organizations or institutes of management, many of which discuss monitoring and evaluation in their training programs.

3. The Economic Development Institute cooperated with the Royal Scientific Society in Jordan and the Arab Planning Institute in Kuwait to develop monitoring and evaluation training within the framework of project planning and management courses for the English-speaking Arab countries.

4. The EDI article by Al-Bazzaz and Bamberger is a synthesis of experiences in the organization of monitoring and evaluation courses and seminars in Pakistan (1987), Laos (1988), Malaysia (1988 and 1990), Tunis (1988), Kuwait (1988), Jordan (1989), and Viet Nam (1989).

# Glossary of Technical Terms

ANNUAL DEVELOPMENT PROGRAM (ADP)
An annual development plan, used by many developing countries, that identifies
and prioritizes the projects for which public investment resources (both national
and foreign) will be approved.

BENEFICIARY ASSESSMENT
Method used to assess the perspectives of intended or actual beneficiaries of a
project. Concerned with the attitudes of different groups to proposed projects;
designed to obtain feedback during project implementation, or to assess
beneficiaries' opinions about how they have been affected by a project. These
objectives have their origins in participant observation and the desire to "listen to
people" (Salmen 1987). (See Chapter 10.)

CASE STUDY
Case studies permit an in-depth analysis or description of how programs or projects
operate and how they are affected by the social, economic, and political environment
in which they operate (Yin 1984). There are a wide range of case study methods but
a common feature is that they concentrate on a small number of cases (individuals,
communities, schools, and so on), which they examine in depth, normally through
qualitative rather than quantitative methods. Cases can examine one moment in
time or one event, or they can be used to examine processes that evolve over long
periods of time. (See Chapters 5 and 10.)

> SINGLE-SITE STUDY. Analysis of data from a single project or organization. The study
> may be conducted at one point in time or may involve continuous observation over time
> (Miles and Huberman 1984).

MULTISITE STUDY. Analysis of data from a number of different communities or organizations. This requires the development of simple matrixes to permit cross-site comparisons.

## COMMUNITY FORA

An extension of the key informant approach, except that the whole community is consulted on the issues of primary concern in the evaluation. In a large community, a number of separate fora—often based on sex, age, or cultural groupings—may be organized. (See Chapters 5 and 10.)

## CONFIDENCE INTERVAL

The range in which one can be confident (with a certain defined probability) that the true value of the mean lies. (See Chapter 11.)

## CONTROL GROUP

A group selected in an experimental or quasi-experimental design to represent the conditions of the experimental group if they had not been exposed to a project.

NONEQUIVALENT CONTROL GROUP. Because most projects do not randomly select the individuals or communities who will receive interventions, it is normally not possible to select a control group with exactly the same characteristics as the intervention or experimental group. Consequently any postintervention differences between the control and experimental groups cannot be automatically attributed to the effects of the project. A number of design and statistical procedures are available to adjust for the initial differences between the two groups. (See Chapters 8, 9, and 11.)

## COST-BENEFIT ANALYSIS  (See Economic Analysis.)

## COST-EFFECTIVENESS ANALYSIS

Provides information on the costs of producing a given output (for example, the construction of houses) or service (for example, vaccination) through alternative delivery systems. (See Chapter 4.)

## DIAGNOSTIC STUDIES

Provide information on the characteristics of a community or group at a particular point in time (for example, when a project is being considered or initiated) and analyze the causes of problems identified. (See Chapter 5.)

## ECONOMIC ANALYSIS

Defined as the study of the macroeconomic significance of microeconomic projects (Sang 1988). Compares projects on the basis of their true costs and benefits to society.

## ECONOMIC RATE OF RETURN (ERR)

The return obtained on the resources invested in a project when the true economic costs and benefits are calculated and discounted at a rate reflecting the "opportunity cost of capital" (that is, the best alternative use of the resources). Projects would normally be accepted only if the internal economic rate of return (IRR) is greater than the opportunity cost of capital (often assumed to be 10 or 12 percent).

EVALUABILITY ASSESSMENT
Assessment of the proposed project evaluation design to determine whether it would be technically possible to evaluate outputs and impacts in the way proposed in the evaluation design. This assessment often results in a much simpler evaluation design as it demonstrates that the proposed more sophisticated and expensive design would not, in fact, be able to produce the intended results. (See Chapter 2, page 40.)

EVALUATION
An external activity that consists of assessing (a) the appropriateness of a project's design and implementation methods in achieving both a specific objective and more general development objectives; (b) a project's results, both intended and unintended; and (c) the factors affecting the level and distribution of the benefits produced. (See Chapter 1, pages 12–14.)

> IMPACT EVALUATION (or Summative Evaluation). Assessing the extent to which a project has produced its intended effects and the extent to which the observed changes can be attributed to the presence of the project. This frequently involves the use of an *experimental* or *quasi-experimental* design. That is, control groups are used to eliminate (or control for) the influence of external factors or events that might have produced the observed changes. Frequently, the evaluation will also assess the distributional effects of the project to determine whether the benefits were obtained by the intended target groups. (See Chapters 8 and 9.)
>
> PROCESS EVALUATION (See Formative Evaluation.)
>
> PROSPECTIVE EVALUATION. Synthesizes monitoring and evaluation information from earlier studies to assess the likely outcomes of impacts of new projects. Although widely used in the United States (Chelimsky 1987, 1988) and other industrial nations, prospective evaluations have been little used in developing countries. They are thought to have considerable potential in the latter. (See Chapter 2, page 63.)

EXPOSURE (to project inputs and benefits)
Defining the kinds and levels of inputs and benefits accessible to, and actually enjoyed by, different sectors of the project target group. When projects offer a range of different services that become available to different groups at different points of time, it is common to find that different beneficiaries have been exposed to significantly different packages of services. (See Chapter 9.)

FORMATIVE EVALUATION (or Process Evaluation)
Studies the process of project implementation to assess how effectively the project is being implemented and the effect of implementation on the final outcomes and impacts. (See Chapter 1, pages 12–14; and Chapter 5.)

GAIN SCORE
Term used in the cost-effectiveness analysis of educational and certain other kinds of projects to define the amount of change produced in an intended product (such as reading ability or performance on a mathematics test) as a result of different kinds of project delivery systems. (See Chapter 4, page 145.)

GENDER ANALYSIS
Assessment of the likely differences in the impacts of proposed policies, programs, or projects on women and men. Also used to monitor impacts as a policy/program or project is implemented or to evaluate the impacts once it has become operational. (See Chapter 2, pages 66–71; and Chapter 4.)

IMPACT (Impact Assessment)
The changes produced in a group exposed to an experimental treatment as a result of the project. Project *impact* is distinguished from *total observed change* in the project population. The latter may be due in whole or in part to factors unrelated to the project. (See Chapters 8 and 9.)

> ENVIRONMENTAL IMPACT ASSESSMENT. Analysis conducted during the project preparation phase to assess the likely environmental impacts of a project (Winpenny 1991).

> SOCIAL IMPACT ASSESSMENT. When conducted during project appraisal, social impact assessment is used to assess the likely impact of a project on different social groups and also to assess the feasibility of the project's successful implementation on the basis of the proposed organizational structures, its compatibility with sociocultural norms, and the likely responses of different stakeholder groups. The same techniques can be used to monitor a project's social impacts during implementation or after it has become operational (Finsterbusch 1990).

IMPLEMENTATION
Covers the actual development or construction of the project, up to the point at which it becomes fully operational. Includes the monitoring of all aspects of the work or activity as it proceeds and supervision by "oversight" agencies within the country or by external donors.
   The transformation of project inputs, through the use of a set of implementation methods, to produce a specified volume and quality of project outputs.

IMPLEMENTATION METHODOLOGY
Technical and organizational systems and procedures used to transform the available inputs so as to produce the intended outputs.

INPUTS
Financial, human, and material resources available to implement the project as planned.

INTERNAL ECONOMIC RATE OF RETURN (IRR) (See Economic Rate of Return.)

INTERVENTION (intervention group)
"Interventions" are the services or "treatments" provided by a project. The group receiving the project services is known as the "treatment" or "experimental" group. This contrasts with the "control" group, which does not receive the services. (See Chapters 8 and 9.)

KEY INFORMANTS
People in a community, region, or organization, who, because of their position are able to provide information or insights on some aspects relevant to the project. These informants play a key role in many kinds of qualitative evaluations, but it is important to recognize that they frequently provide a very one-sided perspective, rather than an "objective" description of reality. The evaluator must obtain information from a broad range of key informants who between them reflect all of the main currents in the area under study. (See Chapters 7 and 10.)

LOGICAL FRAMEWORK ANALYSIS (LOGFRAME)
A technique for program planning and monitoring originally developed for the U.S. Agency for International Development. It requires an explicit statement of the changes that a project is supposed to produce, and of each step that must be taken to bring these changes about. Based on a four-stage sequence: the *general goals* to be achieved; the *purpose* of the project (how it will achieve these goals); the *outputs* that are to be produced to fulfill this purpose; and the *inputs* that will be used to achieve these outputs. (See Chapter 3.)

LOGICAL POSITIVISM (See Positivist-Behaviorist Paradigm.)

MANAGEMENT INFORMATION SYSTEM (MIS)
The creation, through a well-designed monitoring system, of regular feedback to management at the project and central agency level, on all key aspects of a project. In some countries, such as the SETIA system in Malaysia, a central MIS system has been established to make information on all development projects instantly accessible to all central government agencies and line ministries. (See Chapters 4 and 12.)

META-ANALYSIS
Considers all available (evaluation) studies on a particular kind of program or intervention as a population, and takes the finding of each study as an observation point. Then combines all observations to estimate the magnitude and range of effects produced by a particular intervention. The underlying assumption is that the average levels of effect observed in a large number of studies will be more reliable than the findings of an individual study. (See Chapter 2, page 64.)

META-EVALUATION
An "evaluation of an evaluation" (Patton 1980). It has been suggested that the quality and reliability of evaluations should be audited through meta-evaluation in the same way as financial performance is audited (Schwandt and Halpern 1988). (See Chapter 12.)

MODEL
A planned intervention based on explicit theories about how to foster social change or reform, and why that change should be expected. A model of a social program should make explicit how different inputs should lead to certain impacts. Therefore,

a model is a testable hypothesis about a project that can be either refuted or vindicated. (See Chapter 3.)

MONITORING
An *internal project management activity* whose purpose is to ensure that the project achieves its defined objectives within a prescribed time frame and budget. Monitoring provides regular feedback on the progress of project implementation, and on the problems faced during implementation. It consists of operational and administrative activities that track resource acquisition and allocation, the production or the delivery of services, and cost records.

NET PRESENT VALUE (NPV)
The value today of the stream of net benefits produced by a project when these benefits have been discounted at the discount rate being used in the economic analysis. NPV and the Economic Rate of Return (see above) are the two main methods used in economic analysis to estimate project worth.

OBJECTIVE TREE LOGIC
An objective tree is a logical framework linking different levels of results or outcomes according to a causal theory, that a certain set of activities will result in certain program outcomes that will achieve a strategic objective. This concept is applied in logical framework analysis and in similar approaches, such as USAID's PRISM (see below) used to formulate and evaluate longer-term strategic objectives.

OUTPUTS
The services or products that a project delivers to a target population and that are intended to produce the expected impacts.

PANEL (panel study)
Selection of a group of individuals, communities or organizations whose behavior is observed over time. Panels are used to monitor and describe the process of change produced by a project or to observe changes occurring as a result of outside events such as elections or the evolution of a newly established urban squatter settlement. (See Chapters 8 and 9.)

PARADIGM
"A world view, a general perspective, a way of breaking down the complexity of the real world. As such, paradigms are deeply embedded in the socialization of adherents and practitioners; paradigms tell them what is important, legitimate and reasonable. Paradigms are normative, telling the practitioner what to do without the necessity of long existential or epistemological consideration" (Patton 1978).

PARTICIPANT OBSERVATION
Allows the field researcher to become a member of the community or group being studied. She or he tries to understand the community by participating in its activities and by observing how people behave and interact with each other and with outside organizations. The observer tries to become accepted as a neighbor or participant

rather than an outsider, and to *feel* and *experience* the world from the perspective of the community. (See Chapter 10.)

PATH ANALYSIS

Method used to evaluate the contribution of different project components and nonproject factors to observed changes in the project group. A model is created of the sequence of events expected to produce the intended project impacts and the main external factors which might intervene. Multiple regression analysis is then used to estimate "path coefficients," which show the relative importance of the different factors and stages in the process. (See Chapter 3, page 93.)

PHENOMENOLOGY

Analyzes and describes everyday life and its associate state of consciousness. No assumptions are made about social structure or causality. Phenomenology is opposed to positivist methods (see below) and to the assumption that individuals are formed by social forces. Rather, individuals are said to form the social forces.

POSITIVIST-BEHAVIORIST PARADIGM

Derived from the Logical Positivist school of philosophy, which believes that science can only deal with observable entities. In sociology, this has led to the search for observable regularities ("social facts") that can be analyzed independently of the meanings and interpretations that the individuals or groups being observed may attribute to these actions or events.

PRISM: (PROGRAM PERFORMANCE INFORMATION SYSTEM FOR STRATEGIC MANAGEMENT)

PRISM is a program performance monitoring, reporting, and management information system introduced by USAID in 1991 for senior managers both in Washington and in the field. Its purpose is to improve AID's ability to clarify objectives, measure performance, and apply performance information in decisionmaking at all organizational levels. PRISM calls for the routine collection of data by Missions to measure their actual progress in achieving strategic objectives and program outcomes. The approach is similar to logical framework analysis but is applied to the formulation and assessment of strategic objectives to be achieved over a time frame of five to eight years. (See Chapter 2.)

PROGRAM

A series of projects and activities within a particular sector, all of which seek to achieve similar objectives or to provide similar services. For example, a nutrition *program* in a particular country or region may comprise a number of separate *projects* as well as broadly based activities funded out of the national budget.

PROJECT

A discrete package of investments, policies, and institutional and other actions designed to achieve a specific development objective (or set of objectives) within a designated period.

PROJECT CYCLE.  The sequence of stages involved in the planning, implementation, operation and evaluation of a project. (See Chapter 1, page 16; and Chapter 4.)

PROJECT COMPLETION REPORT (PCR)
A report normally required by international aid agencies at the time that project implementation is completed (usually within a certain number of months after the final loan disbursement has been received). The PCR reviews and assesses all aspects of project implementation and compares intended and actual performance with regard to physical implementation, costs, and timing. The report includes lessons learned. Many agencies want it to include a reestimated economic rate of return. (See Chapter 4.)

QUALITATIVE METHODS
Defined as "a particular tradition in social science that fundamentally depends on watching people in their own territory and interaction with them in their own language, on their own terms" (Kirk and Miller 1986). Qualitative approaches emphasize *understanding* reality as it is construed by the persons being studied. In many cases, the researcher is expected to become absorbed in the culture in order to understand the *meaning* of particular activities or beliefs within the context of this culture. Qualitative methodologists are strongly opposed to any effort to isolate a particular event (or "social fact") and to study it independently of the context in which it occurs.

Although this is not an essential condition, most qualitative studies rely on descriptive rather than numerical or statistical analysis. (See Chapter 10.)

QUANTITATIVE METHODS
In most cases, these methods rely on a *structured instrument* (questionnaire or observation guide) to collect *standardized information* on a *carefully selected sample* of individuals, units, or events. The information is then analyzed by statistical procedures to obtain descriptive data on a group, make statistical comparisons between groups, or conduct more complex multivariate analysis.

Frequently, researchers who collect and analyze quantitative data operate within a *positivist-behaviorist* paradigm (see above). The purpose is to identify and analyze observable regularities ("social facts") that can be interpreted independently of the meanings attached to them by the individuals or groups being observed.

QUASI-EXPERIMENTAL DESIGN (QED)
Identifies competing explanations for a program effect and develops research designs to control for these alternatives so that one can assess whether and to what extent the observed changes can be attributed to the project or intervention being evaluated.

In most social evaluations, it is not possible to achieve the degree of scientific rigor obtained in laboratory experiments, and QED provides the closest approximation to the true experimental design available in a particular context.

In most QED, one or more *control groups* (see above) are selected to approximate as closely as possible the characteristics of the experimental group and are used to assess the condition of the experimental group if the project had not taken place. (See Chapter 8.)

RAPID ASSESSMENT (or Rapid Appraisal)

Methods first developed in agriculture and rural development (where they became known as rapid rural appraisal, or RRA) to provide a rapid and cost-effective means of assessing the conditions of a community or area at the time a project was being planned. Since then, they have been extended to provide a rapid method of impact assessment and are now being used widely in other sectors, such as health and nutrition. (See Chapters 4, 7, and 10.)

SAMPLE

A number of people, households, communities, or other units that have been selected in a systematic way and are used to estimate the characteristics of the population from which the units were drawn. In a well-designed sample, sufficient interviews are conducted to ensure that estimates about the mean or distribution of values around the mean can be made with a specified degree of accuracy. (See earlier discussion of confidence intervals and Chapter 11.)

CLUSTER SAMPLE. Clusters of populations such as blocks, neighborhoods, communities, or other easily definable areas. Interviews conducted in a small number of carefully selected clusters can save considerable time and money. Although cluster samples produce statistically less precise estimates, this is usually compensated for by the reduced costs and time.

PURPOSIVE SAMPLE. Respondent selected in a nonrandom way, according to characteristics of concern to a particular study. Although this is a much more economical way to obtain information, caution must be exercised in making generalizations because the sample is not representative of the total population from which respondents are drawn.

RANDOM SAMPLE. Each unit has an equal chance of being selected. Generalizations can therefore be made directly from the sample to the population from which it was drawn without introducing any bias. With more complex forms of random sampling (such as stratified random samples), the probability of each unit's being selected is known; thus, through weighting it is possible to obtain an unbiased population estimate.

STRATIFIED SAMPLE. Reduces the number of interviews required to achieve a required level of statistical precision in the estimation of population attributes. All primary units (households, individuals, and so on) are classified into groups according to a clearly definable attribute such as age, sex, or household income. Samples of a size sufficient to ensure a required degree of statistical precision are then selected from each stratum. After the findings for each stratum have been analyzed separately, weighting procedures are used to estimate the population parameters.

Stratification can help reduce the total number of interviews required to ensure a specified degree of precision when the attributes being studied vary greatly from one stratum to another, when there is little variation within each stratum, and when some strata represent a relatively small proportion of the total population.

LOT QUALITY ACCEPTANCE SAMPLING (LQAS). A sampling technique that uses some of the principles of industrial quality control to reduce significantly the size of samples required to monitor the performance of health centers and other service delivery units.

### SAMPLE PRECISION
Refers to the range in which, for a given degree of statistical confidence, the true value of a population characteristic (such as the mean) is estimated to lie. Precision can be defined as the range divided by the mean. The precision of an estimate can be increased by increasing the sample size. (See Chapter 11, page 362.)

### SECONDARY DATA
Data that already exist in the form of published reports or project files, which can be used for evaluation purposes. (See Chapters 7 and 10.)

### SOCIAL COSTS OF ADJUSTMENT
Many developing countries have been forced to introduce broad programs of economic reform and structural adjustment to correct deeply entrenched economic and administrative factors that have inhibited growth. Many of these programs produce, at least in the short run, substantial reductions in public sector employment, cutbacks in public services, and rapid increases in prices of essential products. A major area of recent evaluation research is to assess the social costs of these programs, particularly on the poor and vulnerable groups. (See Chapter 3, page 99.)

### SOCIAL (DEVELOPMENT) PROGRAMS
The broad range of programs designed to improve the quality of life by improving the capacity of citizens to participate fully in social, economic, and political activities at the local and national levels. Programs may focus on improving physical well-being (health, nutrition); providing access to services (housing, water supply, local transportation); protecting vulnerable groups from some of the adverse consequences of economic reform and structural adjustment; or providing education, literacy, and employment and income-generating opportunities (vocational and technical training, credit, integrated rural development, and small business development). (See Chapter 1, page 8.)

### STAKEHOLDERS
Groups that have an interest in the outcome of a project or program and consequently in the orientation, interpretation, and dissemination of the monitoring and evaluation studies. (See Chapter 4, page 113.)

### STRUCTURED LEARNING
Structured Learning is a systematic way to learn from the experience of ongoing projects or sector programs and policies, and to utilize this knowledge to improve the way in which future projects, programs and policies are formulated, implemented, and evaluated. (See Chapter 3.)

SUMMATIVE EVALUATION (See Impact Evaluation.)

SUSTAINABILITY

Refers either to projects or the process of development. *Project* sustainability is the capacity of a project to continue to deliver its intended benefits or services throughout its intended economic life. *Sustainable development* refers to the management of natural and human resources in a way that maximizes the benefits to present generations while maintaining the potential to meet the needs of future generations. (See Chapter 6.)

> SUSTAINABILITY INDEX. Different indicators of sustainability are rated on a 5-point scale. The sum of these ratings can be used to produce a sustainability score that can be used to compare different projects or to assess changes in the sustainability of one project at different points in its development cycle. (See Chapter 6.)

SYSTEMS ANALYSIS

The use of graphical and mathematical techniques to describe the process of project implementation and to assess factors affecting project outcomes. It is extensively used for planning and monitoring health and infrastructure programs, among others. (See Chapter 3, page 83.)

THREATS TO VALIDITY

Factors that can affect or distort the findings of an experiment and thus can threaten the validity of the interpretations, because quasi-experimental designs (see above) are not able to satisfy all the requirements of a true design. Cook and Campbell (1979) identified four main groups of threats to validity. (See Chapter 8.)

> CONSTRUCT VALIDITY. Different causal explanations can be given to statistically significant relationships between the exposure to a project and observed changes in the variables that the project is intended to affect. For example, one researcher may conclude that the increased family income of residents in a new housing project shows that living in a better neighborhood makes it easier to obtain a better job. Another may conclude that increased housing expenditures may force secondary workers to come into the labor force.

> INTERNAL VALIDITY. Statistically significant differences between the project and experimental groups are not due to the effects of the project but to a third variable that could not be adequately controlled. For example, it is sometimes argued that increased income of participants in small business credit programs is not due to the provision of credit per se but to the fact that projects tend to attract more motivated people who would probably have succeeded even without the project. It is usually not possible to control for *motivation* in the selection of project and control groups.

> EXTERNAL VALIDITY. The impact of a project is erroneously attributed to the project interventions rather than to external factors (such as employment conditions, other projects, favorable climatic conditions, etc). Consequently it is wrongly inferred that the project would produce the same outcomes if implemented in another location or region.

STATISTICAL CONCLUSION VALIDITY. The impact of a project is erroneously attributed to the fact that the statistical tests were wrongly applied or interpreted. For example, a statistical test with insufficient *power* may have been said to identify an effect.

## TRIANGULATION

The degree of confidence in the findings of an evaluation can be greatly increased by comparing information and estimates obtained from different methods of data collection. The systematic use and comparison of independent data collection methods is known as "triangulation." (See Chapter 7, page 225.)

## UNOBTRUSIVE METHODS (OF DATA COLLECTION)

A major problem in evaluation, or other kinds of social research, is that the act of collecting data changes the behavior and the responses of the subject or community. Evidence of illegal activities is removed, community leaders behave more democratically, children are dressed in their best clothes, or mothers begin to feed children better kinds of food. Unobtrusive measures seek to observe the community and collect data in ways that reduce this "reactivity." Methods include direct observation, photography, automatic recorders, acting as a member of the community, or using community members to help collect the information. (See Chapters 7 and 10.)

# References

Abt, Clark. 1976. *Evaluation of Social Programs*. Beverly Hills, Calif.: Sage.

Acharya, Meena, and Lynn Bennett. 1981. *Women and the Subsistence Sector: Economic Participation and Household Decisionmaking in Nepal*. World Bank Staff Working Paper 526. Washington, D.C.

Achen, Christopher. 1982. *Interpreting and Using Regression*. Quantitative Applications in the Social Sciences 29. Beverly Hills, Calif.: Sage.

African Development Bank, UNDP, and World Bank. 1990. *The Social Dimensions of Adjustment in Africa: A Policy Agenda*. Washington, D.C.: World Bank.

Ahmad, Yusuf, Salah El Serafy, and Ernst Lutz. 1989. *Environmental Accounting for Sustainable Development*. Washington D.C.: World Bank.

Ahmed, Viqar, and Michael Bamberger. 1989. *Monitoring and Evaluating Development Projects: The South Asian Experience*. Seminar Report Series. Washington, D.C.: World Bank, Economic Development Institute.

Al-Bazzaz, Mehdi. 1989. *Tunisia Second Urban Development Project*. EDI Case 605/025. Washington, D.C.: World Bank.

Al-Bazzaz, Mehdi, and Michael Bamberger. 1990. "Seminar on Monitoring and Evaluation of Development Projects and Project Sustainability." *EDI Review*. January 1990.

American Council of Voluntary Agencies for Foreign Service (ACVAFS). 1983. *Evaluation Sourcebook for Private and Voluntary Organizations*. New York.

Asher, Herbert. 1983. *Causal Modeling*. 2d ed. Quantitative Applications in the Social Sciences 3. Beverly Hills, Calif.: Sage.

Asian Development Bank. 1988. *Sector Paper on Rural Development*. Manila.

————. 1990. "Ex-Post Evaluation at the Asian Development Bank." In *Monitoring and Evaluation of Development Projects: The East Asian Experience*. Kuala Lumpur: INTAN.

————. 1991. *Guidelines for Social Analysis of Bank Projects*. Manila.

Azad, Nandini. 1986. *Empowering Women Workers: The WWF Experiment in Madras, India*. Working Women's Forum (published in collaboration with UNICEF).

Babbie, Earle. 1973. *Survey Research Methods*. Belmont, Calif.: Wadsworth.

Bamberger, Michael. 1968. "A Problem of Political Integration in Latin America: Barrios of Venezuela." *International Affairs* 44(4).

————. 1988a. *Community Participation, Development Planning and Project Management*. Policy Seminar Report Series 13. Washington, D.C.: World Bank, Economic Development Institute.

————. 1988b. "The Politics of Evaluation in Developing Countries." Paper presented at the American Evaluation Association Annual Meeting, New Orleans, October.

————. 1989. "The Monitoring and Evaluation of Public Sector Programs in Asia: Why Are Development Programs Monitored but Not Evaluated?" *Evaluation Review* 13(1):223–42.

————. 1991. "Approaches to Gender and Poverty: World Bank Experiences and Implications for Socialist Countries." In Rita Raj-Hashim and Noeleen Heyzer, ed., *Gender, Economic Growth and Poverty*. Kuala Lumpur: Asian and Pacific Development Centre.

————. 1992. "Seminar on the Design and Management of Sustainable Poverty Alleviation Projects: Recommended Curriculum and Readings." *EDI Review*.

Bamberger, Michael, and Abdul Aziz. 1993. *The Design and Management of Sustainable Poverty Alleviation Programs; the South Asian Experience*. EDI Seminar Series. Washington, D.C.: World Bank, Economic Development Institute.

Bamberger, Michael, and Shabbir Cheema. 1990. *Project Sustainability: Cases from Bangaldesh and Experience from Asia*. Seminar Paper Series. Washington, D.C.: World Bank, Economic Development Institute.

Bamberger, Michael, and Margaret Earle. 1971. "Factors Affecting the Success of a Family Planning Program in a Low-Income Neighborhood of Caracas." *Studies in Family Planning* 12(8).

Bamberger, Michael, Edgardo Gonzalez-Polio, and Umnuay Sae-Hau. 1982. *Evaluation of Sites and Services Projects: The Experience from El Salvador*. World Bank Staff Working Paper 549. Washington, D.C.

Bamberger, Michael, and Eleanor Hewitt. 1986. "Monitoring and Evaluating Urban Development Programs: A Handbook for Managers and Researchers." World Bank Technical Paper 53. Washington, D.C.

Bamberger, Michael, and Daniel Kaufmann. 1984. *Patterns of Income Formation and Expenditures among the Urban Poor of Cartagena: Final Report on World Bank Research Project 672-57*. Washington, D.C.: World Bank.

Bamberger, Michael, Daniel Kaufmann, and Eduardo Velez. 1984. *Research and Methodology of the Study of Interhousehold Transfers in Cartagena.* Operations Policy Staff Discussion Paper WUDD 57. Washington, D.C.: World Bank.

Bamberger, Michael, and Otterbein, Julie. 1982. "Designing a Questionnaire for Longitudinal Impact Studies." Urban and Regional Report 82-5. World Bank, Urban and Regional Economics Division. Washington, D.C.

Bamberger, Michael, and Scott Parris. 1984. *The Structure of Social Networks in the Zona Sur Oriental of Cartagena.* Operations Policy Staff Discussion Paper WUDD 50. Washington, D.C.: World Bank.

Bamberger, Michael, Bishwapura Sanyal, and Nelson Valverde. 1982. *Evaluation of Sites and Services Projects: The Experience from Lusaka, Zambia.* World Bank Staff Working Paper 548. Washington, D.C.

Bamberger, Michael, and Khalid Shams. 1990. *Community Participation, Project Management and Sustainability.* Kuala Lumpur: Asian and Pacific Development Centre.

Bangladesh Rural Advancement Committee (BRAC). 1983. *The Net: Power Structure in Ten Villages.* Dhaka.

———. 1990. "A Tale of Two Wings." Dhaka.

Barkdoll, Gerald, and Bell, James, eds. 1989. *Evaluation and the Federal Decision Maker: New Directions for Program Evaluation.* San Francisco: Jossey-Bass.

Barkdoll, Gerald, and Douglas Sporn. 1989. "Five Strategies for Successful In-House Evaluations." In J. Wholey, K. Newcomer, and Associates, eds., *Improving Government Performance: Evaluation Strategies for Strengthening Public Agencies and Programs.* San Francisco: Jossey-Bass.

Bartoleme, Leo. 1978. *Viviencia y Trabjo en las Zonas Urban y Periurbanas de Posadas a Ser Afectadas por la Represa de Yacyreta.* Posadas, Argentina: Entidad Binacional Yacyreta.

Basu, P. K. 1988. *An Approach to the Monitoring and Evaluation of Programme Implementation in India.* Washington, D.C.: World Bank, Economic Development Institute.

Baum, Warren, and Stokes Tolbert. 1985. *Investing in Development: Lessons from World Bank Experience.* New York: Oxford University Press.

Becker, H. S. 1958. "Problems of Inference and Proof in Participant Observation." *American Sociological Review* 23:652–60.

———. 1979. "Do Photographs Tell the Truth?" In Thomas Cook and Charles Reichardt, eds., *Qualitative and Quantitative Methods in Evaluation Research.* Beverly Hills, Calif.: Sage.

Bell, James 1989. "Using Short-Term Evaluation Tools." In J. Wholey, K. Newcomer, and Associates, eds., *Improving Government Performance: Evaluation Strategies for Strengthening Public Agencies and Programs.* San Francisco: Jossey-Bass.

Bertrand, J. T., P. Russell-Brown, E. Landry, D. Murray, S. Norville, and Y. Rotschell. 1986. "A Test of Two Strategies for Delaying a Second Pregnancy in Teenage

Mothers in Barbados: Final Report." New Orleans, La.: Tulane University Medical Center, School of Public Health and Tropical Medicine.

Birdsall, Nancy. 1982a. *Child Schooling and the Measurement of Living Standards.* Washington, D.C.: World Bank.

————. 1982b. "Strategies for Analyzing Effects of User Charges in the Social Sectors." World Bank, Washington, D.C. Processed.

Blalock, Hubert. 1965. *Statistics for Social Research.* New York: John Wiley.

————. 1979. *Social Statistics.* 2d ed. rev. New York: McGraw-Hill.

Blalock, Hubert, and Ann Blalock. 1968. *Methodology in Social Research.* New York: McGraw-Hill.

Boateng, O., K. Uwusi, R. Kanbur, and A. McKay. 1990 *A Poverty Profile for Ghana 1987–88.* Social Dimensions of Adjustment Working Paper 5. Washington, D.C: World Bank.

Boeninger, Edgardo. 1992. "Economic Policy Change and Government Processes." In Geoffrey Lamb and Rachel Weaving, eds., *Managing Policy Reform in the Real World: Asian Experiences.* Economic Development Institute Seminar Series. Washington D.C.: World Bank.

Bogdan, R. 1972. *Participant Observation in Organizational Settings.* Syracuse, N.Y.: Syracuse University Press.

Bogdan, R., and S. Taylor. 1975. "Introduction to Qualitative Research Methods." New York: John Wiley.

Boissevain, Jeremy. 1974. *Friends of Friends: Networks, Manipulators and Coalitions.* New York: St. Martin's Press.

Boruch, R.F., and W. Wothke, eds. 1985. *Randomization and Field Experimentation.* New Directions for Program Evaluation 28. San Francisco: Jossey-Bass.

Boswell, D. M. 1971. "Personal Crises and the Mobilization of Social Networks." In J. C. Mitchell, ed., *Social Networks in Urban Situations.* Manchester: Manchester University Press.

Bottrall, Anthony. 1981. *Comparative Study of the Management and Organization of Irrigation Projects.* World Bank Staff Working Paper 458. Wahington, D.C.

Bougon, Michael. 1983. "Uncovering Cognitive Maps: The Self Q." In Gareth Morgan, ed., *Beyond Method: Strategies for Social Research.* Beverly Hills, Calif.: Sage.

Briscoe and others. 1986. *Evaluating Health Impact: Water Supply, Sanitation and Hygene Education.* Ottawa. International Development Research Centre.

Brown, L. R., and P. Shaw. 1982. *Six Steps to a Sustainable Society.* Washington, D.C.: World Watch Institute.

Bruyn, S. 1966. *Human Perspective in Sociology.* Englewood Cliffs, N.J.: Prentice-Hall.

Burns, L., and Grebler, L. 1977. *The Housing of Nations: Analysis and Policy in a Comparative Framework.* New York: John Wiley.

Buvonic, Mayra, Nadia Youseff, and Barbara Von Elm. 1978. "Women-Headed Households: The Ignored Factor in Development Planning." International Center for the Study of Women. Paper prepared for the Agency for International Development.

Caldwell, J. C. 1986. "Routes to Low Mortality in Poor Countries." *Population and Development Review* 12(2): 395–413.

Campbell, D. T., and A. E. Erlebacker. 1970. "How Regression Artifacts in Quasi-experimental Evaluations Can Mistakenly Make Contemporary Education Look Harmful." In J. Hellmuth, ed., *Compensatory Education: A National Debate*, vol. 3. New York: Brunner-Mazel.

Campbell, D. T., and R. Levine. 1970. "Field Manual Anthropology." In R. Naroll and R. Cohen, eds., *A Handbook of Method in Cultural Anthroplogy*. New York: Natural History Press.

Campbell, D., and J. Stanley. 1966. *Experimental and Quasi-Experimental Designs for Research*. Chicago: Rand McNally.

Canadian International Development Agency (CIDA). 1985. *A Practical Guide for Conducting Project Evaluations*. Hull: Program Evaluation Division, Policy Branch.

Carlson, Ronald, and Anabel Crane. 1989. "Planning and Managing Useful Evaluations." In J. Wholely, K. Newcomer, and Associates, eds., *Improving Government Performance: Evaluation Strategies for Strengthening Public Agencies and Programs*. San Francisco: Jossey-Bass.

Carnoy, M. 1975. "The Economic Costs and Returns to Educational Television." *Economic Development and Cultural Change* 23 (January):207–48.

Casley, Dennis, and Denis Lury. 1982. *Monitoring and Evaluation of Agricultural Projects*. Baltimore, Md.: Johns Hopkins University Press.

Casley, Dennis, and Krishna Kumar. 1987. *Project Monitoring and Evaluation in Agriculture*. Baltimore, Md.: Johns Hopkins University Press.

———. 1988. *The Collection, Analysis and Use of Monitoring and Evaluation Data*. Baltimore, Md.: Johns Hopkins University Press.

Cassell, J. C. 1974. "Community Diagnosis." In A. R. Oman, ed., *Community Medicine in Developing Countries*. New York: Springer.

Centre for Integrated Rural Development for Asia and the Pacific. 1985. "Monitoring and Evaluation Arrangements and Techniques in Rural Development." Dhaka, Bangladesh.

Centre for Science and Environment. 1985. *The State of India's Environment 1984–85: The Second Citizen's Report*. New Delhi.

Cernea, Michael. 1991. *Putting People First: Sociological Variables in Rural Development*. 2d ed. New York: Oxford University Press.

Cernea, Michael, and Benjamin Tepping. 1977. *A System for Monitoring and Evaluating Agricultural Extension Projects*. World Bank Staff Working Paper 272. Washington, D.C.: World Bank.

Chambers, R. 1979. "Shortcut Methods in Information Gathering for Rural Development Projects." Processed.

———. 1983. *Rural Development: Putting the Last First.* New York: Longman.

———. 1985. "Short-cut Methods for Gathering Social Information for Rural Development Projects." In Michael Cernea, ed., *Putting People First: Sociological Variables in Rural Development.* New York: Oxford University Press.

———. 1991. "Shortcut and Participatory Methods for Gaining Social Information for Projects." In Michael Cernea, ed., *Putting People First: Sociological Variables in Rural Development,* 2d ed. New York: Oxford University Press.

Chander, Ramesh, Christian Grootaert, and Graham Pyatt. 1980. *Living Standards Surveys in Developing Countries.* Living Standards Measurement Study Working Paper 1. Washington, D.C.: World Bank.

Cheema, Shabbir. 1986. *Reaching the Urban Poor: Project Implementation in Developing Countries.* Boulder, Colo.: Westview Press.

Chelimsky, Eleanor. 1987. "Linking Program Evaluations to User Needs." In Dennis Palumbo, ed., *The Politics of Program Evaluation.* Beverly Hills, Calif.: Sage.

———. 1988. *Evaluation and Public Policy: The Use of Evaluation.* Washington, D.C.: World Bank, Economic Development Institute.

Chelimsky, Eleanor, and Linda Morra. 1984. "Evaluation Synthesis for the Legislative User." In Yeaton and Wortman, eds., *Issues in Data Synthesis.* New Directions for Program Evaluation 24. San Francisco: Jossey-Bass.

Cicourel, Aaron 1981. "The Role of Cognitive-Linguistic Concepts in Understanding Everyday Social Interactions." *Annual Review of Sociology* 7:87–106.

Clark, Mari. 1993. *Household Economic Strategies and Support Networks of the Poor in Kenya: A Literature Review.* Washington, D.C.: World Bank, Economic Development Institute.

Cochran, W. C. 1963. *Sampling Techniques.* New York: Wiley.

Cohen, J., and C. Cohen. 1975. *Applied Multiple-Regression/ Correlation Analysis for the Behavioural Sciences.* Hillsdale, N.J.: Lawrence Erlbaum Associates.

Collins, R. 1981. "The Microfoundations of Macro-Sociology." *American Journal of Sociology* 86(5):984–1014.

Conner, R. 1978. "Selecting a Control Group: An Analysis of the Randomization Process in 12 Social Reform Projects." *Evaluation Studies Annual Review* 3:104–53.

Converse, Jean, and Stanley Presser. 1986. *Survey Questions: Handcrafting the Standardized Questionnaire.* Quantitative Applications in the Social Sciences 63. Beverly Hills, Calif.: Sage.

Conway, G. R. 1983. *Agrosystem Analysis.* ICCET Series E, no. 1. London: Imperial College.

Cook, T., and D. Campbell. 1979. *Quasi Experimentation: Design and Analysis Issues for Field Setting.* Chicago: Rand McNally.

Cook, Thomas, and Charles Reichardt. 1979. *Qualitative and Quantitative Methods in Evaluation Research.* Beverly Hills, Calif.: Sage.

Cooper, Lauren. 1981. *Designing the Sites and Services Plot Allocation Process: Lessons from Project Experience.* World Bank Technical Paper 3. Washington, D.C.

Cordray, David, ed. 1985. *Utilizing Prior Research in Evaluation Planning.* New Directions for Program Evaluation 27. San Francisco: Jossey-Bass.

Cornia, Giovanni Andrea, Richard Jolly, and Francis Stewart. 1987. *Adjustment with a Human Face: Protecting the Vulnerable and Promoting Growth.* 2 vols. A study by UNICEF. Oxford. Clarendon Press.

Cowan, C., L. Murphy, and J. Weiner. 1978. *Effects of Supplemental Questions on Victimization Estimates from the National Crime Survey.* Proceedings of the American Statistical Association, Section on Survey Research Methods. Washington, D.C. American Statistical Association.

Davis, Barbara Gross. ed. 1986. *Teaching of Evaluation across the Disciplines.* New Directions for Program Evaluation 29. San Francisco: Jossey-Bass.

Davis, Ted, and Isabelle Schirmer, eds. 1987. *Sustainability Issues in Agricultural Development.* Proceedings of the Seventh Agriculture Sector Symposium. Washington D.C.: World Bank.

Deaton, Angus. 1980. *Measurement of Welfare: Theory and Practical Guidelines.* Living Standards Measurement Study. Washington, D.C.: World Bank.

Deaton, Angus, and Anne Case. *Analysis of Household Expenditures.* Living Standards Measurement Study. Washington, D.C.: World Bank.

Dennis, Michael and Robert Boruch. 1989. "Randomized Experiments for Planning and Testing Projects in Developing Countries." *Evaluation Review* 13(3):292–309.

Denzin, N. K. 1978. *The Research Act.* New York: McGraw-Hill.

Derlien, Hans-Ulrich. 1990. "Genesis and Structure of Evaluation Efforts in Comparative Perspective." In Ray Rist, ed., *Program Evaluation and the Management of Government: Patterns and Prospects.* New Brunswick, N.J.: Transaction.

de Soto, Hernan. 1989. *The Other Path: The Invisible Revolution in the Third World.* New York:Harper and Row.

Diaz-Guerrero, R. I., D. B. Reyes-Lagunes, W. H. Witzke, and Holzman. 1976. "Plaza Sesamo in Mexico: An Evaluation." *Journal of Communication* 26 (Spring):145–54.

Dilts, Russ, E. Moning, V. T. Riza, and Soekirman. 1989. "Indonesian Experience in Beneficiary Participation for Small-Scale Irrigation Development." Paper presented in the APDC/EDI Seminar, "Community Participation in Project Management." Kuala Lumpur. July 1988.

Dodge, H. F., and H. G. Romig. 1959. *Sampling Inspection Tables: Single and Double Sampling.* New York: John Wiley.

Dreitzel. H. P. 1970. *Recent Sociology.* Vol. 2: *Introduction.* London: Macmillan.

Duncan, Otis, David Featherman, and Beverly Duncan. 1972. *Socio-economic Background and Achievement.* New York: Seminar Press.

Emerson, R. 1981. "Observational Field Work." *Annual Review of Sociology* 7:351–78.

Epstein, A. L. 1969. "The Network and Urban Social Organization." In J. C. Mitchell, ed., *Social Networks in Urban Situations*. Manchester: Manchester University Press.

Erickson, K. T. 1967. "A Comment on Disguised Observation in Sociology." *Social Problems* 14 (Spring):366–73.

Esman, Milton, and Norman Uphoff. 1984. *Local Organizations: Intermediaries in Rural Development*. Ithca, N.Y.: Cornell University Press.

Evaluation Research Society Standards Committee. 1982. "Evaluation Research Society Standards for Program Evaluation." In Peter Rossi, ed., *Standards for Evaluation Practice*. New Directions for Program Evaluation 15. San Francisco: Jossey-Bass.

Fairweather, G., and L. Tornatsky. 1977. *Experimental Methods for Social Policy Research*. Chicago: Rand McNally.

Fernandez-Palacios, Marisa, and Michael Bamberger. 1984. *An Economic Evaluation of Low-cost Housing Options in El Salvador*. Water and Urban Development Department Discussion Paper. Washington, D.C.: World Bank.

Ferrero, C., and S. Boada-Martinez. 1985. "Transparencias sobre Evaluacion del Programa de Salud Rural de Costa Rica." Pan American Health Organization, Washington, D.C.

Festinger, L., H. Riecken, and S. Schachter. 1964. *When Prophecy Fails*. New York: Harper Torchbooks.

Finsterbusch, Kurt, Jasper Ingersoll, and Lynn Llewellyn, eds. 1990. *Methods for Social Analysis in Developing Countries*. Social Impact Assessment Series 17. Boulder, Colo.: Westview Press.

Fishman, Michael. 1989. "Evaluation and Congress." In Gerald Barkdoll and James Bell, eds., *Evaluation and the Federal Decision Maker*. San Francisco: Jossey-Bass.

Follain, J., and E. Jimenez. 1982. "The Demand for Housing Characteristics in Three Developing Countries: Colombia, Korea and the Philippines." Metropolitan Studies Program. World Bank, Washington, D.C.

Freeman, Howard, Peter Rossi, and Sonia Wright. 1979. "Evaluating Social Projects in Developing Countries." Organization for Economic Cooperation and Development, Paris.

Friedman, J., and D. Weinberg. 1980. "The Demand for Rental Housing: Evidence from the Housing Allowance Demand Experiment." *Journal of Urban Economics*.

Fundacion Salvadorena de Desarrollo y Vivienda Minima (FSDVM). 1976. *Evaluation of the Causes of Absenteeism and Withdrawal of Families Selected for the "La Periquera" Project in Santa Ana*. FSDVM Report 1. San Salvador, El Salvador.

———. 1977a. "Analysis of the Development Process of the El Pepeto Project." San Salvador, El Salvador.

———. 1977b. *La efectividad de la cooperativa como medio de cambio social y la definicion de las alternativas de accion para el programa de empresas comunitarias*. San Salvador.

————. 1978. "Estimation of Housing Demand in Apopa, San Salvador." San Salvador, El Salvador.

————. 1979. "Analysis of Progressive Development and Self-Help Housing." San Salvador, El Salvador.

Gans, H. 1967. *The Levittowners: Ways of Life and Politics in a New Suburban Community*. London: Allen Lane.

Garaycochea, Ignacio. 1990. "The Methodology of Social Development Evaluation." In Marsden and Oakley, eds., *Evaluating Social Development Projects*. Development Guidelines 5. Oxford: OXFAM.

Garfinkle, Harold. 1967. *Studies in Ethnomethodology*. Englewood Cliffs, N.J.: Prentice-Hall.

German Development Agency (GTZ). 1987. *ZOPP: An Introduction to the Method*. Frankfurt am Main.

Gittinger, J. P. 1982. *Economic Analysis of Agricultural Projects*. Baltimore, Md.: Johns Hopkins University Press.

Getubig, Ismael, and A. J. Ledesma, eds. 1988. *Voices from the Culture of Silence: The Most Disadvantaged Groups in Asian Agriculture*. Kuala Lumpur: Asian and Pacific Development Centre.

Goffman, E. 1961. *Essays on the Social Structure of Mental Patients and Other Inmates*. New York. Doubleday.

Goldberg, L. R. 1965. "Diagnosticians vs. Diagnostic Signs: The Diagnosis of Psychosis vs. Neurosis from the MMPI." *Psychological Monographs* 9:602.

Goma, A., M. Mwafi, A. Nagaty, M. El Rafie, S. Nasser, A. Kielman, and N. Hirschorn. 1988. "Impact of the National Control of Diarrhoeal Diseases Project on Infant and Child Mortality in Dakhalia, Egypt." *Lancet* (July 16): 145–48.

Gomez, F. 1985. "Community-based Distribution: The Case of Colombia." In M. Warner and others, eds., *Health and Family Planning in Community-Based Distribution Programs*. Boulder, Colo.: Westview Press.

Gonzalez-Polio, Edgardo, Juan Serarols, James Richard, and Michael Bamberger. 1977. *Diagnostico Sobre la Situation de Vivienda Popular en Usulutan y sus implicaciones para el proyecto "El Naranjo."* San Salvador: Salvadoran Low Cost Housing Foundation.

Gonzalez-Vega, C. 1985. "Health Improvements in Costa Rica: The Socio-Economic Background." Paper delivered at the Rockefeller Conference, Bellagio, Italy.

Gow, David. 1990. "Rapid Rural Appraisal: Social Science as Investigative Journalism." In Kurt Finsterbusch, Jasper Ingersoll, and Lynn Llewellyn, eds., *Methods for Social Analysis in Developing Countries*. Social Impact Assessment Series 17. Boulder, Colo.: Westview Press.

Gran, Guy. 1983. *Development by People: Citizen Construction of a Just World*. New York: Praeger.

Grimes, O. 1976. *Housing for Low-income Urban Families: Economics and Policy in the Developing World*. Baltimore, Md.: Johns Hopkins University Press.

Grootaert, Christiaan. 1982. *The Conceptual Basis of Measures of Household Welfare and their Implied Survey Data Requirements*. Living Standards Measurement Study Working Paper 19. Washington, D.C.: World Bank.

Grootaert, Christiaan, and K. F. Cheung. 1980. *Household Expenditure Surveys: Some Methodological Issues*. Living Standards Measurement Study. Washington, D.C.: World Bank.

Grootaert, Christiaan, and Ravi Kanbur. 1990. *Policy-Oriented Analysis of Poverty and the Social Dimensions of Structural Adjustment: A Methodology and Proposed Application to Cote d'Ivoire 1985–88*. Social Dimensions of Adjustment in Sub-Sahran Africa Policy Analysis Series. Washington, D.C.: World Bank.

Grootaert, Christiaan, and Timothy Marchant. 1991. *The Social Dimensions of Adjustment Priority Survey: An Instrument for the Rapid Identification and Monitoring of Policy Target Groups*. Social Dimensions of Adjustment Working Paper 12. Washington, D.C.: World Bank.

Grosh, Margaret. 1992. *From Platitudes to Practice: Targeting Social Programs in Latin America* Vols. 1 and 2. Regional Studies Program. Latin America and the Caribbean Technical Department. Washington D.C.: World Bank.

Guba, Egon. 1978. *Towards a Methodology of Naturalistic Enquiry in Educational Evaluation*. CSE Monograph Series in Evaluation 8. Los Angeles: University of California Center for the Study of Evaluation.

Guba, Egon, and Yvonna Lincoln. 1987. "The Countenances of Fourth Generation Evaluation: Description, Judgement and Negotiation." In Dennis Palumbo, ed., *The Politics of Program Evaluation*. Beverly Hills, Calif.: Sage.

HAM-BIRF. 1983. "Design for an Evaluation of an Artisan Credit Program." Honorable Alcaldia Municipal. La Paz, Bolivia.

Harbison, Ralph, and Erik Hanushek. 1992. *Educational Performance of the Poor: Lessons from Rural Northeast Brazil*. New York: Oxford University Press.

Harlan, J. R. 1977. "The Plants and Animals that Nourish Man." In *Scientific American Book, Food and Agriculture*. San Franciso: Freeman.

Hartwig, Frederick, and Brian Dearing. 1979. *Exploratory Data Analysis*. Quantitative Applications in the Social Sciences 16. Beverly Hills, Calif.: Sage.

Hatry, H., R. Winnie, and D. Fisk. 1981. *Practical Program Evaluation for State and Local Governments*. Washington, D.C.: Urban Institute.

Hays, William. 1977. *Statistics for the Social Sciences* New York: Holt, Rinehart and Winston.

Heaver, Richard. 1988. "Improving Family Planning, Health and Nutrition Outreach in India: Lessons from Some World Bank Assisted Projects." New Delhi: World Bank. Processed.

Henderson, R. H., and T. Sundaresan. 1982. "Cluster Sampling to Assess Immuniza-tion Coverage: A Review of Experience with a Simplified Sampling Method." *Bulletin of the World Health Organization* 60:253–60.

Hendricks, Michael. 1981. "Service Delivery Assessment: Qualitative Evaluations at the Cabinet Level." In N. Smith, ed., *Federal Efforts to Develop New Evaluation Methods*. San Francisco: Jossey-Bass.

Herrera, A., and M. Baro. 1978. *Ley y orden en un meson de San Salvador* (Law and order in a meson in San Salvador). San Salavador, El Salvador: Fundacion Salvadorena de Desarrollo y Vivienda Minima.

Heynemann, S., D. Jamison, and Montenegro. 1984. "Textbooks in the Philippines: Evaluation of the Pedagocical Impact of a Nationwide Investment." *Educational Evaluation and Policy Analysis* 6(2).

Heyzer, Noeleen, ed. 1985. *Missing Women: Development Planning in Asia and the Pacific*. Kuala Lumpur: Asian and Pacific Development Centre.

———, ed. 1987. *Women Farmers and Rural Change in Asia: Towards Equal Access and Participation*. Kuala Lumpur: Asian and Pacific Development Centre.

———. 1992. *Gender Issues in Anti-Poverty Programmes in Asia: Experience and Issues*, Washington, D.C.: Economic Development Institute.

Hill, J. M., M. E. Woods, and S. D. Dorsey. 1988. "A Human Development Interven-tion in the Philippines: Effect on Child Morbidity." *Social Science Medicine* 27(11):1183–88.

Hollnsteiner, Mary. 1973. "Reciprocity in the Lowland Philippines." In F. Lynch and A. Guzman, eds., *Four Readings on Philippine Values*. Institute of Philippine Cul-ture. Ateneo de Manila University Press.

Honadle, G. 1979. "Rapid Reconnaissance Approaches to Organizational Analysis for Development Administration." Paper presented at the Conference on Rapid Rural Appraisal held at the Institute for Development Studies, Sussex.

Honadle, George, and Gerry VanSant. 1985. *Implementation for Sustainability: Lessons from Integrated Rural Development*. West Hartford, Conn.: Kumarian Press.

Hunting, Gordon, Manuel Zymelmann, and Godfrey Martin. 1986. *Evaluating Vocational Training Programs: A Practical Guide*. Washington, D.C.: World Bank.

Husserl, Edmund. 1960. *Cartesian Meditations: An Introduction to Phenomenology*. Atlantic Highlands, N.J.: Humanities Press.

Ianni, Francis, and Margaret Terry Orr. 1979. "Toward a Rapprochement of Quan-titative and Qualitative Methodologies." In T. Cook and C. Reichardt, eds., *Qualitative and Quantitative Methods in Evaluation Research*. Beverly Hills, Calif.: Sage.

India, Department of Rural Development. 1990. *Concurrent Evaluation of IRDP: The Main Findings of the Survey for January 1989-December 1989*. Delhi: Ministry of Agriculture.

————, Ministry of Programme Implementation. 1987. *Towards a Goal Oriented Management of Production, Projects and Programmes: Annual Report 1986–87.* New Dehli. India.

————, Programme Evaluation Organization. 1985. *Evaluation Report on Integrated Rural Development Programme.* New Delhi: Government of India Planning Commission.

Ingersoll, Jasper. 1990. "Social Analysis in AID and the World Bank." In Kurt Finsterbusch, Jasper Ingersoll, and Lynn Llewellyn, eds., *Methods for Social Analysis in Developing Countries.* Social Impact Assessment Series 17. Boulder Colo.: Westview Press.

Instituto SER de Investigation. 1981. *Modelo e evaluacion de impacto del programa IPC Linea de Base.* 2 vols. Bogota.

————. 1984. "Diagnostico Evaluativo del Avance del Programa IPC." IFT-072. Bogota.

International Development Research Centre. 1982. *Low Income Urban Shelter Projects: An Annotated Bibliography of Research Funded by IDRC-IBRD.* Ottawa, Canada.

IUCN. 1980. *World Conservation Strategy.* Gland, Switzerland.

Jha, Satish. 1987. "Rural Development in Asia: Issues and Perspectives." *Asian Development Review* 5(1):83–99.

Jimenez, Emmanuel. 1980. *The Economics of Self-Help Housing: Theory and Some Evidence.* Urban and Regional Report 80-16. Washington, D.C.: World Bank, Urban and Regional Economics Division.

————. 1982. "The Value of Squatter Dwellings in Developing Countries." *Economic Development and Cultural Change* 30(4):739–52.

Jimenez, Emmanuel, Bernardo Kugler, and Robin Horn. 1989. "National in-Service Training Systems in Latin America: An Economic Evaluation of Colombia's SENA." *Economic Development and Cultural Change* 37(3):595–610.

Kanbur, Ravi. 1990. *Poverty and the Social Dimensions of Structural Adjustment in Cote D'Ivoire.* Washington, D.C.: World Bank.

Jorgensen, Steen, Margaret Grosh, and Mark Shacter. 1992. *Bolivia's Answer to Poverty, Economic Crisis, and Adjustment: The Emergency Social Fund.* Regional and Sectoral Studies. Washington, D.C.: World Bank.

Kapferer, B. 1973. "Social Network and Conjugal Role in Urban Zambia: Towards a Reformulation of the Bott Hypothesis." In J. Boissevain and J. C. Mitchell, eds., *Network Analysis: Studies in Human Interaction.* The Hague: Mouton.

Kaplan, M. 1973. *Urban Planning in the 1960s: A Design for Irrelevancy.* New York: Praeger.

Katzin, Margaret Fisher. 1973. "The Jamaican Country Higgler." In Lambros Comitas and David Lowenthal, eds., *Work and Family Life: West Indian Perspectives.* New York: Anchor Books.

Kaufmann, Dani. 1982. "Social Interactions as a Strategy of Survival among the Urban Poor: A Theory and Some Evidence." Ph.D. diss. Harvard University, Cambridge, Mass.

Kaufmann, Dani, and David Lindauer. 1980. *Basic Needs, Interhousehold Transfers and the Extended Family*. Urban and Regional Report 80-15. Washington, D.C.: World Bank, Urban and Regional Economics Division.

Kaufman, Daniel, and Michael Bamberger. 1984. *Income Transfers and Urban Projects: Research Findings and Policy Issues*. Water Supply and Urban Development Department Discussion Paper 56. Washington, D.C.: World Bank.

Keare, D., and E. Jimenez. 1983. *Progressive Development and Affordability in the Design of Urban Shelter Projects*. World Bank Staff Working Paper 547. Washington, D.C.

Keare, D., and S. Parris. 1982. *Evaluation of Shelter Programs for the Poor: Principal Findings*. World Bank Staff Working Paper 547. Washington, D.C.

Kennedy, S. D., and J. McMillan. 1979. "Participation under Alternative Housing Allowance Programs: Evidence from the Housing Allowance Demand Experiment." Abt Associates.

Kenya, Central Bureau of Statistics. 1982. "National Urban Household Survey Program, 1980–84: Urban Areas." Nairobi.

Keohane and Nye. 1977. *Power and Interdependence in the International System*. Boston: Little, Brown.

Khan, Adil. 1989. *A South Asian Regional Study on Current Thoughts and Practices in Monitoring and Evaluation Economic Development Institute*. Washington D.C.: World Bank, Economic Development Institute.

_____. 1990. *Monitoring and Evaluation of Development Projects in South East Asia: the Experience of Indonesia, Malaysia, the Philippines and Thailand*. Washington, D.C.: World Bank, Economic Development Institute.

Khan, Akbar Ali, Abdul Muyeed Chowdhury, Md. Aminul Islam Bhuiyan, and A. H .M Nizamuddin. 1987. "Sustainability of Rural Development Projects: A Case Study of Rural Development 1 Project in Bangladesh." Dhaka, Bangladesh Public Administration Training Centre.

Khan, Muhammad Akram. 1991. "Performance Evaluation in Pakistan." Paper presented at a conference on Performance Evaluation in Asia and the Pacific. Kuala Lumpur.

Khun, Thomas. 1970. *The Structure of Scientific Revolutions*. Chicago: University of Chicago Press.

Kielman, A., A. Mobarak, M. Hammamy, A. Goma, S. Abou-El-Saad, R. Lotfi, I. Mazen, and A. Nagarty. 1985. "Control of Deaths from Diarrhoeal Disease in Rural Communities: I. Design of an Intervention Study and Effects on Child Mortality." *Tropical Medicine and Parasitology* 36:191–98.

Kielman, A., A. Nagaty, and C. A. Ajello. 1986. "Control of Deaths from Diarrhoeal Disease in Rural Communities: II. Motivating and Monitoring the Community." *Tropical Medicine and Parasitology* 37:15–21.

Kirk, Jerome, and Marc Miller. 1986. *Reliability and Validity in Qualitative Research.* Beverly Hills, Calif.: Sage.

Kish, Leslie. 1965. *Survey Sampling.* New York: John Wiley.

Knowles, James, and Richard Anker. 1981. "An Analysis of Income Transfers in a Developing Country: The Case of Kenya." *Journal of Development Economics* 8:205–26.

Kumar, Krishna. 1987. *Conducting Group Interviews in Developing Countries.* Program Design and Evaluation Methodology Report 8. Washington, D.C.: U.S. Agency for International Development.

———. 1989. *Conducting Key Informant Interviews in Developing Countries.* Program Design and Methodology Report 13. Washington, D.C.: U.S. Agency for International Development.

———, ed. 1993. *Rapid Appraisal Methods.* Regional and Sectoral Studies. Washington, D.C.: World Bank.

Lamb, Geoffrey, and Rachel Weaving. 1992. *Managing Policy Reform in the Real World: Asian Experiences.* Economic Development Institute Seminar Series. Washington D.C.: World Bank.

Lemeshow, Stanley A., and George Stroh, Jr. 1989. "Quality Assurance Sampling for Evaluating Health Parameters in Developing Countries." *Survey Methodology* 15:71–81.

Lemeshow, Stanley A., Tserkovnyi, J. L. Tulloch, J. E. Dowd, S. K. Lwanga, and J. Keja. "A Computer Simulation of the EPI Survey Strategy." *International Journal of Epidemiology* 14(3):473–81.

Lenski, G., and J. Leggett. 1960. "Caste, Class and Deference in the Research Interview." *American Journal of Sociology* 65:463–67.

Levin, Henry. 1984. *Cost Effectiveness Analysis.* Beverly Hills, Calif.: Sage.

Lewis, Oscar. 1961. *The Children of Sanchez.* New York: Random House.

Lewis-Beck, Michael. 1980. *Applied Regression: An Introduction.* Quantitative Applications in the Social Sciences 22. Beverly Hills, Calif.: Sage.

Liebow, Elliot. 1967. *Tally's Corner.* Boston: Little, Brown.

Light, Richard. 1984. "Six Evaluation Issues That Synthesis Can Resolve Better Than Single Studies." In Yeaton and Wortman, eds., *Issues in Data Synthesis.* New Directions for Program Evaluation 24. San Francisco: Jossey-Bass.

Lindauer, David. 1979. "Sources of Income, Selection Strategies and Project Affordability." World Bank, Urban and Regional Economics Division, Washington, D.C.

Little, Ian, and Mirlees, James. 1974. *Project Appraisal and Planning for Developing Countries.* New York: Basic Books.

———. 1991. "Project Appraisal and Planning Twenty Years On." *World Bank Economic Review.* Suppl.

Lofland, L. 1966. *In the Presence of Strangers: A Study of Behaviour in Public Settings.* Working Paper 19. University of Michigan, Center for Research on Social Organization.

———. 1971. *Analyzing Social Settings: A Guide to Qualitative Observation and Analysis.* Belmont, Calif.: Wadsworth.

Lofland, J., and R. A. Lejeune. 1960. "Initial Interaction of Newcomers in Alcoholics Anonymous: A Field Experiment in Class Symbols and Socialization." *Social Problems* 8:102–11.

Lofland, J., and L. Lofland. 1969. *Deviance and Identity.* Englewood Cliffs, N.J.: Prentice-Hall.

Loft, A., T. F. Anderson, and M. Madsen. 1989. "A Quasi-Experimental Design Based on Regional Variations: Discussion of a Method for Evaluating Outcomes of Medical Practice" *Social Science in Medicine* 28(2):147–54.

Lomnitz, L. 1977. *Networks and Marginality: Life in a Mexican Shantytown.* New York: Academic Press.

Lusaka Housing Project Evaluation Team. 1979. "An Attempt at Assessment of Project Affordability." Lusaka Housing Project Unit. Lusaka, Zambia.

Lycette, M., and K. White. 1989. "Improving Women's Access to Credit in Latin America and the Caribbean." In M. Berger and M. Buvonic, eds., *Women's Ventures: Assistance to the Informal Sector in Latin America.* West Hartford, Conn.: Kumarian Press.

McCall, George, and J. L. Simmons. 1969 . *Issues in Participant Observation: A Text and Reader.* Reading, Mass.: Addison-Wesley.

McCain, L. J., and R. McCleary. 1979. "The Statistical Analysis of the Simple Interrupted Time Series Quasi-Experiment." In T. D. Cook and D. T. Campbell, eds., *Quasi-Experimentation: Design and Analysis Issues for Field Settings.* Chicago: Rand McNally.

McLeary, R., and others. 1979. "How a Regression Artifact Can Make Any Delinquency Interventional Program Look Effective." *Evaluation Studies Annual Review* 4:626–33.

McMillan, Della. 1987. "Monitoring the Evolution of Household Economic Systems over Time in Farming Systems Research." *Development and Change* 18(2):295–314.

———. 1993. "Diversification and Successful Settlement in the River Blindness Control Zone of West Africa." *Human Organization.*

McMillan, Della, Jean-Baptiste Nana, and Kimseyinga Savadogo. 1993. *Settlement and Development in the River Blindness Zone. Case Study: Burkina Faso.* Technical Paper 200. Washington, D.C.: World Bank.

Malpezzi, Stephen. 1984. *Analyzing an Urban Housing Survey: Economic Models and Statistical Techniques.* Water Supply and Urban Development Department Discussion Paper 52. Washington, D.C.: World Bank.

Malpezzi, Stephen, Michael Bamberger, and Stephen Mayo. 1982. *Planning an Urban Housing Survey: Key Issues for Researchers and Program Managers in Developing*

*Countries.* Water Supply and Urban Development Department Discussion Paper 44. Washington, D.C.: World Bank.

Mangin, William. 1967. "Latin American Squatter Settlements: A Problem and a Solution." *Latin American Research Review* 2(3):65–98.

Marsden, David, and Peter, Oakley, eds. 1990. *Evaluating Social Development Projects.* Development Guidelines 5. Oxford: OXFAM.

Martin, Pat. 1989. *Community Participation in Health and Population Programs.* Economic Development Institute Paper 076/004. Washington, D.C.: World Bank.

Matorell, Reynaldo. 1982. *Nutrition and Health Status Indicators: Suggestions for Surveys of the Standard of Living in Developing Countries.* Living Standards Measurement Study. Washington, D.C.: World Bank.

Maya Tech Corporation. 1991. *How to Conduct a Workshop to Integrate Gender Considerations into Development Planning: A Trainers Manual.* Silver Spring, Md.: USAID Office of Women in Development.

Maynard, R., and R. Murname. 1981. "The Effects of Negative Income Tax on School Performance: Results of an Experiment." *Evaluation Studies Annual Review* 6.

Mayo, Stephen. 1983. "Housing Demand in Developing Countries." World Bank, Water Supply and Urban Development Department. Washington, D.C.

Mehran, Farnad. 1980. *Employment Data for the Measurement of Living Standards* Living Standards Measurement Study. Washington, D.C.: World Bank.

Meier, P. 1978. "The Biggest Public Health Experiment Ever: The 1954 Trial of the Salk Poliomyelitis Vaccine." In J.M. Tanur and associates, eds., *Statistics: a Guide to the Unknown.* San Francisco. Holden-Day.

Middleton, John, James Terry, and Deborah Bloch. 1989. *Building Educational Evaluation Capacity in Developing Countries.* Policy, Planning, and Research Working Paper 140. Washington, D.C.: World Bank.

Middleton, R. 1985. "The Philippine Radio Education Project: A Case Study of Decision, Design and Interaction." In M. B. Miles and A. M. Huberman, eds., *Qualitative Data Analysis: A Sourcebook of New Methods.* Beverly Hills, Calif.: Sage.

Miles, M., and A. M. Huberman, eds. 1984. *Qualitative Data Analysis: A Sourcebook of New Methods.* Beverly Hills, Calif.: Sage.

Miller, C. M., and R. G. Knapp. 1979. "Item Inspection Control." In *Evaluating Quality of Care: Analytic Procedures-Monitoring Techniques.* Rockville, Md.: Aspen.

Miller, W. 1958. "Lower Class Culture as a Generating Mileau of Gang Delinquency." *Journal of Social Issues* 14:5–19.

Mitchell, Robert. 1982. "A Note on the Use of the Contingent Valuation Approach to Value Public Services in Developing Nations." World Bank, Country Policy Department, Washington, D.C.

Moffat, R. 1981. "The Labor Reply Response in the Gary Experiment." *Evaluation Studies Annual Review* 6:289–99.

Moock, Joyce. 1978. "The Content and Maintenance of Social Ties between Urban Migrants and Their Home-Based Support Groups: The Maragoli Case." *African Urban Studies* 3.

Moore, J. W., and others. 1978. *Homeboys: Gangs, Drugs and Prison in the Barrios of Los Angeles*. Philadelphia: Temple University Press.

Morgan, Gareth, ed. 1983. *Beyond Method: Strategies for Social Research*. Beverly Hills, Calif.: Sage.

Morris, Lynn Lyons, and Carol Taylor Fitz-Gibbon. 1978. *Evaluator's Handbook*. Beverly Hills, Calif.: Sage.

Moser, Carolyn. 1989. *Approaches to Community Participation in Urban Development Programs in Third World Countries*. Economic Development Institute Study 076/003. Washington, D.C.: World Bank.

Mukras, Mohammed, and Oucho, John. 1982. "Migration, Remittances and Rural Development in Kenya. A Preliminary Report." Nairobi.

Muller, M. 1975. *Actions and Interactions: Social Relationships in a Low-Income Housing Estate in Kitale, Kenya*. Stationsplein, Leiden: Afrika-Studicentrum.

Murdock, G. P. 1967. *Ethnographic Atlas*. Pittsburgh: University of Pittsburgh Press.

Murphy, Josette, and Marchant, Tim. 1988. *Monitoring and Evaluation in Extension Agencies*. Technical Paper 79. Washington, D.C.: World Bank.

Murphy, Josette, and L. Sprey. 1980. "The Volta Valley Authority: Socioeconomic Evolution of a Resettlement Project in Upper Volta." West Lafayette, Ind.: Purdue University, Department of Agricultural Economics.

Nachmias, David, and Chava Nachmias. 1981. *Research Methods in the Social Sciences*. New York: St. Martin's Press.

Naroll, Roaul, and Cohen, Ronald. 1970. *A Handbook on Cultural Anthroplogy*. New York: Natural History Press.

Nathan, R., and others. 1981. *Public Service Employment: A Field Evaluation*. Washington, D.C.: Brookings Institution.

Nelson, N. 1978. "Female-Centered Families: Changing Patterns of Marriage and Family among Buzaa Brewers of Mathare Valley." *African Urban Studies* 3. Michigan State University.

———. 1979. "Women Must Help Each Other: The Operation of Personal Networks among Buzaa Beer Brewers in Mathare Valley, Kenya." In *Women United, Women Divided: Comparative Studies of Ten Contemporary Cultures*. Indiana University Press.

Nepal, V. N., and N. N. Nepal. 1991. "Performance Evaluation System in Nepal: Country Overview." Paper presented at a conference on Performance Evaluation in Asia and the Pacific. Kuala Lumpur.

Newcomer, Kathryn, and Joseph Wholey. 1989. "Evaluation Strategies for Building High-Performance Programs." In J. Wholey, K. Newcomer, and Associates, eds.,

*Improving Government Performance: Evaluation Strategies for Strengthening Public Agencies and Programs*. San Francisco: Jossey-Bass.

Ng, Cecilia, Siti Nor Hamid, and Syed Husin Ali. 1987. "Rural Development Programmes, Women's Participation and Organizations in Malaysia." In Noeleen Heyzer, ed., *Women Farmers and Rural Change in Asia: Towards Sexual Access and Equality*. Kuala Lumpur: Asian and Pacific Development Centre.

Nie, Norman, Hadlai Hull, Jean Jenkins, Karin Steinbrenner and Dale Dent. 1975. *Statistical Package for the Social Sciences*. 2d ed. New York: McGraw-Hill.

Nieves, Isobel. 1979. "Household Arrangements and Multiple Jobs in San Salvador" *Signs: Journal of Women in Culture and Society* 5(1).

Nisbett, R. E., and L. Ross. 1980. *Human Inference: Strategies and Shortcomings of Social Judgement*. Englewood-Cliffs, N.J.: Prentice-Hall.

Nucleo de Acompanhamento e Avaliacão. 1983. *Desenvolvimento da Pesca Artesanal* (Development of Artesan Fishing). Natal, Brazil: World Bank Medium Cities Project.

Operations Research Group Baroda. 1975. "Monitoring and Evaluation Design for the First Madras Urban Project." Madras Metropolitan Development Authority.

Organization for Economic Cooperation and Development (OECD). 1986. *Methods and Procedures in Aid Evaluation*. Paris.

Osborne, David, and Gaebler, Ted. 1992. *Reinventing Government: How the Entrepreneurial Spirit Is Transforming the Public Sector*. New York: Addison-Wesley.

O'Sullivan, Neil. 1993. "Identification and Design of Poverty Alleviation Projects." In Michael Bamberger and Abdul Aziz, eds. 1993. *The Design and Management of Sustainable Poverty Alleviation Programs; The South Asian Experience*. EDI Seminar Series. Washington, D.C.: World Bank, Economic Development Institute.

Overholt, Catherine, Mary Anderson, Kathleen Cloud, and James Austin. 1985. *Gender Roles in Development Projects: A Case Book*. West Hartford, Conn.: Kumarian Press.

Palumbo, Dennis, ed. 1987. *The Politics of Program Evaluation*. Beverly Hills, Calif.: Sage.

Parris, Scott. 1984. *Survival Strategies and Support Networks: An Anthropological Perspective*. Report UDD-58 Urban and Regional Economics Division. Washington, D.C.: World Bank.

Pasteur, David. 1979. *The Management of Squatter Upgrading*. Saxon House. England.

Patton, Michael Q. 1978. *Utilization-Focussed Evaluation*. Beverly Hills, Calif.: Sage.

———. 1980. *Qualitative Evaluation*. Beverly Hills, Calif.: Sage.

———. 1982. *Practical Evaluation*. Beverly Hills, Calif.: Sage.

———. 1987. "Evaluation's Political Inherency: Practical Implications for Design and Use." In Dennis Palumbo, ed., *The Politics of Program Evaluation*. Beverly Hills, Calif.: Sage.

Payne, Stanley. 1951. *The Art of Asking Questions*. Princeton, N.J.: Princeton University Press.

Peattie, Lisa. 1968. *The View from the Barrio*. Ann Arbor: University of Michigan Press.

———. 1981. "Marginal Settlements in Developing Countries." *Annual Review of Sociology*, 157–75.

Perrett, Heli. 1984. "Monitoring and Evaluation of Communication Support Activities in Low-Cost Sanitation Projects." Technical Assistance Group Technical Note 11. UNDP Interregional Project for the International Drinking Water Supply and Sanitation Decade. World Bank, Washington, D.C.

Peru, Population Council. 1986. "An Experimental Study of the Efficiency and Effectiveness of an IUD Insertion and Back-up Component (English summary of first six-month report. PC PES86). Lima, Peru: Population Council.

Pfefferman , Guy, and Griffin, Charles. 1989. *Nutrition and Health Programs in Latin America: Targeting Social Expenditures*. Washington, D.C.: World Bank.

Philippine National Housing Authority. 1978. *A Study of Income and Expenditure Patterns of Households in the Tondo Foreshore Area*. Manila: Research and Analysis Division.

———. 1979a. *A Study of the Community Participation Process in Tondo*. Manila: Research and Analysis Division.

———. 1979b. *A Study of the Impact of the Project on the Physical Environment of Tondo*. Manila: Research and Analysis Division.

———. 1980. *An Evaluation of the Housing Materials Loan Program of the Tondo Foreshore-Dagat Dagatan Development Project*. Manila: Research and Analysis Division.

———. 1981. *The Reblocking Process in Tondo Foreshore*. Manila: Research and Analysis Division.

Polsby, Nelson. 1963. *Community Power and Political Theory*. New Haven, Conn.: Yale University Press.

Practical Concepts Incorporated. 1979. *The Logical Framework: A Manager's Guide to a Scientific Approach to Design and Evaluation*. Washington, D.C.

Psacharopoulos, George, and William Loxley. 1985. *Diversified Secondary Education and Development: Evidence from Colombia and Tanzania*. Baltimore, Md.: Johns Hopkins University Press.

Pugh, Derek. 1983. "Studying Organizational Structure and Process." In Gareth Morgan, ed., *Beyond Method: Strategies for Social Research*. Beverly Hills, Calif.: Sage.

Quigley, John. 1980. *The Distributional Consequences of Stylized Housing Projects: Theory and Empirical Analysis*. Urban and Regional Report 80-18. Washington, D.C.: World Bank, Urban and Regional Economics Department.

Rao, Aruna, Mary Anderson, and Catherine Overholt. 1991. *Gender Analysis in Development Planning: A Case Book*. Hartford, Conn.: Kumarian Press.

Ramanujam, P. 1991. "Performance Evaluation in Sri Lanka: Country Overivew." Paper presented at a conference on Performance Evaluation in Asia and the Pacific. Kuala Lumpur.

Reforma, Mila, and Ricci Obusan. 1981. *Household Networks and Survival Strategies among the Urban Poor: Monetary and Non-monetary Transfers among Selected Families in Tondo.* Urban and Regional Report 81-22. Washington, D.C.: World Bank, Urban and Regional Economics Division.

Reichardt, R. 1979. "The Statistical Analysis of Data from Non-equivalent Group Designs." In T. Cook and D. Campbell, eds., *Quasi Experimentation: Design and Analysis for Field Settings.* Chicago: Rand McNally.

Reichardt, Charles, and Thomas Cook. 1979. "Beyond Quantitative versus Qualitative Methods." In Cook and Reichardt, *Qualitative and Quantitative Methods in Evaluation Research.* Beverly Hills, Calif.: Sage.

Richard, James, and Michael Bamberger. 1977. *Economic Evaluation of Sites and Service Programs and Their Accessibility to Low-income Groups in El Salvador.* Evaluation Report 16. San Salvador: Fundacion Salvadorena de Vivienda Minima.

Rist, Ray, ed., 1990. *Program Evaluation and the Management of Government: Patterns and Prospects across Eight Nations.* London. Transaction.

Roberts, B. 1969. "Politics in a Neighborhood of Guatemala City." *Sociology* 2(2): 185–203.

Robinson, John, Robert Athanasiou, and Kendra Head. 1969. *Measures of Occupational Attitudes and Occupation Characteristics.* Ann Arbor: University of Michigan, Institute for Social Research.

Rogers, Everett. 1962. *Diffusion of Innovations.* New York: Free Press.

Ross, H. L., D. T. Campbell, and G. V. Glass. 1970. "Determining the Social Effects of a Legal Reform: The British 'Breathalizer': Crackdown of 1967." *American Behavioural Scientist*, March/April.

Rossi, P. H., and H. E. Freeman. 1993 *Evaluation: A Systematic Approach.* 5th ed. Beverly Hills, Calif.: Sage.

Rossi, P., and W. Williams. 1972. *Evaluating Social Programs.* New York: Academic Press.

————, eds. 1972. *Evaluating Social Programs: Theory Practice and Politics.* New York: Seminar Press.

Rossi, Peter, and James Wright. 1984. "Evaluation Research: An Assessment." *Annual Review of Sociology* 10:331–52.

Roy, Dunu. 1985. "The Politics of Environment." In *The State of India's Environment 1984–85: Second Citizen's Report.* New Delhi: Centre for Science and Environment.

Ruogu, Li. 1991. "Performance Evaluation of Foreign Financed Projects in China." Paper presented at a conference on Performance Evaluation in Asia and the Pacific. Kuala Lumpur.

Sáenz, L. 1985. *Salud Sin Riqueza: El Caso de Costa Rica.* Costa Rica: Ministry of Health.

Salmen, Lawrence. 1983. *Participant Observer Evaluation of Urban Projects in La Paz, Bolivia and Guayaquil, Ecuador.* Water Supply and Urban Development Department Discussion Paper. Washington, D.C.: World Bank.

———. 1987. *Listen to the People: Participant Observer Evaluation of Development Projects.* New York: Oxford University Press.

———. 1992. "Beneficiary Assessment: An Approach Described." Washington,D.C.: World Bank.

Sang, Heng-Kang. 1988. *Project Evaluation: Techniques and Practices for Developing Countries.* New York: Wilson Pess.

Satia, J. 1993. *The Access of the Poor to Primary Health and Nutrition in South Asia.* Washington, D.C.: World Bank, Economic Development Institute.

Schuman, H., and Jean Presser. 1981. *Questions and Answers in Attitude Surveys: Experiments on Question Form, Wording and Content.* New York: Academic Press.

Schutz, Alfred. 1967. *The Phenomenology of the Social World.* Evanston, Ill.: Northwestern University Press.

Schwandt, Thomas, and Edward Halpern. 1988. *Linking Auditing and MetaEvaluation: Enhancing Quality in Applied Research.* Applied Social Research Methods Series. Beverly Hills, Calif.: Sage.

Scrimshaw, Susan, and Elena Hurtado. 1987. *Rapid Assessment Procedures for Nutrition and Primary Health Care: Anthropological Approaches to Improving Program Effectiveness.* Tokyo: United Nations University.

Scriven, Michael. 1967. *The Methodology of Evaluation.* AERA Monograph Series in Curriculum Evaluation 1. Chicago: Rand McNally.

Searle, Barbara, ed. 1985. *Evaluation in World Bank Education Projects: Lessons from Three Case Studies.* Operations Policy Staff Paper. Washington D.C.: World Bank, Education and Training Department.

Searle, Barbara, P. Matthews, P. Suppes, and J. Friend. 1978. "Formal Evaluation of the Radio Mathematics Program, Nicaragua Grade 1, 1976." In T. D. Cook and associates, eds., *Evaluation Studies Review Annual,* vol 3. Beverly Hills, Calif.: Sage.

Segura, Edilberto. 1985. *Guidelines for Evaluating the Management Information Systems of Industrial Enterprises.* World Bank Technical Paper 47. Washington, D.C.

Selvaraj, N., Mahmod Modisi, and Kiyau Loo Lee. 1988. "Review of Monitoring and Evaluation Training in South East Asia." Paper prepared for an international seminar, "The Design and Management of Monitoring and Evaluation in South East Asia," Kuala Lumpur, INTAN.

Senegal, Bureau d'Evaluation. 1976. *Second Housing Survey—The Control Group from Gran Dakar.* Dakar: Office D'Habitation de Loyer Modere.

———. 1977. *The Target Population of the Sites and Services Project. The Effect of the Selection Process on Some Social and Economic Variables.* Report III-6. Dakar: Office D'Habitation de Loyer Modere.

———. 1978. *Study of Purchasers of Serviced Lots Who Have Not Begun Construction of Their Houses.* Series 3, no. 3. Dakar: Office D'Habitation de Loyer Modere.

————. 1979. *Study of House Construction in the Sites and Services Project*. Series 4, No. 2. Dakar: Office D'Habitation de Loyer Modere.

Siegel, Sidney. 1956. *Non-Parametric Statistics for the Behavioral Sciences*. New York: McGraw-Hill.

Silas, Johan. 1988. "Community Participation and Urban Development: Issues and Experiences in Surabaya." Presented at APDC/EDI seminar, "Community Participation."

Sjamsu, Asmarni, and Rantetana, Marcellus. 1991. "Performance Evaluation as a Management Tool: the Experience of Indonesia." Paper presented at a conference on Performance Evaluation in Asia and the Pacific. Kuala Lumpur.

Slade, Roger, and R. Noronha. 1984. "An Operational Guide to the Monitoring and Evaluation of Social Forestry in India." World Bank, Washington D.C.

Squire, Lyn, and Herman Van der Tak. 1975. *The Economic Analysis of Projects*. Baltimore, Md.: Johns Hopkins University Press.

Stack, Carol. 1974. *All Our Kin: Strategies for Survival in a Black Community*. New York: Harper and Row.

Staub, William. 1990. "The Development and Evolution of Project Benefit Monitoring and Evaluation in Projects Financed by the Asian Development Bank." In INTAN, *Monitoring and Evaluation of Development Projects: The East Asian Experience*. Kuala Lumpur.

Stokke, Olav, ed. 1991a. *Evaluating Development Assistance: Policies and Performance*. London: Frank Cass.

————. 1991b. "Policies, Performance and Trends in Aid Evaluation." In Olav Stokke, ed., *Evaluating Development Assistance: Policies and Performance*. London: Frank Cass.

Strassman, P. 1982. *The Transformation of Urban Housing*. Baltimore, Md.: Johns Hopkins University Press.

Stren, Richard. 1978. *Housing the Urban Poor in Africa. Policy, Politics and Bureaucracy in Mombasa*. Berkeley, Calif.: University of California Institute of International Studies.

Struening, Elmer, and Marilynn Brewer. 1983. *Handbook of Evaluation Research*. Beverly Hills, Calif.: Sage.

Struyk, R., and M. Bendick, eds. 1981. *Housing Vouchers for the Poor: Lessons from a National Experiment*. Washington, D.C.: Urban Institute.

Sudman, Seymor, and Graham Kalton. 1986. "New Developments in the Sampling of Special Populations." *Annual Review of Sociology* 12:401–29.

Sullivan, Jeremiah, Susan Cochrane, and William Kalsbeek. 1982. *Procedures for Collecting and Analyzing Mortality Data in LSMS*. Living Standards Measurement Study. Washington, D.C.: World Bank.

Suttles, Gerald. 1968. *The Social Order of the Slum: Ethnicity and Territoriality in the Inner City*. Chicago: University of Chicago Press.

Thompson, M. S. 1980. *Benefit-Cost Analysis for Program Evaluation*. Beverly Hills, Calif.: Sage.

Tisdell, Clem. 1988. "Sustainable Development: Differing Perspectives of Ecologists and Economists, and Relevance to LDCs." *World Development* 16(3): 373–84.

Tolchin, Susan. 1987. "The Political Uses of Evaluation Research: Cost-Benefit Analysis and the Cotton Dust Standard." In Dennis Palumbo, ed., *The Politics of Program Evaluation*. Beverly Hills, Calif.: Sage.

Turner, C. F., and E. Krauss. 1978. "Fallible Indicators of the Subjective State of the Nation." *American Psychologist* 33:456–70.

Turner, John. 1968. "Uncontrolled Urban Settlement: Problems and Policies." International Social Development.

Unidade de Avaliacao (Campina Grande). 1984. "Estudo Rapido de Acompanhamento de Projeto de Apoio as Atividades Produtivas" ("Rapid Monitoring Study of a Project Providing Support to Productive Activities"). Prefeitura Municipal de Campina Grande, Paraiba, Brazil.

United Nations ACC Task Force on Rural Development. 1984. *Guiding Principles for the Design and Use of Monitoring and Evaluation in Rural Development Projects and Programmes.* Panel on Monitoring and Evaluation. Rome.

United Nations Centre for Human Development. 1992. *The Housing Indicators Program Extensive Survey: Preliminary Results.* Washington, D.C.: World Bank.

———. 1993. *The Housing Indicators Program.* Vol. 1: *Report of the Executive Director.* Washington, D.C.: World Bank.

United Nations Industrial Development Organization (UNIDO). 1972. *Guidelines for Project Evaluation.* New York. United Nations.

United Nations Statistical Office. 1980. *Towards More Effective Measurement of Levels of Living and Review of Work of the United Nations Statistical Office Related to Statistics of Levels of Living.* Living Standards Measurement Study Working Paper 4. Washington, D.C.: World Bank.

Uphoff, Norman. 1986. *Improving International Irrigation Management with Farmer Participation: Getting the Process Right.* Boulder, Colo.: Westview Press.

———. 1988. *Approaches to Community Participation in Agriculture and Rural Development.* Course Note 076/005. Washington, D.C.: World Bank, Economic Development Institute.

U.S. Agency for International Development (USAID). 1980a. *Central America: Small Farmer Cropping Systems.* Impact Evaluation Series 14 (PN-AAH-977). Washington, D.C.

———. 1980b. *Philippines Small-Scale Irrigation.* Impact Evaluation Series 4 (PN-AAH-749). Washington, D.C.

———. 1982. *Assisting Small Business in Francophone Africa—The Entente Fund African Enterprise Program.* PN-AAL-002. Washington, D.C.

———. 1985a. *Agricultural Credit in the Dominican Republic.* Impact Evaluation Series 58 (PN-AAL-048). Washington, D.C.

———. 1985b. *A Synthesis of USAID Experience: Small Farmer Credit 1973–85.* Washington D.C.

————. 1987. *A.I.D Evaluation Handbook*. AID Program Design and Evaluation Methodology Report 7. Washington D.C.

————. 1990. *The Economic and Social Impacts of Girls' Primary Education in Developing Countries*. Advancing Basic Education and Literacy (ABEL) Project. Washington, D.C.: Office of Education and Women in Development.

————. 1991. *Gender and Adjustment*. Washington, D.C.: Office of Women in Development Bureau.

————. 1993. "Strengthening Performance Monitoring and Evaluation in AID. A Progress Report." Office of Education. Washington, D.C.

U.S. General Accounting Office. 1984. "An Evaluation of the 1981 AFDC Changes: Initial Analysis." Washington, D.C.

Valadez, Joseph. 1978. *Forced Resettlement Programs in the Yacyreta Hydroelectric Project: An Appraisal* Chicago. Harza Engineering Co.

————. 1982. "Non-survey Techniques in the Evaluation of Urban Shelter Programs." World Bank, Urban and Regional Economics Division, Washington, D.C.

————. 1984. "Macul: Influences of Taste on the Development of Social and Physical Spaces." *Human Organization* 43:146–54.

————. 1985. "Quantitative and Qualitative Methods for Monitoring and Evaluation." Pan American Health Organization, Washington, D.C.

————. 1991. *Assessing Child Survival Programs in Developing Countries: Testing Lot Quality Assurance Sampling*. Cambridge, Mass.: Harvard University Press.

Valadez, Joseph, and Leisa Weld. 1992. "Maternal Recall Error of Her Child's Vaccination Status in a Developing Country." *American Journal of Public Health* (January).

Valadez, Joseph, Lori DiPrete, and Leisa H. Weld. 1990. "The Impact of an Educational Intervention on Vaccination Service Quality." Harvard Institute for International Development, Cambridge, Mass.

Valadez, Joseph, William Vargas Vargas, and Zoila Rosa Ajiuro Rivera. 1988. "Diagnosis of the Measles Vaccination Subsystem of the Costa Rican Primary Health Care System: Understanding Low Vaccination Coverage and Low Quality Service Delivery." PRICOR II. Rpt. Harvard Institute for International Development, Cambridge, Mass.

Valadez, Joseph, William Vargas Vargas, and Marcia Sell. 1989. "Assessing Mother's Competency in Knowledge, Preparation and Use of Packets of Oral Rehydration Salts." Harvard Institute for International Development, Cambridge, Mass.

Valadez, Joseph, Leisa H. Weld, and William Vargas Vargas. 1990. "The Quality of Maternal and Child Health Care Service Delivery by Community Health Workers in Costa Rica." PRICOR II Rpt. Harvard Institute for International Development, Cambridge, Mass.

Valadez, Joseph, Lori DiPrete Brown, William Vargas Vargas, and David Morley. 1990. "Using Lot Quality Assurance Sampling to Assess Measurements for

Growth Monitoring in a Developing Country's Primary Health Care System." Harvard Institute for International Development, Cambridge, Mass.

Valadez, J. J., and others. 1987. "Quality Control of Primary Health Care in Costa Rica. PRICOR, S&T Health. Washington, D.C.: U.S. Agency for International Development.

Van der Lugt, Robert. 1990. "The Organization of Ex-Post Evaluation in the World Bank and Its Relevance for Asia." In INTAN, *The Monitoring and Evaluation of Development Projects: The East Asian Experience*. Kuala Lumpur.

Van Maanen, John, ed. 1983. *Qualitative Methodology*. Beverly Hills, Calif.: Sage.

Villegas, Hugo. 1978. "Costa Rica: Recursos Humanos y Participación de la Comunidad en los Servicios de Salud en el Medío Rural." *Buletín de la Oficina Sanitíaria Panamericana* 84(1).

Visaria, Pravin. 1980. *Poverty and Living Standards in Asia: An Overview of the Main Results and Lessons of Selected Household Surveys*. Living Standards Measurement Study. Washington, D.C.: World Bank.

Wahab, Mohammed Abdul. 1980. *Income and Expenditure Surveys in Developing Countries: Sample Design and Execution*. Living Standards Measurement Study. Washington, D.C.: World Bank.

Walker, A. L., and C. W. Lidz. 1977. "Methodological Notes on the Employment of Indigenous Observers." In R. S. Weppner, ed., *Street Ethnography*. Beverly Hills, Calif.: Sage.

Wallis, Nicholas. 1989. *Environmental Assessment of Investment Projects and Programs*. Economic Development Institute Working Paper 260/004. Washington, D.C.: World Bank.

Ward, William, Barry Derren, and Emmanuel D'Silva. 1991. *The Economic Analysis of Projects: A Practitioner's Guide*. Economic Development Institute Technical Materials. Washington, D.C.: World Bank.

Webb, E., and others, 1966. *Unobtrusive Measures: Non-reactive Research in the Social Sciences*. Chicago: Rand McNally.

Weidner, B. L., N. K. Nosseir, and C. C. Hughes. 1985. "A Need of Community Education in Development: The Mit Abu El Kom Case." *Social Science in Medicine* 20(12):1259–68.

Weisner, Thomas. 1966. "The Structure of Sociability: Urban Migration and Urban Ties in Kenya." *Urban Anthropology* 5:199–23.

Weiss, Carol. 1970. "The Politicization of Evaluation Research." *Journal of Social Issues* 26(4).

———. 1972a. *Evaluation Research*. Englewood Cliffs, N.J.: Prentice-Hall.

———. 1972b. *Evaluating Action Programs: Readings in Social Action and Education*. Boston: Allyn and Bacon.

———. 1987. "Address to the Annual Meeting of the American Evaluation Association." Kansas City.

Wholey, J. 1979. *Evaluation: Promise and Performance*. Washington, D.C.: Urban Institute.

Wholey, J., K. Newcomer, and Associates, eds. 1989. *Improving Government Performance: Evaluation Strategies for Strengthening Public Agencies and Programs*. San Francisco: Jossey-Bass.

Whyte, W. F. 1955. *Street Corner Society: The Social Structure of an Italian Slum*. Chicago: University of Chicago Press.

Wigg, David. 1993. *And Then Forgot to Tell Us Why . . . A Look at the Campaign against River Blindness in West Africa*. World Bank Development Essays 1. Washington, D.C.

Williams, Walter, and John Evans. 1969. "The Politics of Evaluation: the Case of Head Start." *Annals of the American Academy of Political and Social Science* 385 (September):118–32.

Winpenny, J. T. 1991. *Values for the Environment: A Guide to Economic Appraisal*. London: Her Majesty's Stationer's Office.

Wolf, Frederic. 1986. *Meta-Analysis: Quantitative Methods for Research Synthesis*. Quantitative Applications in the Social Sciences 59. Beverly Hills, Calif.: Sage.

Wood, Donald, and Jane Knight. 1985. *The Collection of Price Data for the Measurement of Living Standards*. Living Standards Measurement Study. Washington, D.C.: World Bank.

World Bank. 1971. *Economic Tests of Project Acceptability*. OPM 2.21. Washington, D.C.

———. 1978a. *Analysis of the Level of Demand for Low-cost Housing in Usulutan (El Salvador)*. Urban and Regional Report ME-2. Washington, D.C., Bank, Urban and Regional Economics Division.

———. 1978b. *The Effectiveness of the Cooperative as a Means of Social and Economic Change*. Urban and Regional Report ME-5. Washington, D.C., Urban and Regional Economics Division.

———. 1978c. *Evaluation of Mutual Assistance and Its Functions within the Process of Social Change*. Washington, D.C.

———. 1980a. *A Study of Income and Expenditure Patterns of Households in the Tondo Foreshore Area*. Summary of a Report prepared by the Research and Analysis Division, Philippines National Housing Authority. Washington, D.C., Urban and Regional Economics Division.

———. 1980b. *Economic Analysis of Projects*. OMS 2.21. Washington, D.C.

———. 1983. *World Development Report*. New York: Oxford University Press.

———. 1985. *Sustainability of Projects: First Review of Experience*. Washington, D.C., Operations Evaluation Department.

———. 1986. *Sustainability of Projects: Review of Experience in the Fertilizer Subsector*. Washington, D.C., Operations Evaluation Department.

———. 1987. *The Twelfth Annual Review of Project Performance Results*. Washington, D.C., Operations Evaluation Department.

————. 1988. *Rural Development: World Bank Experience 1965–86.* Washington, D.C., Operations and Evaluation Department.

————. 1989a. *China: Women in Development.* China Department Country Assessment Paper. Washington, D.C.

————. 1989b. *Impact Evaluation Report: Sustainability of the First and Second Education Projects.* Washington, D.C., Operations Evaluation Department.

————. 1990a. *Annual Review of Evaluation Results 1988.* Washington, D.C., Operations Evaluation Department.

————. 1990b. *Bangladesh: Strategies for Enhancing the Role of Women in Economic Development.* Washington, D.C.

————. 1990c. *The Social Dimensions of Adjustment in Africa: A Policy Agenda.* Washington, D.C.

————. 1990d. *World Development Report 1990.* New York: Oxford University Press.

————. 1991a. *Annual Report on Operations Evaluation (FY91).* Washington, D.C., Operations Evaluation Department.

————. 1991b. *Gender and Poverty in India: Issues and Opportunities Concerning Women in the Indian Economy.* Washington, D.C.

————. 1991c. *The Sustainability of Investment Projects in Education.* Washington, D.C., Operations Evaluation Department.

————. 1991d. *Forestry: The World Bank's Experience* Washington, D.C., Operations Evaluation Department.

————. 1992a. "Economic Analysis of Projects: Towards a Results-Oriented Approach to Evaluation." ECON Report (draft). Washington, D.C.

————. 1992b. *Population and the World Bank: Implications from Eight Case Studies.* Washington, D.C., Operations Evaluation Department.

————. 1992c. "Poverty Handbook." World Bank, Washington, D.C.

————. 1992d. *World Bank Approaches to the Environment in Brazil: A Review of Selected Projects.* Operations Evaluation Departmnet. Report 10039.

————. 1992e. *World Development Report: Development and the Environment.* Washington, D.C.

————. 1993b. *Early Experiences with Involuntary Resettlement: Impact Evaluation on India: Maharashtra Irrigation II Project* Operations Evaluation Department Report 12133. Washington, D.C.

————. 1993 *Early Experiences with Involuntary Resettlement: Impact Evaluation on India: Karnataka Irrigation Project.* Operations Evaluation Department Report 12132. Washington, D.C.

————. 1993. *Early Experience with Involuntary Resettlement: Impact Evaluation on Thailand. Khao Laem Hydroelectric.* Operations Evaluation Department Report 12131. Washington, D.C.

————. 1993 *Early Experience with Involuntary Resettlement: Overview.* Operations Evaluation Department Report 12142. Washington, D.C.

World Health Organization Expanded Programme on Immunization. n.d. *Training for Mid-Level Managers: Evaluate Vaccination Coverage.*

World Health Organization. 1983. *Minimum Evaluation Procedures for Water Supply and Sanitation Projects.*

World Resources Institute. 1990. *The State of the World 1990.* Washington, D.C.

Wyon, John, and John Gordon. 1971. *The Khanna Study.* Cambridge, Mass.: Harvard University Press.

Yayha, Saad. 1982. *House Registration Handbook: A Model for Registering Houses and Plots in Unplanned Settlements.* World Bank Technical Paper 4. Washington, D.C.

Yeaton, William, and Paul Wortman, eds. 1984. *Issues in Data Synthesis.* New Directions for Program Evaluation 24. San Francisco: Jossey-Bass.

Yin, Robert. 1984. *Case Study Research: Design and Methods.* Beverly Hills, Calif.: Sage.

# Index

*(Page numbers in italics indicate material in tables, figures, or boxes.)*

Federal Annual Development Plan (India), 3

Financial Management Initiative (England 1983), 127

First Integrated Rural Development Project (Bangladesh), 208n; purpose and methodology of, 202–3; quantitative objectives of, 189, 203; sustainability assessment of, *195*, 199, 204–6

Florianopolis, Brazil, 356

*Forestry: The World Bank Experience* (World Bank 1991d), 54

Foundation for Liberty and Democracy, 429

Gantt chart, 84, 121, *122*

Gender analysis, 11, 45; agricultural modernization requiring, 66–67, 69; in Bangladesh, *68;* in design phase, 148–49, *150, 151;* four components of, 70–71; in implementation phase, *152, 153;* structural adjustment requiring, 70

German Development Agency (GTZ): ZOPP planning version by, 87, 91

Grameen Bank (Bangladesh), 191

Guayaquil, Ecuador, 176, 355–56

Haiti, 219

Health data: as project impact measurement, 325–27

Health programs: assessment criteria for, 390–91; attitude scale studies of, 300–301; econometric analysis of, 275–76; key informants in, 349–50; LQAS used in, 390–98; quasi-experimental design in, 233–34, 239; sample estimates for, 364–65; simplified impact evaluation of, 259

Hedonic methods: for environmental impact assessment, 199

Highways Design Model (World Bank), 105

HIV/AIDS control projects, 154

Household head: definitions for, 324; as measurement issue, 321, 328n; panel sampling of, 376

Household income: direct observation of, 346–47; measurement of, 321–23, 372

Households: definitions for, 323–24; sampling of, 375–77. *See also* Samples

Household size data: measurement of, 369–71

Housing Indicators Program (United Nations Centre for Human Settlements 1993), 105, 106–8

Housing projects: quasi-experimental design in, 234, 237–38, 256–57; simplified impact evaluations of, 259–61, 268, 269

Human capital approach: to environmental impact assessment, 198–99

Impact evaluation: of Bolivian Social Investment Fund, 275–76; clients' use of, 23, *24;* control group in, 372–73; data collection for, 213, 214, 215–18, 295–96; of EDURURAL, 280–85; limitations on simplified, 266–70; limited demand for, 28, 405, 418, 423–24; NGOs' experience in, 428–29; problems in, 28, 211–13, 221–23; purpose and results of, 50–51, *52,* 368, 372; questions required for, 302–5; rapid assessment method of, 210, 211; simplified, 224, 258–66; strengthening of simplified, 270–74; using before-and-after comparisons, 263–64; using meta-analysis, 64–65; weaknesses of conventional, 210; of West Africa River Blindness